Bali: *Sekala and Niskala*

Volume I: *Essays on Religion, Ritual, and Art*

BALI:
SEKALA
AND
NISKALA

VOLUME I:
ESSAYS ON RELIGION,
RITUAL, AND ART

Fred B. Eiseman, Jr.

with two chapters by
Margaret Eiseman

 PERIPLUS
EDITIONS

A version of the material in this book appeared in
Bali: Sekala & Niskala Volumes I, II, and III
published by Fred B. Eiseman, Jr. in Bali.

Publisher Eric M. Oey
Edited by David Pickell
Designed by David Pickell and Peter Ivey
Cover by Peter Ivey
Cover painting by I Dewa Ketut Baru
(A) Cintya, the inconceivable God, with the world-turtle and
the two *nagas;* watercolor and ink on cloth. 1988

Published by Periplus Editions (HK) Ltd.

Distributors:

Australia:	
New South Wales:	R & A Book Agency,
	Unit 1, 56-72 John Street Leichhardt 2040
S.E. Queensland:	Book Outlet Agencies
	49 Prosser Street, Riverhills 4074 Brisbane
Victoria & S.A.:	Ken Pryse & Associates,
	156 Collins Street, Melbourne 3000
Western Australia:	Edwards Book Agencies,
	Unit 4, 48 May Street, Bayswater 6053
Benelux:	Nilsson & Lamm B.V.,
	Pampuslaan 212-214, 1382 JS Weesp, The Netherlands
Hong Kong & Taiwan:	Asia Publishers Services Ltd.,
	16/F, Wing Fat Commercial Building,
	218 Aberdeen Main Road, Hong Kong
Indonesia:	C.V. Java Books,
	P.O. Box 55 JKCP, Jakarta 10510
Japan:	Charles E. Tuttle Co. Inc,
	1-21-13, Seki, Tama-ku, Kawasaki-shi,
	Kanagawa-ken 214, Japan
Singapore & Malaysia:	Berkeley Books Pte. Ltd., 5 Little Road,
	#08-01 Cemtex Industrial Building, Singapore 536983
United Kingdom:	GeoCenter U.K. Ltd., The Viables Center,
	Harrow Way, Basingstoke, Hampshire RG22 4BJ
United States:	The Crossing Press, 97 Hangar Way,
	Watsonville CA 95076

First printing 1990
Second printing 1992
Third printing 1994
Fourth printing 1996

Printed in Indonesia
ISBN 0-945971-03-6

The drawings appearing throughout this volume are by I Nyoman Sukartha

TO MY WIFE MAGGIE, whose encouragement, patience, and interest kept me going. I thank her for enduring all the months that I had to spend away from home. But she knew very well that if she had not allowed me to do this I would have been even harder to get along with than usual. And I thank her for helping me, both in the field and at home, with the gathering of information and photographs, and in the preparation of the text. In a very real sense, this book is not mine, but ours.

AND TO I WAYAN BUDIASA, of Jimbaran, Bali, my good friend and assistant. There is literally not a paragraph in this book that is not a direct result of Budi's help. His valuable, loyal, and efficient assistance is hereby recognized. Budi and I have worked together for more than ten years now, and our relationship has become more like that of father and son than of worker and employer. He has helped me learn to understand his culture as I have helped him learn to understand mine. We have both grown wiser and, I think, have become better human beings as a result of such mutual understanding.

Contents

PART III: ANNIVERSARIES AND TEMPLES

PART IV: THE PERFORMING ARTS

Introduction

MY WIFE MAGGIE AND I first came to Bali in 1961. At that time my only knowledge of the word was from a song in "South Pacific." As a former professional musician, Maggie insisted that we visit Bali because she had heard that its pentatonic music had influenced some important modern Western composers. That was when the summit of Gunung Agung was still pointed; when no motorbikes intruded among the bicycles and *dokars;* when there was no Hotel Bali Beach; no jets landing at the airport; no "Barong Show" at Batubulan; no cassettes; plenty of fried chicken, but not from Kentucky; no gigantic tourist buses; no traffic jams.

Much has intervened between that first glimpse of Bali and the present edition of *Bali: Sekala and Niskala.* After almost annual visits to Bali in the course of world travels, the island grew to be one of the principal destinations of our trips, and we extended our stays to several weeks, a month, several months. Soon Bali became the only destination.

Fortunately the first person we met on that first visit was Njoman Oka, primus inter pares of the small group of professional Balinese guides. We had been told about him before our arrival, and during our two-week visit he kept us busy night and day with adventures and information. He has remained our close friend and advisor ever since. Then, quite by chance, we met I Wayan Budiasa, "Budi," a young taxi and *bemo* driver who spoke almost no English. His desire to learn English and become a licensed guide was as great as our desire to learn about Bali. His friends became our friends. And his village, Jimbaran, became our adopted village. We gained new insights and perspectives. Bali's attractions, initially geographical, began to include and then concentrate upon cultural phenomena and personal relationships.

As former teachers, we started to feel the urge to share some of our experiences with others. Even then there was no dearth of books about Bali. But they were either written in Dutch or were intended for the in-and-out visitor who had little time to spend on the island and no particular urge to probe the inner workings of this complex culture. I saw a gap. And I began by researching and writing magazine articles. Perhaps the most important of these was one on the great 1979 Eka Dasa Rudra ceremonies for *National Geographic.* I followed this with a series of articles for the in-flight magazines of various airlines — Qantas, Singapore Airlines,

Philippine Airlines, Garuda, and others — plus articles in other publications devoted to Asian matters.

Then one day several years ago I happened to run across my friend Andy Toth. Andy — Dr. Toth — is an expert on music theory who now teaches at ASTI in Denpasar. Andy said he had seen some of my pieces and they interested he and his friends. But the magazines were no longer available. He suggested I round up all the articles and make them available under one cover. What you have here is the result of Andy's suggestion.

Over the course of four years I wrote three long volumes of *Bali: Sekala and Niskala.* I did not limit myself to the articles that had already appeared, but as new topics suggested themselves, I followed them up. The first volume, with 35 chapters, was published in Denpasar in 1985. In it Maggie wrote the chapters (which appear here) on *wayang kulit* and traditional *gamelan,* since that is her specialty. The second volume came out in 1986, with 24 more chapters. A small run of plain-vanilla editions of these two volumes met with modest sales in the hotels and book stores of Denpasar, Kuta, and Sanur. I had the materials ready for a third volume when I was asked by Eric Oey if his press, Periplus Editions, could publish these books and three others I was then working on. Of course, I agreed at once.

I completed the 28 chapters of Volume III in the spring of 1988, but it was never offered for sale in anything other than a photocopied edition for a few friends and scholars. Rather, Eric determined to put all three volumes into the hands of a capable editor who would try to transform what was essentially a series of unconnected essays into a coherent and organized whole. David Pickell has done this job extremely well, I think.

We decided to enliven the newly edited and revised series by commissioning an artist to prepare illustrations. By good fortune, Budi and I located Drs. I Nyoman Sukartha, a well known Denpasar artist who has taught at the Sekolah Menengah Seni Rupa Bali since 1973. In addition to his teaching, Drs. Sukartha is a painter, sculptor, mapmaker, and a creator of *wayang kulit* puppets. His work has been exhibited at art festivals and exhibitions in Bali as well as Europe.

Drs. Sukartha, 37, is from Ulakan in the district of Karangasem in northeastern Bali, although he makes his home in Denpasar. He graduated in 1968 from the Sekolah Teknologi Negeri in Denpasar, and completed his high school work in 1971 at the Sekolah Seni Rupa Indonesia in Denpasar. He entered the Faculty of Technology at Universitas Udayana in Bali in 1972 and received his Doctorandus degree in Art in 1983. While at the university he taught art at SSRI and, after graduating, taught at the university. Drs. Sukartha is married to Ni Putu Ariasih, from Manggis in Karangasem, and they have two boys and a girl.

As indicated above, this book had its origins in a series of independent essays, written at different times and for different audiences. Even when the articles are collected and edited to provide as much coherence as possible, they are still, to a considerable degree, independent essays. Each chapter can be understood without reference to the others, which makes for a certain amount of repetition. And although all the essays are about the same culture, there is no theme or story line. The editor has wisely decided not to try to change the basic structure of the original essays. No apologies need be made for that fact.

A word about spelling. Balinese spelling varies widely. One reason is that there are almost no works written in Balinese using the Roman alphabet. Budi and I searched all of the principal bookstores in Denpasar — our harvest was a handful of paperbacks on specialized subjects, plus a few books for elementary and junior high school students. And most Balinese writers do not use a dictionary, but rather spell words as they hear them. Another source of variation is that many Balinese words come from Sanskrit, which can be accurately romanized only by using diacritical marks. The Balinese, who never use the special sounds represented by the diacritics in the spoken language, do not bother with the marks in their written works. (In this volume, I will stick to the Balinese spelling — closer to the true sound in Balinese — using, for example, *Siwa* instead of *Shiva* or *Siva*.)

Thus the few authoritative dictionaries of the Balinese language must serve as standards. I recommend to the interested reader the following three dictionaries, which I have constantly used as references: *Kamus Bali-Indonesia*, published in 1978 by the Balinese Office of Education; Father J. Kersten's *Bahasa Bali* (Balinese-Indonesian) published by Penerbit Nusa Indah in Ende, Flores, in 1984; and *Dictionary of Balinese-English* by Dr. C.C. Barber, Aberdeen University, 1979.

It will be useful to the reader to understand how and why the material in this book was gathered and written. The reader is always at the mercy of the prejudices, methods, and special points of view of the writer, and should be provided with a caveat lector right from the start. I am not a trained anthropologist and neither my method nor my writing style strictly follows the accepted norms of the profession. This has its advantages and disadvantages. It probably means that some of my conclusions could not withstand the harsh light of professional criticism. But it also means that my style can be more relaxed, informal, and therefore readable by one who himself is not a trained anthropologist.

My home in Bali, where I spend six months of a year, was in the house compound of my close friend and associate Budi. The story of my long relationship with Budi, a guide by profession, need not be recounted here. Budi's house compound is in Jimbaran, a village of some 12,000 people on the narrowest part of the isthmus connecting the Bukit to the main part of the island. I am the only foreign resident of Jimbaran. Recently two small hotels have been built in the village, but visitors have little contact with the villagers. Other than Budi, who spent two years at my house in Scottsdale, Arizona perfecting his English, noboby in the village can speak English. Most of the villagers are fishermen, tailors, salt makers, truckers, drivers, or are engaged in various other forms of small business. Jimbaran, and the dry limestone Bukit in general, is not "typical" of the Bali seen by most visitors. There is no handicraft industry other than a few small shell jewelry factories. There is no irrigation water and therefore no rice cultivation. It is a world away from the tourist meccas of Ubud, Kuta, Sanur, and Nusa Dua.

When I first came to Jimbaran I was a novelty, of course; an unfamiliar unintelligibility. As the years passed I have made the transition to a familiar unintelligibility to some and a familiar intelligibility to many. I have entered freely into village activities, dancing at temple festivals, chopping up food for feasts, participating in the *barong* society's activities, helping at temple festivals, teaching English to high school students, and, in short, trying to become as much a part of Jimbaran life as possible.

The reader may suspect that I have somehow worked my way into Jimbaran society in order to learn its secrets with the purpose of writing about them — not an unknown practice among anthropologists. This is not my intent. I live in Jimbaran because I like it there. It is very much my home — perhaps even more my home than the one in Scottsdale. Many of the villagers are my close friends. We have learned from each other, but I value them foremost as people, not informants. I have begun to learn to live in their cultural setting and within their set of values. And I think that my neighbors recognize that my effort is to be as much a part of their culture as possible — not to gather information on interesting "phenomena." At least they pay me the compliment of ignoring my presence. When they started doing that, I felt that we had arrived at a condition of mutual respect and understanding.

I have adopted Balinese Hinduism. I was not converted to Hinduism. Quite the contrary, I was like the character in Molière's *Le Bourgeois Gentilhomme* who realized that he had been speaking prose all his life and didn't know it. I had been practicing a philosophical form of Hinduism since adolescence and never realized that my beliefs were consistent with a large organized body of religion.

I investigate and write about Bali for the sheer joy of learning new things and to help others understand what I have learned. More than a little of this imperative can be traced to my 20 plus years as a schoolteacher. And my talents in investigation, such as they are, are perhaps the result of my education as a chemical engineer and the subject of my teaching — physics and chemistry.

There are a few important points the reader of this series must keep firmly in mind. Anyone who purports to write about "the way it is in Bali" is either ignorant or a liar. One would think that local variations in culture on such a tiny island would be insignificant. That is not the case. One of the first things a careful investigator learns is the principle of *desa kala patra*: that whatever one learns in Bali is largely determined by *where* he is, *when* he is there, and the *circumstances* under which the learning occurs.

Since I live about six months of each year in Jimbaran, my observations are strongly influenced by practice in that particular village. In effect, this book is really about Jimbaran, Bali and should be titled: *Jimbaran: Sekala and Niskala*. Years ago I set out to learn as much as I could about Indonesia. A decade of experience later, I decided to narrow my field to just Bali. Another decade later I thought I had better concentrate upon South Bali. A couple of years ago the field narrowed to Jimbaran. It is now becoming apparent that I had better focus only upon South Jimbaran. I have tried to gather information from as wide a variety of places as possible. My informants have been sought from Gilimanuk to Nusa Penida, Pecatu to Singaraja. But I make no apologies for the probable deviations of that which I report from what one might find elsewhere on the island.

There are many people I would like to thank. Budi, of course, makes countless contributions to my work. But his greatest assets are his ability to find informants, and his enthusiasm for extracting information from them. Our sources vary from university professors to *balians*; rice farmers to engineers; heads of government offices to sellers of *jamu*; master craftsmen, peddlers, waiters, builders, philosophers, *pedandas*, and housewives. The only requirement is that the people are willing to share their information. And Budi has a knack for prying out information without coloring it with his own preconceptions. This did not come naturally to him; it is not a common Balinese trait.

Budi's importance to me cannot be overestimated. But his wife Ni Wayan Lidawati also has been extremely important in my education. She is my dance teacher, and has been an invaluable source of information on a great variety of subjects. Wati works at the Rumah Sakit Umum Pusat, the public hospital, in Denpasar. She is also a part-time seller, an accomplished cook, an expert maker of offerings, a former professional classical dancer, a dance instructor, and a mother. Since I have known her and her large family since before she and Budi married, I have had a good opportunity to see how matches are made. And since her own family lives in Denpasar, I have had a chance to compare life in the big city to that in Jimbaran.

When one's subject of study is people and their ideas, every person becomes a subject of study and a source of information — whether the contact is a formal interview or idle gossip over a cup of coffee. It would be impossible for me to acknowlege my debt to the thousands of people who have helped me since my arrival in 1961. If any of them should read these lines, I can only offer my sincere thanks. However, my most valuable contacts and sources have been the ordinary people of Jimbaran — not the professors and specialists and experts, just the sorts of people you might meet in your own town. They run the market, cure the sick, clean up the garbage, harvest the fish, make the salt, hoe the fields, sew the clothes, dance in the temples, sell cakes and coffee in the *warungs,* drive the trucks and *bemos,* bury the dead, and usher the newly born into the world. They are kind to me and share their lives with me. They discuss their problems and their joys with me. This is how I have learned.

The one area where Budi's help has been other than a complete boon in in my mastery of the Balinese language. Were it not for Budi I would probably be much more fluent than I am — his command of English and his skill at translation has somewhat spoiled me in this regard. I regularly study Balinese for one or two hours every day with Budi. But his ability to help me in my work has made it unnecessary for me to learn to speak Balinese really well, and his acting as a translator has made my work so much more efficient that — without him — it would have taken several lifetimes to do what I have done.

Finally, I would like to single out Maggie and Budi once again for thanks. Maggie has had almost as great a role in the writing of this book as I. She read all of the manuscripts, criticized, corrected, and offered suggestions. And, as mentioned above, she wrote two of the chapters herself. As for Budi, my feelings toward him are evident in the dedication of this book and in frequent remarks in the text. Except in the most technical interpretation of the term, the authorship of this work is ours — Maggie's, Budi's, and mine.

Fred B. Eiseman, Jr.
December, 1988
Jimbaran, Bali

PART I

Religion in Bali

CHAPTER 1

Kaja and Kelod

SPATIAL AND SPIRITUAL ORIENTATION

IN THE WEST ONE IS ACCUSTOMED TO A WORLD BUILT UPON OPPOSITES: sacred and profane, positive and negative, constructive and destructive, male and female. The Balinese also recognize this polarity, which they call *rwa bineda*. But in the Judeo-Christian tradition, these opposites are presented as mutually exclusive choices: either one does/is good, or one does/is evil. In the Hindu-Balinese scheme, this division is neither so stark, nor at all exclusive. And it includes what can be considered a third position, "center," which balances the other two.

In Bali, the position of mankind is one between good and evil or, more appropriately stated, in a state of coexistence with them. Mankind's job is not to destroy evil. Nothing in the teachings of Balinese Hinduism requires or even mentions this. Evil is a part of the whole, and good is a part of the whole. Neither can exist without the other. Instead, the life of any Balinese is devoted to maintaining a balance between these opposing forces — maintaining an equilibrium so that neither gets the upper hand. This notion of three forces, overlapping and interdependent, the three together constituting a whole, lies close to the center of Hindu theology. Even the most casual tourist learns of the Hindu triad — Brahma, Wisnu, and Siwa. But this is only one of the myriad tripartite classifications that organize Balinese society. This grouping by threes, or *tri hita krana*, governs ideology and activities as grand as cosmology, and as humble as building a toilet.

For most busy Westerners the airport is where the freeway arrow points; north is where you ski in the winter; "up" is a button on the elevator. We don't assign special importance to orientation, except possibly to choose a house for its nice view. Direction is instrumental in the West. "How do I get to the hospital?" Answer: "Head down the street *that way* (pointing), and turn *that way* (pointing)." And except to the extent that it enables us to get where we"re going, a sense of direction means little to us. But orientation is exceedingly important to the Balinese. In Bali, a direction describes a vector not just in physical space, but in cultural, religious, and social "space" as well. As a result, every Balinese seems to possess a built-in sense of direction. And if for some reason this feeling is lacking, the individual is visibly uncomfortable and disoriented.

A few years ago my friend and associate I Wayan Budiasa came to live at my home in the United States. He arrived about noon in early winter when the sun was low and in the south. From then on, that direction was east to him because in Bali, just a few degrees south of the equator, the sun is near the horizon only at sunrise and sunset. He quickly learned, intellectually, that this direction was south, not east, but he *felt* that it was east, and no amount of intellectualizing could change that first visual impression. He learned to *say* south, but he still *felt* east. It bothered him for the entire two years that he lived in the United States.

ORIENTATION IN BALI begins with the sacred mountain, Gunung Agung, which stands 3,142 meters high in the eastern central part of the island. Gunung (Mount) Agung is the dwelling place of the Hindu gods. Toward the mountain is called *kaja*. Because Gunung Agung is in a fairly central location, *kaja* is a variable direction. It is north for inhabitants of South Bali and south for those who live in North Bali. Whether north or south, it is always "up," the sacred direction toward God. Antipodal to *kaja* is *kelod*, seaward, toward the lower elevations and away from the holy mountain. *Kelod* is "down," less sacred than *kaja*, even impure. The second-most sacred direction, after *kaja*, is *kangin*, "east," the direction from which the sun, an important manifestation of God, rises. *Kangin's* opposite to the west, *kauh*, is correspondingly less sacred.

The eight compass directions consist of four cardinal points — *kaja, kangin, kelod, kauh* — and their intercardinal divisions — *kaja-kangin, kelod-kauh*, etc. To these are added the position, center. In each of these nine directions dwells a separately-named aspect of God, each aspect having its associated color and characteristics. Sometimes the symbolism is extended to cover all three dimensional space by adding two more directions, up and down. For example, once every hundred years an enormous islandwide ceremony is held to exorcise evil forces, to drive them off into the eleven directions of all space. The name of this ceremony, Eka Dasa Rudra, comes from the Sanskrit expression for eleven, *eka dasa*. (See CHAPTER 21.)

This *kaja/kelod*, sacred/profane, high/low concept is deeply ingrained in the Balinese psyche. Villages are aligned *kaja-kelod*. The cemetery and the temple called Pura Dalem, dedicated to Siwa, or to his wife, Durga, are located at the *kelod* end. And the villagers locate the Pura Puseh, the temple dedicated to Wisnu, on the *kaja*, upslope end. Each temple, and there are tens of thousands of them in Bali, is itself oriented *kaja-kelod*. The most sacred inner part of the temple, containing the holy shrines, is *kaja* and higher than, and divided by a gate from, the more secular courtyards of the temple complex.

Every house compound is oriented *kaja-kelod*. The family temple is in

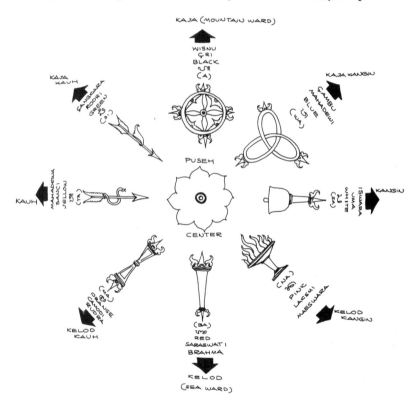

THE BALINESE COMPASS, WITH DIRECTIONAL SYMBOLISM

the most sacred position, *kaja-kangin*. The head of the household lives in the most *kaja* building in the compound. Everyone sleeps with his or her head toward either *kaja* or *kangin*, the sacred directions for the head that together are called *luan*. The directions for the feet, *kelod* or *kauh*, are called *teben*. One would not put a door or a clothes closet on the *luan* side of the bedroom. The kitchen and granary are *kelod*. Furthest *kelod*, often *kelod-kauh*, are the animal pens and the garbage dump.

To understand orientation on Bali, one must make what may at first seem to be a very fine distinction between "direction" and "place." Since *kelod,* towards the sea, is the direction away from the seat of purity, the assumption is sometimes made that the sea is the least sacred place of all. This is an error. In fact, the Balinese consider the sea to be a place of exceptional purity. Directions are relative, not absolute. *Kelod* is an impure direction. A man dumps garbage and keeps his pigs at the *kelod* end of his house compound. His family temple is at the *kaja-kangin* corner. Yet this same man's neighbor, who lives directly *kaja,* dumps his garbage and keeps his pigs at the *kelod* end of *his* house compound — just over the dividing wall from the most sacred part of his neighbor's house.

The daily attitudes and behavior of the Balinese reflect this highly oriented, directional space. In situations in which Westerners would point or say "left" or "right," or "here" or "there," the Balinese use compass directions. If a group of men are carrying a heavy load that must be placed in a particular spot they will shout to each other: "A little more *kaja* — now a bit *kangin* — there, now, set it down." If you visit a friend and are invited into his home he may say: "Come *kaja* and sit down next to me in this chair to the *kauh.*" When giving directions for travel a Balinese will always say something like: "Go a little farther *kangin,* turn *kaja* at the crossroads, and you will find his house on the *kauh* side of the road."

THIS INTERLOCKING SET OF HORIZONTAL AND VERTICAL ORIENTATIONS is a consequence of the Hindu conception of cosmic structure and organization. Man is a tiny part of the overall Hindu-Balinese universe, but he contains its structure in microcosm. Man's body has three parts — head, body, and feet — just as the universe, macrocosm, has three parts: the upper world of God and heaven, the middle world of man, and the underworld. Man is a kind of scale model of the universe, with exactly the same structure — as is the island of Bali, and each village, temple, house compound, building, and occupant on it. The interlocking, related structures and orientations produce balance, the goal of Hinduism. Unless a Balinese can orient himself properly in this universe of balance, dictated by *kaja* and *kelod,* up and down, he feels uncomfortable and lost because he is not in harmony with his environment and the forces of good and evil within it. His gyroscope is not set. There is nothing to guide him.

The Balinese conceptualize the entire universe, the macrocosmos, as being structured on three levels. In the middle is the world of man, called *bhuwah* (sometimes spelled *buwah*) or *bhuwah loka* in Sanskrit. Above lies heaven, *suarga,* to which man's spirit will return after death, cremation, and purification, finally to be reincarnated in another physical form in *bhuwah.* Heaven is the realm of the prime mover, Ida Sanghyang Widi

Wasa, and the positive forces of the cosmos, the division called *swah,* or *swah loka.* The highest level of *swah, moksa,* or *nirwana,* is that state to which an exceedingly pure and holy spirit can aspire — once there freed from the ceaseless cycle of life, death, and rebirth.

Below the world of man is *bhur,* or *bhur loka,* the location of hell, *neraka,* where man's spirit is punished for its earthly misdeeds. This punishment is meted according to the principle of *karma-pala,* where every earthly deed, karma, results inevitably in a *pala* ("fruit"), which may be punishment in hell or reward in heaven, or usually, since man's deeds are sometimes good, sometimes bad, both. *Bhur* is also the dwelling place of Bedawang Nala, the world turtle, who carries the earth on his back and whose restless stirrings produce Bali's frequent earthquakes. The name is derived from *wedawang,* "boiling water," and *nala,* "fire," the mixture that constitutes the magma that finds its way to the surface through Bali's many volcanoes. Bedawang Nala is always accompanied by the two dragon-snakes, Naga Basuki and Naga Anantaboga, which represent man's earthly needs — safety, food, shelter, and clothing. *Bhur* is also the dwelling place of the negative forces of the world, the evil spirits called *bhutas* and *kalas,* which ceaselessly interfere with man's peaceful daily routines and attempt to upset the equilibrium between positive and negative forces that man so painstakingly tries to maintain.

The *bhur-bhuwah-swah* triptych is found everywhere in Bali. Every temple has a stone or brick, or today sometimes concrete, *padmasana,* a shrine that represents the macrocosmos, with turtle and dragons below, the empty seat of *surya,* the sun, on top, and the world of man in between. Many Balinese cremation ceremonies feature gaudily decorated towers, *wadah,* with the same symbolism. The details of the *wadah* may be clearly, and sometimes colorfully, depicted: leafy forests, mountains, and a kind of house representing *bhuwah* in the middle; a series of tiered roofs representing *mahameru,* the holy world-mountain, on top; and the world-turtle, the *nagas* entwined about him, representing *bhur* below.

The cycle of life has three divisions: birth, life, and death. A newborn baby whose spirit has just arrived from heaven is treated like a god. Similarly, a very old person, whose spirit will shortly return again to heaven, is shown the greatest respect — like that accorded holy people. Everywhere one finds triple shrines, triple niches, and triple platforms of lotus leaves made of stone, brick, or wood to accommodate the Hindu triad.

The structure of man, the microcosmos, is divided into three parts corresponding to those of the macrocosmos. In fact, the same Sanskrit word, *bhuana,* is used to describe both man's body and the universe. The former is *bhuana alit,* the small body, the latter *bhuana agung,* the large body. The three divisions of man are: head, body, and feet. The head is holy, the seat of the soul. A waitress at a tourist restaurant apologizes before putting a flower behind your ear, as does the barber before he begins his work. You never see a Balinese ruffle up a child's hair in greeting, as is so common in the West. Holy offerings are invariably carried on the head, as is holy water. Conversely the feet are dirty, being in contact with the earth and antipodal to the head. Pointing with a foot or stepping on or over an offering or other sacred object is a dreadful breach of etiquette. For an ordinary person to position himself at a higher elevation than a high priest or a holy object, such as a temporary residence of a god or deified ancestor, is not only rude but sacrilegious. When a sacred object, such as the mythic Barong, is present the Balinese audience sits on the ground. Many Balinese will not enter a two-story building, lest something impure be located over their heads.

Clothing is considered dirty and profane, even when it has been carefully washed. This is especially true of women's clothing that may have been contaminated by menstrual blood. The Balinese consider that menstruation makes a woman unclean and impure, and during her period she cannot participate in any sort of religious activity. The clothes worn by a woman at the time of childbirth, which may be bloodstained, are especially impure, and are often dried in a place away from other clothes. Putting clothes on a temple wall is a sacrilege. No Balinese would ever walk under a clothesline on which clothes are hung out to dry — even men's clothes, because some of them may have been in contact with the lower, less pure, parts of the body. Even *watching* someone else walk under drying clothes gives some Balinese headaches. In the past, Balinese farmers would string up a rope around their fields to prevent trespassing. To insure that nobody would dare duck under the rope, dirty clothes were tied to it.

Even the Balinese language reflects a division into three levels that have spatial referents. One uses low, or common Balinese when speaking to family and close friends. Medium Balinese is for strangers and people of higher caste. And high, or refined Balinese is used when speaking to high priests or when referring to sacred objects or ceremonies. Other investigators may find even more than three divisions, but even those will be subsets of the three major categories. The three levels are not just different dialects of the same basic language. For example, the word for water is *yeh* in common Balinese, *toya* in medium, and *tirtha* in high Balinese. Common and high Balinese are based upon two completely different linguistic origins, with the medium language, in many cases, a kind of combination of the two.

Many common nouns are acceptable in all three levels. But verbs relating to human actions, and nouns that refer to body parts and human activities, are quite different in the three levels. It is considered very improper to address a stranger in low Balinese, even though he or she is just a seller in a market stall. And, since few ordinary people are fluent in high Balinese, it is common, when seeking the services of a high priest, to take along a scholarly friend who is fluent. Interestingly enough, the high priest, well educated and knowledgeable, speaks to all lower people in the rough familiar tongue, whereas the commoner, often illiterate, is expected to speak all three levels of the language.

THE BALINESE VILLAGE is not just a collection of houses and public buildings and stores. Rather, like man, the cosmos, and the language, it too has three parts. It has a *kaja*-oriented head, upslope and hence higher than the rest of the village. It has a *kelod*-oriented foot; lower because nearer the sea. Its main body is in the middle, where most of the daily activities of the people occur. And there are three temples. In the center is the village temple, the Pura Desa, the original temple of the first settlers, hence dedicated to Brahma, the creator. In the *kaja* direction is the Pura Puseh, dedicated to Wisnu, the preserver of life, since the life-giving waters come from the mountains and Wisnu is always associated with water. In the *kelod* direction is the village cemetery and the Pura Dalem, sometimes incorrectly called the "death temple," dedicated to Siwa, dissolver and recycler of the spirit, or to Durga, Siwa's wife.

Each temple itself is divided into three parts. In the upslope, *kaja*, direction is the *jeroan*, the inner sanctum, which contains the sacred shrines. It is clearly divided from the rest of the temple by a wall and a huge gate, the *kori agung*, decorated with a prominent carving of a leering face, *bhoma*, whose fangs and bulging eyes keep evil forces away from the holiest part of the temple. If the land is relatively flat the *jeroan* is elevated by a built-up base of stone or earth. The middle section of the temple is called *jaba tengah*, and serves as a transitional area between sacred and secular spaces. It contains storage rooms, the temple kitchen, and pavilions for arranging offerings before they are taken into the sacred *jeroan*. Separated from the middle area by another wall and a large split gate, the *candi bentar*, is the most *kelod*, hence the lowest and least sacred courtyard. It is called *jaba*, meaning "outside." Here secular activities are permitted: food stalls are set up at festival time and people relax, play cards, eat, and chat.

In each of the three temple areas only specific kinds of artistic performances are permitted during the usual three-day period of an anniversary festival. Only the most sacred performances of music and dance, called *wali*, are permitted in the *jeroan*. These are usually quite serious productions and attendance is limited to those of appropriate status and position. Performances of the middle courtyard are classified as *bebali*, and are more dramatic and secular in nature than the performances of the inner temple, but still have considerable religious significance. In the outer temple one finds secular performances, called *balih-balihan*, presented chiefly to entertain a human audience. There are very few traditional dances or other performances that do not have some sort of religious significance.

Every Balinese belongs to a neighborhood association, the *banjar*, which has from one hundred to several hundred members. Each *banjar* has a meeting hall, the *bale banjar*, which is always divided into three parts: the *banjar* temple, the secular meeting place, and the kitchen.

In a manner exactly analogous to these public structures, every traditional Balinese house compound compound is organized into three divisions. The family temple, like the *jeroan*, separated by a wall and gate, is built in the *kaja-kangin* corner of the compound. The family living quarters, usually consisting of several separate buildings called *bales*, form the middle of the unit. Most *kelod* in this section are the kitchen and the rice barn. And most *kelod* of all, constituting the third and most profane part of the compound, are the animal pen, the *kandang*, and the garbage pit. Within the house compound, each building displays an analogous structure — roof, the "head"; pillars, the "body"; and foundation, the "feet."

Before a *bale* is occupied, the Balinese purify it, a ceremony of offerings and special prayers bringing it to life. Today this same practice is observed even when a building is not a traditional *bale*, but is constructed of modern materials. After the ceremony, the house is no longer a mere collection of wood, stone, and roofing materials, but is a living analog of the tripartite Balinese world. On auspicious occasions, the house is decorated just as a Balinese would dress. A colorful strip of cloth, the *ider-ider*, is wrapped around the roof of the *bale*, just like the traditional head cloth, the *udeng*, that all Balinese men wear. The body-pillars are decorated with colored cloth, *pangaput sasaka*, just like the skirtlike *saput* that men wear wrapped around their loins on ceremonial occasions. The personification of the house points out the theological principle implicit in the Balinese organization by threes. The replication of analogous trinities is not just a convenient way to organize the world; it is a way to epitomize the organic connectedness and interrelatedness of all things, natural and artificial. For example, not only does a Balinese home exhibit the same tripartite structure as a human being, but it also is created in accord with the organic proportions of its owner.

The layout, size, and proportions of all buildings within the house compound are dictated by a complex series of rules called *asta kosala kosali*. The home, a living thing, must be harmonious with the body of the family patriarch. It is only natural, therefore, that the system of measurements by which the *bale* is constructed should be based upon the microcosmos, the body, itself. The same is true for all other traditional Balinese structures, not just *bales* in the house compound.

Before the traditional Balinese architect, the *undagi*, does anything else, he takes various measurements from the body of the head of the household. The most important measurements are those governing the construction of the pillars, for it is their dimensions that will control the size of the buildings. The principal measurements are the length of the index finger, the width of the little finger, the width of the three middle fingers, and the width of the second joint of the index finger. From these measurements, a set of three notched bamboo sticks, called *gagulak,* are made, and these are used as measuring sticks for the pillars of the *bale* and associated structures. The basic measurements for the layout of the house compound are taken from the length and width of the owner's foot. The outside wall dimensions are determined by the span of his outstretched arms and the distance from elbow to outstretched thumb. The architect himself may bring the building to life when it is completed, or he may require the services of a priest if he does not know the proper prayers and procedures. The living trees that have been chopped down to make the pillars, the long grass that has been cut for the roof thatch, and other materials of construction, once assembled according to dimensions taken from a human body, are themselves brought to life, reincarnated, as a living house.

ORGANIZATION BY THREES MAY SEEM QUITE STRANGE to the Western visitor. Certainly, Christianity has its trinity and groupings by three are not unknown in the West. But our thought is much more dualistic, we are much more accustomed to paired opposites. In our thought, social relations, and politics, we seek resolution between two Manichean sides — us and them, pro and con, good and bad. When we balance our arguments, what we really do is subtract the "cons" from the "pros" and go with the remainder. This is fundamentally different from the Hindu-Balinese. They do not seek resolution as such, their worldview is not based on conflict + resolution = "progress." They seek to better organize and balance their lives around fixed ideas, already centuries old.

CHAPTER 2

Hinduism

THE INDIAN ROOTS OF BALINESE RELIGION

THE VIVID ACCOUNTS OF JOURNALISTS AND TRAVELERS who visited India after the British conquest have greatly colored popular Western notions of Hinduism. Hoping to arouse interest, these writers emphasized the more lurid and sensational aspects of some of the Hindu sects: suttee, burning of the deceased's wife (or wives) upon his funeral pyre; drenching idols with goat's blood; temples with frescoes of erotic art; ritual prostitution; the contortions of the practitioners of yoga; the strict rules of caste, including untouchability — and on and on. Nobody can deny that these practices existed and, in a few cases, still do exist. But they are not at all central to the fundamentals and philosophy of Hinduism. The Hinduism that came to Bali with the Javanese Majapahit dynasty was not a particularly glamorous sect. The official name of Balinese Hinduism is Agama Hindu or Hindu Dharma. Agama means "religion"; dharma does not slip into place very easily. In fact, understanding the concept of dharma is really the most straightforward way to understanding the basic philosophy of Hinduism.

Hinduism is founded on the belief that there is order in the world, that the universe is not random. Left entirely to itself, any natural system will tend toward a state of maximum disorder: rocks roll downhill, cold things warm up, living cells die. There exists everywhere in the universe a disordering force. Because order does exist, there must be an equivalent organizing force. What Hinduism seeks is an equilibrium, a balance, between these two forces or tendencies. Order is personified as the gods, *dewa* and *dewi*, or *bhatara* and *bhatari*. Disorder is personified as the earth demons, *bhutas* and *kalas*. One can think of order as good, or positive, and disorder as evil, or negative. Or you can call order dharma, and disorder adharma.

Hinduism is largely concerned with dharma, the organizing force that maintains order. Dharma is the organization that governs the universe as a whole, the relationships between various parts of the universe, and actions within the various parts of the universe. Hinduism recognizes the universe as an ordered whole of which each person, each animal, and each thing is an integral part. And each of these parts stands in a definite and established relationship to every other part — this relationship is dharma. A Hindu feels that his actions, his karma, must be in harmony with his dharma, "duty" or "order." A Hindu cannot look at the world from the point of view of his own interests, without regard for those of his fellow men, his fellow living creatures, and his fellow inanimate objects. His karma must be related to them and to his own dharma. If his karma fulfills his dharma, he contributes toward order and harmony. If it does not, he contributes toward disorder, chaos, and adharma.

The extent to which one's karma fulfills one's own particular dharma governs the future of one's atman, "spirit." Karma that does not fit with one's dharma produces suffering — either at the moment of inappropriate behavior or at some future time or in some future life. The only salvation for dharma is that the ordering force be kept at least as strong as the disordering force, so as to maintain equilibrium. Local pockets of prevailing disorder may form, and every effort must be made to insure that these pockets do not spread to other areas that are in equilibrium, lest adharma prevail generally. An example of a pocket of adharma on Bali might be a volcanic eruption, an illness, or a *leyak* (witch). Such pockets are generally only ephemeral. Local pockets of prevailing dharma may also form, and one must take quick advantage of them, because they too are but ripples on the sea, quick to fade. An example of a pocket of dharma might be an *odalan* (temple festival), a new grandson, or a *pedanda* (priest).

A Hindu lives according to dharma. He or she tries to respond to desire, *kama*, with action, karma, that is appropriate to the dharma. The key word is "appropriate." One does not "do good deeds" as a Hindu, one "behaves appropriately." Upon death, one's atman will be reborn into another corporeal vehicle, the station of which — animal, priest, farmer, etc. — will have been determined by the degree to which one's karma was proper to one's dharma. This cycle of reincarnation, samsara, will continue until the spirit is freed from all desire. Only then is the atman freed from the necessity of rebirth. At that point the spirit reaches a state called *moksa*. Then the atman fuses with the unmoved mover of the universe, representing both ordering and disordering forces, both order and disorder: Ida Sanghyang Widhi Wasa. The sacred Hindu texts refer to this mover as *brahman*.

People may lead lives in which the result of their activities is destructive, producing adharma and disorganization. For their efforts they will be

SIWA RIDING HIS VEHICLE, NANDI THE BULL

rewarded with the fruit, *pala*, of punishment in the now and the hereafter, and rebirth of their spirit in a shell stationed in a lower order of life. People can live with desire, if they are content with its transitory nature. But they can only do so if they understand three principals: *kama*, the desire itself; dharma, the laws governing the proper fulfillment of the desire; and *artha*, the means by which one achieves the lawful desire. Another choice, available to only a very few people, is the total avoidance of any form of desire, which will ultimately lead one's spirit to *moksa* and fusion with the unmoved mover. This third choice is the one chosen by ascetic Hindus, particularly in India. The five fundamentals of Hindu philosophy are: *brahman,* the one God; atman, the imperishable spirit; samsara, reincarnation; *karma-pala,* action and resulting reward and punishment; *moksa,* uniting with God after the disappearance of desire. These are called the Panca Crada, or "five principles."

A HIGHLY EVOLVED CULTURE flourished as far back as 3000 B.C. along the banks of the river Sindhu, now called Indus, in what is now Pakistan. It is from this name, Sindhu, that the word Hindu derives. The existence of this early civilization has come to light only in the past 60 years or so, with excavations at Harappa and Mohenjodaro, not far upriver from modern Karachi. Until this find historians supposed that the invading Aryans from eastern Europe civilized India. But the cities they discovered had broad, paved streets, sophisticated water supplies, sewage disposal, active markets, and spacious homes some 5,000 years ago. As well as the inhabitants of the Harappan cities, societies of unknown origin were living in India before the Aryan invasion. Their religion was animistic, and their world was full of demons, spirits, and forces that they struggled mightily to control through magical incantation and prayer.

The Aryans were a hardy, light-skinned, warlike people who lived in the vicinity of the Caspian Sea. Some migrated to what is now Iran. Some went farther east to northern India, seeking pasture land for their cattle. These were not the Aryans of Nazi mythology — the blue-eyed, fair-haired master race. They were lighter in skin color than the indigenous tribes whose territories they invaded, the Nagas and Dravidians. And they must have been considerably more skilled at warfare, because it did not take them long to overcome the natives and establish themselves as rulers. Historians date the Aryan migration at some time around 1600 B.C.

The Aryans had a pantheon of nature gods, which constituted a religion we call Vedism. Indra was one of the more powerful gods, the wielder of thunderbolts and lightning and the god of storms and war. Agni was the god of the fire that the Aryans used to perform their religious sacrifices. Rudra was god of the strong harsh winds. Sita was god of the furrow of the plowed field. Varuna was god of the earth. Savitar was the giver of life; and Surya, sometimes called Mitra or Wisnu, was god of the sun. Dyaus, the personification of the sky itself, was perhaps the most important of the early Vedic gods. The Sanskrit word *deva,* or *dewa,* originally meant "bright." It later came to mean "divine." Since the names of these deities were handed down to us in the Sanskrit language, and since many Sanskrit sounds do not occur in English, spellings vary.

We know a great deal about the religion and daily affairs of the Aryans because a substantial body of written material has survived. These are the Vedas, books that Hindus, both Indian and Balinese, consider to be divinely inspired and sacred. But the Vedas were oral texts, and were not recorded for many hundreds of years after they were created. They were composed as songs and hymns. The ancestral script of all Indian writing was not devised until the eighth or ninth centuries before the common era, yet it is estimated that the Vedas were sung at least 1,000 years earlier. Even after writing became commonplace in India the people preferred to have their sacred works transmitted orally, and it never occurred to them to have them written down. Only merchants and bankers kept written records. Four of what were probably dozens of Vedas have survived to this day:

THE RIG-VEDA. The oldest religious "text" in the world, this Veda was likely composed sometime between 1500 and 900 B.C. It is a collection of 1,028 hymns to be used at the religious sacrifices of the Aryan aristocrats.

THE SAMA-VEDA. Sometimes called "The Knowledge of the Melodies," the Sama-Veda is a collection of some of the verses of the Rig-Veda that have been arranged for religious purposes.

THE YAJUR-VEDA. Considered to be not as old as the Rig-Veda by some 200 years, the Yajur-Veda contains sacrificial formulas, in prose and poetry, for the use of the priests of lesser importance.

THE ARTAVA-VEDA. The most recent Veda, the Artava-Veda contains mostly magic spells and formulas in verse. This Veda has many non-Aryan elements, and scholars consider it to be the product of a less sophisticated source.

Each of the four Vedas has four parts:

1) Mantras, or hymns
2) Brahmanas, appendices to the mantras, manuals for priests
3) Aranyaka, appendices to the Brahmanas, manuals for forest meditation
4) Upanishads, also appendices to the Brahmanas, confidential sources for the study of philosophers

These works were composed at different times. The Brahmanas date from about 800 to 600 B.C., and the oldest Upanishads overlap the most recent Brahmanas. Taken as a whole, these are the components of what is referred to as the Vedic literature. The language in which they were originally composed and sung is unknown. As they come to us they are written in fairly sophisticated Sanskrit, which is obviously not an artifact of such an ancient civilization. But, the roots of these sacred works undoubtedly date back a thousand years or more into the untraceable shadows of pre-Aryan times. The Rig-Veda is the only one of the four that can be called a work of literature, as opposed to a work of magic, philosophy, or religion. Its hymns praise the various objects that the Aryans worshiped, forces of nature such as the sky, the earth, the sun and moon, rain, and so on. Some are prayers for long life, fertility, and rain. Some are poems of wonder. The religion of the people who composed the Vedas and Brahmanas and Upanishads was not Hinduism. But several hymns in the Rig-Veda give a hint at what was to become the main thrust of Hinduism centuries later. One is a hymn of creation in which the universe is described before anything existed in it — that is, anything except what is translated as "that one thing," or "the only one." This is *brahman,* the unmoved mover, the unknown knower. This theme of *brahman* is taken up at great length in the Upanishads, but it has roots in the earliest of all the Vedas.

SOME DEFINITIONS

BRAHMA — the manifestation of the supreme god as creator of all living things. Brahma was not an important part of the Aryan pantheon, but evolved into prominence at a later time.

BRAHMAN — a member of the priestly class or caste, in Aryan times and today. *Brahman* refers to the unknown and unknowable soul of the world, or god as the spirit that pervades the universe.

BRAHMANA — the priestly class or caste just like Brahman. But, as explained above, the word also refers to a group of Vedic materials that is concerned with manuals of rituals and prayer.

BRAHMIN — a term that is also used to mean any member of the priestly class or caste, whether a priest or not. It also has a more general meaning in English, "blue-blood" or "aristocrat."

The second very interesting hymn in the Rig-Veda is called the "Hymn to Purusha." The word *purusha* or *purusa* literally means "person" or "man." But it also means *brahman*, "god." This hymn is one of the first statements of the religious concept in which the god becomes a victim of sacrifice. From this primordial immolation of the supreme god came forth all human beings. And the hymn describes how from the mouth of Purusha came the Brahmanas, from his arms came the Ksatriya, from his thighs the Wesya, and from his feet the Sudra — the four castes of Bali. Remember that this text is the earliest religious work in the world, created at least 4,000 years before the Portuguese invaders applied their word "casta" to the social structure of India.

What we see in the Vedas, taken apart from the Upanishads and Brahmanas that are grouped within them, is an emphasis upon the powerful forces of nature and a personification and deification of them. The essential intent of the Vedic prayers was to maintain order — to monitor the usual course of natural affairs and happenings so that by imitating them they might continue forever. The Aryans had an open society. There were classes, but these were not rigid castes. Upward (and downward) mobility was possible, depending upon individual worth and achievement. The ruling class was that of the warriors. Next in status and prestige came that group known, even then, as Brahmanas — the priests whose responsibility it was to maintain balance by offering sacrifices and prayers to *brahman* and the nature gods. Apparently Vedism's principal religious ceremonies involved sacrifice to the gods using fire as the medium to carry the offerings. There were no permanent temples or shrines or idols. Unlike later Hinduism, the Vedic Brahmanas were quite below the warrior class, acting merely as those who officiated at rituals, with no political power.

One of the most sacred hymns of the Rig-Veda is called the Gayatri. It was whispered into the ear of an upper class boy by a priest at the climax of the initiation ceremony in which the boy was inducted as a full member of his class and society. The Sudras — workers and servants — and those lower were not allowed to undergo this ceremony and, in fact, could not even hear the sacred text. This was a very ancient rite, dating far earlier than the Aryan invasion. The verse is addressed to the god of the sun, Savitar:

> Tat Savitur vareniam
> bhargo devasya dhimahi
> dhiyo yo nah pracodayat.

"Let us think on the lovely splendor of the god Savitar, that he may inspire our minds."

Doubtless this means nothing to you, unless you are a Balinese Hindu. If you are, you will immediately recognize it as the opening of that very important mantra called the Trisandhya. It is considered so important that, for example, it is recited every day when the Denpasar television station, TVRI, opens its broadcast schedule. Virtually every Balinese knows at least the opening four or five lines. And it comes from the most sacred verse of the most ancient religious text extant.

The Upanishads mark the real beginnings of Hinduism. The name comes from the Sanskrit words *upa*, meaning "near," and *shad*, "to sit." "Sitting near" refers to the relationship between teacher and student. More than 100 Upanishads have been printed in Sanskrit, and their total length is about the same as that of the Old and New Testaments of the Bible combined. Their constant, relentless theme is that of *brahman* and atman. Atman is usually translated as "soul" or "spirit"; it is the essence of a person. It is not the mind or the individuality, but rather that which is described as a formless, silent depth of being. The first lesson of the Upanishads is that the essence of a person is his atman. The second lesson is the acceptance and understanding of the concept of *brahman,* as previously described. And the final and most important teaching is that atman and *brahman* are one and the same. This is really the essential teaching of Hinduism. You can strip away all the externals — the offerings, the prayers, the ceremonies, the temples — everything. Because it is the concept of the unity of *brahman* and atman that has as its natural consequences the special attitudes that Hindus have about the nature, purpose, and importance of life, death, the world of man, and the universe.

One of the most famous dialogues between teacher and student in the Upanishads is found in the Chandogya Upanishad. Here we find the teacher explaining by parable the doctrine of the identity of atman and *brahman.* He asks the student to bring him the fruit of a nearby tree and break it open. The student is asked what he sees within. He replies that he sees tiny seeds. And the teacher then asks him to break open one of them and tell what he sees. He replies that he does not see anything. The teacher replies that the subtle essence that the student does not perceive is the very essence upon which the fruit tree exists.

"That which is the subtle essence, in it all that exists has its self. It is the true. It is the self. And you, my son: *tat twam asi.*"

This last phrase is often quoted as being the very pith of Hinduism. It means "You are that." In other words, your atman and that of the tree, and that of *brahman* are one and the same. You, the individual, are identical with the ultimate principle of things — *brahman.* After the Upanishads we can say that Hinduism, as we now know it, really began. The world of the nature gods began to disappear from the thinking of the philosophers, and an internalization of thought began which led to the rather abstract ideas of atman and *brahman*. The Vedic literature, however, was not very accessible because it was written in obscure, allegorical language and guarded by the priests. The flowering of popular Hinduism really began with the creation of a body of literature that was readily available and could be understood by the average person.

THE FIRST HINDU EPIC POEMS began to appear in the beginning of the last millennium before the common era. The two greatest epics of Hindu literature, the Mahabharata and the Ramayana, were hugely influential. They were lessons in morality; they were entertainment; they were subjects for discussion; and they presented an opportunity for the average person to appreciate how important a role the ideas of Hinduism played in the life of gods, legendary heroes and heroines, and men and women. Even today the epics provide great entertainment. They describe enough wild battles to keep even the most somnolent awake. The heroic exploits they relate will warm the heart of the most adventurous. Three thousand years after they were composed, one has only to visit a *wayang kulit* — shadow puppet — performance in one of the villages in Bali and see the rapt attention of the audience to understand the grip that these wonderful stories have upon Hindus even today.

But within the Ramayana and Mahabharata are contained passages that are extremely sacred to even the most learned Hindu. And the most sacred of all is the Bhagavad-Gita. This long passage of the Mahabharata is a kind of lecture given by Krishna to Arjuna, who is about to lead his family into battle with his cousins. Krishna is Arjuna's friend and charioteer, and when Arjuna hesitates to do battle with the family, Krishna reveals himself as Wisnu and proceeds to offer at some length some of the central lessons that were first developed in the Upanishads. The average Hindu could now get a glimmer of what his religion was all about, because these pronouncements were being made not by a high caste, remote, and unapproachable priest, but by one of the heroes of a popular story that was being recited or sung by a local or traveling bard. The epics humanized Hinduism 2,500 years ago, and they appear to be just as effective now as they were then.

The story of the Mahabharata is long and very complex. The action takes place in north central India, not far north of the present New Delhi, a region then called Kuruksetra. Dhritarashtra and Pandu were the sons of the mighty hero Bharata (hence the name of the story, "Great Bharata"). Dhritarashtra, the elder of the two, fell heir to the Kuru Kingdom, the capital of which was Hastinapura. But Dhritarashtra was blind, which meant that he could not rule. So his younger brother Pandu took over the throne. Then Pandu was afflicted with a curse and had to give up the kingdom and

ARJUNA AND HIS CHARIOTEER, KRISHNA

flee to the mountains with his two wives — leaving the blind Dhritarashtra in charge. Pandu had five children, the Pandawas, by various wives. They were Yudhisthira, Bhima, Arjuna, and the twins Nakula and Sahadeva. They were quite young when Pandu died, and they were taken to Hastinapura to be educated with their 100 cousins, the children of Dhritarashtra, called the Kurus or Korawas.

When he grew up, Yudhisthira, the eldest of the Pandawas, was determined to be heir apparent. But the sons of Dhritarashtra, led by the eldest, Duryodhana, did not like the Pandawas, resented their presence, and plotted against them. Duryodhana could not force the Pandawas to leave because his father, because of his blindness, was not really king. The Kurus made a number of attempts on the lives of the Pandawa brothers, so the Pandawas decided to leave and made their way around the countryside. Along the way, at the kingdom of the Pancalas, Arjuna won Princess Draupadi in a contest, and she promptly became the wife of all five jointly. Here too the brothers met their great future friend Krishna, head of the Yadavas. Shortly thereafter Dhritarashtra decided to give up his throne, called the five brothers home, and split the kingdom evenly between them and his sons, the Kurus. The Pandawas built a new capital city at Indraprastha. But the Kurus were still resentful. Duryodhana invited Yudhisthira to a game of dice and, assisted by his uncle Sakuni who was a master of cheating, won the entire kingdom, all five brothers, and Draupadi. The Pandawas agreed to go into exile for thirteen years, spend their last year incognito, and then return to Duryodhana who would return their kingdom to them. This they did, and at the end of the thirteen years, demanded their lands from Duryodhana. He refused.

War was declared, and each side summoned its allies from all over India — even China and Bactria. The two huge armies faced each other on the plains of Delhi. At this point Arjuna hesitated to go into battle against family and friends, and Krishna revealed himself as Wisnu, telling Arjuna that his business was the deed, not the result, and that the right course must be chosen according to circumstances, without considering personal interest or sentiment (the Bhagavad-Gita). The war lasted 18 days, and at the end virtually the only survivors were the five Pandawas and Krishna. Yudhisthira became king and the five ruled happily for a long time in peace. Finally Yudhisthira gave up the throne, putting Arjuna's grandson in his place, and, with Draupadi, the brothers climbed Mount Meru and entered heaven. As indicated, there are many diversions to the story between dramatic scenes, and there is every indication that the epic began as a simple story and grew by accretion over the years.

The Ramayana is much shorter than the Mahabharata and includes fewer diversions. According to tradition it was composed by one man, the sage Valmiki, who lived at the same time as Rama. The scene of the story is the capital of the kingdom of Kosala, named Ayodhya. Dasaratha, king of Kosala, had four sons by three wives. Of these sons, Rama and Laksmana were the most famous. The four boys attended the court of a nearby king, where Rama won the hand of the king's daughter, Sita, at an archery contest. Rama and Sita were married and lived happily at Ayodhya with Dasaratha. When Dasaratha grew old he named Rama as his heir. But Dasaratha's second wife, Kaikeyi, reminded Rama of a promise the aging king had made to her many years ago, namely that her own son Bharata be named king and that Rama be banished. In spite of the protests of Dasaratha and Bharata, Rama insisted upon fulfilling his father's promise and took Sita and Laksmana into exile in the forest. Dasaratha died, and Bharata took over the rule, but only until such time as Rama might return.

While in the forest of Dandaka, Rama killed many demons who were bothering local ascetics and villagers. A beautiful princess from the South, Surpanakha, met Rama wandering in the forest, fell in love with him, and tried to seduce him, but Rama remained true to Sita. Furious at Rama, Surpanakha sought revenge by asking her demon brother, Rawana, king of Langka (Ceylon) to come and kidnap Sita. He did so, distracting Rama and Laksmana by changing himself into a golden deer, which Laksmana chased, temporarily abandoning his guardianship of the safety of Sita. Rawana took Sita back to Langka. Rama and Laksmana, aided by the monkey king, Sugriva, and his general, Hanuman, and by Rawana's brother, Vibhishana, raised a large army and journeyed to the strait separating Langka from India. Hanuman was sent ahead to scout out Langka, and, leaping over the strait, found her in Rawana's palace. With his monkey army, Rama built a causeway of stones across the strait, invaded Langka, and, after a great battle, killed Rawana and rescued Sita.

Although Sita had not yielded to Rawana, she had, in fact, lived in his palace, and so she could not be accepted as a wife by Rama, according to sacred law. She threw herself on a funeral pyre in despair, but Agni, the god of fire, would not accept her. This proved her innocence well enough to Rama, who returned with her to Ayodhya, where Bharata gave up the throne and Rama reigned in his rightful place. However, the people of Ayodhya were upset because of Sita's living at Rawana's house, and they suspected her of impurities, in spite of the trial by fire. So Rama had to banish her to the forest, even though he knew of her innocence. After bearing two of Rama's children, Sita called upon her mother, the earth, to take her back, whereupon she was swallowed up. And Rama returned to heaven and resumed his identity as Wisnu. It must be remembered that Sita means "furrow," and that Sita was a goddess of the furrow in Aryan times.

These two stories are too well known to warrant further analysis here. The Mahabharata is by far the longer of the two, containing more than 100,000 verses, most of them of 32 syllables each, making a work that is about three times as large as the entire King James Bible. The central theme, the war between the Pandawas and their cousins, the Korawas, apparently did have a basis in historical fact, probably having occurred some time around 900 B.C. But this war is only the outline of the story. Between the stories that lead up to the battle and the battle scenes themselves is woven a vast complex of totally unrelated episodes that may or may not involve some of the characters of the main story.

One of the most popular subjects for *wayang kulit* is the story of Bhima Suci, in which Bhima, one of the five Pandawas brothers, is sent by his teacher to find a certain important kind of holy water. The story is quite simple in and of itself. It involves Bhima's encounters in heaven with a number of people who have been sent there for reward and punishment according to their karma. The discussion surrounds what they did in their previous lives to merit such reward or punishment. And this, of course, offers a theological and moral lesson. But in the context of entertainment by a professional entertainer-teacher, the *dalang* puppet master, the lesson is easily learned by the audience. These methods of education are so effective that the Indonesian Government today uses the *wayang kulit* to teach secular duties like family planning and conservation of resources. (See CHAPTER 28.)

The Hindu epics are not the only source of popular Hindu inspiration. Over the millennium straddling the beginning of the common era, 500 B.C. to A.D. 500, there arose a huge body of what are called the Puranas — the old stories. There are 18 of them, and the total text is four times longer than even the Mahabharata — more than 400,000 couplets. These stories were written specifically for ordinary people so that they might learn about their religion and history. Creation is explained, as is the periodic evolution and dissolution of the world. The doctrine of karma is dealt with at some length. Transmigration, the seven heavens, the twenty-one hells and punishments therein, and much more are treated in these long works. Some of the materials are taken from the two major epic poems. All of them are written in intelligible, popular language without pretense to superior literary form. Thus they admirably fulfill their function as a means of popular education in a world that lacked it.

THE POST-UPANISHAD FLOWERING OF HINDUISM saw profound changes in the way the people looked at God. To the fore came the concept of the Trimurti, or "three shapes" — the Hindu triad Brahma, Wisnu, and Siwa. Wisnu was resurrected from a role as a rather minor sun god in the Aryan pantheon. Brahma was given a supreme position of importance as creator, but was not given sufficient attributes so that he attracted followers or attention. He remains still in the background as an attribute of God, impersonal, intangible and distant from the ordinary person — important, but detached. Wisnu's role represents the bright side of Hindu life. Wisnu is the approachable helper of man who has come to man's aid nine times in the past (the avatars) when danger threatened on earth. Wisnu is a bit like the Virgin Mary of the Christians — not an "earth mother," but an aspect of divinity that seems human and reachable, sympathetic and understanding. Wisnu's incarnations as Krishna and Rama are enormously important to, and popular with, Hindus. Rama especially seems like the ideal man, the hero who devotes his life to avenging a wrong against great odds.

The worship of Siwa seems to be one of the oldest elements in India, if not in Hinduism. The presence at Mohenjodaro of the most common symbol of Siwa, the phallic *linggam,* led excavators there to conclude that the Harappans did indeed worship Siwa — perhaps 2,500 years before the Upanishads and the epics. But Siwa did not play an important role in the pantheon of the Aryans. Taken literally, the word Siwa means "propitious." This is a euphemism, since Siwa is that aspect of God involving death and destruction. In India the two most important Hindu sects are those who worship Wisnu as their principal deity and those who worship Siwa.

In Bali Siwaism is by far the more important of the two. Hindu man, faced with the overwhelming problems of life, sees Siwa as a vigorous force that energetically breaks down everything that Wisnu has protected and Brahma has produced. Why the *linggam* as the symbol of Siwa? The *linggam* is a phallus — symbolic of creativity, not of destruction. Should

this not be the symbol of Brahma, the creator? Siwa is often depicted in statues as performing a dance. It may seem odd that the arch destroyer is dancing. But to a Hindu, death is almost the same as rebirth, and rebirth is the frustration of death. In the Hindu mind this balance of forces seems perfectly natural. Siwa is not only a destroyer, but also a creator, and the dance is an accompaniment to the perpetual dissolving and reforming of the world. The creative or reproductive nature of Siwa is often personified as Siwa's wife, Durga, sometimes called Uma, Parwati or Kali. This has some significance to Balinese Hinduism, since the common figure of Rangda is similar in many ways to Durga. This goddess is not only the ruler of death and destruction, but also of motherhood. There is nothing obscene about phallic symbols to the Hindus. Siwaism is a system of beliefs which requires the most extreme self-discipline, asceticism, and intellectualism. Ghandi once wrote that the first time he learned that *linggams* were obscene was when he was studying a missionary's book.

THERE ARE MANY WAYS TO ACHIEVE LIBERATION, *MOKSA.* One is by meditation. That is rather restricted to intellectuals, because it involves close contact with *brahman.* It is called *jnanamarga.* A second is by ordinary prayers and by making offerings. This is called *bhaktimarga.* And a third is by doing something that will please God, such as creating fine artwork, performing sacred music and dances, and so on, according to one's talents. This is called *karma marga.*

Alternatively, one may look at the three ways of worshiping, the Tri Pramana. The first is pure dogmatism, Agama Pramana. This means simply doing what you are told to do by heads that are presumably wiser than your own. A second is by studying, questioning, and drawing conclusions from that study — Anumana Pramana. And the third route is by meditation, Pratyaksa Prama. All of these methods are equally valid and acceptable, according to the abilities of the devotee. There is no "best" way to achieve liberation. Liberation may be easier for an unschooled farmer to achieve by following dogma than it is for a Brahmana to achieve by meditation. It all depends upon his feelings and how he goes about it.

CHAPTER 3

Caste and Clan

BRAHMANA, KSATRIYA, WESYA, AND SUDRA

OF ALL THE ASPECTS OF HINDUISM, CASTE IS THE LEAST UNDERSTOOD and the most execrated. The caste system of India, with its outcastes, the untouchables, is often compared in the popular imagination of the West to political systems of discrimination, like apartheid in South Africa, or "Jim Crow" in the United States. A Westerner finds the rigidity of caste, and the cruelty of untouchability, to be by definition unjust. But caste is not a government policy, it is a complex system of social organization historically based on social function — smith, farmer, priest, etc. — which eventually became entwined with Hindu doctrine.

The word "caste," as applied to the ordering of Hindu society, comes from the Portuguese, who upon arriving in India in 1498 used the word *casta*, "division," to refer to the stratification of Indian society. But caste is not the same as class, or station, or "division" in a Western society. It is the manifestation on an individual level of an elaborate web of cultural organization in Hindu society wherein balance and propriety are privileged concepts. Caste is the social codification of dharma. Caste lies outside, or perhaps deeper than, political organization by governments. Both the Indian and the Indonesian governments have "banned" discrimination by caste. But in India, and in Bali, caste is too ingrained to disappear by edict.

Away from the offices, or schools, caste in Bali is still quite important. "Where do you sit?" a polite way of asking, "What is your caste?" is the first or second question a Balinese will ask upon meeting a stranger. Caste prerogatives are maintained, in address and codes of deference, and individuals associate more freely and often with those of their own caste than with others. Although there are those in Bali who would seek to reform the system,

for the most part the Balinese accept the social organization of caste. In a
sense, caste in Bali can be understood as something like the Renaissance
system of patronage. There is a dual obligation between members of lower
and upper castes. Most Sudra — the lowest caste — families have one or
more related Brahmana families to whom they turn in the case of special
need, usually of a religious nature. The lower caste people are said to be the
sisya, pupils, or disciples, of their upper caste *surya*, literally "sun," meaning
patron. It is the obligation of the *surya* family to help, just as it is the obligation of the lower caste family to defer and offer a token, food and offerings, for the services. There is obvious gratitude on the part of the Sudra
family and obvious satisfaction on the part of their *surya* — they have been
able to fulfill their duty as Brahmana. Some examples of this relationship:

1) When a *pratima* — a small ceremonial statue — needs repainting,
or when a *barong* mask needs to be repaired, a village always asks a
Brahmana to do the work because he knows how to protect himself
against the power of the objects that he is dealing with. When some
of the masks used for performances in our village needed repairs, a
Brahmana man from Sanur spent upwards of two or three weeks, six
hours a day, repainting them.
2) When there is a cremation, the *surya* is called upon to perform the
final rites of opening the shroud, pouring holy water from various
sources on the remains, and arranging the various offerings in and
around the sarcophagus.
3) When an important house purification is to take place, a new
shrine built, a building dedicated, invariably a *surya* is called in to
help make offerings and present them in the proper fashion.
4) When a family temple anniversary is to be celebrated, often as not
the *surya* group will be asked to read from the sacred scripts, the *lontars,* and also to provide someone who can translate the Old Balinese
or Sanskrit into the vernacular.

Bali has four castes, listed here in order of ascending privilege: Sudra,
Wesya, Ksatriya, and Brahmana. And within these are further subdivisions,
some specific to areas of the island and some based on Hindu strictures
such as those relating to marriage outside of caste. Partly overlapping these
categories, but also with an organizing structure of its own, is the clan system, which is laid out according to genealogy, historical occupation, and
caste. The organization of social and religious station in Bali is Byzantine in
its complexity, and can probably only be partly understood by a Westerner.

CASTE PREDATES THE HINDU RELIGION ITSELF. Since early Vedic times

Indian society recognized distinct classes, and the social order that Westerners call "caste" in both India and Bali owes its origin to Vedic ideas that are 4,000 years old. According to the Rig-Veda, the world's oldest liturgical text:

> When they divided Purusa, how many portions did they make? What do they call his mouth, his arms? What do they call his thighs and feet?
> The Brahmin was his mouth, of both his arms was the Ksatriya made. His thighs became the Wesya, from his feet the Sudra was produced.
> — *Rig-Veda 10.90*

The "Hymn to Purusa" — the word *purusa*, which literally means "man," is here used in a figurative way to refer to *brahman,* the prime mover — is the most ancient reference to the four divisions of Aryan, pre-Hindu, society. In the text these divisions are called *warna*, which originally meant "color" but came to mean "station," implying choice of occupation. The choice of the word *warna* undoubtedly had its origins in the fact that the Aryans were lighter in skin color than the native tribes of India, but there was no concept of closed caste among those who practiced Vedism. The four ancient *warnas* were the same as the castes in Bali today. There were priests, the Brahmanas, and there were rulers, the Ksatriya, and these two, jockeying with each other for the most exalted status, traded control over society for many centuries until, at last, the Brahmanas won out some 2,500 years ago.

Aryan society also made room for the Wesya, fairly close to the top, but not very close. They were allowed into the fold of the "twice-born" as the adult upper classes were known. They were merchants, not rulers or priests. At the bottom were the Sudras, who could not be initiated, but who were still Aryans. Their job was to help the other three *warnas.* There was mobility between the four *warnas,* and merit or demerit could result in a change of station. Way at the bottom of the ladder were the outcastes or untouchables. These people had no status whatsoever. The members of this unfortunate group were pre–Aryan invasion native tribes and Aryans who had violated their dharma, or "duty," so violently that they could no longer be admitted to society. The Aryans had no notion that any of the four *warna* was "better" than the rest, they were all considered necessary. The Rig-Veda suggests that just as a man has head, shoulders, thighs, and feet, none of these being much good by itself, so does society need all four of its parts in order to function. The highest two *warnas* enjoyed privileges that the lower two did not, but that was as far as discrimination went.

SOME DEFINITIONS

WARNA. "Color." Specifically, in our discussion, skin color. Later *warna* came to mean "order" of society, implying profession.

WARGA. "Family," or "clan." It refers to the group to which one belongs by birth.

WANGSA. "Descent," in the genealogical sense, or lineage.

CASTE. Derived from the Portuguese word *casta*, which, in turn, comes from the Latin *castus*, meaning "pure." It implies division, through birth and heredity, according to unchangeable laws.

DHARMA. In the present context dharma means traditional duties, according to one's class, profession, or status.

KARMA. "Deeds." It refers to one's actual deeds during life, as contrasted with what those deeds should be according to dharma.

GUNA. "Aptitude" or talent for a particular profession or task.

Notions of caste can also be traced to the Bhagavad-Gita, meaning "Celestial Song," the part of the epic Mahabharata that is considered one of the most sublime and sacred of all the Hindu writings. It describes an episode that takes place just before the culminating battle between the Pandawas and their cousins the Kurus. Arjuna, one of the five Pandawa brothers, hesitates before the battle and tells his close friend and charioteer, Krishna, that he cannot bring himself to kill relatives and former friends. Krishna thereupon reveals himself as Wisnu and instructs Arjuna.

> I have created the four-fold order according to the divisions of aptitude (*guna*) and work (karma). Though I am its creator, I am incapable of action or change.
> — *Book 4, Verse 13*

This statement, taken by itself, implies that anyone could claim to be a member of one of the four *warna*, birthright notwithstanding, simply upon the basis of his or her choice of profession. A class that is determined by temperament and vocation is not a class determined by birth and heredity (*jati*). It appears here that Krishna means that conduct is the only determining feature of *warna*.

Better is one's own law (dharma) though imperfectly carried out than the law of another carried out perfectly. Better is death in the fulfillment of one's own law, than prosperity in the law of another.
— *Book 3, Verse 35*

One's own law (dharma) imperfectly observed is better than another's law carried out with perfection. As long as one does the work set by nature, he does not incur blame.
— *Book 18, Verse 47*

The meaning of the last two verses, combined with that of the first one, is taken by scholars to be that division into *warna* is made once and for all time by birth. And Brahmanas, Ksatriyas, Wesyas, and Sudras will continue to belong to the class in which they were born. Thus, a member of a particular *warna* should not have the choice of taking up the profession meant for another *warna*, nor should he have the latitude to adopt a *warna* of choice. These texts suggest that the term *warna* evolved — as Vedism gave way to Hinduism — from a reference to the complexions of those in different social classes to a meaning that is very much like *wangsa*, or inherited descent. The word started out based on adopted vocation — priest, warrior-ruler, tradesman, or helper — and ended up meaning a fixed social class one is born into.

The Bhagavad-Gita is by no means the only source for this set of teachings. Other parts of the Mahabharata contain similar ideas, as does the Code of Manu. The essence of what Krishna is telling Arjuna is that he, Arjuna, having the *warna* of a Ksatriya, has, therefore, the duty, the dharma, to go ahead and fight, even it means killing friends and relatives. This duty transcends the self and must be carried out in the spirit of disinterestedness, without regard for one's own personal feelings. And only in that way can the man of disinterested action reach *brahman*.

The essence of the relationship between dharma and karma (deeds), sheds some light on how Vedic notions of *warna*, flexible and based on chosen occupation, evolved into the the more rigid Hindu idea of *wangsa*, or birthright-based classes. Krishna suggests a propriety of action, a matching of karma to dharma in order to achieve one's religious destiny, liberation. But dharma, Krishna says, depends on — is determined by — *warn a*, itself a matter not of choice, but of birthright. In this manner, a Hindu's future course of action is fairly well mapped out for him if he wishes to achieve liberation. Today, this map is in part provided by caste.

THERE WERE FOUR *WARNAS* IN VEDIC DAYS. And there are still four. But in the years between the writing of the Bhagavad-Gita, perhaps 200 B.C., to the coming of the British to India in 1690, Hindu society became stratified

A PEDANDA SIWA, A BRAHMANA PRIEST, IN PRAYER

in an entirely different way. And the unfortunate and confusing problem is that the same non-Indian word — "caste" — used to refer to stratification by *warna* is also commonly used to refer to this second type of stratification. As Hinduism evolved, social stratification gradually developed along the lines of what may be called guilds, craft groups, or trade groups. By 1690 there were hundreds of them. Most had three characteristics in common: marriage was only legitimate within the group; food was only to be received from and eaten in the presence of members of the same or of a higher group; each man was to live by the trade or profession of his own group and not take up that of another group. Indian society had groups of every conceivable calling: dyers, musicians, grave diggers, jewelers, cultivators, weavers, cowherds, leather workers, potters, liquor sellers, and hundreds of others. And, just as in the case of stratification by *warna*, each of these groups had its own set of rules, or dharma.

The craft groups of India were more than just clubs, or guilds. They were sources of support in time of need and crisis. They were sources of money when it was needed. They meant ready assistance when there was a field to plow or a wedding to prepare for. In Bali today, the *banjars*, village organizations, play an analogous role. Without this assistance and support a Balinese today, or a Hindu at any time during the past 2,000 years, would be a helpless drifter, cut off from the support and help of family and friends. The system provides a functional social structure.

For those of the lower orders, life was much more affected by position relative to other classes of lower orders than it was by position relative to the higher *warnas*. There was often as much discrimination and exclusiveness exhibited between, say, leather workers (who handled the skin of the sacred cow) and weavers as there was between government officials and businessmen. And not only the lower classes suffered fragmentation. Stratification developed among the Brahmanas, Ksatriyas, and Wesyas. Priests who dealt exclusively with ceremonies concerning death rites, for example, were lower on the totem pole than those dealing with what were considered to be less polluting activities.

When introduced by the Portuguese, "caste" became a convenient word, quickly adopted by the Hindus themselves and later by the British, to describe both *warna* and trade group. Thus the Vedic "Brahmana," a class of priests anyone with the proper interest and talent could join, ended up the Hindu "Brahmana," a caste determined by birth. The regulations of caste were elaborate, involving dietary prohibitions, complex rules regarding just how close a person of inferior caste could come to one of higher caste, rules about touching each other, eating or drinking out of the same container or with the same utensils, and innumerable more.

The rules made distinctions between internal and external pollution. It was proper for a Brahmana to eat a fruit that had been handled by a Sudra, because the pollution could be washed off. But it was not proper for him to eat food that had been cooked in water that the Sudra had touched, since this internal stain could not be washed away. Some of these laws seem to us today to be sound rules for hygiene. Others sound like frantic efforts to maintain the purity of the group. Some seem arbitrary, as if conceived just to make the group different. People whose profession required the destruction of life, for example those who pressed oil from living seeds, were quite far down the line of prestige. Yet those who sold the oil and who were not involved with killing anything were greatly respected. Some clothes washers who laundered the apparel of the untouchables — about as low a job as you could get — were even considered to be un*see*able — and had to operate only by night. And so stratified did the strata themselves become that even the outcastes had outcastes.

The coming of the British meant a great change in the way people in India lived. Instead of small craft groups and cottage industry, factories, armies, and government offices arose in which individuals could hardly be expected to observe the very strict rules and regulations of caste. These changing social conditions made it difficult, and it is especially difficult today, for the children of a person of high caste to adopt the same profession of their father. It is now often necessary for a person to change professions, such as when a businessman or professional man is called upon to enter government. In other words, the caste system, however bad or good it has been, was created for a social order quite different from that of today, and shows many signs of changing.

WHEN THE MAJAPAHIT FLED JAVA in the fourteenth century, they brought caste — as well as the rest of Hinduism — to Bali. Bali has four castes, although each is subdivided, which are analogous to the Vedic *warna* — Brahmana, Ksatriya, Wesya, and Sudra. All castes are stratified, and, to make matters worse, the terminology differs from area to area in Bali. Popular books on Bali suggest that there is an orderly classification, by birth, of four groups of people, each of whom can easily be identified by his name, and each of whom has a certain function: the Brahmanas to preach and teach, the Ksatriyas to govern, the Wesyas to run the shops, and the Sudras to do the dirty work. This is a great simplification. There are four castes, true, but they are subdivided and fragmented into dozens of status groups. And the clan system, woven within and without caste, offers hundreds more.

The Brahmanas on Bali, all said to be descendants of Pedanda Wawu Rauh, have five divisions: Kemenuh, Manuaba, Keniten, Mas, and Antapan. Ostensibly the descendants of one man, the groups are each named for the various areas from which Wawu Rauh's wives came. The first three are in Java, and the last two in Bali. All five are considered to be of the same level, but the younger Brahmanas are subordinate to the older ones. All have the same status, and, supposedly, all believe themselves to be of equal importance. Men are named Ida Bagus and women Ida Ayu, or Dayu for short.

If a Brahmana man marries a Ksatriya woman, his caste remains the same. If he is a *pedanda,* a priest, both man and wife have the same status. If a Brahmana man marries a Wesya woman, his status is unchanged, but the woman keeps her Wesya title — often, but not always, Gusti. In the past, if the descendants of the male Brahmana progenitor kept on marrying Wesya women, after three marriages in the descent line the man's caste dropped to Wesya. This had been a strict rule, but it is not often followed nowadays. In some areas, a person can only be called Ida Bagus or Ida Ayu if both mother and father are bona fide, pure-blood Brahmana. If the mother is lower in caste than the father, the child may be called Gusti or Gusti Bagus, or if a woman, Ida Made or Ida Putu.

The situation gets more complex with the Ksatriya caste. This historically has been the caste of rulers, who tend to be extremely jealous of title, status, and prerogative. There has been continued strife between the two highest castes over which of the two was superior. The pendulum has tended to swing toward the rulers and warriors — Ksatriya — in time of war and toward the priests and scholars — Brahmana — in time of peace.

Today in Bali, Ksatriyas will tell you that they and the Brahmanas are equal in status. But this is not exactly true. If a Ksatriya dies a Brahmana can pray toward his corpse, but the reverse is not allowed. Brahmanas certainly convey privately the attitude that their caste is "primus inter pares," first among equals, even though they may publicly shun preeminence. But at the same time it is said that those of the two upper castes who understand *paridan, surudan,* and *lungsuran* — important rites concerning offerings — will always be equal. To make matters even more complex, there is even such a thing as the Ksatriya equivalent of a Brahmana holy man, the *pedanda.* Such a person undergoes the same intensive study and training as a Brahmana, but his title is *begawan.* There are only three of them functioning today — in Klungkung, Ketewel, and Kapal.

The capital of Javanese influence over Bali became Gelgel, near Klungkung, and thus Ksatriya Dalem of Gelgel was considered the most important ruler. There were complex rules for name changing in the case of marriage with a lower caste, which add a second title to Ksatriya. The list of titles, in descending order of importance, is: Predewa, Pengakan, Bagus, and Prasangiang. The children of the first Ksatriya Dalem are called by the same name. If one of these marries a Wesya or Sudra, his status doesn't change, but his children are called Ksatriya Predewa, as are their children. And that title remains the same until someone marries a person of lower caste, in which case the names of their children go down another notch on the above list. Today, this practice has been abandoned.

Shortly after Ksatriya Dalem settled in Gelgel, Erlangga established himself as the raja of Kediri, one of the sections of East Java. Erlangga, who had a Balinese father and a Javanese mother, sent an army to Bali under the leadership of a king named Meruti, who conquered the Gelgel area. Meruti established one of his men as the ruler of the area with the title of Dewa Agung. This Dewa Agung had two children. The first had the title of Cokorda, the second Anak Agung. And these titles remained with their off-spring, all down the genealogical lineage, getting more and more complex as occasional marriages with lower caste people forced minor changes in status. The names persist today, but hardly anyone pays any attention to them except within the *puri*, the home of the former ruler of each area.

The Wesya arrived with the other castes from Java in the form of three groups: Tan Kober, Tan Kaur, and Tan Mundur, which have meanings ranging from "willing" to "brave." In those days all were called Gusti. But, there was another Gusti branch, Gusti Para Arya, that came from the Dalem of Klungkung. The Dalem was ordered to come to Bali from Java to rule, and his ministers, *patih*, were given his name. Most Wesyas are named Gusti, but not all are, because the word has now come to mean not only the member of a caste but also the member of a certain type of clan.

One sometimes hears the name "Ngurah" for a Wesya. The story is told of the reestablishment of the raja in Buleleng in the middle and late 1930s. The raja wanted badly to revert to the old names and habits of privilege. He took for himself the title of I Gusti Putu Jelantik. Near his house there was a hill, and he observed that, as he passed to and from home, people who stood on the hill to watch him were actually higher than he was. So, he had the hill cut off. To get even, the people nearby changed their names to Ngurah, which gave them more prestige than before and which was their only way of getting back at their ruler.

There are some people who have names that begin with the prefix Si, for example "Si Made So-and-So." This is an abbreviation of "Gusi" (not to be confused with "Gusti"). The name signifies a status above that of Sudra, but somewhat below that of regular Wesya. People with such a name are often the children of a mixed-caste marriage, the woman being of higher caste than her husband. Of course, many Gustis are the result of people who *ngraradang,* lose caste because of marriage to someone of lower caste.

The Sudra are basically those who are left, the "outsiders" of the Tri Wangsa. This group today, and in the past, constitutes some 90 percent of Bali's population. The Sudra in Bali are also sometimes called the Jaba, a word that comes from Jawi ("Java") and means, generally, "outsider." This, of course, is more than a little ironic because the *triwangsa,* and the rest of Hinduism, came to the original inhabitants of Bali by way of the Javanese.

CLAN PROVIDES YET ANOTHER SOCIAL STRUCTURE IN BALI, sometimes overlapping caste divisions, sometimes forming a separate but equal net-work. The proper Balinese word for "clan," derived from Sanskrit, is *warga*. The English "clan" seems to mean the same thing — an organization or group that shares a common lineage. There are at least 22 of these clans in Bali. In some cases the membership is restricted by caste. In other words, if you are a Brahmana you can't be a member of the Pasek clan. In others, clans cut across caste boundaries. Good examples are the various clans with names prefixed by "Arya," which implies lineage dating from that culture in pre-Hindu India — a lineage that may or may not be valid. Some would substitute the list of clans for the list of castes, because it is more democratic and because it lends a certain amount of prestige to the lower born, who need it most. But most Balinese consider that caste and clan are two different types of classification and do not equate them.

THE CLANS

Brahmana	Arya Kenceng
Ksatrya Dalem	Arya Belog
Ksatrya Taman Bali	Arya Gajah Para
Ksatrya Manggis	Arya Pinatih
Pasek	Arya Goto Waringen
Pula Sari	Arya Tan Mundur
Pande	Arya Tan Kaur
Kayu Selem	Arya Tan Kober
Sangging	Arya Sidemen
Batu Gaing	Arya Sentong
Arya Kepakisan	Arya Dalancang

Some of these clans — those that are also castes, or subcategories of castes — have already been mentioned. By far the biggest and most important is the Warga Pasek, to which about 60 percent of the Balinese people belong. It has a formal organization, called Maha Gotra Pasek Sanak Sapta Resi, and encompasses dozens of branches organized according to locality. The last word is sometimes spelled Rsi. The Pasek organization has many responsibilities, not the least of which is the administration of four very sacred and important temples. These are located in the places where four Brahmanas from East Java settled after they were invited to come to Bali in the tenth century to resolve religious disputes. One is Pura Ratu Pasek at Besakih, the second Pura Dasar Bhuwana Gelgel, the third Pura Sila Yukti, near Padang Bai, and the fourth Pura Lempuyang Madia near Amlapura. The Paseks trace their origin back to the Brahmana caste. Indeed, one genealogical chart shows them descending not just from Brahmanas, but from Hyang Brahma — the creator. There is an allied organization in East Java called Kepakisan, and another in Central Java called Paku Buwono, coming from the word *buwana,* a person who occupies the world.

There are those who say (and those who deny) that the word "Pasek" comes from the Balinese verb *macek,* "to nail." The story is that Empu Geni Jaya (*empu,* sometimes spelled *mpu,* means "sage," and is used as an epithet of great veneration) was one of the four Brahmanas from Java who were invited to come to Bali to solve the problems that were being caused by the native tribes, the Bali Aga.

Empu Geni Jaya had seven children, all of whom became *empu* in their own right. And these seven are the founders of the Pasek clan, from whom it derives its official name. The "Sapta Rsi" of Maha Gotra Pasek Sanak Sapta Rsi means "seven *rsi*" or "seven *empu.*" *Gotra* is an interesting term that was used as early as Vedic times. Originally it meant "a herd of cows," but its meaning changed so as to be roughly synonymous with "clan." So the full title of the organization is: The Great Pasek Clan, Children of the Seven Holy Sages. None of the seven *rsi* was himself a Pasek. But some of their descendants were given the task by Majapahit rulers of Bali of taking care of the temples and the areas in which they lived. By extension, the word *macek* came to mean "nail" in the sense of "to make the area steady," and the people who were appointed to do this became known as Paseks. And, according to this account, these same seven descendants of Empu Geni Jaya were the ancestors of the Pande clan. Some of the descendants of the Sapta Rsi fell in love with lower class women, lost their status as Brahmanas, and became known instead as Aryas. That did not lower their status as *rsi,* but their class changed from that of Brahmana to Arya, a clan category that overlaps three castes — Ksatriya to Sudra.

How vital in the life of an average Balinese is his membership in one or another of the dozens of Pasek groups? Not very. He is aware of his clan, but he probably could not tell you of its origin or meaning. He knows that he has ties to certain Pasek temples, but, chances are, he could not tell you specifically which ones. Occasionally he will go to a Pasek temple to pray.

The cohesion of the much smaller Pande clan seems to be considerably greater. They too have a central organization: Maha Semaya Warga Pande. Since earliest times there has been in the popular mind something magical about metal and those who are skilled in its forging. This was the origin of the clan of smiths, the Pande. You cannot become a Pande by learning how to be a smith. Of course, you can"t become a Pasek either — you have to be born into the clan. Nor if you are a Pande are you compelled, or even expected, to be a smith. Obviously the need for producing objects of metal on a local scale has diminished considerably in the past decades. But, that does not prevent the Pandes from having a feeling of being special people.

In addition to the central organizations of Paseks and Pandes, several other clans have similar groups. The Ksatrya Taman Bali Clan is organized under the Maha Gotra Tirta Harum Taman Bali. There is an organization called Para Gotra Sentanan Dalem Tarukan, and an interesting group called Keluarga Besar Pasek Kayu Selem — or literally, the "Large Black Wood Pasek Family." This last bears some explanation.

Empu Semeru was one of the four Brahmanas who was invited to come to Bali to help solve the problems mentioned above, and he founded Pura Ratu Pasek at Besakih. Empu Semeru, it is said, made two statues of human beings. One was fashioned from the tamarind tree, the dark wood of which is called *kayu selem*. *Selem* is Balinese for "dark" or "black." The other was made from the wood of the jackfruit tree, the wood of which is called *kayu putih* because of its light color. He then brought these statues to life and sent them out into the world, where they became the parents of the Bali Aga, those people who claim to have been living in Bali long before the advent of Hindus, Javanese, Indians, or anyone else. The various descendants of *kayu putih* and *kayu selem* have become mixed up now, and few Bali Aga individuals know to which group to trace their ancestry.

SOME BALINESE WOULD LIKE TO REFORM THE CASTE SYSTEM, essentially turning the clock way back to caste's ancestor, *warna*. They argue that a Sudra who has been appointed to a high government post and who is, say, a *bupati*, head of one of the eight districts of Bali, has every right to be treated as a Ksatriya, since he is performing work that is the duty of a Ksatriya — ruling. They say that a man born of Brahmana parents who is tending bar at a hotel has no right to be considered as Brahmana because he is not fulfilling the dharma of a Brahmana. Others object to this, saying that the quotations from the holy scriptures given earlier in this chapter indicate that *warna* is fixed and strict, and that a person born into one cannot hope to enter another. Temperament is just as vital as birth. One cannot be a priest or a ruler or a shopkeeper or a helper unless his temperament, his *guna,* is suited to this job.

Perhaps it would be more realistic to do away with the idea of *warn a* altogether and come up with a concept of a single class — the *biasa,* or "usual." Everyone would be treated equally, regardless of birth. Those who showed an aptitude for the priesthood and who were willing to assume its duties and responsibilities would be the Brahmanas. Those who had the qualifications for running a store would be the Wesyas, and so on. Perhaps this would be a more "fair" way of organizing society. But Bali has been part of the Republic of Indonesia for only a few decades. And caste in Bali, whatever one's opinion of it, has been a very crucial part of the Hindu-Balinese social and cultural organization for more than 500 years. Caste, I think it is fair to assume, is going to be around for quite a while still.

CHAPTER 4

Bali's Other Faiths

BUDDHISM, CHRISTIANITY, AND ISLAM

BALI IS AN ISLAND OF HINDUS in the largest Muslim country in the world. Whereas more than 90 percent of Indonesians practice Islam, the same proportion of Bali's population practices Balinese Hinduism. In fact, captivated by the colorful pageants of Hinduism, the short-term visitor is likely to overlook the presence of minority religions on the island. None is common, but Buddhists, Muslims, Dutch Reformed Protestants, and Catholics have each created small communities on Bali.

Indonesian law, based upon the Pancasila, or "five principles," grants freedom of worship in the republic. But the first of the five *silas* specifically states that the government is based upon belief in one, all-powerful God. This rule has resulted in a lack of recognition by the central government in Jakarta and the Department of Religion of those religions whose beliefs do not clearly include this concept. Although some Indonesians practice religions that emphasize philosophy and meditation rather than theology, these religions are not officially recognized, and their public practice is discouraged. Some rather liberal or atypical religions are simply banned. Such is the case with the Church of Jesus Christ of Latter Day Saints (Mormon church) and the Hare Krishna movement.

Although non-Hindu Balinese are indeed few, it is perhaps strange that there are any, because for a Balinese Hindu to convert requires a separation not just from a theology, but from the entire social and cultural network of Balinese society. It is difficult, to the point of impossibility, to determine in Bali exactly where religion stops and other social and cultural forms — entertainment, agricultural planning, work, childbirth, rites of passage — begin. When a Balinese separates himself from his religion, he also risks being cut off from the entire cultural web of his village.

Officials of the various alternative religions to whom I spoke were well aware of the potential difficulties. Most will not accept candidates for entrance into their churches until they have gone through a long period of education. This education not only involves matters of doctrine in the new religion, but also makes it quite clear to the candidate what he can expect as a consequence of his defection. Some churches will not accept a convert if it is obvious that he will not be able to make the adjustment. Also, though the various groups of non-Hindu faithful in Bali are extremely small minorities on an islandwide basis, each is concentrated in a few communities where their members are the majority. Under these circumstances the problems of social and economic isolation and discrimination are minimized, and the chances are good that the non-Hindus will be able to exist happily with their Hindu neighbors.

DISTRIBUTION OF RELIGIONS IN BALI BY KABUPATEN

Kabupaten	Hindu	Buddhist	Muslim	Catholic	Protestant
Badung	459,828	5,885	37,042	6,387	8,236
Bangli	165,112	355	781	-	53
Buleleng	454,905	4,070	33,933	623	1,444
Gianyar	309,278	784	756	93	128
Jembrana	156,159	632	38,071	2,195	2,110
Karangasem	315,962	179	9,788	62	175
Klungkung	147,675	-	3,114	50	178
Tabanan	338,282	1,369	4,775	473	636
TOTALS	2,347,201	13,274	128,260	9,883	12,960
PERCENT	93.4	0.5	5.1	0.4	0.5

TOTAL POPULATION: 2,511,570

From Kanwil Agama Propinsi Bali, 1985/1986

BUDDHISM INCLUDES A VERY BROAD SPECTRUM of religious practices, ranging from strict and contemplative monasticism to belief in an elaborate infrastructure of deities, religious paraphernalia, offerings, and something approaching the most baroque of all heavens, complete with angels and pearly gates. There are, however, basically two schools: Hinayana Buddhism, "the small vehicle," and Mahayana, "the large vehicle." The terminology comes from the Mahayana Buddhists, and practicioners of Hinayana Buddhism prefer Theravada, "the doctrine of elders." Theravada is the more austere of the two schools, focusing on the Buddha's ethical teachings, and its practice requires rigorous asceticism and study. Buddhists of the Theravada school are today found chiefly in Burma, Sri Lanka, and

Thailand. Mahayana Buddhism, practiced in China, Japan, and Vietnam, is by far the larger school, and includes the deification of Buddha in a large Hindu-like pantheon of gods. Many other branches exist, the most famous of which include the Hindu-Tantric Buddhism of Tibet and Nepal, and the Zen Buddhism of Japan.

Both forms of Buddhism have had a historical presence in Bali. There is evidence that the infamous Mayadenawa, whose defeat by the armies of Indra is celebrated in the Hindu Balinese festival of Galungan, was a Theravada Buddhist. But dates are unknown, and the actual existence of Mayadenawa is still debated. The legend goes, however, that he imposed what the Balinese believed to be deity-less Buddhism upon the Hindus of Bali, closing their temples and forcing them to renounce all religion but his own. The texts refer to his religion as "atheism," and Indra's triumph over Mayadenawa is taken to be symbolic of the triumph of Hindu right and law, dharma, over a godless, lawless existence, adharma. One authority states that Theravada Buddhism came to Bali as early as the fifth century A.D., but no written records in Bali date back that far. It has also been suggested that Mahayana Buddhists from Sriwijaya set up a kingdom in Bali in about A.D. 955 because the first king of the Bali Sriwijaya dynasty founded Pura Tirtha Empul at Tampak Siring. Buddhism's main influence on Bali has been through Balinese Hinduism, which in many ways is so thoroughly mixed up with Buddhism that separating the two is virtually impossible.

Siddhartha Gautama Buddha was born a Hindu in the sixth century B.C. and during the 80 years of his life became an aescetic and enunciated a new doctrine that won many followers. He almost surely saw himself as a Hindu, albeit one seeking reforms. He was concerned more with ethics than theology, and did not see himself as a god. And the differences between Hinduism and the religion of, particularly, Mahayana Buddhists is even today relatively slight. The variations within each of the religions are as extreme as those between them.

The Hindu-Balinese religion came from the Javanese Majapahit, and the religion of this dynasty was heavily influenced by Mahayana Buddhism. Trade with India brought Hinduism and, probably partly from Sriwijaya and partly from India itself, Buddhism. Hinduism and Mahayana Buddhism became so intertwined in Majapahit East Java that it became impossible to separate their characteristics. The religion of the Majapahit should more accurately be called Siwaism, since its emphasis — in the Hindu triad, Brahma, Wisnu, and Siwa — was upon Siwa, God as dissolver and recycler of life. To be even more accurate, it should be called a Siwaist-Buddhist kingdom because of the mixing of the two religions. The king of Majapahit, it is said, used two helpers when he performed important religious ceremonies: one a Siwaist priest, the other Buddhist. Empu Kuturan, who came to Bali from Java in A.D. 1019 and greatly influenced the island's religion, was a Mahayana Buddhist, according to some authorities. And Danghyang Nirartha, otherwise known as Pedanda Wawuh Rauh or Dwijendra, was a Siwa-Buddhist. When the Majapahit empire fell and its survivors fled to Bali, the import was not just Hinduism, but an alloy of Siwaist Hinduism and Mahayana Buddhism.

The Suthasoma is a great Mahayana Buddhist epic poem composed in Central Java at the time when Buddhism was mixing with Siwaist Hinduism. The poem, in part, tries to point out the essential sameness of the two religions. The following verse is quite well known:

> Rwa neka dhatu wiwnuwus ware Buddha wiswa
> Bhineka rawka ring apan kena parwanosen
> Mangkang jinatwa kalawan Siwa tatwa tunggal
> Bhineka tunggal ika tan hana dharma mangrwa

> "The one substance is called two, namely Buddha or Siwa
> They say it is different, but how can it be divided by two
> Such is how the teaching of Buddha and Siwa became one
> It is different, but it is one, there are not two truths"

Especially significant is the line *Bhineka tunggal ika,* "It is different, but it is one." This is the motto of Indonesia, emblazoned on the Garuda Pancasila, the coat of arms, below the *garuda.* It is a message of unity much like e pluribus unum, "out of many, one," in the United States. The phrase as it originated in the Suthasoma was a statement of the fundamental similarities of Siwaism and Buddhism — but it was meant as a statement of unity for the two religions. Buddhism and Siwaism in Java thus peacefully mixed to such an extent that it is quite difficult to separate them and identify native elements of each. This was the state of the faith when it arrived in Bali where, after receiving a dose of local animism, the mixture remains.

Many Balinese make no distinctions between the Hinduism that they practice and Buddhism. In fact, Buddha is considered a perfectly legitimate companion of the usual Hindu gods. In the temple of Pura Ulunsiwi in Jimbaran there are two doors on the east side of the large *meru,* one for Siwa and one for Buddha. The *pemangku* (priest) of Pura Ulunsiwi said he considers Siwa to be higher than Buddha, likening their relative stature to that between a first- and a second-born son. There are no statues of Buddha in the temple, however. But the main entrance gate of the Pura Puseh–Pura Desa at Batubulan, a few meters from the daily *barong* show, is guarded on each side by classic statues of Buddha in the sitting position. And to the left and right of the Buddha statues are the usual carvings of

Brahma, Indra, Sambu, Bayu, and Kala. Among those Hindus who emphasize Wisnu, Buddha is considered to have been absorbed into Wisnu as the
last of his earthly avatars. Wisnu has had nine of these incarnations, including Rama and Krishna. There is one yet to come. This doctrine of the
absorption of Buddha contributed to the decline and virtual elimination of
Buddhism in India.

Most Balinese Hindu *pedandas* are *pedanda* Siwa. But there are a few
pedanda Buddha. A *pedanda* Siwa wears his hair in what is called an
agelung, a circle on top of the head, whereas a *pedanda* Buddha wears his
hair *acukur asipat aking*, cut to just below the ear. The tall hat of the
pedanda Siwa, called a *ketu* or *bawa*, is decorated with the *nawa senajata*,
the weapons of the nine directions, whereas that of a *pedanda* Buddha is
often red and is very highly decorated. The *pedanda* Buddha has a special
brass instrument called a *bajra* that he holds in his right hand while he is
using his bell in the left hand.

The *pedanda* Buddha, however, is not a Buddhist. He is a Siwa-
Buddhist, the same as a *pedanda* Siwa. Each complements the other.
Originally each was responsible for different types of ceremonies. Today
either can perform any ceremony, except that, at very large ceremonies,
there is a special type of offering for each to dedicate. Whether a family
choses one or the other generally depends upon tradition or, more likely,
upon which one lives nearby. The *pedanda* Buddha makes a distinction
between the founder of Buddhism, Gautama, who was not a god, and
Dewa Buddha, who is. Dewa Buddha is similar to Dewa Siwa and should
not be identified with the man, Gautama, before his enlightenment and
deification. A *pedanda* Buddha feels closer to a *pedanda* Siwa and Siwaism
than he does to the Buddhist religion.

However, when one of the princes of Thailand visited Bali not long ago,
my friend the late Ida Pedanda Padang Tawang, a *pedanda* Buddha from
Krambitan, lead the Buddhist ceremony to welcome the prince — in a
Hindu temple. There is a community named Budakeling in the
Karangasem area that is said to be pure Mahayana Buddhist. But the resident *pedanda* Buddha, Ida Pedanda Wayan Datah, said he is not *agama*
("religion") Buddha, but a Buddhist in the sense that all Balinese Hindus
are Buddhist. He said that as a *pedanda* Buddha, he uses a little *puja*
("worship") Siwa and a lot of *puja* Buddha in his mantras, whereas a
pedanda Siwa uses the opposite.

There is something approaching classical Buddhism in Bali. Biku Giri
Rahito is the head of Buddha Dharma, the officially recognized Buddhist
religion for all of Indonesia. The word *biku* is equivalent to "monk." Biku
Giri presides over a Buddhist temple, called a *wihara*, at the village of
Banjar. Giri was a Brahmana, Ida Bagus Giri, before he became a monk. He

studied in Semarang, was ordained in Bangkok in 1966, and returned to Bali to build a *wihara* at Yeh Panas, near the present site at Banjar. The Banjar *wihara* was built earlier, in 1956. It is a cool, restful place, built around a garden on the top of a hill away from the main part of the village.

Giri, sixtyish, wears saffron robes and has his head shaved just like the monks in Bangkok. He studied Theravada Buddhism in Thailand, but says that he practices Buddha Dharma without a trademark or the limitations of classification. His practices are, however, much closer to what most people classify as Theravada than to the Mahayana school. He said his goal is to teach people the classic eight-fold path of Buddhism. He welcomes everyone at his *wihara*, which has become the center of a sizable group of Buddhists in the Banjar-Singaraja area. He himself pays respects to his ancestors in his Hindu family temple, and he welcomes Hindus who come to the *wihara* to learn, meditate, and return to their Hinduism. He said the principal difference between Hinduism and Buddhism is that Hinduism stresses *yadnya,* "rites," whereas Buddhism does not.

BALI HAS A SIZABLE CHINESE POPULATION and Chinese influence upon Balinese culture is far greater than most people realize. Before Indonesian independence in 1950, there were a number of Chinese temples scattered around the island. The temples were called *klentengs* — probably an onomatopoeic word from the sound of the bell used — or sometimes *bio,* "a place to pray," or *kongco,* "a manifestation of a holy person." The religion practiced at these temples was Confucianism, commonly called Khonghucu.

But the founding of the republic brought some problems. *Sila* number one of the Pancasila specifies Indonesians must be, at least philosophically, monotheistic — Confucianism does not recognize a deity. And the Chinese in Indonesia face a certain amount of general discrimination by the government, because Jakarta identified Chinese-Indonesians with communism, a bogey on the archipelago at least since the 1965 coup attempt by the Indonesian Communist Party. There is also a more general resentment of the Chinese in Indonesia because they are chiefly merchants, clustered in the large cities, and are, as a group, better off than the population at large.

The Department of Religion does not recognize Confucianism as an accepted religion in Indonesia. There is a nongovernmental Confucian organization headquartered in Solo, central Java — Majelis Tinggi Agama Khonghucu Indonesia, or MATAKIN. MATAKIN claims that, prior to the 1965 abortive coup, the government officially decreed *six* acceptable religions in Indonesia, including Confucianism. The group claims that this decree was never rescinded. The official position of the Department of Religion, as previously indicated, is that there are, and always were, five. According to MATAKIN, Agama Khonghucu as practiced in Indonesia is not the same as the classical Confucianism practiced in China. It says that its teachings comply fully with the Pancasila and department policies.

Be that as it may, many Chinese felt that they were under great pressure to join one of the five accepted religions, and most chose Buddhism, considering it to be closer to their original belief than any of the other four. There are *klentengs* at Blabatuh, Denpasar, Gianyar, Kuta, Singaraja (two), Tabanan, and Tanjung Benoa. And the Chinese communities in the Banjar, Blahbutuh, Kuta, and Tabanan areas have converted their *klentengs* into Buddhist *wiharas* and call themselves Theravada Buddhists. Some of the other *klentengs* have expressed desires to do the same, but, at the present writing have not yet done so.

Although a statue of Buddha has been added and Buddhist worship takes place at the *wiharas* in Blahbatuh, Kuta, and Tabanan, they are in a separate building from the existing *klenteng*. The places for Khonghucu worship are still there. Watching devotees pray one evening, I could not keep myself from thinking that there was considerably more emphasis upon prayers at the older Khonghucu shrines than in the Buddhist part. Some of those connected with the *klentengs* that have not yet been converted also speak of their beliefs as Buddhist. But one gets the feeling that these statements are being made more to convince others than to express a true belief. Members of some of the other *klentengs* make no bones about their Confucian philosophy.

ISLAM IS SECOND IN POPULARITY in Bali only to Hinduism, yet throughout the island there is little variation in Muslim practice. There are 180 mosques, and none is considered more important than the others. Most Balinese Muslims are Sunnis. Sunni Muslims approve the historical order of the first four caliphs after Mohammed as the rightful line of succession of leadership and accept the Sunna, a body of traditional law based upon the teachings and practices of Mohammed, as the authoritative supplement to the Koran. A few on the island belong to the Shiite sect, called "Syah" in Indonesia. The latter have separate mosques from the Sunnis and do not generally mix with them.

Balinese Muslims observe the same general rules as do people in other Islamic parts of the world. Almost all read the Koran in Arabic, although few can actually write in this language, and near the mosques one hears the Muezzin's call to prayer five times a day. One never sees Muslims praying in open, public areas, as is the case in some countries. The usual prohibitions against alcoholic beverages and pork are taught. Muslims are encouraged to dress conservatively and cover their bodies, and Islamic law dictates that no Muslim should possess an image of any sort of life form, human or otherwise, painting or statue. Most Muslim men wear the traditional brimless black hat, called *pici* or *peci*, or sometimes *songkok* in Indonesian. It is really more of a national hat than a Muslim hat, however. There are no Mullahs in Bali. Teachers are called *kiyai* and have no political power, as do Mullahs in other countries. There are no missionaries. In Bali no attempt is made to solicit members or compete with other faiths.

Sixty thousand to seventy thousand Indonesians make the pilgrimage, Ibadan Haji, to Mecca each year, and Balinese Muslims join their fellows. The cost in 1987 was Rp 3.25 million (U.S. $2,000), all inclusive, for a 35-day trip. The national airline, Garuda Indonesia, had six wide-body jets in Haji service. Indonesia that year sent the fourth largest number of pilgrims to Saudi Arabia, behind only Iran, Egypt, and Turkey.

THERE IS AN INTERESTING, AND LITTLE-KNOWN, STORY about the early days of the Protestant missionaries on Bali. One of the first tasks of the missionaries was to provide a translation of the Bible into Balinese, which brought up a serious problem: What Balinese word should be used for "God"? The term *brahman* (not to be confused with Brahma — part of the triad) was familiar and had entered Hinduism in very ancient times. But *brahman* was considered a rather too philosophical concept of the soul of the universe — "the unmoved mover." Nobody in Bali worshiped *brahman*, nor did they then have a name for a single, all-powerful god.

So these first missionaries had to invent a suitable Balinese name for their Christian God. The name could not be too close to Hinduism, since, after all, these people were trying to convert Balinese from Hinduism. Sang Hyang Tuduh (*tuduh* means "fate," or "command") was considered. So was Sang Hyang Pramakawi, which was based upon the notion of *kawitan*, or ancestral lineage. They finally settled on Sang Hyang Widi as a more neutral word. *Widi* (sometimes spelled *widhi*) was a Balinese word in use at that time with a number of meanings having to do with fate, destiny, or good luck — especially at gambling. A losing gambler would say "*sing la widi*" meaning that he had no luck. The word *pawidi* means "lucky," and in other contexts, "knowledge," "feeling," or "compel." In Jane Belo's *Trance in Bali*, written in the 1930s, *widi* is mentioned as being more or less synonymous with *dewa*, the usual generalized word for a god.

After its use in the Bible, the term became popular — and not just with Christians. After the wars for independence and the adoption of the Pancasila as the basis for the Republic of Indonesia, Hindu officials felt that they should promulgate a term that would clearly show that Balinese Hindus did believe in a single, all-powerful god. Since there was no such term, it was only natural to chose the same one that the Christians had picked twenty years earlier and which was in common usage. And today one hears Sang Hyang Widi everywhere, probably without realizing that it was not an important part of Balinese Hindu religion until fairly recently.

The Dutch arrived in the East Indies at the end of the sixteenth century and set up a trading organization, the Vereenigde Oostindische Compagnie (VOC), or Dutch East India Company. Article 177 of the Dutch Colonial Code of 1850 stated that no missionary work could be done in any part of Indonesia, and the Dutch Reformed Church, with the trade interests of the VOC in mind, agreed not to disrupt the Islamic society of Java. This was much to the chagrin of the Catholics, who were trying to establish a foothold in the Indies. As early as 1630 the raja of Klungkung had asked for two priests, and two Jesuits arrived in 1636. But they did not last long, and the Dutch destroyed their records. After years of indecision, in 1854 the Governor General divided up the Lesser Sunda Islands for the missionaries. The Catholics were awarded Flores and the middle part of Timor. The Protestants got most of the rest — including Bali.

The first Christian missionary to Bali was an Englishman, the Reverend Ennis, who arrived in 1838 and left shortly thereafter. The Dutch Utrecht Missionary Society sent a missionary in 1865 who also left in frustration. In 1866, the society sent a missionary who was to convert the first Balinese to the Christian faith, Reverend van Eck. Van Eck converted his servant, Gusti Wayang Nurat Karangasem, and baptized him as Nicodemus. This was van Eck's only success, however, and his increasingly disquieted sponsors finally sent two others, including the Reverend J. de Vroom. These two, under a mandate to achieve results and finding little success, found themselves preaching with increased fervor to their single convert. For his part, Nicodemus found himself in a steadily worsening position. He was shunned by his Hindu peers, and the new preachers were fastening on him with a panicked intensity. In 1881, he had de Vroom murdered. Nicodemus was rounded up, displayed in a cage around the villages, and then executed by the Dutch in Jakarta. Bali was closed to all missionaries.

In the 1920s tourists began to come to Bali and the Dutch saw what was rapidly becoming a profitable tourist industry. Fearful that Bali, one of their prize attractions, would lose its culture in the wake of missionaries, the Dutch government rejected missionary applications from various Christian churches. But in 1929, Tsang To Han, a Chinese evangelist of the Hong Kong–based Christian and Missionary Alliance, was granted permission to come to Bali to minister to two Chinese Christians who had recently arrived. He was supposed to work only with the Chinese, but his efforts there were unsuccessful. But it so happened that a Javanese mystic had come to Bali in 1927 and founded a small group of followers. He was later removed by the Dutch, but his group remained. Hearing of Tsang's new religion, the group invited him to visit their village, thinking that he was the successor to their founder. Tsang did so, and the result was the baptism

THE CATHOLIC CHURCH IN DENPASAR

of eleven Christians in 1931.

From then on, Christianity spread rapidly throughout Bali. But Tsang's insensitivity to Hinduism made him unpopular and he was expelled in 1933. By this time almost 300 Balinese had been baptized, and they then found themselves without a leader. It took considerable persuasion, but the Governor General finally allowed the Dutch Reformed Church to come to minister to those converted by the Christian and Missionary Alliance. The new group called itself Gereja Kristen Protestan di Bali, GKPB. It has grown to the point where there are, in 1988, about 6,000 members in Bali. About twice that many have moved to other islands of Indonesia, notably Sulawesi, where they have joined another synod of the Dutch Reformed Church. The Dutch Reformed Church, of which the GKPB is a part, had its origins in the reformation activities of John Calvin in the middle of the sixteenth century. It followed the progress of empire in the Indies and is today the largest of the Protestant churches in Indonesia.

GKPB has been under the direction of Dr. I Wayan Mastra since 1972. Dr. Mastra, a Balinese, took his theological training in the United States. GKPB operates 56 churches with 25 pastors, all of them Balinese. Services are conducted in Bahasa Indonesia in most areas, but in the Balinese language in rural areas. Synod headquarters are in Denpasar. Dr. Mastra is a firm believer in a contextualized service. He feels that a conversion to his church should be a religious conversion, not a cultural conversion. "The Gospel is like water," Dr. Mastra said. "It can be held in a glass, in a cup, or in a coconut shell." Several of the GKPB churches have Balinese *gong* and dance groups, and the church operates four schools.

The showpiece of the GKPB is a new church at Belimbing Sari. This village is far off the beaten path, near Gilimanuk in extreme West Bali. A sizable Christian population is located here because, in the early days, the Dutch thought Christianity would corrupt Balinese culture and in 1939 more or less banished the missionaries and their flocks to remote Belimbing Sari. The GKPB took this opportunity to set up a training school there for church members who wished to go on missions to other islands, thus preparing them for the jungle conditions they would meet. Belimbing Sari is now a sizable community.

The present church, designed by an Australian architect and built at a cost of Rp 100 million, was dedicated in 1981, although it is still far from completion. One approaches it through a Balinese style split gate decorated with a few crosses done in *paras* (tuff) and brick. One then ascends a long flight of steps to the main gate, done in the Balinese style. There are ponds of water surrounding the path with water flowing through them. The church itself is oval in plan and is open to the air on all sides. The language of the services alternates — one week in Indonesian, one week in Balinese. Church members are encouraged to bring gifts of food to the church on holy days, but instead of offering them to God, Balinese style, they share the gifts with each other. The church boasts a membership of 185 families.

Other Protestant organizations in Bali include a second (much smaller) synod of the Dutch Reformed Church, an evangelical church, a fundamentalist church, a church for Chinese Christians, and a Reformed church where the services are given in *Batak*. There are also a few more radical

Protestant sects in Bali, not sanctioned by the government, including Pentecostals, Seventh Day Adventists, Christ is the Answer, and the Hong Kong–based House of Gospel.

ALTHOUGH CATHOLICS HAVE ENJOYED A PRESENCE IN INDONESIA since the days of Spanish and Portuguese colonialism, Catholic missionaries were firmly banned from Bali until 1935. Catholic schools had been established in Java, and there was some hope of introducing them to Bali, even without missionaries. But Cokorda Sukawati, the first representative from Bali in the Dutch Parliament in Jakarta, was dead set against any Catholic influence, and his vote was influential in continuing the ban.

In 1935, a permit was finally issued for one Catholic and one Protestant missionary to come to Bali, provided they agreed not to do any proselytizing. Their assignments were to take care of those who had already been converted. The Bishop of Ende, in Flores, sent Father J. Kersten. Those Christians who had originally been under the guidance of Tsang To Han came to Father Kersten and asked him to help them, as Tsang had been forced to leave Bali. Kersten hesitated, because he was not supposed to do missionary work, and he did not want trouble. But finally he acceded to the group's desires and in 1936 he established the first Catholic church in Tuka. This area has now become the stronghold of the Catholics in Bali.

In 1947 Father Peter Shadeg, an American, was invited to come to Bali. After five months in Flores waiting out the ban, he arrived in Bali, where he helped start clinics and schools in Singaraja. But again, anti-missionary pressure was building in Jakarta. The post-independence political climate was volatile, and the head of what was then called East Indonesia, who was Balinese, led the fight to keep his native island free of missionary influence. The Protestants, already well-established, backed him. Finally, a delegation went to President Sukarno with the problem. Sukarno said that Indonesia was now an independent country and that people could believe as they pleased within the confines of the constitution. Article 177 of the old Dutch code was repealed, and missionaries were free to enter. In 1953 Father Shadeg moved to Tangkeb, not far from Tuka, where Father Kersten's Catholic settlement had been.

Indonesia has 32 Catholic dioceses — in Indonesian, *keuskupan* — one of which oversees Bali and Lombok. Father Vitalis Djebarus, SVD, is the Bishop, with offices in Denpasar. There are 70 places of church worship and 18 priests. Father Shadeg is the only non-Indonesian priest. There is a beginning seminary in Tuka, but most pastors attend the seminary in Java. Services are given in Balinese in the countryside and in Bahasa Indonesia in the villages. Only the New Testament has been translated into Balinese as of this writing.

As it does in many parts of the world, the Catholic Church in Bali places a great emphasis upon education. Father Shadeg is a respected scholar, maintains a large library at his headquarters in Tuka, and is the author of a widely used Balinese-English dictionary. The most startling of the Catholic educational institutions is the Swastiastu Foundation in Denpasar. The school has students from kindergarten through high school, with kindergarten branches in Tangeb and Kuta. Kuta also has a primary school.

The most unusual Catholic Church in Bali is Gereja Katolik Santa Maria Immaculata in Tabanan. The front is an enormous wall in Balinese style — except a Virgin Mary and Jesus adorn the gate in place of the usual Balinese *bhoma*. Crosses are represented as square planes pierced by spires. The guardians are two two-meter *paras* angels, with traditional Balinese dress, looking very much like *legong* dancers. The octagonal church building is about twenty meters in diameter, airy and open. The roof is arched, with flat panels of wood laid out in diagonals. Paintings of the stations of the cross around the octagon are done in a Goya-like elongated style. The style is not Balinese, but the figures in the paintings are dressed in traditional Balinese clothes.

THE REPUBLIC OF INDONESIA HAS A DEPARTMENT OF RELIGION, and officially recognizes five religions: Buddhism, Catholicism, Hinduism, Islam, and Protestantism. The headquarters of the department are in Jakarta, but each province has a local *kanwil*, a branch office. There are also non-governmental, advisory bodies for each religion: WALUBI, (Per)walian Umat Buddha Indonesia (Buddhist); MAWI, Majelis Agung Wali Gereja Indonesia (Catholic); PHD, Parisada Hindu Dharma (Hindu); MUI, Majelis Ulama Indonesia (Islam); PGI, Persatuan Gereja-gereja Indonesia (Protestant). Each of these organizations has an office in the same building in Jakarta, and they work together on common problems in a group called Wadah Musyawarah Antar Umat Beragama, a kind of inter-religious council.

CHAPTER 5

Holy Water

SUBSTANCE AND SYMBOL

HOLY WATER IS AN AGENT OF THE POWER OF A GOD, a container of mysterious force. It can cleanse spiritual impurities, fend off evil forces, and render the recipient immune to the attacks of negative, or demonic, influences. In Bali, holy water is not a symbol, or something abstract — it is a *sekala* container of a *niskala* power, and, as such, is sacred and holy in and of itself. The water strengthens and purifies everything it touches. Although there are many kinds and potencies of holy water, no matter where or by whom it is made and no matter whether its quantity is great or small, holy water is always a sacred and powerful agent.

Holy water accompanies every act of Hindu-Balinese worship, from individual devotion at a household shrine to islandwide ceremonies. Theoretically, the practice of using holy water in Hindu ritual derives from a famous passage in the Bhagavad-Gita, an episode in the vast Hindu epic, the Mahabharata. The Bhagavad-Gita is a lecture, given by Krishna to the human hero Arjuna, that has come to be one of the most basic texts on Hindu worship. In Major Book Six, Minor Book 63, Chapter 9, Verse 26, Krishna says:

> If one disciplined soul proffers to me with love a leaf,
> a flower, fruit, or water, I accept this offering of love from him.

These two lines provide the theological basis for holy water, and the practice of preparing flower and food offerings.

The Balinese call holy water *toya*, from the Medium Balinese word for "water," and often the High Balinese *tirtha* will be used. These are never confused with ordinary water, however, which everyone calls by its low Balinese name, *yeh*. The uses and potency of holy water vary according to how it is made, its source, and who makes it. The more powerful the mantras used to make it, the more mystic energy it contains. The more sacred the place from which it is obtained, the greater the sanctity of the holy water. The more exalted the status of the person who makes it, the greater its magical power. Holy water is used in many different ways, and need not always be of the most powerful variety. The supply kept in the several shrines of family temples need not come from as remote or high as source as, say, the holy water needed for a cremation or a temple festival. And sometimes holy water from a specific temple might be preferred, because that temple emphasizes a particular manifestation of the Hindu deity and that manifestation is the one to whom an appeal is being made. All holy water is sacred, but some kinds are more powerful, or more appropriate in a given situation, than others.

Holy water requires special handling; it must be treated with respect and deference. The most powerful holy water from the most sacred source, prepared with the most magical mantras by the most exalted priest loses its power if treated casually or disrespectfully. On the other hand, clean water from the well of a house compound, placed in a new container in the shrine of an ordinary family temple becomes powerful and effective holy water if the feelings of the user toward it are properly reverent. When preparing even such simple holy water, one must wear traditional clothing, be freshly bathed, and have a mind uncluttered with confusing or impure thoughts.

The most important rule to follow is that the holy water must be stored in a clean container and must be handled with great respect. People often use a *bungbung* — a section of bamboo culm closed at one end and open at the other — to transport holy water. Ordinary large glass jars, with loose-fitting glass tops, are quite commonly used. Villagers often transport holy water in ordinary drinking glasses or bottles. These should theoretically be brand new and unused, but it is sufficient that they be thoroughly clean if a new one is not available. Even empty Coke bottles will do in emergency, if thoroughly washed before use. Typical red clay pots are often used for temporary storage in temples where demand for holy water is great. But they are not used for holy water in household shrines because they are porous, and the water eventually seeps out.

Any container of holy water is always held and passed to others using only the right hand. If possible, one should also grasp his right elbow with his left hand while doing so. The container should be held as high as possible as it is being handled, preferably higher than the heads of others nearby. During many of the temple ceremonies in our village, containers of holy water are carried on the heads of women to a temporary shrine just outside the main temple gate. There the *pemangkus,* lay priests, sit on the ground facing the shrine and the holy water. Everyone nearby squats or sits to be lower than the holy water and other sacred objects in the shrine.

Vertical position is a function of status. In transit a container with holy water is carried on the head. In its final resting position it is placed in as high a position as possible in a place where it will not be disturbed or contaminated. If placed on the floor, stepped over, or handled excessively, holy water will lose its mystical power and be rendered ineffective. And the one who has thus defiled it becomes *pramada,* insubordinate, and is vulnerable to the negative aspects of the holy water's mystical power. Containers of holy water are usually stored in the shrines of family and public temples. During large and important temple festivals, when a great quantity of holy water is needed, the containers are kept in a very tall temporary shrine called *sanggar agung* made of bamboo poles. This shrine is a common feature of temple ceremonies of various kinds. The *sanggar agung* is both a shrine to *surya,* the sun, and an elevated resting place for holy water.

HINDU PRIESTS, *PEDANDAS,* MAKE HOLY WATER early every morning. The ceremony, called *maweda,* involves chanting certain mantras over water taken from his family temple. Together with the mantras, the *pedanda* performs a series of *mudras,* or hand gestures, and gestures using his bell and other paraphernalia such as a brazier. Commonly the *pedanda* holds a flower in his right hand, clasps his right hand in his left, recites the mantra, and then throws the flower into the bowl of water. Before he can do this, he must cleanse his own body and mind, virtually hypnotizing himself into a state of communion with the gods.

There are three basic types of holy water made in this way by *pedandas.* To purify the body, he prepares *pangelukatan pabersihan* — the first word from *lukat,* meaning "purify," and the second from *bersih* or *bresih,* meaning "clean" or "holy." *Prayascita* is a type of holy water used to make one's thoughts steady, holy, and pure. And *tirtha biu kawonan* will drive bad thoughts away. There are many ways to make this variety. In rites for people, *manusa yadnya,* such as an *oton* "birthday," tooth filing, or a wedding, there will be a need for all three.

A lay priest, *pemangku,* always makes holy water for his own temple. Many *pemangkus* classify the holy water that they make into two types, *toya pengalukatan* and *toya pabersihan,* which are made in more or less the same manner as that used by *pedandas. Pemangkus,* however, do not have the spiritual power of *pedandas* and do not know the most powerful mantras. Since a *pemangku* is associated with a particular temple, the holy water he makes contains the power of the specific god or gods that make their homes in the temple. This holy water is not only important for use in the local temple. This water might be sought by those who seek the specific powers of one of these gods or manifestations.

Pedandas and *pemangkus* are not the only ones who can prepare holy water. The *dalang*, the puppet master of the *wayang kulit* shadow puppet performance, is regularly called upon to make holy water. This often takes place during a special daytime performance of the puppet theater. After completing the ordinary presentation — which is often abbreviated in these daytime shows — the *dalang* prepares the holy water, using special mantras and often dipping the sticks from one or more of his puppets into the water in front of him. Holy water so prepared is often called *toya panyudamalan*, from the word *sudamala*, meaning "purified." This particular *toya* will often be used to purify an individual whose life has been affected by acts that took place on inauspicious days. Sometimes this ceremony, called a *wayang lemah*, is a normal part of a temple anniversary festival, and the holy water the *dalang* prepares is used the same as a *pedanda*'s holy water.

Holy water for local use in temples is quite regularly made by simply leaving a container of clean water in each of the shrines of the temple. Some *pemangkus* know no mantras at all. And it is not necessary to use them, provided the water and container are clean and the thoughts and feelings are proper. The container used is called a *jun tandeg*, a fired red clay jar about 25 centimeters in diameter. There is one in each shrine, from which it is never removed. No flowers are put into the container, as they would spoil and contaminate the water. Each container is covered, and usually a small offering adorns the top. The containers are refilled at intervals of about one week. Many individuals use this method to prepare their everyday holy water in their own family temples. The source of water makes no difference so long as it is pure and clean. The Balinese call it *toya ning*, the second word meaning "clear," in the sense of being unmuddied.

Every shrine, no matter how small, should have some sort of plain water container in it. There are three types, each made of red clay. The *jun* is a round pot with a flat bottom, about 13 centimeters across, with a flared rim. It is covered with a round clay cover, concave side up. The *caratan* is much smaller, and shaped like a traditional drinking cup with a small, open top and a spout on one side. The *coblong* is a small, flat-bottomed bowl about eight centimeters across and four deep. Every shrine must have at least one of these, and the larger have all three. The container should be filled on every important day, such as Kajeng Keliwon, Tilem, Purnama, and other special religious occasions. The water is not considered to be holy water. It is not sprinkled on anything or drunk. It is a kind of symbolic drink for the god of the shrine.

An individual can prepare a kind of holy water for cleansing himself from impurities suffered as the result of contact with a dead body or from some other similar circumstance. This is necessary, for example, when a member of the village *banjar* organization has helped with the washing of a body before burial. This washing leaves him *sebel,* ceremonially unclean, and he must purify himself with holy water. Upon arriving home, he will draw some water from the family well and throw it on the roof of the kitchen, allowing the drops to run off his body and catching some in a rice steamer. This is holy water from Brahma, the god of kitchens, and is called *pamarisudan cuntaka.* This cleansing is sufficient to allow him to go any-where in the house compound except for the family temple — he must still avoid the temple for three days. The deceased's family members are *sebel* for a much longer period of time — in many villages, 42 days.

Important to this source of holy water is the special nature of the *lalang* thatch used to make the kitchen roof. *Lalang* is considered to have been the first plant to appear in the world, and to have received the holy water of everlasting life at the time of the birth of Garuda and Naga in the Hindu Adiparwa stories. Thus water in contact with *lalang* becomes holy water. If there is no holy water with which to wash his hands before praying in a temple, a Balinese will walk over to the nearest shrine or building with a *lalang* roof and touch it with his right hand. This has the same effect as holy water. Today most kitchen roofs are covered with tile rather than long grass, but the symbolism, and the practice, is still widely observed.

MAKING AND DISPENSING HOLY WATER is one of a *pedanda's* chief duties. By tradition a *pedanda* develops a kind of clientele, and an extended family group will usually use the same *pedanda* for all its needs. There is no hard and fast rule about this, but it is generally true. Before independence, vil-lagers were utterly dependent upon the *geriya* — "benefactor" — for their religious sustenance, one of the most important aspects of which is as a source of holy water. Even today some will accuse *pedandas* of trying to exert a monopoly on the religious needs of their clients, called *sisya,* for pri-vate gain. Those who come to seek holy water always bring presents and offerings and a suitable — usually modest — amount of money. In defense of the mutuality of this relationship is the well-known saying: "Pedanda sing dadi ngakuwin sisya. Sakewala sisya dadi ngakuwin pedanda." Translation: "A *pedanda* may not claim clients. But clients may claim a *pedanda.*"

The trip to the *pedanda* to get the holy water is usually inspired by some forthcoming ceremony, but there is nothing to prevent an individual from seeking holy water for his own or his family's own purposes. An individual family will keep a supply of holy water in a shrine in the family temple, and sometimes this is obtained from a *pedanda.* Many people in our village call it *toya ida* and use it to purify themselves before leaving to pray at an *odalan* or before setting out on a pilgrimage to a distant temple.

A special terminology is used to request holy water. One does not "seek" or "get" holy water. Instead the verb *nunas* applies, which translates to something like "beg," or "ask to be favored with." The implication is that a person of lower status or caste is asking to be favored with something only a high caste person can provide. In the case of something very important such as holy water prepared by a *pedanda,* the recipient shows that he is grateful for the gift, which he, a person of lower status, is not worthy of on his own. This same diction, incidentally, is used when obtaining food from others.

A *pedanda* will usually have holy water on hand, as he knows who his *sisya* are and what their needs might be. But getting holy water from a *pemangku* is often a more complicated process. One must usually go to the home of the *pemangku* and get him. The holy man must dress properly and offer his own prayers and offerings. Then those who have come for the *toya* must make ready the offerings, often elaborate, that they have brought from home. The group then prays at the principal shrines of the temple. Only after all this is accomplished is the holy water obtained. The *pemangku* is always given a suitable gift and a small amount of money.

Families often go to temples a considerable distance from their village to obtain holy water, either because of tradition, or because of a special religious attachment to a distant temple. Although *pemangkus* are supposed to be available in or near the temple most of the time, and most live next door, they are not always available to make holy water. This could be a most disappointing state of affairs if a family, laden with heavy offerings, has made a trip of several hours or a day. To insure that this does not happen, the family will *ngendek,* from *endek,* "to tie" — meaning they will send a messenger to give the *pemangku* three days notice of their arrival.

For special ceremonies, holy water is sought at particularly sacred springs or sources, a favorite being Bali's sacred mountain, Gunung Agung. The source at Gunung Agung is a spring that is actually not near the top at all, but is a kind of water hole or small pond located at the base of the last rocky ascent to the peak. For really big ceremonies holy water may be brought from even more exotic sources. For the islandwide Eka Dasa Rudra exorcism held in 1979, holy water was brought from Mount Semeru in Java, Mount Rinjani in Lombok, and even from the Ganges River. (See CHAPTER 21.)

The holy water from some temples is considered particularly desirable or appropriate. The *toya* from Pura Mutering Jagat Dalem Sidakarya, just east of Sesetan in South Denpasar, is a favorite for important ceremonies. The name of the temple is derived from a phrase meaning "the work can be done," and holy water from Pura Sidakarya is said to insure that any cere-

PEMANGKU GIVING HOLY WATER TO A WORSHIPER

mony in which it is used will be effective. In the Jimbaran area, Pura Sakenan on Turtle Island is a favorite source of holy water. So is Pura Luhur Uluwatu. And Pura Danu Batur's connection with irrigation and wet rice fields makes it a regular source for any number of villages.

When a ceremony is held that requires the use of holy water from distant shrines, each *bungbung* of holy water, upon arrival, is placed in a tall temporary shrine, called *panggungan,* outside of the gate of the temple. During the main part of the ceremony these various containers are transferred to a second temporary shrine, the *sanggar agung,* inside the temple. At the climax of the ceremony, the holy water containers are taken down, and each is carried on a person's head to a pavilion where all the waters are mixed together. Then the *pemangkus* of the temples administer it to themselves, sprinkle it on the shrines of the temple, and administer it to the worshipers present in the temple. Each family may take a container of the blended holy waters home to their own family temple.

Holy water is commonly obtained from the temple well. Not all temples have wells, but the water from those that do can be considered as holy water — even without further prayers or offerings. However, as our local *pedanda* put it, such water is *durung sah,* "not yet valid." It is perfectly fine, however, for most purposes. Many villages, including Jimbaran, have sacred wells, usually called *beji,* from which holy water can be obtained. These wells are always surrounded by stone or concrete enclosures so that the water within cannot be contaminated.

At Pura Luhur Lempuyang, on top of a mountain near Karangasem, there is a small grove of thin bamboo plants. Cutting open one of the culms reveals a small amount of a liquid. After prayers are offered to the grove, this fluid can be mixed with clean water to produce holy water. In some ceremonies, the water within an unripe coconut can be used as holy water. Even ocean water can sometimes be holy, particularly for use in rites that affect sea temples and fishermen. (This is just one contradiction of the oft-repeated, but false, adage that the Balinese consider the sea unclean.)

Very large quantities of holy water can be prepared by simply putting a small amount of holy water into a large container of clean water that has not been sanctified. The resulting mixture has the same mystical power as that of the small amount of holy water put into it. Enormous amounts of holy water were required at Besakih during the months that preceded the climax of the Eka Dasa Rudra ceremony. There was even holy water on tap at that time, running from a large container of clean water into which smaller amounts of holy water were added from time to time.

ONE OF THE MOST IMPORTANT USES OF HOLY WATER is to anoint the faithful during a temple ceremony. When the family comes to a temple to pray, the wife always brings an offering. It may be very large and elaborate, or it may consist simply of a small *canang* for each member of the family. She also brings a small container with which to carry holy water back to the family temple. She leaves the offerings and container at the shrine in front of the worshipers, where they sit in a queue to be consecrated by the *pemangku*. She picks up already blessed *canangs* for her family, and she and the family then sit down to pray. To purify their minds and bodies, the worshipers first dip their hands into a small half coconut shell of holy water, called a *kocor*. There is almost always one nearby on the ground, or someone may be asked to pass one. The *kocors* are kept filled by the *pemangkus*.

Then everyone prays. Each person usually has a *canang* on the ground in front of him and a lighted stick of incense that is stuck into the ground next to the *canang*. It is best to pray five times. One holds one's palms together, thumbs pointed at or touching the forehead, hands raised high so that the fingers point straight up. Men sit cross-legged; women kneel, sitting on their heels. For the first and fifth prayers the hands are empty. For the second, third, and fourth prayers, a flower from the *canang* is held between the tips of the fingers. The first and last prayers are to Sanghyang Widi. The second and third are to Surya Raditya, Hyang Widhi Wasa, and Dewa Samudaya. There is some variation on the list, depending upon the circumstances. And a great many people who pray just do so, without thinking about directing their prayers to a specific god. When finished praying, the worshiper waits to receive holy water from the *pemangku*.

The *pemangku* carries holy water in a coconut shell dipper, a *cedok*. The *cedok* is always held high in the right hand, with left palm touching the elbow. The worshiper holds his hands out, palm upward on each side. The *pemangku* grasps a flower that is floating in the *cedok* between the first and second fingers of his right hand and sprinkles the worshiper three times by twisting his wrist. This sprinkling is called *ngitisin*. After one has been sprinkled, one is *maketis,* in low Balinese, or *sirat,* in the medium form.

The worshiper now puts his hands in the *nunas* or begging position. The right hand is cupped and held on top of the left palm, both palms up. The *pemangku* places a bit of the holy water in the worshiper's palm either by pouring it from the *cedok* or by dripping it from the flower used to sprinkle the holy water. After each placement of the water in his palm, the worshiper sips it into his mouth and swallows it. This is done three times. A fourth, and often a fifth or even sixth delivery of holy water is wiped on the face and sprinkled on the head by the worshiper. After this *nunas tirtha,* the *pemangku* usually sprinkles the worshiper once or several times more and gives him a small dab of wet rice, called *bija*. This is received in the right hand, transferred to the left, and then a bit of it is pressed with the right hand against the temples, forehead, and throat, and a grain or two is swallowed. The *pemangku* may give the worshiper the flower that was used to sprinkle the holy water, in which case it is stuck in the head band, or placed behind one ear. The worshiper may now rise and leave, being careful not to step in front of others who are praying. The *pemangku* pours the leftover holy water into a *kocor* and returns to the shrine to get more.

Usually the *pemangku* sprinkles three or four people at once with his holy water and pours a little in each of the palms of all of them in turn, one after the other, returning to the first one after the last in line. Sometimes the holy water is in a large container instead of a *cedok*. Sometimes a clay or metal drinking bottle, *caratan,* is used instead of a *cedok* or other container. If a little child is praying, he normally sits in the lap of one of his parents, who then holds the baby's hands in the proper position and brings the water up to his mouth at the proper time. Children learn to do this for themselves at a very early age.

At the *odalans* of the larger or most important temples, there is such a throng of worshipers that a great many *pemangkus* are required. The worshiper may not even have the opportunity to get a *canang* from the shrine in front. In that case, anticipating the problem, he brings his own, and his own incense. In such cases, the *pemangku* may simply give a *cedok* of holy water to the worshiper, who then sprinkles himself and his family and pours the holy water into his own palm and theirs. By watching how a *pemangku* obtains the holy water from the vessel at the front of the shrine, one knows what to do. Usually, when a *pemangku* refills his *cedok,* he holds it up, says a prayer, and sprinkles a little of the holy water toward the shrine three times. He then sprinkles some toward himself. This, in effect, establishes a communication between the god of the shrine and the holy water. If this has already been done, the person who receives the holy water from the *pemangku* can go ahead and use it at once. If not, the recipient must himself establish the link with the god of the shrine in the same fashion before he can use the holy water. When the family has finished praying, the wife goes up to the shrine, retrieves her offering tray and her container filled with the holy water of the shrine, and everyone leaves the inner temple to go home or socialize with friends nearby.

On some occasions there is no opportunity for a worshiper to *nunas toya.* Such is the case when a temple is so full of worshipers, and when time and space are so limited, that to treat each individual separately would be impossible. In such an event, one of the *pemangkus* sprinkles holy water over the entire group using a brush like implement called a *lis.* A *lis* is made from a bundle of immature coconut leaves — *busung* — which are cut into elaborate and symbolic patterns. The exact patterns used and the number of leaves per *lis* are specified by tradition. Most *lis* are about 10 centimeters across, and up to 75 centimeters long. The leaves are bound together at one end, forming a kind of handle into which is thrust a flower and a special variety of rice container made from coconut leaf called *ketipat*. The free ends are temporarily held together by a cover. When put into use, this cover is symbolically cut by striking it with a knife three times. The *pemangku* now removes the cover, dips the free end into a container of holy water and begins sprinkling. Using a large container of holy water and a big *lis* a *pemangku* can sprinkle a great many worshipers with holy water. It is a common sight to see this in the larger ceremonies — hundreds of people seated on the ground, the *pemangku* walking among them, spraying holy water as if he were sowing seeds.

A *lis* is often used to sprinkle holy water on offerings. One of the most beautiful and moving sights that one can see in our village is the *ngaturan piodalan* ceremony, which takes place late in the evening after the public has prayed at one of the major temples. A dozen or more of our village *pemangkus* are seated in a line, facing the principal shrine. In front of them are piles of offerings, placed on raised clay trays called *dulang*. A large jar of well-water is handy. Braziers pour out fragrant smoke, joined by bundles of lighted incense. The village *gong* plays nearby. Each *pemangku* then takes a flower in his right hand and his bell in his left and begins to chant his mantras. As a mantra is completed, each *pemangku* flips his flower into the water and begins a new prayer. In this way the water is changed to holy water and is now ready to be sprinkled on the offerings. An assistant hands the *pemangku* of the Pura Dalem, the leader of the group, a *lis*. He shakes it three times at the shrine, hands it back to an assistant who strikes it with his knife, removes the cap, and hands it back again — he then dips the *lis* into the newly made holy water and sprinkles the assembled offerings. Then the assistants sprinkle all of the shrines of the temple, the holy water is mixed with more water, and the *pemangkus* distribute the holy water.

Another important kind of holy water sprinkler is that used by *pedandas*. It is usually called *penyiratan tirtha*. The word is derived from the verb *sirat*, which means "sprinkle water." It is a silver tube about 25 centimeters long and about 2 centimeters in diameter, tapering slightly toward the top. The *penyiratan tirtha* is stuffed with each of three special grass headbands, and a white frangipani flower is thrust into the top of the tube. The *pedanda* holds the sprinkler in his right hand and uses it from time to time throughout most of the ceremonies that he performs, dipping the bottom end into the holy water that he has prepared and flipping it onto the offerings that lie in front of him on his platform.

One very important use of holy water occurs on the occasion of an all-village purification ceremony, held on the last day of the Balinese lunar year, which almost invariably falls some time in March. The purification ceremony — called *melis* or *melasti* — takes the form of a procession to the sea or to some nearby source of water, which may be a holy spring or well or lake. The processioners carry *pratimas*, small wooden statues that serve as temporary resting places for deities and ancestors during the ceremony. After various welcoming and purification ceremonies are performed, all the *pratimas* are carried to the water source. In the case of our village, this means to the beach, about a kilometer away. The procession is a very colorful sight. Umbrellas shade each *pratima*. Banners and flags wave. Women carry holy water from every temple. The *gong* provides marching music. All the villagers are dressed in their best traditional clothing and join the procession at its end.

When the procession reaches the beach, the *pemangkus* prepare a batch of holy water on the spot, using the water carried from the temple and some from the ocean. The sanctity of the ocean water comes from the Pamuteran Mandara Giri myth, sometimes called "The Churning of the Sea of Milk." In the myth, Tirtha Amertha, the holy water of eternal life, was prepared by the combined energies of the gods and demons by using the largest mountain as a whisk and mixing all sorts of earthly effluvia into the ocean. (See CHAPTER 6.) The sea purified the ingredients and finally cast up the Tirtha Amertha, which the gods drank, becoming immortal. But the gods did not get all of this mystic water from the sea, and all seawater still contains it, giving the sea the power to purify and sanctify.

HOLY WATER IS SO ESSENTIAL TO BALINESE LIFE that it is impossible to list all its uses. Those who are sick are made well by *balians* or *pemangkus* or *pedandas* who clean the spirits of their patients with holy water. A Balinese undergoes such a cleansing before and after any major trip. Every one of the rites of passage involves the use of holy water. Shrines are sprinkled with it every day. Those who go into trance are brought back from this state with holy water. One of the most sacred and most popular stories portrayed in the *wayang kulit* shadow play, "Bima Suarga," is the story of how Bima was sent in quest of holy water.

And one of the most devastating things that can happen to a family is to be denied access to holy water from the village temples. This is the common punishment for a person who has been expelled from his *banjar* because of failure to comply with the religious or customary laws. Because it is so serious, it is not a common punishment. It means, in effect, that the person so expelled is ritually dead. And this applies not only to him, but to all members of his family and all close relations.

CHAPTER 6

The Sea of Milk
CREATING THE MYTHIC ELIXIR OF LIFE

THIS STORY COMES FROM THE MAHABHARATA, and relates the creation of
the first Tirtha Amertha, or holy water. A long work describing the war
between the Pandawas and the Kurus — described in an earlier chapter —
the Mahabharata is also full of asides, fables, and tales that add interest to
the story. Our tale here is from "The Book of the Beginning," chapter 5,
verses 15 to 17. In the epic it has no formal title, but this popular story is
called "Pamuteran Mandara Giri" by the Balinese, literally, "The Spinning
of Mount Mandara."

The narrator is a professional bard, telling his story to an audience of
noble hermits — "ascetics" — who live in the forest. Saunaka is the leader
of this group. Our story opens when two princesses see a great horse
approach. It is a world-horse that has the power to fly through the air. But
when Saunaka asks about the horse's origin, the narrator launches into the
tale of the churning of the Sea of Milk, and the horse is quickly forgotten.

NOW, O ASCETIC, the two sisters saw the horse named Ucaisrawa approach,
the stallion of priceless value that was cheered by all the gods when it
sprang from the Sea of Milk from which it had been churned. It was a
wonderful horse, greatest of steeds, having enormous strength, splendid,
always young, holy, and having all marks of excellence.

Saunaka asked the bard to tell him about how the gods churned the sea
and to narrate the circumstances surrounding the birth of the horse.

The bard said that there is a great mountain, Mount Meru, that shines
like glowing cinders, and from its peak comes a radiance equal to that of
the sun. It is a wonderful ornament of gold that the gods cherish, of enor-

mous size, but those who are not worthy cannot reach it. Huge beasts of prey roam on Mount Meru and herbs of magical power grow on it. It is so high that it covers the vault of the sky. It has many rivers and trees, and flocks of beautiful birds sing on its slopes. The gods climbed this mountain of boundless height and sat down to talk about how they might get the Tirtha Amertha, the holy water that gives everlasting life.

Wisnu said to Brahma that, in order to get the Tirtha Amertha, both the gods and the demons would have to churn the sea. And while this sea is being churned many good things would come forth, and finally the Tirtha Amertha would appear. So the gods and demons went to Sangkadwipa, the location of Mount Mandara, and found this huge mountain overgrown with forests in which many birds called and many tusked animals and other beasts of prey were to be seen. It was the playground of both gods and demons. It rose 11,000 *yojana* into the sky and was 1,000 *yojana* in diameter. [Note: a *yojana* is 100,000 *depa*, the distance between a man's outstretched hands — thus Mount Mandara is 2 million kilometers high!]

It was the intention of the gods and demons to churn the sea with Mount Mandara, but, try as they might, they could not budge it. So they went to Wisnu and Brahma and asked them to help, since all would benefit from the result. At once Wisnu called up Naga Anantaboga [the great snake] from the world below and ordered him to uproot Mount Mandara. And so the *naga* wrapped himself around the mountain and succeeded in pulling it up. And the gods and demons carried Mount Mandara to the Sea of Milk where they told Hyang Segara, god of the oceans, what their intentions were. Segara consented, provided that he could get some of the Tirtha Amertha too. But when the mountain was placed in the Sea of Milk it sank out of sight. So the gods summoned Akupara, king of the turtles, and asked him to be the support of the mountain while they were churning, to which the turtle agreed. Indra sat on top of the mountain to keep it from being dislodged by the churning.

The other snake, Naga Basuki, offered to let his body be used as a rope with which to spin the mountain. So Basuki wrapped himself around Mount Mandara and all the gods took hold of the tail, while all the demons held the head. Anantaboga stayed by Wisnu and kept Basuki's head steady while the gods and demons pulled back and forth. As the churning proceeded, smoke and fire and poison came from the mouth of Basuki, which made the gods and especially the demons very tired from the heat of the fire and the great effort used to twist the mountain.

As the gods and demons were strong, they worked very hard, trying to outdo each other. The force of their work caused rocks to rain down from the mountain, and the trees of the great forest fell all over the place. Their crashing together caused great fires to be started, and sparks rained every-

where. A great roar like that of thunder issued from the depths of the sea.
The wild animals fled from the burning forest, and the elephants and
rhinoceroses and other animals were crushed by the falling trees and fell
into the sea. All the fish and other marine creatures were crushed by the
weight of the mountain and died as the sea bubbled and boiled from the

THE CHURNING OF THE SEA OF MILK

churning and from the poison that issued from Basuki's mouth. Saps and
resins oozed from the burning trees of the forests and ran into the sea, as
did the plants and flowers that had grown on the sides of the mountain.
The birds that once lived on the mountain slopes were killed and fell into
the sea. Great gusts of wind shook the air as the mountain was spun.

Seeing the fatigue and heat exhaustion of the demons and gods, Indra
meditated, and at once clouds and lightning appeared, shielding the workers from the sun and causing rain to fall in torrents, putting out the fires
and giving shade. The saps and resins and juices of the trees and flowers
and herbs ran into the sea along with the water from the rain. And now the
water of the sea turned into milk. And from this Sea of Milk butter, mixed
with fragrant essences, floated upward to the surface. But still there was no
Tirtha Amertha. The gods and demons, very tired by now, stopped and
asked Brahma to intercede with Wisnu, god of the waters, so that he could

KALA RAUH EATING THE SUN

help them. Brahma did as he was asked, and Wisnu granted renewed energy to those who were churning. Hearing his command, the gods and
demons got to work again with renewed energy.

And suddenly, as they churned the Sea of Milk, a sun of 100,000 rays
arose from the Sea, followed by the bright, cool moon. And the goddess
Sri emerged from the sea, clothed in white robes. And the goddess of
liquor arose from the sea, as did the white horse, Ucaisrawa. The great
jewel named Kastuba that Wisnu now wears on his chest — the jewel that
can grant any wish — also emerged. All of these things went to where the
gods were standing and watching. And finally there arose the beautiful
goddess Danwantari, carrying the white gourd named Kamandalu, which
held the Tirtha Amertha.

As soon as the demons saw the Tirtha Amertha they screeched, "It is
ours!" and took it from Danwantari, claiming that it belonged to the
demons, not the gods. But Wisnu was equal to the occasion. He changed
himself into a beautiful girl and approached the demons as they were taking
the Tirtha Amertha home. The demons liked pretty girls, so they paid a lot
of attention to Wisnu in disguise. They carried her on their backs, and they
gave her the container full of Tirtha Amertha to carry. As soon as he was

given the Tirtha Amertha, Wisnu assumed his proper form and ran away with the Tirtha Amertha back to the gods, who hastily drank of it, thereby achieving immortality.

In the confusion a demon by the name of Kala Rauh disguised himself as a god and took a mouthful of Tirtha Amertha. The Sun and Moon, who saw what was happening, told Wisnu, who at once took up his magic discus-like Cakra, hurled it at Kala Rauh, and cut off his head. But Rauh had already half swallowed some of the Tirtha Amertha, which had just reached his throat. Thus his head was immortal, but the Tirtha Amertha had not yet reached his body, so it died at once and fell with a crash to the ground. The head of Kala Rauh roared frighteningly at the Sun and Moon for giving him away. And he began to chase them. And even to this day Kala Rauh chases them, and whenever he catches one or the other he swallows them up, causing an eclipse.

Discovering their loss, the demons attacked the gods, and a terrible and ferocious and gruesome battle ensued. The demons, cut by the spears and swords, and shattered by the lances and clubs, vomited buckets of blood, and their bodies fell everywhere along the shores of the sea where the battle occurred. Heads severed by the lances rolled along the ground like nuggets of gold. Everywhere screams were heard by the thousands as the opposing sides shouted and gave encouragement to their friends.

Seeing the terrible battle, Wisnu meditated, and at once his discus, Cakra, began to cut its burning, razorlike path through the sky as Wisnu with arms like elephant trunks hurled it at the enemy. The Cakra tore apart thousands of the demons, drinking their blood greedily. But the demons, undaunted, hammered the gods with mountains, and some of the gods fled to the sky. From there they caused giant wooded mountains to come thundering down on to the enemy, crushing them and crashing into them and causing terror in their ranks. The earth shook from the pounding. The god Nara made the sky dark with his arrows that had golden tips. Pressed mightily by the gods, the demons finally were forced to flee into the sea or to dig into the ground.

AND, HAVING WON, the gods returned to Mount Mandara and placed it with great honor on its original resting place. They dispersed the clouds to their homes and cleared the area of the blood that drenched the plains and mountains. The gods hid the Tirtha Amertha and rejoiced at their victory.

CHAPTER 7

Bujangga Wesnawe
ICONOCLASTIC FOLLOWERS OF WISNU

THE BUJANGGA WESNAWE are a small, but iconoclastic Hindu sect —
Wisnuists on an island of Siwaists, disbelievers in caste in a caste-conscious
society, ceremonially austere on an island where grand and lavish displays of
faith are exalted. The Wesnawe suffer from a kind of second-class status
from religious authorities and others who feel that their priests deviate
rather widely from the main stream of official Balinese Hinduism, and
Wesnawe priests, Ida Bujangga Rsi, are not given the status and publicity
accorded to the more conservative priests, the *pedandas*. Even in the ceremonies where the priority of a Wisnu-based sect should be recognized, for
example in administering the *caru* purification rites, the Balinese just as
often to turn to a *sengguhu*, a religious man with neither the training nor
the background of a Wesnawe, but whom most Balinese assume to be just
as qualified.

The Bujangga Wesnawe people are a clan or sect that considers itself to
be caste-less, tracing its doctrine to pre-Hindu Vedic notions of *warna* —
literally "color," but meaning order, or profession — instead of fixed caste.
Caste in Vedic, and Wesnawe, doctrine is based on one's profession. Thus a
teacher or priest is a Brahmana only as long as he is a teacher or priest.
According to the Wesnawe, the origin of their group dates back to the time
of the Upanishads, some 500 to 800 years before the common era.

The story is told that, much like the founding of Buddhism, Wesnawism
was a reaction to abuses of prestige and status by high caste Hindus.
Establishing the doctrine of rigid, birth-based caste was seen to be chief
among the abuses. Reform-minded Hindu philosophers, from their study
of the Vedas, found that the religious practices of the time were in clear

violation of the teachings. One of these Wedanta philosophers, Ramanuja, wrote extensively of the relationship between the Vedas and the practices of a rigid caste system. His principal thesis expounded upon the equality of man. A large number of Hindus were attracted to his philosophy and teaching, and under his guidance formed a group that called itself Waisnawa (or Wesnawa, or Wesnawe) and held itself to be entirely outside of any caste at all.

By the time Hinduism came to Indonesia, about the fourth century A.D., Hinduism, Wesnawism, and Buddhism had separated in India. But in Indonesia there was a more general fusing of these basically similar religions. Hinduism and Buddhism united in Central Java in about the ninth century. And Siwaism from South India and this Hindu-Buddhism fused to become the religion of the Majapahit empire in East Java.

When Empu Kuturan, a Hindu (some claim he was a Buddhist), came to Bali in about A.D. 1019, he found nine separate religious sects but no caste system. According to the Wesnawe, each kept itself separate from the others and maintained its identity. And each believed itself to be superior to the others. Empu Kuturan organized a meeting of the leaders of the nine sects at Samuan Tiga, near the village of Pejeng. The result of this meeting was a fusion of the nine sects into three: Buddhist, Siwaist, and Wesnawist. These were called the Trisadhaka (or Trisedaka). Every major ceremony was supposed to be led by three priests, one from each of the sects.

After the coming of the great priest Danghyang Nirartha, about A.D. 1550, caste appeared in Bali for the first time. The descendants of Danghyang Nirartha were all Brahmanas who consolidated their power and began a reaction against the Wesnawes. Before this time the king had three advisor-priests: Brahmana, Buddhist, and Wesnawist. The result of this was the ejection of the Wesnawes from their equality with the other two sects. No longer were their priests allowed to advise the king.

THIS, AT LEAST, IS HOW THE WESNAWE TELL THE STORY. The group steadfastly maintained its position as being outside of caste and continued to preach the equality of man, diverging from conventional religious law (*adat*) in many respects. They did not believe in punishment for mixed-caste marriages. They tried to simplify the complex system of rituals followed by other groups. They made offerings, but many fewer than those of the other Hindus. Their cremations were relatively brief, and simple, affairs. These deviations did not please the more traditional Hindu priests, for it threatened to erode their authority. Thus the Wesnawes found themselves not only outside of caste, but also outside of the mainstream of power in the Hindu hierarchy — which is where they are today.

The Balinese religious authorities officially sanction about ten to 12

Bujangga Wesnawe priests, the Ida Bujangga Rsi. Their training is always from another, older Ida Bujangga Rsi, never by a Siwaist or Buddhist *pedanda*. The status of an Ida Bujangga Rsi is more or less equal to that of a *pedanda* Siwa or *pedanda* Buddha — but with the emphasis on "less." Though the very largest Balinese Hindu ceremonies require all three, the *pedanda* Siwa sits highest, the *pedanda* Buddha somewhat lower, and the *rsi* the lowest. In such ceremonies, for example the enormous *taur agung* that concluded the islandwide Eka Dasa Rudra ceremony in 1979, each has his own special duty. That of the Ida Bujangga Rsi is to lead the ceremonies knows as *caru*, or sacrifice. (See CHAPTER 20.) The three use different mantras, but their goal is essentially the same.

When an officially recognized Ida Bujangga Rsi is not working with the other two types of *pedandas* he is considered capable of performing all of the ceremonies of Balinese Hinduism — all five of the *yadnyas*. Whether he or a *pedanda* would be called upon to perform a particular ceremony depends only upon the feeling of the person who is putting on the ceremony. But even a *pedanda,* when asked to perform a *caru* ceremony, will frequently refer the potential client to an Ida Bujangga Rsi.

The Bujangga Wesnawe sect feels a strong tie to the Hindu God incarnated as Wisnu, rather than as Siwa or Brahman. The name "Wesnawe" reflects this attachment. The predominance of Siwaist *pedandas* in Bali can be traced to the fact that the chief Hindu influences felt in the archipelago came from South Indian — Siwaist — traders. The worship of Wisnu took hold in North India and the North Indians influenced Java, and later Bali, very little. Wisnu is known as the preserver. His duties are to protect and safeguard the world and its creatures and to purify them. And the *caru* ceremony is a purification rite — thus the strong association between Bujangga Wesnawe priests and sacrifices.

AN IDA BUJANGGA RSI OFTEN INHERITS THE DUTY from his parents. Or the people in his area might feel the need for a Bujangga Wesnawe priest and ask some qualified person to begin his training. A person may simply feel the urge and study on his own or with a teacher. But only one of Bujangga Wesnawe lineage can become a full-fledged *rsi*. An outsider can study the *lontars* and can apprentice himself to a *rsi*. And, if successful, he can lead the same ceremonies. But he cannot be called a *rsi*. Rather, he is called a *penganut wesnawe*, the first word coming from *anut*, meaning "to follow."

Another way to becoming a *rsi* is through sickness. If someone gets very sick, the family may go to a *balian*, a traditional healer, to *matakon di baase* — literally, "ask something from the rice" — in order to determine the cause and cure of the sickness. If the affliction is serious enough, the *balian* may tell the person that he should learn the powers of an Ida

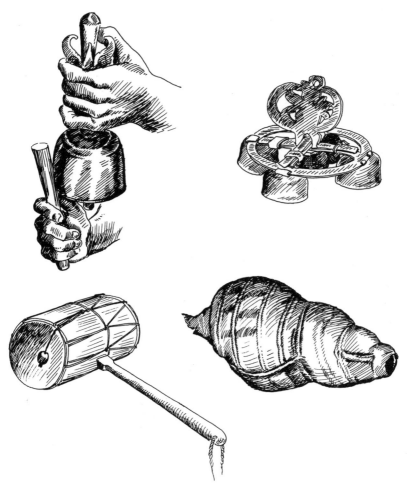

CLOCKWISE FROM TOP LEFT:
BAJRA UTER, GENTORAG, SUNGU, AND KETEPLOK

Bujangga Rsi to combat the spirits hounding him. This is the same route by which a good many *balians* and *pemangkus* — lay priests — have come to their professions.

In order to function officially as a Bujangga Wesnawe priest, a *rsi* must apply to the Parisada Hindu Dharma, the Hindu dharma committee that is the official overseer of the Hindu religion in Bali. The same rule applies to prospective *pedandas*. The applicant must meet certain standards and satisfy the *parisada* that he is qualified to fulfill his duties.

A Bujangga Wesnawe priest dresses somewhat differently from a *pedan-*

da. Although he wears the tall hat of the *pedanda,* the *bawa* or *ketu,* his is undecorated. He wears his hair in a curl on the back of his head, *apusung,* rather than on top of his head as is the case with a *pedanda* Siwa. A *rsi* also uses unique tools or instruments in his ceremonies. One is a very large conch shell, called *sungu.* It is blown in the manner of a trumpet, giving off a loud sound full of tones. Some *rsi* have several, the higher-pitched ones considered female; the lower-pitched, male.

The *ketiplug* or *keteplok* is a small, hand-held *rsi* drum. It is mounted on a wooden handle and the entire apparatus look like a hammer. A small weight is fastened by a short length of string to the equator of the drum. To sound the instrument, the handle is held upright and the head twisted rapidly back and forth, the weight thus striking alternate faces of the drum. The *rsi* also uses a frame of bronze bells called a *gentorang.* This instrument usually contains five individual bells of different tones, all of them rung at once by shaking the *gentorang's* frame.

The fourth instrument is a special bell called *bajra uter.* The word *bajra* comes from *vajira,* Sanskrit for "club" or "mace." This bell is one of the *nawa senjata* — "nine weapons" — carried by the gods of the nine directions. *Bajra* is the weapon of Iswara, god of the east. A *pedanda* Buddha uses a small bronze *bajra* in his right hand. Arjuna in the Mahabharata wears a *bajra* bracelet as a symbol of the Hindu triad. The *bajra uter* is not shaken as is an ordinary bell. It is sounded by rubbing the edge with a piece of wood, usually sandalwood. One end of the stick is pressed against the lip of the bell and then swept in a circular motion around the circumference of the bell, always in contact with the surface. This rubbing motion excites the sounding of the bell — like rubbing the edge of a crystal wine glass with a wet finger — which continues as long as the circular motion continues. It is a remarkably pure, penetrating tone.

A *bajra uter* is extremely difficult to make. One cannot just take an ordinary bell, stroke it with a piece of wood, and expect it to work. In fact, it is only by accident that a smith produces one. I once asked a smith to make one for me and he told me that he had made only one or two in his whole life, and those by pure accident. He said that he always tests his bells to see if they will respond to rubbing with a piece of wood, but that the result is almost invariably a failure. He promised to let me know if he made one.

Two years passed, and I had almost forgotten about the arrangement. Then one day he arrived at my house in Jimbaran proudly bearing my new *bajra uter.* He had made more than 200 bells since my visit, he said. And he had just succeeded in making a *bajra uter.* If I didn't want it (at a rather steep price) then there were several others who did. He demonstrated it using a wooden screwdriver handle. It was a lovely sound, and I bought it on the spot. I had a piece of sandalwood cut and polished for the rubbing stick. And I discovered that a little violin bow rosin applied to the wooden stick allows the sound to be produced more easily. Interestingly enough, I have asked several villagers if they would like to try the instrument, and they usually decline. The reason given is that this is such an unusual sort of object that it must have some kind of mystical force connected with it, and few are willing to risk an encounter with it.

The *bajra uter* is used by the Bujangga priest himself or his assistant in all ceremonies that he conducts. The other four are only used in *caru* ceremonies to send invitations to particular demons, *bhutas* and *kalas,* and are normally sounded by the assistants of the priest. These are often sounded near the end of the ceremony, raising a great din, as if the sound were intended to drive the evil spirits away rather than attract them.

Like *pedandas,* the Ida Bujangga Rsi have *sisya,* clients, who traditionally come to them in time of need. No formal agreement binds them, it is merely a matter of tradition. Of course the services of a Bujangga priest are available to anyone, *sisya* or not.

THE MYTH OF MAYADENAWA, which provides some of the background for the important Galungan ceremony, is part of Bujangga lore as well. Mayadenawa's name is invariably associated with atheism, and, hence, evil. He was the son of a rich, powerful, and benevolent king who ruled in the area called Balingkang (or Bali Kang), north of Kintamani, partway down into the Batur crater just east of Penulisan. Mayadenawa was powerful and very evil, and could turn himself into all manner of shapes or make himself invisible. He imposed his godless regime upon all of Bali, destroyed the temples, punished those who worshiped their gods, banned religious festivals, and so on. As a result, disaster struck. Crops withered and died. Streams dried up. Hordes of rodents appeared. The people got sick, and were starving. The priests appealed to Indra, who came to earth with a great army to chase and kill Mayadenawa.

One of the mightiest of the battles between the two armies was brought to a halt by sunset. That night, while the army of Indra was sleeping peacefully in its camp. Mayadenawa sneaked into the camp and created a pool of poisonous water nearby. So that he would not be detected, he was very careful not to make any noise, carefully walking on the sides of his feet. ("Footprint" in Balinese is *tampak; siring* means "edge." The place where this happened is known today as Tampak Siring.) The next morning Indra's army awoke, found the water nearby, and drank of it. Everyone became violently sick. Indra used his magic power and created a large spring of fresh, clear water that was able to cure the sickness of his army. The spring is called Tirtha Empul — *empul* is Kawi for a big spring of water.

Mayadenawa now fled from Indra, changing his shape from place to place. Finally he changed himself into a large *paras* rock. Indra shot the rock with his magic arrow and killed Mayadenawa. His blood flowed out of the rock down a hill and formed the river Pekerisan. Indra cursed the river, saying that, although its waters would allow rice to grow well, if the rice were harvested it would become bloody and smell like a corpse. This curse was to last for 1,000 years. It appears that the Balinese viewed the Pekerisan with considerable misgivings up until rather recently because of this curse. The death of the arch-villain Mayadenawa took place on Rebo, Wednesday, of the 11th week, Dunggulan, of the Balinese Pawukon calendar — a day called Galungan. Today Galungan is celebrated, some say, as the victory of religion over atheism, the triumph of good over evil, the saving of the world from the forces of darkness.

Myths being what they are, some of the members of the Bujangga Wesnawe clan feel that Mayadenawa actually was a member of, or was used to symbolize, their sect. Perhaps Mayadenawa was just a Bujangga Wesnawe priest who was more interested in meditation and thought than he was in ritual and display — perhaps his "atheism" was nothing more than a less lavish and more ascetic version of Hinduism. Perhaps, the Wesnawe say, it was the entrenched Siwaist priesthood, motivated by jealousy and anxious to defend their own positions, who spread the word that Mayadenawa, a Bujangga Wesnawe, was the evil anti-god. (The Wesnawe are not alone in feeling this — some Theravada Buddhists cite the story as an attack on their own spare and meditative form of worship.)

Adherents of the Bujangga Wesnawe–Mayadenawa connection cite as evidence the name Mayadenawa itself. *Maya* means "illusion," something that is lost and cannot be seen. *Danu* is Balinese for "lake" or "water." *Danawa* are the followers of the water, Wisnu is the god associated with water — hence *danawa* are the followers of Wisnu. And Mayadenawa means that the followers of Wisnu, the Bujangga Wesnawe, disappeared. This, they say, refers to the loss of prestige and influence of the Bujangga Wesnawe at the hands of the conservative Siwaist priesthood.

There is another myth that relates to the Wesnawe, and to the *sengguhu* with which they are often lumped, and points out another way the Wesnawe have come to have an unfavorable image. The Balinese often confuse the Wesnawe and *sengguhu*, the latter a kind of self-trained priest who is often called upon to perform less important, or sacrificial ceremonies. And like the Wesnawe, the *sengguhu* claim to be caste-less. They call themselves *jero gede*, sometimes *rsi*, and use instruments that resemble those of the Wesnawe. But the *sengguhu*, in contrast to the Wesnawe *rsi*, are neither certified by any religious authorities nor, in fact, are they very often well-trained. They are something of imposters.

According to the myth, one day the great Pedanda Danhyang Nirartha, also known as Dwijendra and as Pedanda Sakti Wawu Rauh, was not at his home. Some people came to his house and asked him to lead a ceremony. They were met by one of the *pedanda's* followers and assistants, whose name was I Guto. I Guto had learned the mantras and was able to lead ceremonies because he had followed his master for a long time. The people who had come to the house of the *pedanda* had not met the priest before, and they naturally assumed that I Guto was Danghyang Nirartha. I Guto told them that, indeed, he was the *pedanda,* and led the ceremony that they had asked for.

As soon as the ceremony had ended, the master himself appeared upon the scene. He was very angry with his student for pretending that he was a *pedanda.* And the people were very angry with him for deceiving them. They called him Sengguhu, derived from the word *sengguh,* which means "regard as," or "suspect." The people regarded this man as a real *pedanda,* but, in fact, he was a fraud and an imposter. Danghyang Nirartha told the man that he could perform only the lowest ceremonies for the lowest caste — *caru* ceremonies for the lowest caste people, the Sudras.

THIS, THEN, IS HOW THE TERM *SENGGUHU* came to have such negative implications. And by association, in the popular mind of the Balinese and because of the ceremonies they are often called upon to perform, the Wesnawe as well. Even the *sengguhu* don't always deserve their reputation, as some are not *pedandas* or *rsi* only in name — in terms of knowledge and seriousness, they are true priests. There are *sengguhu* at Keramas and at Angkeling near Gianyar, Sukawati, Tegeh Kuri, Bon Biyu, and at Sibang Kaja on the road to Mambal and at Tonja just north of Denpasar. These cover the full spectrum from what I consider to be outright charlatans to those who are, except for credentials, the equivalent of regular Bujangga Wesnawe priests.

There are bona fide Bujangga Wesnawe priests at Banjar Titih in Denpasar, at Tegal Cankring in Negara, at Tembahu, at Takmung near Klungkung, at Nyit Dah, at Tegal, at Pejaten in the Kediri area northwest of Denpasar, at Gabogan south of Bajra, and at Gunung Sari near Penebel. There are families of Wesnawe priests in Buleleng, but no living priests.

CHAPTER 8

Masters of Steel

THE POWERFUL PANDE CLAN OF SMITHS

THE PANDES — LITERALLY, "SMITHS" — are a fairly small, but very tightly knit clan group in Bali. The historical importance of their craft, particularly in the shaping of the magically charged, and (unfortunately) very practical kris daggers, gave this group of low caste artisans a status that seemed to fall outside the usual dictates of caste. And today, this clan is still fiercely proud, the most conservative in its ranks refusing the religious authority of the Brahmana priests — some, claiming ancestry preceding Hinduism, even creating a sort of hybrid religion of their own.

Hinduism was an import to Bali, brought by members of the Hindu-Javanese Majapahit kingdom. In the period of this East Java kingdom's collapse, 1478 to 1520, increasing numbers of Majapahit royalty settled in Bali. The caste system the Javanese brought was the *triwangsa:* Brahmana priests, Ksatriya rulers and princes, and Wesya merchants. The lowest of the four original Vedic "classes," the Sudra, was not part of the Hindu-Javanese scheme, but the indigenous Balinese came to be considered the Sudra. The Sudra are often called *jaba,* "outsider," a term that fits well with the historical record. Ironically, although the Sudra were outside the caste system, the caste members, who were Javanese, were the real outsiders. (The irony is doubled because *jaba* comes from "Java," which is how it came to mean "outsider.") The Sudra were the large majority 500 years ago and still represent well over 90 percent of Bali's population.

Caste brought with it an increased cultural emphasis on status, and the prestige caste offered was a powerful attraction to the essentially caste-less Sudra. Though officially frowned upon, some married into the *triwangsa,* a method no doubt made possible by the vast disproportion between the numbers of *triwangsa* and Sudra. Some of the caste-less group opposed the Javanization of Bali and withdrew to the isolated regions of the island, either voluntarily or by force. These Bali Aga, left to themselves, continued according to the old ways and religion. There were also groups within the Sudra who could claim status apart from caste — among these were the metalworkers.

THE EARLIEST AVAILABLE WRITINGS FROM INDONESIA, not just Bali, show that those who worked with metals were held to be something of a group apart. Metals had magical power, and craftsmen with the skills to work metal enjoyed the respect and awe of their peers. From the days when the prevailing religious beliefs on the islands were animistic, metal was revered and feared for its exceptional capabilities, and those who worked it were either brave, or powerful, or both. The smiths on Bali were called, generally, *pande,* the most influential among them being the blacksmiths: *pande wesi,* or *pande besi*. Although the Pande clan did not exist, even in the earliest days the *pande* had considerable political power, including the right to seat representatives on the governing bodies of the *desa* (village). To maintain their position of prestige, the smiths kept their techniques secret and saw to it that marriage would take place only within their own professional group.

With the development of a Hindu-Javanese state in Bali, a system of Ksatriya kings and their Brahmana priests replaced the traditional *desa* government. But the rulers were acutely aware of the magical power that the smiths possessed. They knew the strength of the new government depended to a large extent upon the work of the smiths — their products were the means to political stability. The rulers patronized the *pandes,* making their work an adjunct of the government and giving the smiths a place in the *puri,* the palace of the king's family.

During the period these changes were taking place, sometime between the 15th and 16th centuries, the Pande clan inscribed its own history in a *lontar,* a formal religious document, called the Prasasti Sira Pande Empu. Many clan groups wrote *lontars* during this time as a way to codify, and amplify, their right to a status greater than that of mere Sudra. These *lontars,* which are still read today, offer histories that are vivid, exaggerated, and full of hubris. The Pandes' is no exception.

The Prasasti Sira Pande Empu outlines a mythology that seems to predate Hinduism. It describes the creation by Brahma, but the Brahma here appears less like that of the Hindu triad, and more like the Vedic god of fire, Agni. Emphasizing fire, of course, makes sense for the Pande, who have always considered fire as their special instrument, from which much of their power was derived. And yet the Pande adopted the color red, which is always associated with the *trimurthi* god Brahma. The Pande temple at

Pura Besakih is decorated in red. And Pande men often wear red articles of clothing, such as *udeng* (head band), and *saput* (waist cloth), when participating in ceremonies.

In the early Hindu myths, asceticism and meditation commonly result in the creation of life, and in the Pande *lontar* these actions by Brahma created a man called Empu Pradah. *Empu* here is an epithet of high distinction, meaning "sage." But, the Indonesian word *empu* also refers to a master craftsman — especially to one who is skilled at forging kris. In the *lontar*, Empu Pradah is proclaimed the first head of the Pande clan. The document also includes a declaration of independence of sorts. It clearly states that the Brahmanas obtained their knowledge and power from the Pande, and establishes the Pandes as older than the Brahmanas and of greater power

A PANDE FORGES A METAL TOOL

and prestige. It also stipulates that Pandes are not permitted to obtain holy water from *pedandas* because, in effect, the Brahmana priests are the younger brothers of the Pandes, and, for that reason should be subservient to them. The *lontar* also includes various warnings to other caste-less people that they should not follow the teachings of the Brahmanas and Ksatriyas, but rather emulate the Pandes. The document is anti-Brahmana, anti-establishment, and loaded with pro-Pande propaganda.

According to their own history, the Pande came to Bali with the Majapahit exodus. They are said to have landed at Gunung Beratan in West Bali, between Gilimanuk, where the present ferry terminal is located, and Pulaki. From there the clan migrated to Lake Beratan, near Bedugul. The Pandes built the Pura Beratan temple on the lake shore, according to their history, or at least an important shrine there. From here the clan spread throughout Bali. One very important and very conservative group moved to what is now Banjar Beratan in the south part of Singaraja. Another important group went to Marga. Others went to Klungkung, Karangasem, Gianyar, and Celuk.

Historians who have examined the Prasasti Sira Pande Empu conclude that the general style was copied from the same sorts of documents written at about the same time to legitimate other organizations. Many of the mantras in it are copied directly from the mantras of the *pedandas*. The tone, they say, is much more Hindu-Javanese than Hindu-Balinese. This, combined with the Pande's own suggestion that they came from Java, would appear to weaken the Pande argument that their greater importance is based on a longer history in Bali. But had the Pandes claimed to have been in existence long before the advent of Hinduism in Bali, which is doubtless the case, they would have in fact weakened their position, since the Hindu-Javanese were now in control of the government. Their claim to an older *divine* origin — from the fire god — was what helped legitimate their point that they were older, and hence more prestigious than the Brahmanas.

Some of the Pande clan follow the regular rituals of Balinese Hinduism as dictated by the *triwangsa*, obtaining their holy water from *pedandas*, praying at regular temples, and observing the routines that are followed by just about everyone else in Bali. But the conservative Pandes do not obtain holy water from *pedandas*, maintaining that they are senior to the Brahmanas, not vice versa. And some of them have a very pronounced anti-*pedanda* bias. This has caused some problems.

The Pande people accuse *pedandas* in some areas of fomenting discrimination against them. And individual *pedandas* are sometimes criticized by Pandes because they require that their clients, *sisya*, obtain holy water exclusively from that *pedanda* himself, not from any other *pedanda*. The

Pandes accuse the Brahmana priests of profiteering from the dispensation of holy water and of trying to monopolize clients. For their part, the *pedandas* tell non-Pandes not to associate with the clan — because the Pandes do not obtain holy water from *pedandas,* and are thus ritually impure. Non-Pande people may come to help Pande families within a *banjar,* if help is required, but they are asked by the *pedandas* not to accept offers of food and other refreshments. It is said that in Gianyar a *pedanda* asks if there are any Pande men present before distributing holy water at a ceremony. If there are, they are asked to leave.

In the years before the Eka Dasa Rudra, a huge, islandwide exorcism ceremony that took place at Besakih in 1979, the government had always sent a Brahmana priest to officiate at ceremonies at the Pande temple at Besakih. Just before the Eka Dasa Rudra ceremonies began, the central Pande organization sent a letter to the organizing committee saying that the Pandes would not accept a *pedanda* to officiate at the temple. And, the letter continued, if the committee did send a *pedanda,* he would have to perform his ceremonies outside of the Pande temple. A *pedanda* was not sent. There are records of bitter village conflicts in which Pande families were denied the right to bury their dead in the village cemetery because the families did not obtain holy water from *pedandas,* and the villagers said the unpurified bodies would contaminate the cemetery.

The most conservative Pande areas have their own temples and their own *pemangkus* — lay Pande priests — who officiate at special Pande ceremonies and who make their own holy water for use only by Pande people. There is such a *pemangku* in the Pura Beratan complex and another at Banjar Beratan in Singaraja. As citizens of the village, the Pande are obligated to go with everyone else to the three village temples, the Kahyangan Tiga, or at least to the Pura Desa-Bale Agung and to the Pura Dalem. This keeps some measure of harmony within their villages. But their principal ties are to the Pande temples. If they can avoid the holy water of the Pedandas at the village temples, they do so.

THERE ARE NO SHRINES OR STATUES in a Pande temple. The only object of worship is Ratu Pande — Empu Pradah, the founder of the clan. Brahma does not dominate Pande life except while the Pande smith is working as a smith. For the Pande, the *sad kahyangan,* the six most important directional temples in Bali, are combined into a single temple. Pande people do not worship at the customary *sad kahyangan* temples used by most other Balinese Hindus. There is now only one ordained Pande priest, Empu Santa Budhi, who lives in Kediri, near the city of Tabanan. He officiates at ceremonies for the local Pande organization, Banjar Beratan Pandes, in Singaraja. He is quite an old man, as of this writing, and it is not clear who, if anyone, will succeed him when he dies. The *empu* uses a typical *pedanda ketu,* "crown," which is tall and red, and a bell.

Another man leads Pande ceremonies on the island. He represents a curious mix of Buddhism, Hinduism, and, if it can be called this, "Pandeism." Thirty or so years ago some of the Singaraja Pande leaders felt the need for proclaiming themselves to be something other than Hindu, since they considered their fundamental beliefs to be different enough from Hinduism to warrant making a distinction. Although they knew very little about Buddhism, they decided it was similar to Hinduism, but sufficiently different — they forthwith proclaimed themselves to be Buddhists. Under the guidance of this group the Buddhist *stupa* was built in the 1950s just outside the entrance to the main temple at Pura Beratan, near Bedugul, on the shores of Lake Beratan. The *stupa* is a rather imposing structure. It is quite easily visible from the main entrance to Pura Danu Beratan, at the northwest corner of the temple complex. It is still used by the Beratan Pandes — though they no longer proclaim themselves to be Buddhists.

But the Pande mentioned above, Sri Pandita Buddha Raksita, knowing of the Buddhist claims of his relatives, went to Semarang, Java, to study Buddhism. He later returned to Bali and studied under the Biku Giri, Bali's only Buddhist monk. The man is called by the Karangasem Pande families to officiate as a priest, particularly for cremation ceremonies. He uses Hindu mantras, but he recites them in the language used by the Buddhists. He can lead any ceremonies in Karangasem, but not in Beratan. Typical of the iconoclastic Pandes, it is said that his Buddhism has nothing to do with his being or not being a Pande priest.

More information on the Pande clan can be found in an excellent article by the Dutch anthropologist Roelof Goris, "The Position of the *Pande Wesi* (1929)," which appears in the recently reprinted *Bali: Studies in Life, Thought, and Ritual,* Wertheim, W.F., ed. W. van Hoeve Ltd. Amsterdam, 1984. Pages 289 to 299.

PART II

Ritual and Magic

CHAPTER 9

Rites of Passage
BALINESE LIFE CYCLE CEREMONIES

RITES OF PASSAGE IN BALI are not the celebrations of achievement we are used to in the West — the proud father dangling a set of car keys at the climax of the graduation dinner; the teary-eyed mother coming down from the attic with grandmother's china on the eve of her daughter's wedding; the office buddies buying 21 beers for their friend on his birthday. Certainly the emotion represented by these acts is not missing in Bali. But rites of passage in Bali, like almost everything else on the island, have a deeply religious purpose — they mark, with sometimes elaborate purification ceremonies, the passage from the innocent and inherently godlike child to the duty-bound and vulnerable adult.

Rites of passage usually coincide with observable physical events — birth, cutting of teeth, puberty, marriage — which may lead an observer to conclude that each rite is a separate entity with a separate aim. This is only superficially true. The basic aim of all the rites is to purify and provide the individual with the appropriate spiritual energy to exist peacefully, productively, and healthfully in a dangerous world. The demands upon an individual increase as he or she matures, as does the individual's capability of acting and chosing from among alternatives. In short, life becomes more difficult. Rites of passage, which are all purification rites, seek to increase the individual's inventory of *kesaktian,* "spiritual energy," so that he or she will be able to live correctly and successfully.

Almost all rites of passage fall under the category of Hindu-Balinese ritual called *manusa yadnya* (sometimes, *manusia*). The *manusa yadnya* are ceremonies that focus on the human being — *manusa* — and seek to protect and purify the individual from the time that the body is first formed in the womb until, but not including, death. Sometimes death ceremonies are considered rites of passage, and these fall into a separate category, *pitra yadnya*. Although the *manusa yadnya* are concerned with *manusa*, it would be a mistake to think that these are strictly "human" or individual rites. The Hindu-Balinese universe is too interrelated. For example, essential during all rites of passage ceremonies are the *kanda empat*, the four spiritual siblings, physically represented by the amniotic fluid, blood, vernix caseosa, and placenta that are "born" with the child, but spiritually much more complex. A ceremony for a *manusa* is a ceremony for his or her *kanda empat* as well, and they must be specifically included and mentioned by name. At different stages in the individual's life the *kanda empat* assume different attributes, and confer different powers. Rites of passage seek also to maximize the contribution of this spiritual family. (See CHAPTER 10.)

EVERY *MANUSA YADNYA* CEREMONY consists of four basic sub-ceremonies. These four have different forms and names in different parts of Bali, and the various parts receive varying degrees of emphasis in different communities. But at least some version of each of the four is considered essential. *Mabiakala* (sometimes *mabiakaonan*) is a component of all *yadnya*, not just *manusa yadnya*. This is a sacrifice to the evil spirits, the *bhutas* and *kalas,* so that they will be sated and not disturb or corrupt the ceremony. In fact, the sacrifice and rites of *mabiakala* ask for their blessings and protection. When the time comes to waft the essence of the offerings toward the gods, some of this is directed to the back or to the side — for the *bhutas* and *kalas.*

A second essential component of *manusa yadnya* rites is the *majayajaya* (sometimes *malukatan*) — *jaya* means "prosperity"; *malukatan* means "purify." This can be very simple, consisting of only a small offering and sprinkling with holy water, but more often than not it is much more elaborate. A medium-sized *majayajaya* is often called *eteh-eteh madudus alit,* and the largest are called *eteh-eteh madudus agung.* These names come from *padudusan,* which is one of the most important offerings used in the ceremony. Whether this part of the ceremony will be modest or elaborate depends upon the wishes of the family, and these, in turn, are often limited by the family's finances. A large ceremony is quite expensive, and some *manusa yadnya* rites are delayed until several families can combine their resources and put on a really big and extravagant event. This may mean a wait of several years. Most Balinese feel that they should put on as large a ceremony as possible; in Bali, small and modest do not connote sanctity. It is always the bigger the better.

A *majayajaya* ritual has quite a few parts. When I had my teeth filed, in accordance with the traditional Hindu-Balinese rite of passage, the *pedan-*

da, who conducted the ceremonies determined that I needed to have a full-blown *eteh-eteh madudus agung.* The ceremony involved 14 distinct rituals:

1. *Nakep taluh* or *maisuh-isuh:* I was told to put my hands on an egg that was contained in the offering called *isuh-isuh.* The egg is a symbol of development of the mind and body.

2. *Matepung tawar: Tepung tawar* is an offering that consists of five tiny triangular coconut leaf containers, *celemik,* on a coconut leaf tray. Each *celemik* is filled with a different kind of food, all chopped up very fine, including leaves from the *dapdap* tree, coconut oil, rice powder, and turmeric. The offering was placed in my upturned palms and then the contents were smeared on my hands. This is a purification offering, cleaning away all sins and stains of the body.

3. *Melis:* Holy water was sprinkled over the offerings and over me and some was rubbed on my hands.

4. *Mapedudusan:* Holy water was sprinkled over my body. The water was poured into a *penguskusan,* a conical rice steamer, which has a sieve at the small end and served in this case as a sprinkler.

5. *Magunting bok* or *penebak bok:* "Cutting hair." Since the head of an infant exits the womb first — except in the case of a breech birth — it is the part that first contacts what the Balinese call the "dirty" part of the mother, her genitalia. This ceremony "cleans" the impurities one's head received at birth. A little of my hair was cut and put into a long, woven container called a *blayag.* The hair was cut three times, once on each side and once in back. A fan-shaped offering was put into the container with the hair, and the *blayag* was then placed inside a yellow coconut. This coconut, during the actual filing, was the repository of the filings and my saliva. When the ceremony ended, it was wrapped in a cloth and given to me. I was directed to throw it into the sea so that its power would reach me wherever in the world I was. While the hair cutting was taking place a *jinah sandangan,* a little bamboo cage containing 1,100 Chinese coins, was put in my lap as a symbol of the money to buy my permission to cut my hair.

6. *Ngekeh* and *masolsolan: Ngekeh* refers to a chick scratching; *solsol* is a duck bill. Four colors of rice: red, white, black, and yellow, were put on both of my hands, palms up, and on my forehead. A white duck was held to my forehead to eat the rice there. As it did so it took dirty

things from my mind and body. A small chick was then held so that it could scratch the rice from my palms, scratching the bad things away from my body.

7. *Matirtha pengelukatan:* A type of holy water called *tirtha peng-elukatan* was administered to me by the *pedanda*.

8. *Matirtha pabersihan:* Also the administration of holy water, only this kind was specifically for spiritual purification.

9. *Makerewista:* A *kerewista* is a head band made from three strands of long grass, with the pistil of a hibiscus flower tied in front. The *pedanda* placed it on my head as a place for the Hindu supreme diety, Sang Hyang Widhi. The *kerewista* is similar to the usual Balinese headband, the *udeng,* which has the same function.

10. *Mahasma:* Uncooked rice was put on my forehead three times, symbolizing "food for thought." Some was also put on each side of my head to insure that I will hear only good things.

11. *Maselimpet:* A *selimpet* is a long cord made of three strands of yarn: red, white, and black, symbolizing the Hindu triad, the *trimurthi.* A Chinese coin is tied to each end. The *pedanda* passed it behind my body and under my arms, and then crossed it over my chest. This cord was to help tie my mind into a good way of thinking.

12. *Natab tuhan yang maha esa:* I wafted smoke from a clay brazier over my entire body to cleanse it.

13. *Padamaran:* A *damar* is a traditional coconut oil lamp; I wafted smoke from it toward my eyes to wake them up and make them bright. I also wafted smoke from the *pedanda's* brass lantern.

14. *Natab suwaran:* As the *pedanda* sounded his bell I wafted its sound toward my ears so that only good sounds would enter them henceforth.

The third part of every *manusa yadnya* ceremony is called *natab* and *ngayab*, wafting. (Note that several of the *majayajaya* ceremonies involved this action as well.) *Ngayab* refers to wafting the essence of an offering toward a deity, away from oneself. *Natab* refers to wafting the essence toward a person — either toward oneself, if one is the subject of a *manusa yadnya* ceremony, or toward a small child, if he is the subject and cannot do this himself. The offerings used for *ngayab* and *natab* are called, respectively, *ayaban* and *tataban*. Usually each consists of a group of offerings. One uses both hands to *natab*, palms toward oneself. To *ngayab* usually only one hand, or sometimes a small basket called a *saab*, is used. *Manusa yadnya* ceremonies emphasize *natab*, since the purpose of the ritual is to imbue an individual with spiritual power. Most other *yadnyas* feature *ngayab*, since they are chiefly directed toward deities.

The *pedanda* or *pemangku* leading the ceremony first dedicates the offerings to the Nawa Sanga, the gods of the nine directions. The person for whom the ceremony is being given now wafts the essence of the offerings toward himself. In so doing the nine gods are invited to enter his body and convey their power to him. Each of the nine gods is known to dwell in a particular place in the body, as follows:

N: Wisnu; *bile*

NW: Sangkara; *spleen*   NE: Sambu; *diaphragm*

W: Mahadewa; *ungsilan**   C: Siwa; *tumpuking ati**   E: Iswara; *heart*

SW: Rudra; *intestines*   SE: Mahesora; *lungs*

S: Brahma; *liver*

*no specific location in the body

The final essential part of a *manusa yadnya* ceremony is prayer, *muspa*. This takes place either before *majayajaya* — in which case the prayers are offered to Surya Raditya, the sun — or after *natab* — in which case the prayers are to the deified ancestors. In the latter case one asks for a symbolic foot washing which, in effect, is a washing of the feet of Sang Hyang Widhi, since he has entered one's body in the course of the ceremonies.

THERE ARE 13 DIFFERENT *MANUSA YADNYA* CEREMONIES, beginning with the materialization of the fetus into a lifelike form and ending with marriage and possible later purification. The names of these ceremonies vary somewhat from place to place, and the degree of elaborateness depends upon the caste and wealth of the family involved. Rich, high caste families may ask a *pedanda* to officiate; poor, low caste families are content with a local religious healer, a *balian*. The larger ceremonies are occasions of great extravagance, with decorations, many guests, lavish banquets, and entertainment. The more humble ceremonies may involve only immediate members of the family and may last only a few minutes. The 13 rites are:

1. *Pegedong-gedongan:* Six months after conception
2. Birth ceremonies
3. *Kepus pungsed:* The umbilical cord falls off
4. *Ngelepas hawon:* Twelve days after birth
5. *Tutug kambuhan:* Forty-two days after birth
6. *Telubulan:* Three "months" (105 days) after birth
7. *Oton:* Six "months" (210 days) after birth
8. *Ngempugin:* Adult teeth begin to appear
9. *Maketus:* Last milk tooth falls out
10. *Munggah daa/teruna:* Puberty
11. *Mapandes:* Tooth filing
12. *Pawiwahan:* Marriage
13. *Pawintenan:* Purification for study

Local village tradition often dictates the content of some of these ceremonies. For example, in some areas a baby is given a name at the age of three months, whereas in others the name is given at the *oton* ceremony. Some families ignore those ceremonies that are considered to be of lesser importance. In some cases, rites of passage, or parts of them, are delayed long past the date when they would normally be performed so that they can be combined with *manusa yadnya* ceremonies for other members of the extended family to make possible a larger ceremony. Obviously delay is not possible in some cases.

Whatever the scale of the ceremony, it is a time for joy in the family. In the case of the large ceremonies everyone looks forward to the busy preparations and the excitement of the actual day of the ceremony. Teams of hired offerings experts may work for days to prepare for the event. The extended family or the village organization, the *banjar,* may be asked to help prepare food for guests. The house compound is transformed into a crowded wonderland of lovely offerings, bright colors, and enticing smells. Everyone dresses in his very best traditional clothes — especially the honoree who, if he is a child, may be wearing something other than Western style baby clothes for the first time. On the other hand, for a small, poor family, many of these rites of passage are merely short interruptions in the routine of the day.

Because of the considerable variations in all rites of passage ceremonies, it is both impossible and useless to attempt to give descriptions of the rituals and offerings of each. Thus I will give a brief outline, using a few examples from my personal experience, of the philosophy behind each of the *manusa yadnas.*

PEGEDONG-GEDONGAN. This should be given after the fetus is about six months old, but before birth. By this time the embryo has a definite human form and the *kanda empat* are already standing guard. It is said that the craving of the mother for sour foods, *ngidam,* is one signal that the fetus is old enough for this ceremony. *Gedong* means "building," and it is thought that the name of the ceremony derives from a group of prayers — sometimes referred to as a building — that are used. This ceremony is for the parents and the ever-present *kanda empat* as well as the fetus. The rite is a purification, and the prayers are directed toward the hope that the child will be strong and healthy, and live a long and useful life. The parents are cautioned not to use coarse or sharp language. The mother must observe specific prohibitions, and the father is encouraged to read from the Ramayana and Mahabharata. This ceremony should be held in the bathing area of the house compound.

BIRTH CEREMONIES. The ceremonies at birth constitute the second rite of passage. They are directed almost entirely toward the *kanda empat* rather than toward the newborn child itself. They are most concerned with the placenta, the *ari-ari,* which is the only one of the *kanda empat* that does not vanish at birth. The placenta is washed, placed in a yellow coconut upon which the *ongkara* and other symbols have been inscribed, wrapped in a white cloth, and buried by the front door of the parents' house. One cannot overestimate the importance of the regard that a Balinese person has for the place where his placenta is buried. Wherever he may live, that burial spot is his true home, and he is unhappy if he is far away from it. Offerings are regularly placed on the rock, especially on the day Kajeng Keliwon according to the Pawukon anniversary calendar, when evil spirits are about. The baby's bathwater is supposed to be dumped on it every day. A little food destined for the baby should be put on the rock before the baby is fed. This is particularly true of the mother's milk. Just after birth is considered a time of great danger for the mother and the baby. They are said to smell of blood (*alid*), like fresh meat, for a period of two days. This is likely to attract spooks, *leyaks,* and neither can go outside. The baby is weak and is easy prey for negative influences. Everything is done to protect it from harm. (See CHAPTER 10.)

KEPUS PUNGSED. The third set of ceremonies (also called, in high Balinese, *kepus puser*) occurs when the umbilical cord drops. After birth the parents of the child are ceremonially impure, *sebel,* and cannot take part in any sort of religious activity. The father is *sebel* until the umbilical cord drops off.

The mother is *sebel* for 42 days, but she cannot even enter her kitchen until the falling off of the umbilical cord. The umbilical cord is the last physical link to the *kanda empat*. When it drops, the connection becomes spiritual and mystical. (Another name for the ceremony is *penelahan*, from *telah*, "finished.") The umbilical cord is wrapped in a piece of new cloth and put inside of a *ketipat kukur*, a little woven offering shaped like a turtle dove (*kurkur*). This is hung over the bed of the baby. A small shrine, a *kumara*, is constructed and hung over the baby's bed. The shrine is to Sanghyang Panca Kumara, one of Siwa's children. According to mythology, Kumara's older brother Gana was going to kill him and Kumara asked Siwa for help. Siwa protected Kumara from his brother Gana, but in exchange Siwa ordered Sanghyang Kumara to be the guardian of all babies until they have lost their milk teeth.

Because the baby is itself *sebel* until 42 days after birth, a *balian* will not go near it to perform any ceremonies related to the *kepus pungsed*. Instead, he gives instructions to the family. My friend and assistant Budi was told to prepare a special ceremony for his newborn son on the occasion of the falling off of the umbilical cord. Actually, the ceremony had to occur not necessarily on the actual date of the falling off of the cord, but on the Triwara (three-day week) date of the baby's birthday that immediately followed the *kepus pungsed*. Budi's child was born on Kajeng, the last day of the three-day week, so the offering had to be made on the first Kajeng after the *kepus pungsed*.

Budi had to perform a *banten babajangan*, which is a special ceremony to protect the baby from *bajangs*, which are sort of negative characteristics generated by the *kanda empat*. (There are 108 kinds of *bajangs*, each bringing a specific "vice" — sleepiness, kleptomania, stupidity, etc.) The *bajangs* leave permanently 42 days after birth. In Budi's case, the *balian* told him to collect a number of different kinds of leaves, including those from a *dapdap* tree, considered magical, as well as two spices called *kesuna jangu*. The *balian* provided Budi with some pieces of *lontar* palm leaf over which he had said special mantras, and gave him specific instructions. Budi had to rise before dawn to sacrifice and grill a speckled chicken for the main offering, and his mother had to prepare a great many smaller offerings. Budi's wife Wathi could make no offerings at all because she was *sebel*. The baby was first washed. Budi chewed up the spices and spat them onto the *lontar*. He then wrapped it up, tied it with red, blue, and white thread, spat on it again, and attached it to his son's right wrist as a little bracelet. He chewed more of the spices and a special leaf on which a mantra was written and spat the mixture on the baby's forehead three times. He did the same for each foot. Then the little cylinder was placed in the *kumara* shrine in the bedroom.

NGELEPAS HAWON. When the baby is 12 days old another ceremony should be performed, although some families omit it. Most people simply call the ceremony *upacara roras rahina,* "12-day ceremony," and it is usually a relatively minor affair. The reason for the ceremony has to do with the numerological importance of *12.* Three, five, seven, and 12 are the most important numbers for the Balinese. On the 12th day, offerings are made for the baby in the kitchen, the home of Brahma, at the well, the location of Wisnu, and in the family temple, the place of Bhatara Guru. This cere-mony is the first at which the baby receives holy water. Sometimes the occasion is used to determine the nature of the spirit that has recently been re-born into the baby. In this case, a *balian* is hired who goes into trance to divine which of the family's ancestors has been reborn into the child. Wealthy families often hire entertainment, such as a *joged* dancer or a *wayang lumah* puppet show.

TUTUG KAMBUHAN. This ceremony is important for both the mother and the child. Sometimes called *bulan pitung dina,* "one month and seven days," the ceremony signals the end of the mother's 42-day *sebel* period and the departure of the dangerous *bajangs.* (One "month," according to the Pawukon ceremonial calendar, is 35 days.) In some parts of Bali two baby chickens, called *pitik,* one male and one female, are appointed as guardians for the baby, substituting for the *bajang.* Neither they nor their offspring may be used as an offering. In some areas the ceremony required that these chicks be stolen, and from this practice arose another name for the ceremony, *macolong* — from *colong,* "steal." Colong is also the name of one of the *bajangs,* who is believed to be a thief. It is felt that if this partic-ular *bajang* departs, the baby will never be a thief when he grows up.

TELUBULAN. One of the most important of the early rites of passage takes place three months after birth. Again, this is a 35-day Balinese "month." *Telubulan* means "three months." Sometimes the ceremony is called *nyambutin,* from *sambutan,* one of the principal offerings used. This is usu-ally a large, and therefore expensive, ceremony, so it is not unusual for some families to delay it. I know of people who have not had the three-month ceremony until they were adults. There is considerable variation from place to place in the content of this ceremony. In some villages several of the rites are delayed until the *oton,* which takes place three months later. In other villages, ceremonies that usually take place at the time of the *oton* are carried out at the three-month ceremony.

The *balian* or priest will usually give the child his or her name at the *telubulan.* In some areas it is customary to pretend that the gods have named the child — it is written on a piece of *lontar* and tucked into one of the offerings. But everyone knows that the mother and father sneaked the name in. Unlike the Western custom, this name is not permanent. It will be in general use only until the child marries and has his or her own children. Then the name will disappear from use and he will be called "father of..." or she will be called "mother of..." — with the child's name filling in the blank. The usual word for "father of" is Pan, but in our village some families use the term Guru. Thus, Budi's real name is no longer used. In fact, for a stranger to call him "Budi" would be a serious breach of manners. He is Gurun Aris, since his first child's name is Aris.

Usually the *telubulan* features a big feast for family and friends, who arrive with gifts. There may be musical entertainment. The baby is dressed up in his first *pangangge adat*, traditional Balinese clothing. The first part of the ceremony takes place in the family temple, if possible. Very often there is an image made of a child, complete with clothing. After the ceremony this image is thrown away out on the street or near the bathing place. The idea is that evil spirits will think the effigy is the child and focus their powers on it, leaving the real baby alone. An egg is rolled over the baby's body to give it strength and vitality. Lengths of rough cotton string are placed over the baby's head and tied around each wrist, to give long life. Adjourning to the traditional *bale* in the house compound, the child is given its first jewelry — often a silver anklet or bracelet. And, the baby now acquires one of its principal weapons against evil spirits: a little amulet, often made of silver or copper, containing the dried up umbilical cord. An amulet of any sort is called a *sasikapan*. The amulet box itself should have two guards, one on each side. To the baby's left should be an old Balinese coin; to the right should be a tiger's tooth, to protect against black magic. If such a rare object can be obtained it is just a cross section, never the whole tooth.

OTON. The *oton*, the child's first "birthday," is likely to be the most elaborate of the rites of passage since birth. The Pawukon is only six (35-day) months long. Thus a Balinese will have almost two *otons* each Gregorian year. The Pawukon day is the salient anniversary for a Balinese, and everyone knows their *oton* — although many have forgotten, or never even knew, their Gregorian calendar birthdate. The *oton* ceremonies are usually carried out in the house compound's traditional *bale*. The great piles of offerings are placed on a table in the pavilion. The pillars are decorated with waistcloths and headbands, just as if they were people. The eves are hung with bright *ider-ider,* cloth strips painted gold. Above the piled offerings a white cloth, the *leluur,* is hung to symbolize the sky. Chairs are set up for the mother, holding the child, and the *balian,* and the rest of the family watches from the side. As with other rites of passage, the principal

A BABY TOUCHES THE GROUND AT HIS OTON

purpose of the *oton* is purification and providing spiritual strength to the child. If the family can afford it, the ceremony is accompanied by a feast, guests, decorations, music, and all the other gay accompaniments. Even a modest *oton* might cost several hundred thousand rupiah.

At *oton* time the baby is allowed to touch the ground for the first time. Having recently descended from the home of the gods, he has been treated somewhat like a god since birth. The name for "great grandchild" is the same as the name for "great grandparent" — *kumpi*. They are both close to heaven. Children who die before their milk teeth fall out are buried in a cemetery away from adults and, because they are still in a sense divine, burial ceremonies for them are minimal. But now, at age six months, the baby is losing its godlike status and is joining the human race. In some villages a mark is made on the ground with rice flour, the baby is placed upon it, and he is then covered for a short time with a cock cage. This symbolizes the amnion of the child — the membrane in which he was born. If, for some reason, the *oton* is delayed until the person is too large to fit underneath, the cock cage is present anyway. In Jimbaran, a village with many fishermen, a throwing net, *jala*, is tossed over the mother and child, accomplishing the same purpose.

The baby usually is provided with a little metal cap, *pupuk*, to protect the fontanel. This is to prevent evil spirits from entering. Very often the family provides a clay water bowl, *pane*, that contains small fish. The child's hands are put into the water to simulate his success at getting the material things he needs from life. The hair-cutting ceremony that was described earlier in this chapter is usually performed at this time. Often the parents take this opportunity to shave the baby's head clean, leaving only a little tuft in front. It is believed that the hair will be more beautiful if allowed to grow out again. In some villages the mother holds a large banana bud in her arms like a baby, and the father holds a bundle of Chinese coins. The mother then "buys" her child, offering to exchange the money for the real infant, and throws the banana bud away. It the area where I live it is customary to celebrate both the second and third *oton*, although on a smaller scale than the first. After that there may be no ceremonies at all, although some families continue to prepare small offerings for the family temple.

MAKETUS. This ceremony is occasioned by the falling out of the child's milk teeth; *maketus* comes from *ketus* — loss of baby teeth. This is considered to be a rather minor ceremony, often omitted. Prayers are offered to Surya, Brahma and Dewi Sri asking that the new teeth be beautiful, even, clean, and strong. Permanent teeth are the sign that the child is no longer like a god and has fully joined the human race. After this the child is treated just like any other person. Sometimes the ceremony is called *makupak*, meaning "burst" or "break open." Although this is an important rite of passage, the ceremony is usually not very large and may very well be omitted. The child, no longer a baby, is now capable of study and learning, and prayers are offered so that he will succeed. The child is no longer allowed to have certain kinds of protective offerings made for him and is, for the first time, allowed to partake of the important purification offerings, *prayascita* and *pabiakalaan* — the first for the body, both interior and exterior, the second to prevent danger from *bhutas* and *kalas*. Sanghyang Kumara, who has guarded the child from the shrine in the bedroom, is now dismissed, and the child is put under the protection of his deified ancestors.

[PAPINTONANG.] After the milk teeth drop, many years pass without an important *manusa yadnya* rite. The child matures, takes up the normal routines of Balinese family life, is given gradually increasing responsibilities, and begins his school career. During this period the family often decides to introduce the growing child to the deities of his village. In our village this event, not a *yadnya* rite, is called *papintonang*. It must be reported to the village deities that this person is now a member of the community and is obligated to show respect to them. And at the same time the deities are asked to give their help and protection to the new citizen of their village.

MANGGAH DAA and MANGGAH TERUNA. Puberty, the first menstruation of a girl or by the deepening of the voice of a boy and the obvious development of the genitals, is the occasion of the *manggah daa* ("virgin girl") or *teruna* ("virgin boy") ceremony. It is also sometimes called *ngaraja swala* or *menek kelih* for boys. The ceremony is most often given only for the girls of the family, since changes in their physical and biological status are more pronounced than those of boys. This may be a very elaborate ceremony, with all the trimmings, in the case of a wealthy high caste family, or it may pass almost unnoticed in the case of poor low caste people. The ritual emphasis here is two-fold. One involves what is sometimes thought of as "marriage" with Sanghyang Semara-Ratih, the bisexual symbol of sexual union. Semara-Ratih is also the symbol of beauty and is able to guarantee success in all ventures, cure sickness, and chase away evil. The second emphasis is upon attaining skill in the household chores that every Balinese girl must master — pounding rice, grinding spices, cooking rice, and so on. And the girl may go through the motions of these actions with real props. Along with the sexual features of the ceremony go prayers that the girl will be of high moral standards and will raise her family in such a way that they will be righteous and pure.

The most important part of this ceremony is for the person to present the offerings called *biakala* and *prayascita,* which, as previously described, ward off evil spirits and purify the body, then to pray in the kitchen, and finally to "natab" the offering of a type called *sayut*. This is an offering made to the deified ancestors and is for the purpose of asking their blessings, to pray for happiness and success, and to ward off evil. In the case of a girl the offering is called *sayut sabuh rah,* "spattering of blood," and in the case of a boy *sayut ngeraja singha,* "lion king." And finally, there must be a ceremony and offering called *pedadarian* made for Semara Ratih on top of the bed — which includes some obvious sexual symbolism.

MAPANDES. The tooth-filing ceremony is crucial. While a certain implication in the ceremony is the beautification of the honoree — the front teeth

are evened out — the filing is a symbolic balancing of the *sad ripu,* six personality characteristics, much like the Western humors, that must be put in
balance. (See CHAPTER 11.)

PAWIWAHAN. The last *manusa yadnya* ceremony that most Balinese are
likely to experience is that of marriage, *pawiwahan,* less formally called
nganten. The most common form of marriage in Bali is elopement, *ngero -
rod* or *malaib.* The man and woman arrange to meet somewhere out of
sight of the girl's parents and spend the night together at a friend's house,
with sufficient publicity that people find out what is going on. Under these
circumstances the girl cannot return to her parents and resume her normal
life. In almost all cases the girl's parents are not in the least surprised. They
pretend to be outraged at the impoliteness of the boy and his family for
plotting the downfall of their daughter. But usually the whole thing is
planned to avoid the very expensive ceremonies that would have to have
been put on had the couple been married by the mutual consent of the two
families. This "arranged" sort of wedding is called *mamadik,* and it is
expensive because of the large ceremonies and offerings involved.

An elopement usually requires only modest ceremonies. The morning
after the event a local *pemangku* performs a simple ceremony called
makala-kalaan, which is something like a small civil wedding in the West.
It is a very private affair, and the couple wear only the simplest of traditional
Balinese clothes. They are now legally married. Normally, however, the
family of the boy puts on a more elaborate and formal wedding ceremony
in which everyone dresses up in traditional Balinese clothing and a *balian*
or *pemangku* presides. This ceremony is not as important as the private
one, and is devoted mostly to purification. But it does involve a mandatory
offering called *jerimpen tegeh.* The name means different things in different
parts of Bali. Where I live it is an elaborate offering that contains some
meat, as well as an assortment of extra, small offerings off to one side,
including cones of rice, peanuts, and five white threads.

The boy's family generally has a reception for friends of the couple who
were not invited to the traditional ceremony. The reception is strictly
Western style. Everyone wears ordinary clothes, there is socializing and
good fun, presents are brought by the guests, and a buffet dinner is served.
The family of the girl is not invited to either of these ceremonies — of
course they are "mad" at the boy for stealing their daughter. Three days
after the wedding the family of the boy visits the family of the girl, at whose
house the *ketipat bantal* ceremony is performed. At this ceremony, the two
families "make up."

The general philosophy of a Balinese wedding ceremony is not much
different from that of one held in the West. The priest or *balian* in charge

asks Ida Sang Hyang Widhi to witness the union of the couple. It is made clear that the two unite freely and take full responsibility for the consequences of their wedding. The mantras and offerings are designed to purify the sperm and the egg and hope that the two will be free of bad influences and not bothered by *bhutas* and *kalas* until they unite to form the embryo. And it is hoped that they will be endowed with the power to produce a good offspring. It is also stated that the couple must follow the teachings and laws of the Balinese-Hindu religion, raise their families accordingly, and help their older parents while they are still alive.

The *lontars* specify eight different kinds of marriages, depending upon the characteristics of the bride and the groom. And the person in charge of the ceremonies is warned not to perform the union unless he is sure the wedding is one of the two types out of the eight that is likely to succeed.

If the wedding is not of the elopement type, a larger and more formal ceremony called *madengen-dengen* must take place. It may not be omitted. Unlike a ceremony following elopement, this takes place in the family temple of the groom's family. As with the *makalakalaan* ceremony, it calls upon God to witness the union of the two and to bless the egg and sperm so that the children will be strong internally and externally. A few days later there will also be the same sort of *ketipat bantal* ceremony.

A Balinese wedding ceremony will likely include lots more than what has been described. It may very well be that the bride or the groom or both have never had some of their other *manusa yadnya* ceremonies performed. In that case, the necessary ceremonies are performed by the presiding priest or *balian* at the time of the wedding. Any of all of the various ceremonies mentioned above in connection with the *mabiakala* and *majayajaya* ceremonies may take place at the same time as the wedding ceremony as well — cutting of hair, being pecked by a duck and scratched by a chicken, and so on. Those are all purifications, or, in the case of *mabiakala,* sacrifices for the *bhutas* and *kalas,* and are not connected with the marriage itself.

It may be that the couple has had all of these ceremonies previously, but it has been decided that they should have them all over again to ensure the proper purification. If the family can afford it, this is not unusual. These ceremonies are normally done in the large traditional *bale* in the house compound. The priest or *balian* sits on a chair facing stacks of offerings. The bride and groom sit on each side. When the *mabiakala* and *majaya-jaya* ceremonies are complete, everyone adjourns to the family temple for the actual marriage. As with most Balinese ceremonies, there is nothing sad or solemn about these occasions. The participants joke and laugh with each other and with spectators. If the *pemangku* or *balian* is well known to the participants he joins in with the fun when he is not praying. The pecking of rice by the duck is always an occasion for a lot of fun.

PAWINTENAN. This *manusa yadnya* ceremony is not experienced by many people. It is a mental and spiritual purification and preparation for those who wish to embark on a study of religion. Such a task requires contact with powerful and mysterious forces and a person so doing must be well prepared. There are several kinds of *pawintenan* ceremonies. One group, long, complex, and expensive ceremonies, are for those who seek to become a *pemangku* or *pedanda*. The other group consists of *pawintenan* ceremonies for anyone wishing to pursue a course of study in religion, ethics, tooth filings, offerings, traditional architecture, and other religious specializations. I had my first *pawintenan* at the time I became a Balinese Hindu. And I had a second one at the time of my tooth filing, since I had continued to pursue the study of Balinese religion. A person can have as many *pawintenans* as he sees fit. The ceremony is not large or complex. It involves prayers and offerings for three gods: Betara Guru, as a guide and teacher; Betara Gana, as protector and eliminator of obstacles; and Dewi Saraswati, as administrator of knowledge. There are two major offerings, one large one for Saraswati, and a small *pawintenan* offering. The usual *manusa yadnya* rituals of prayer, *natab,* and *ngayab* endow the candidate with the necessary power to pursue his study.

Kanda Empat

THE FOUR SPIRIT GUARDIANS

WHEN A BALINESE CHILD IS BORN, the family pays an enormous amount of attention to the *ari-ari,* the placenta. Immediately upon birth, they rush it to the family home, wash it in clean water spiced with a little turmeric, wrap it in a clean white cloth, and tie the whole together with the black string made from sugar palm fiber. Then they place the carefully bundled *ari-ari* in a specially prepared coconut, with an *ongkara* symbol cut into the top half, and an *ahkara* cut into the bottom. The coconut containing the placenta is then buried outside the main entrance to the baby's home — if the baby is a boy, a member of the father's family places the coconut in the ground to the right of the front door; if a girl, one of the mother's relatives does the same on the left. The relatives place a large black rock on top of the site and plant a thorny *pandanus* there to protect it from animals. Offerings are placed in a temporary shrine beside the burial hole.

The *ari-ari* is one of the *kanda empat,* "four siblings" — *empat* meaning "four" and *kanda* probably coming from the Indonesian *kakanda,* "older brother," or "older sister." The other three are: *yeh nyom,* amniotic fluid; *rah* (or *getih* in common Balinese), blood; and *lamas,* or *banah,* the vernix caseosa, a kind of natural yellow salve that coats the newborn. The four are also sometimes called the *catur sanak,* with a meaning much like "quadruplets," or *nyama catur,* "family of four."

The process of birth is thought of as follows: the *yeh nyom* opens the door for the baby to exit, the *lamas* and *rah* help on each side, and the *ari-ari* pushes from the rear, coming out after the baby (hence *ari* — "*younger* sibling"). Of course, the fluid, blood, and vernix disappear at once. Their physical remains are disposed of unceremoniously. The greatest attention, as described above, is paid to the *ari-ari,* since it is the only one of the four that is substantial. But all four are considered to have considerable power and spiritual presence, and are the focus of considerable lore and symbolism in Bali.

Why? The four brothers of the newborn boy, or four sisters of the newborn girl, were born with the baby and will remain with him or her for the rest of his or her life and with the spirit after death. They have the power to be of immeasurable help — to protect the baby from sickness; to ward off evil spirits; to insure that he or she grows into a healthy, strong adult. The power of the *kanda empat* continues through adulthood, helping out at work, guarding against enemies — particularly at night — and finally accompanying the spirit to heaven to testify to the good *karma* that the person has built up over his or her lifetime.

But — the *kanda empat* will do these things if and only if their fifth member, the person himself, treats them properly. They must be accorded respect and ceremony. The nursing mother should spill a few drops of milk from her breast upon the place where the placenta is buried. When the baby is bathed, the bathwater should go on top of the rock that protects the placenta. Any ceremony for the baby, or later, the adult, should be accompanied by the same ceremony for the *kanda empat.* When one goes to sleep at night he should say goodnight to his brothers, or she should say goodnight to her sisters — and in the morning thank them for guarding during the night. The *kanda empat* must be treated just like members of the family. When a death occurs in some wealthy families, a separate small cremation tower is built for the four brothers or sisters of the deceased.

Power in Bali is always double-edged. If one does not accord the proper respect to the *kanda empat,* they can cause great harm to their sibling — unhappiness, disease, failure in business, an accident, susceptibility to witchcraft — almost anything imaginably bad. Going one step further, if one is respectful of one's four siblings, if they are treated properly and with reverence, their power can be turned to one's own purposes — for good or for evil. With the *kanda empat*'s help one can become a *leyak* (spook), and perform black magic. One can force them to cause sickness and accidents to enemies, and bring wealth to oneself. One can use their power to transform into various shapes, to fly through the air, to menace. Or they can help achieve dharma, assist in meditation, bring understanding, hasten Hindu liberation, *moksa.* In other words, they can do either good or evil, or both.

The Balinese recognize four varieties of *kanda empat. Kanda empat rare* are the siblings who accompany the birth of the baby. From these come the others. The *kanda empat bhuta,* are those whose power may be turned toward evil or, conceivably, toward the antidote of black magic, so-

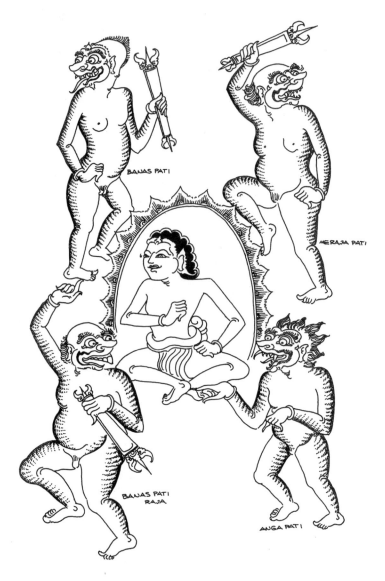

THE KANDA EMPAT BHUTA

called white magic. *Kanda empat bhuta* also help with such mundane activities as eating, and will assist a person making religious sacrifices. *Kanda empat dewa* are the four siblings whose power has been turned toward helping their fifth brother or sister in meditation and achieving *moksa*. And *kanda empat sari* are those turned toward helping intellectually growth, power through knowledge. Everyone has all four of these. In Bali, once a child loses its baby teeth, *maketus,* it has passed that point where it still enjoys the protection of heaven, and requires all four kinds of *kanda empat,* in proportion to its needs.

THE NAMES FOR THE *KANDA EMPAT* CHANGE as the fifth brother or sister develops. They even have different names in the womb. They switch to four new names at birth, and acquire still more names in the ordinary course of events. They are said to inhabit various places in the body of their brother or sister. They enter and exit through known routes. A vast body of terminology describes these names, places, routes, shapes, appearances, and so on. The four siblings are conceived with the child and at first are called *babu sugian, babu lembana, babu abra,* and *babu kerere.* At birth, these names change:

> *babu sugian* becomes *sang anggapati*
> *babu lembana* becomes *sang mrajapati*
> *babu abra* becomes *sang banaspati*
> *babu kekere* becomes *sang banaspati raja*

The five are arranged in directional and color order as follows:

KAJA
yeh nyom
Apah
black
Anggapati

KAUH	PUSEH	KANGIN
lamas	*bayi**	*ari-ari*
Pertiwi	Akasa	Bayu
yellow		white
Banaspati		Banaspati Raja

KELOD
rah
Teja
red
Mrajapati

*The baby itself

Each of the *kanda empat* has a place of residence and a place of entrance to and exit from the body:

ANGGAPATI enters through the eyes, lives in the heart, leaves through the mouth, has the form of wind, and has the characteristics of being a poet

MRAJAPATI enters through the mouth, lives in the liver, leaves through the ears, has the form of fire, and has the characteristics of friendship

BANASPATI enters through the nostrils, lives in the kidneys, leaves through the eyes, has the form of earth, and has the characteristics of intelligence and compassion

BANASPATI RAJA enters through the ears, lives in the bile, leaves through the nostrils, has the form of breath, and has the characteristic of strength

The above chart is used only with reference to the *buana alit,* the body of the human himself. We start at the top, because the *yeh nyom* comes out of the mother first. If we are to refer our discussion to the *buana agung,* the body of the universe, we have to start at the east, where the sun rises and proceed clockwise around the circle:

Banaspati Raja

Banaspati   Anggapati

Mrajapati

These four are the best-known names for the *kanda empat*. There are many, many more, however. The names Anggapati, Mrajapati, Banaspati, and Banaspati Raja are generally associated with *kanda empat bhuta*. The story is that Betari Uma, the wife of Siwa, left her characteristics and nature on earth when she went to her husband. Her earthly characteristics were changed into life forms by Brahma and became four shapes or forms called the *kanda empat bhuta*. Each was given a place and told how to live:

ANGGAPATI lives in the body of humans and other creatures and uses as food people who are weak or have bad feelings.

MRAJAPATI lives in the graveyard and at the main crossroads. He eats corpses if they were buried at the wrong time or people who give ceremonies at the wrong time according to the reckoning of auspicious days.

BANASPATI lives in rivers and in big stones. He eats people who take a nap at noon or walk around at noon or just after sunset.

BANASPATI RAJA lives in big trees like *kepuh* or *rangdu* (the survivor of a former pair of *kepuh* trees — the death of one of these *kepuhs* is thought to be an extremely fey, *tenget,* sign). He eats people who cut or climb trees on inauspicious days.

Each of the 4 has 27 *bajang* ("young"). Taken together the group — 4 times 27, or 108 — is called *nyama* ("family") *bajang.* Each *bajang* has certain characteristics, for example sleepiness or stupidity. One of them, *bajang colong,* makes the child want to be a thief (*colong* means "to steal"). The *nyama bajang* are likely to bother the baby. At age 1 month and 7 days (42 days, using a Balinese month), it is time to send the *nyama bajang* back home. This involves obtaining a *pitik,* a replacement for the *bajang,* consisting of a male and female chicken. The birds — sometimes they must be stolen — are used in a special ceremony called the *mecolong.* A special offering is made to *bajang colong* so that he will be sure to leave the baby alone, who will then have no desire to be a thief. (See CHAPTER 9.)

IN 1937, WOLFGANG WECK, A DUTCH PHYSICIAN who was then chief medical officer for Bali and neighboring Lombok, wrote a book called *Pengetahuan Tentang Penyembuhan Dan Pekerti Rakyat di Bali* (Knowledge Concerning Recovery and Behavior of the People of Bali), a study of the healing arts of *balians,* native practitioners of herbal and spiritual medicine. In the book, written in Bahasa Indonesia, he reports an allegorical explanation for the *kanda empat.*

The Hindu deity Sanghyang Widhi decided to make four manifestations of himself, gods, so that he could be recognized by man. First he made a male person with a white color, Sang Hyang Kartika, that would later become Iswara. Then he made Sang Hyang Garga, ruddy, who would later become Brahma. Then he made Sang Hyang Metri, who had a yellow appearance, who would become Mahadewa. And then he made Sang Hyang Kurusia, black skinned, who would become Wisnu. Sang Hyang Widhi then gave each one a special duty — the result of their combined efforts being the creation of the world.

But his children refused his orders, and were therefore cursed. He turned Kartika into a *bhuta,* a demon, with the shape of a Raksasa — bulging eyes and tusks — and sent him east with a new name, Sang Kala Banaspati Raja. Sang Garga was turned into a tiger, ordered south, and renamed Sang Hyang Kala Yampati, or Anggapati. Sang Merti was sent west as a snake, now called Sang Hyang Kala Angaspati. And Sang Kurusia, recast as a crocodile, was sent north to be called Sang Hyang Mrajapati.

At that time, Bhatara Siwa and his wife, Bhatari Uma, created the world and the people upon it. The four cursed gods asked forgiveness and Sanghyang Widhi, manifested as Siwa, accepted the apologies of the four disobedient *dewas*. Siwa ordered them to organize and run the world for the humans upon it. These first people, called *manusa sakti*, had very strange shapes (the gods thought), much like the king of the Raksasas, with round eyes, rays like the rising sun, and long tusks. When the people had been created, Sanghyang Widhi greeted them:

> Among the living things that I have made, you are very different than the others. You can make good or bad things. You can create happiness or unhappiness. You can possess evil, material greed, anger, egotism, and even become a *leyak* and use many bad kinds of poisons. But you can also behave well and create good things: wisdom; learning; love; and you can behave so that there is satisfaction and happiness. All these powers were given to you by me.

Then Sanghyang Widhi ordered the four errant *dewas,* now called Sang Hyang Kala Yampati, to accompany the *manusia sakti* wherever they wished to go and give them whatever they wanted, whether good or evil. The four repeated to the *manusa sakti* that which God had ordered them to do, and asked what the people wanted of them. The *manusa sakti* said that the gods should go with them throughout the world and organize the people, *dewas,* and *bhutas,* all good and all evil, so that the evil of the world could be wiped out. The four gods replied:

> What you say is good. But do not just pretend. If you can follow what you say, we will accompany you and take care of you, day and night. You must know that we are part of your family, male or female. Two of us would like to stay in your heart, and two of us would like to stay outside in your magical power. Remember this well. If you forget your promises we will cause trouble for you.

Then the four disappeared and entered the bodies of the humans. The white one, Sang Kartika, as a *raksasa,* entered the heart and was called Bhatara Putih. Sang Garga, as a tiger, red in color, entered the liver and was called Bhatara Jaksa Bang. Sang Merti, a yellow snake, entered the kidneys and was called Bhatara Pita. And Sang Kurusia, the black crocodile, entered the bile or gall and was called Bhatara Ireng.

BEFORE GOING TO BED ONE MUST CALL ONE's *KANDA EMPAT* by their names, tell them that you are going to sleep, and ask them to keep watch. When a person goes to bathe he must invite his brothers to join him with prayers. When the rites of passage are performed for an individual — those connected with maturing, tooth filing, marriage, and even cremation, the *kanda empat* of the person for whom the ceremony is being given must be included as well as the person himself. They must be given food and drink when one is drinking or eating. A thoughtful person spills a little of his coffee or *brem* or Coca-Cola on the ground before drinking it himself. Every housewife puts offerings out in front of the gate on days like Kajeng Keliwon when these spirits are afoot. Offerings are put at the crossroads where they often live. A bit of food is placed on the ground for them just before it is served to the people. If treated properly, the *kanda empat bhuta* will cheerfully act as guardian spirits and will help their brother in many ways. They must, however, be called by name, and the human brother must face in the proper direction when calling each one separately. If these precautions are not taken, these spirits can cause a person to fall victim to his lusts and passions, lose his friends, and get mired in frustration.

CHAPTER 11

Tooth Filing

AN IMPORTANT COMING OF AGE RITUAL

THE NAME OF THE CEREMONY IS DESCRIPTIVE, but hardly explanatory. This is, perhaps, why the wife of a visiting foreign dignitary, when told of this practice, exclaimed: "Oh, do they still do *that* here?"

Yes, they still do *that* in Bali. To everyone. But do not confuse tooth filing with some sinister vision of Dracula-like sharpened teeth. In fact, the procedure produces just the opposite, dulling the front teeth to diminish the savage characteristics of their owner. The ceremony is called *matatah,* from the word *natah,* to "chisel" or "carve." The same word in high Balinese is *mapandes,* and another common synonym is *masangih,* from *sangih,* to "file." Sometimes the Indonesian *potong gigi* — "to cut teeth" — will be used. The person who files the teeth is called *sangging,* the same word used for "painter" or "artist."

Tooth filing, together with prenatal rites, birth ceremonies, various ceremonies for the young baby, and marriage, is one of the rituals known as *manusa yadnya.* These are an important category of the Panca Yadna ("Five Rituals") that every Balinese Hindu absolutely must have performed to insure an orderly transition of his or her spirit from birth to death and later reincarnation. Six to 18 years old is considered the best age for tooth filing — before marriage, but for girls, after the first menstruation. Better late than never though, and it is not unusual for people in their 60s to have their teeth filed. If a person dies before having held the ceremony, the family sometimes has it done to the corpse before burial. It is that necessary.

Why is *matatah* so important? As a group, the Balinese look with disgust and fear upon coarse behavior, coarse appearance, and coarse feelings. The Balinese word is *kasar.* It is quite synonymous with "bad," even "evil." The opposite adjective is *alus* — "refined" — characteristic of a lofty being. One needs only to glance at any of the old style wood or stone carvings, paint- ings, or *wayang kulit* puppets to see what characterizes good guys and bad guys in the Balinese mind. The bad ones look coarse, and sport long fangs and bulging eyes and bellies. The refined ones are gentle looking, effemi- nate, with dainty features.

Of course animals are coarse — in aspect, behavior, and position (on the ground, the place of the lowest of the low) — and Balinese animals, except for the cow, are not loved and coddled. Some, like dogs, are tolerated for their usefulness. Anything resembling animal behavior is frowned upon — even a baby crawling on all fours. A special coarse language is reserved for talking about animal activities, such as eating, and it would be a gross insult to use this language to refer to a human being's actions.

Balinese Hinduism can be very highly symbolic, and the one characteris- tic that epitomizes uncivilized, uncouth, coarse disposition is protruding canine teeth. The Balinese call them *caling*, "fangs." If one wishes to be rid of his coarse behavior, then it is only natural that this be done symbolically by filing the canine teeth until all *kasar* traces have been smoothed out.

According to tradition and the *lontars*, a *sangging* for tooth filing must be of the Brahmana caste. Today lower caste people, even Sudras, will per- form the ceremony and *balians* — special low caste shamans — regularly perform the task. However, most families still prefer to call in one of their Brahmana *suryas* (patrons) to do the job. After all, the filing of the teeth is but a slight modification of the *buana alit*, the temporary shell of the spirit. Much more important is the religious substance of the ceremony — rid- ding the individual's spirit of its negative traits, the *sad ripu* — literally, the "six enemies."

Balinese Hindus believe that the disposition of an individual is con- trolled by three *gunas*, called the Triguna Sakti. The Guna Satwam results in a disposition that is calm, quiet, and directed toward honesty, wisdom, righteousness, and nobility; the Guna Rajas causes dynamic, lustful, vain, violent, disturbing behavior; and the Guna Tamas makes one passive and lazy, enjoying the benefit of the work that others do without wanting to work oneself.

From these last two come the "six enemies" which will lead a person into misery, grief, and suffering, both in this world and the next. Something like Saint Gregory's Seven Deadly Sins, the *sad ripu* are essen- tially weaknesses of the flesh: *kama* ("lust"), *loba* ("greed"), *krodha* ("anger"), *mada* ("drunkeness"), *moha* ("confusion"), and *matsarya* ("jealousy"). Reducing the influence of these six will help an individual live a healthy, well-adjusted existence as part of a closely knit family and com- munity, and this behavior will insure reincarnation into a better future life.

SINCE TOOTH FILING IS SO IMPORTANT, no expense is spared to turn the ceremony into an elaborate and festive event. The deified ancestors of the family are invited to attend and lend their support. The house compound is decked out to the limit of the family's finances. Guests are invited; visitors from out of town accommodated; musicians hired; offerings made; a high caste tooth filer — perhaps even a high priest — is invited to supervise the proceedings; and the finest clothing is provided for those who are to participate. The *matatah*, in short, is very expensive. Because of the cost, today tooth filing is almost always an adjunct, although an important adjunct, of another ceremony — perhaps a wedding or cremation.

The ceremony has implications beyond Hindu doctrine. The Balinese, male and female alike, just don't find long canine teeth aesthetically pleasing. Tooth filing is a kind of beautification rite. Of course, like everything else in Bali, there is a god of beauty, Dewa Kama, or Sanghyang Semara Ratih. The god of tooth filing, both male and female, is an image of Dewa Kama — Arda Nare Swari. Arda Nare Swari has many names, shapes, colors, places of residence and attributes. The picture of Arda Nare Swari shows Ananga in the East, colored white; Sanghyang Semara, with a symbolism of mixed colors, in the center; and Dewa Kama, or Dewi Ratih, golden yellow and armed with a bow and arrow, at the nadir.

Dewa Kama is believed to bring success in all efforts, cure sickness, chase away evil, and provide the beauty of flowers. In honor of this god, the *matatah* ceremony should take place in a *bale gading*, literally, "ivory pavilion." *Gading* means "ivory," and it also means "canine tooth." A special *teteg* offering accompanies the ceremony, larger than usual and shaped like Dewa Kama. This offering, often called Semara Ratih, is a gift to *widiadara-widiadari* which, freely translated, means "knowledge of male and female." The *widiadara* and *widiadari* are sort of male and female spirits. The *matatah* both lessens the *sad ripu* and symbolically — and physically — prepares the person undergoing the ceremony to attract someone of the opposite sex.

No Balinese schedules an event as important as a tooth filing without consulting someone to choose an auspicious day. When this has been done, the extended family picks those who are to participate. Tooth filings are not held very often, and in a large family there may be dozens of candidates, perhaps even a hundred or more remote cousins, in-laws, children, and siblings. A ceremony of this size will require the services of several tooth filers and involve half a day or more of work.

On the day of the *matatah*, the house compound is gaily decorated, the *bale* wrapped and hung with gold cloth. A *gong* plays, and when the actual ceremony takes place one or a pair of *gender wayang*, the instruments used to accompany the shadow puppet shows, take over. White cardboard boxes

DEWI RATIH

MEKA

BUNGKAK NYUH GADING

KIKIR

SANGIAN

PALU

TEBU

PAHAT

DAPDAP

THE ACCOUTERMENTS OF A TOOTH FILING

of snacks and a bottle of tea are proffered to guests at the door. Friends of the family each bring a small present and sign the guest register. Men may be reading from the sacred *lontars*. An army of community members is chopping away at enough meat and spices to feed a hundred or more later on. Offerings are everywhere. Guests are greeted by the family in a kind of receiving line. It is a noisy, colorful gathering.

The filees are dressed in their very finest traditional clothing. Boys are wrapped in a wide piece of *songket,* gold brocade, that reaches from armpits to knees, with a sash of yellow tied around the waist and a kris dagger slung across the back. Girls wear their lovely traditional *kambens,* their upper bodies wrapped tightly in many meters of cloth strips. They are crowned with fragrant flowers and gold leaves are wound in their hair. Both boys and girls may wear makeup. Parents bustle here and there dressing their children, most of whom are full of nervous apprehension.

If a *pedanda* presides he summons the group of boys and girls and blesses them with a mantra and holy water. The teeth and the individual are symbolically "killed" during the tooth-filing procedure. This is a moment of weakness — when enemies can do harm — and the one getting filed needs all the support he or she can get. There are stories of people who had all of their teeth drop out shortly after the ceremony. One is, in short, vulnerable and needs help and protection. Friends and relatives stay close by.

The *sangging* or *pedanda* kills the teeth by tapping with a small hammer a little metal rod, a *peet,* that he places upon one of the upper teeth. *Peet* is the word for a carver's chisel. The *pedanda* also draws the symbol *ang* on the right upper canine and *ah* on the left, symbolizing male and female, mother and father. The "drawing" is really a symbolic gesture, done with a ring called *bungkung masasoca mirah,* or *bungkung mamata mirah.* The real killing is done by a mantra. The *pedanda* goes through this procedure for each candidate as he or she files up to him for blessings and holy water.

The boys and girls lie on a woven mat upon which has been inscribed the figure of Semara Ratih, also representing male and female. Semara is the moon; Candra is male and Ratih is female. The inscriptions today are done with a rather untraditional felt marker. The *sangging* opens a yellow coconut, empties it of its water, and inscribes upon it the magic symbol, the *ongkara.* Tools are laid out, mouthwash is made ready, and a large offering, the *canang oyodan,* is brought close by. The coconut acts as a spittoon nearby. A silver bowl of holy water and a white cloth are at the ready.

Each candidate stands at the end of the bed opposite from where the *sangging* will work. They hold out their hands to receive a prayer, and waft the essence of the offerings toward themselves. The kris worn by the boy must be removed. The candidate takes off his or her sandals, climbs onto the bed, and receives another mantra and more holy water. He or she then lies down on the bed and is covered with decorated cloths. Parents and close relatives crowd around to put their hands on the boy or girl to ward off evil.

Meanwhile the guests have assembled below the elevated *bale,* chatting, perhaps taking pictures, and listening to the *gender wayang.* This is a pair of xylophone-like percussion instruments with a softer tone and a more peaceful sonority than the sharp, ringing notes of the usual village *gong. Gender* are used in the performance of the *wayang kulit* shadow play. And in the tooth-filing ceremony they provide a calming accompaniment for the events that are unfolding.

The *sangging* puts a small cylinder of sugarcane in the patient's mouth, wedged between the teeth, to keep the jaws open and prevent an inadvertent display of *sad ripu* upon his fingers. As with most Balinese ceremonies, it is not a solemn moment. The *sangging* may joke with his patient as he works — the equivalent of a dentist making small talk to divert the attention of the patient. He then takes his small file, *kikir,* and with his index finger on the flat of the file, sets to work filing. The only teeth that are modified are the two canine teeth in the upper jaw and the four incisors between them — six teeth, one for each *ripu.*

THE AMOUNT OF FILING DONE depends upon the wishes of the individual. The gesture is purely symbolic, and can consist of just a few quick strokes. Some people use the opportunity to really have their teeth filed even. If so, the *sangging* proceeds in easy stages, allowing the person to sit up occasionally and view the progress in a mirror. When it is over, and it takes only a few minutes, the boy or girl spits the saliva containing the filings into the yellow coconut. If there is any bleeding, the *sangging* rubs betel leaf on the teeth to staunch it, and then he brings the teeth to life once again with a mantra. The much-relieved patient receives a mouthwash of honey, sandalwood powder, lime, turmeric, *areca* nut, betel leaf, *gambir,* and water. Part is swallowed and part spat into the coconut. In some places the newly filed person is required to step down from the *bale* upon a large round offering called *peningkeben.* And, although ceremonies are to follow, he or she must change clothes — it would not do to celebrate in the same clothes in which one has "died."

After prayers in the family temple, the ceremony ends for the boys and girls. Traditionally there were, and sometimes today still are, preludes and postludes to a tooth filing, traditions left over from another era when jobs and school did not interfere. A person whose teeth were to be filed was isolated for three days before the ceremony and given a mixture of rice powder and spices to rub on his or her body to clean it. After the ceremony one had to eat a traditional food called *padamal,* consisting of foods of the six different tastes: *pait* ("bitter"), *manis* ("sweet"), *pakeh* ("salty"), *lalah* ("spicy"), *masem* ("sour"), and *nyangluh* ("burned taste"). And for the three days following the ceremony, a person could not go out, nor could he or she drink or eat hot things because this would cause the teeth to take a bad shape. The Balinese use a word here that means "wrinkled." The yellow coconut with the filings and saliva must be buried near the most important shrine in the family temple which insures that its power will always be close to the individual.

I WENT THROUGH THE CEREMONY DESCRIBED ABOVE. People have asked me why I had my teeth filed. I have adopted Balinese Hinduism and decided to probe rather deeply into its philosophical depths. Those who helped me, especially those in the Department of Religion, felt that I should be suitably fortified and purified lest what I was learning could harm me. They suggested that I have a *pawintenan* ceremony performed over me by the same *pedanda* who inducted me into Hinduism several years ago. A *pawintenan* is a kind of purification, generally only performed for adults who are exposing themselves to potentially dangerous situations.

I went to my *pedanda*, Ida Pedanda Gede Manuaba Sidantha, at Geriya Panti in Denpasar, and explained the situation. He agreed to perform the ceremony. But he pointed out that performing one of the more advanced purification ceremonies on a person who has not had the preliminaries is rather like building the roof of a house before its foundation. He would, he said, only perform the *pawintenan* if he could also perform first all of the other preliminary ceremonies that Balinese undergo from conception to the normal adult time of *pawintenan*. One of these preliminaries was the tooth filing.

CHAPTER 12

Cremation in Bali

FIERY PASSAGE TO THE AFTERLIFE

A HUGE CROWD SWARMS THE STREETS. A shouting, laughing horde of men shoulders gaudy platforms and life-size animal statues, weaving with their burdens in a crazy path. There are water fights, and boisterous horseplay. The animals spin around riotously and tilt precariously. A long, white cloth strung out over the heads of dozens of people leads a gigantic tower, borne by even more men. Women carry objects in silver bowls on their heads.

The procession heads for a secluded glade where piles of ornate offerings, a small percussion orchestra, and dancers await its arrival. Circling several times, the bearers deposit their burdens, and the backs of the animal statues are torn open. Crowds of onlookers gather around, a white bundle is practically torn from the tower and laid inside the hollow animal. Attendants pack the animal's hollow torso with cloths and paraphernalia, and pour it full of liquid.

A crackling noise, a few licks of flame, and the tower and wooden beast flare up in a great, blazing pyre.

A BALINESE CREMATION IS A DRAMATIC EVENT, but one that leaves many casual onlookers puzzled. Where is the body? Why is everyone so happy? Why all the horseplay? What kind of death rite is this after all? The cremation, as witnessed by most visitors, is just one afternoon of weeks, sometimes months, of ceremonies and preparations. A Balinese cremation is a big event, and almost none of it has anything to do with a dead body.

Many cultures focus their death rituals upon the body itself, and cremation is merely a sanitary way to reduce the body to a form that can be easily installed in a permanent memorial, to be visited with flowers upon suitable anniversaries. In some Christian sects the actual physical remains of especially holy people are often preserved, enshrined in churches, and worshipped. Miraculous powers may be attributed to them. Some countries are in the habit of pickling their national leaders, who are then dressed, powdered, and placed on display under glass.

But in Bali the body is nothing more than an impure, temporary shell, having no significance at all, except as the container of the soul and its anchor to earth. All thoughts at the time of death are concentrated upon the spirit and its passage to heaven. The body is just there to be disposed of, and that as quickly as possible. Instead of grieving, the Balinese prefer to throw a great celebration, in the process hastening their dead friend's soul to oneness with god.

In the Hindu-Balinese cosmology, the body of man is but a microcosm of the universe, made up of the same five elements: air, earth, fire, water, and space. These constitute — temporarily — a place for atman, the immortal soul. After the body's death, this soul, according to the principles of samsara (reincarnation), will find a home in another form. Before this it might go through a kind of hell, *neraka*, spend some time in heaven, *suarga*, or even ascend to a state of ultimate oneness with God, *moksa*.

But the soul of someone who dies cannot immediately leave the body. At first, the *atman* hovers near the body, sometimes as a ghost that can bother the deceased's family. Only after the body's five elements have been returned to the macrocosm by burning can the soul completely detach itself from the body. The series of ceremonies that are involved with returning the *panca maha butha*, the five elements, is called, in common Balinese, *pengabenan*. *Ngaben* is derived from *abu*, "ashes." In higher Balinese the preparations are called *palebonan*. What we call "cremation" is only the climax of *pengabenan*, and there must always follow a second, complementary series of ceremonies in which the now-released soul is returned to God.

HINDU-BALINESE DEATH RITES CAN BE VERY SIMPLE. A corpse can be cremated and its soul released quickly and without much fuss — so long as a few basic offerings and preparations are made. But cremations are never simple. There is a pervasive belief that no expense must be spared in this final sendoff of the soul, as any skimping would constitute disrespect. And since this soul will shortly become a deified ancestor, with great power to help or hurt, a cheap funeral is considered a very bad way to start off this relationship. And not only the spirits are impressed by a grand cremation. A good ceremony will win a family status and prestige in the village. The vanity of man comes into play even upon the stage of death. The rule seems to be that every family provides as grand a cremation as it can afford — perhaps even more than it can afford — in terms of time and money.

Even a medium-large cremation today may cost thousands of dollars, severely taxing the family resources. The ceremony and the preparations for it may require the services of hundreds of people over a period of weeks or even months. The Balinese "family" that organizes this event is not just mother, father, and children, but an army of relatives — siblings, cousins, uncles, aunts, in-laws, children, and grandchildren. All these people must cease their regular jobs and concentrate upon the death rites. The higher castes are expected to provide extra-elaborate ceremonies, which may be difficult for them because wealth no longer necessarily accompanies high caste. Because of these factors, it is very common for poorer people to hold a simple ceremony of preparation and cleansing, and then bury the corpse in the village cemetery with no cremation at all. Eventually, when sufficient funds have been accumulated, a properly grand cremation will be held.

Sometimes a poor family will ask a wealthier family that has scheduled a grand cremation if it can join the ceremony, thus sparing itself much of the expense. It is not unknown for dozens, or even hundreds, of bodies to join in the shared glory of a particularly important or rich person's cremation. Years may elapse between the death of a person and his cremation — perhaps even a decade or more. During this time the spirit never strays far from the body and may bother the family in various ways as it seeks total release toward God and heaven. Every family tries to cremate its dead as soon as possible, but only the wealthy can do so immediately.

If a priest, or a descendant of a former ruler or of a royal family, has died, burial in the ground is considered to be inappropriate. The body is preserved and kept lying in state in a pavilion in the family house compound, an extremely expensive procedure. Fresh offerings must be made daily. The services of a high priest, *pedanda,* must be engaged. The body must be under 24-hour guard. Music and other entertainment must be commissioned. Symbolic daily meals must be provided for the body, plus snacks and coffee or tea. A mirror, comb, and toothbrush are laid nearby. Even if the cremation is planned right away, the preparations can take so long that this lying in state may go on for weeks or even months.

In fact, even if the family has the money and the preparations get underway forthwith, just about every body is going to spend some time waiting, because in Bali, the calendar is the final authority on everything. And not all days are suitable for cremations. The complex formulas of the Balinese calendars show auspicious days for such things as journeying south (not the same auspicious day for traveling, say, north), harvesting rice, burning trash, building a house, going to market, getting married, cutting down a tree, and, of course, holding a cremation. So an expert on such matters has to be consulted in order to set the day of the final rites. And that day may be months away.

When the big day is finally picked, an unbelievably complex, interlocking series of preparations is set into motion. And yet, in spite of the thousands of little details that must be attended to, there is no checklist of tasks, no boss who assigns jobs and sees that they are carried out. Somehow it all works out, in typical cooperative Balinese fashion.

Temporary structures for shrines, shelters, and shade must be built and roofed with coconut leaf mats. Several days may be required just to cut the coconut leaves — and this with a whole gang of men. Offerings must be made every day because there are so many ceremonies that precede the cremation itself, and the number required for the final event itself is staggering. Some are small, requiring only a few minutes' effort. But others are large and involve the preparation of great quantities of food. Gaily decorated, colored rice cakes are molded and fried in coconut oil. These are in the shapes of people, boats, flowers, and animals. Ducks and pigs are slaughtered and cooked. High offerings are made by skewering a variety of fruits, eggs, cakes, and meats on a banana stem pole. For a medium-size cremation perhaps two dozen or three dozen women will work all day long for several weeks just making offerings.

The offerings provide symbolic pleasure to the deified ancestors, and to the spirit that will be shortly released to God. They satisfy the hunger of the evil spirits, the *bhutas* and *kalas,* who stand greedily by, ready to interfere in man's every activity. Most important, however, the offerings will implore God to purify the spirit and return it to earth in an appropriately higher and purer form.

The family's open pavilions must be decorated with brocades. Temporary electric wires and lights must be strung up. Often the entire house compound is temporarily roofed over. Chairs for guests must be rented or borrowed. A *pedanda* — a priest — has to be engaged for many of the preliminary ceremonies as well as for the final cremation. One or more musical groups must be hired, as must dancers and *wayang kulit* shadow puppeteers.

Every reasonably large cremation will have at least one animal-shaped sarcophagus, life-sized or even larger. The sarcophagi of those of highest caste is called a *lembu,* a bull for a man and a cow for a woman. Other forms are specified for lower castes — a lion, a deer, or a fish-elephant, the *gajah mina.* But always there have to be four feet — which symbolize the four spiritual siblings, the *kanda empat.* The bull, as the vehicle of Siwa, is the most prestigious. Siwa is that aspect of God that symbolizes death, destruction, and the recycling of the spirit. Bulls are sometimes used as sarcophaguses in lower caste cremations. These cases are attributable to a family or a clan having given service long ago to a higher caste ruler or patron, in return for which the family was granted the bull privilege.

The animal coffin is cut from a solid tree trunk, hollowed out by hand, and built with a removable back section into which the corpse will be put. The whimsical Balinese never omit a single anatomical detail, often over-emphasizing the sex organs — sometimes even making the bull's penis movable. The figure is covered with paper and then with cloth — black for bulls, yellow for cows, and then covered with a gaudy assortment of col-ored cotton wool, mirrors, colored paper cutouts, tinsel, and glitter. The animal is then mounted on a platform of bamboo poles so it can be carried by a large group of men.

A cremation tower, called a *wadah,* or *bade,* is built. The tower repre-sents the Balinese universe, with Badawang Nala, the world-turtle, at its base, surrounded by the two dragon-snakes, Naga Basuki and Naga Anantaboga. These represent the physical needs of mortal man — the for-mer symbolizing safety, the latter perpetual food, clothing, and shelter. Every man-microcosm has its two accompanying *nagas,* but they are no longer needed after death. In the cremation of descendants of a royal family one sometimes sees a separate snake-dragon, perhaps 50 or more meters long, accompanying the procession. This is Naga Banda, the dragon that binds or ties man, granted only to royalty according to an ancient legend, and symbolizing the two dragons mentioned above. Naga Banda is symbol-ically killed by a flower-tipped arrow from the bow of the attending *pedan-da,* symbolizing the release of the spirit from its earthly physical needs and from its sins.

The turtle and the snake-dragons live in the lower world, *bhur.* Above *bhur* in Balinese cosmology is the word of man, *bwah,* represented on the cremation tower by leafy forests and mountains. At the very top is the world of heaven, *swah,* built of successive tiers of little roofs of receding size, like those found on the pagoda-like *merus,* found in some temples. These tiers represent the 11 levels of heaven and the world-mountain, Maha Meru. Only royal families may put 11 tiers on their towers. The lower castes are allowed nine, down to five or seven for the lowest caste.

Between heaven and earth on the tower is a houselike structure, the *bale balean,* with four posts, again symbolizing the *kanda empat.* This *bale balean* has a protruding shelf on which the body is placed for transporta-tion from the house compound to the cemetery. This is done only if the body has not been buried. If it has, an effigy takes its place — it would be improper to put a body that has been in contact with the unclean earth in such an elevated and holy place. The effigy is a fan-shaped object, about 40 centimeters high, made of sandalwood, wrapped in a cloth, and decorated.

On the back of the tower is a big, grotesque mask, *bhoma,* the same fanged face that stares down from the main gate of most Balinese temples to scare away the evil spirits. *Bhoma* on the tower has huge, outstretched

A BULL SARCOPHAGUS

wings, often with a span of several meters. Sometimes a photograph of the deceased is attached to the back of the tower.

The height of the tower is limited not only by expense, but more mundanely, by the height of the electric and telephone lines under which it must pass. A wealthy family may even pay the electric company to remove the wires temporarily if an extra high (and prestigious) tower is to be used.

I once was present at a cremation procession when a rather high tower was in use, but the power lines were left in place. I noted that one of the members of the procession carried a very long bamboo pole with a T-shaped piece on top. I wondered what the ceremonial significance of this pole was until I saw it being used to hoist the power lines up just a bit so that the tower could pass beneath. If a tower is too high to climb, a separate bamboo ramp is built as well. For wealthy families of high caste, the *wadah* may be 10 to 20 meters high, or even more, requiring a hundred men to carry. A family can buy towers and sarcophagi from people who specialize in their manufacture, or hire special craftsmen, or make the items themselves. Whichever the case, a lot of money is involved.

If the body to be cremated has been previously buried, it is dug up in the cemetery. Often very little remains — perhaps just a few bones or fragments of bones. These are washed, wrapped in a white cloth, and placed in a temporary shrine in the cemetery. A buried body, having been in the impure earth, is never carried to the family home. Ceremonies that take place in the home concentrate on an effigy of the body, the *adegan* (a place where spirits reside).

Holy water is essential to any Balinese ceremony. A cremation requires large quantities of it to be obtained from sacred springs and temples. A coconut oil lamp, spherical and covered with a white cloth, is hung on a tall bamboo pole outside the family house compound, together with a similarly constructed bird. The lamp is kept lit until the cremation day to guide the wandering soul back to its home. Invitations are printed, addressed, and sent to friends and family. Villagers are expected to bring quantities of rice to help feed workers and guests. For lower caste families, higher caste patrons come to help with the preparation of the more complex offerings and effigies. These patrons, in turn, must be given gifts, and special trips are made to their homes by large delegations from the deceased's family after the cremation. Usually a kind of life-size doll, the *ukur*, is made from old Chinese coins tied through their center holes with white thread. The doll represents the skeleton, nerves, and muscles. It is carried to the cemetery in the tower, transferred to the cremation vehicle, and burned.

Meanwhile, dozens, perhaps hundreds, of volunteer workers must be fed two or three meals a day, constantly supplied with cigarettes and betel chew ingredients, and treated to coffee, tea, and rice cake snacks every hour or so. A small army of women does nothing all day long except cook and prepare food for the workers and serve them.

In North Bali, a great procession, the *madeeng*, is held on the day preceding the cremation. Members of the family dress in their very finest traditional clothes, with gold leaves wound in their hair, gold and silver brocade cloths wrapped around their bodies, and long white trains dragging on the ground. The procession has no particular religious significance — it is just part of the spectacle. The *madeeng* is led by the *dawang-dawang,* a pair of grotesque, prancing figures, made up on tall frameworks of bamboo that fit over the heads of carriers. Some say the figures represent the parents the deceased will soon meet; others say they are strictly for entertainment.

A special percussion orchestra plays for cremations, and for no other event in Bali. It features an ancient instrument called a *gambang,* a large xylophone with bamboo keys, struck by a man who holds two wooden hammers in each hand. The orchestra usually has four of them, plus one *saron,* a more conventional bronze-keyed instrument. The musicians play either at the house compound or at the cemetery. A troupe of dancers is often hired to perform the sacred *baris gede.* Dressed in the magical checkered *poleng* cloth and peculiar tall, pyramidal hats, their gestures imitate soldiers in battle as they symbolically guard the spirit from evil influences.

Crowds begin arriving early on the day of the cremation, which usually begins, in South Bali, about noon. All members of the deceased's neighborhood association, his *banjar,* are obliged to assemble, very informally dressed, in front of the house compound where the sarcophaguses and *wadah* are lined up in the street. No weeping or sorrow is evident. It is a joyful event. The soul is about to be sent to that most desirable of all places, *suarga,* and it will soon be on its way toward deification. In fact, weeping might disturb the spirit and make its departure difficult. It is a time for merriment — the culmination of all of the many preparations, and for a grand sendoff of the soul to a better life in a better world. In North Bali there may even be water fights, in which nobody is exempt from a thorough drenching with water from a muddy ditch.

If the body has been kept in the family house compound it is boisterously snatched up and fought over as it is carried up the ramp and bound to the *wadah* on the shelf in the *bale balean,* amid much pushing, shoving, and laughter. The body or effigy is then covered with the *rurub kajeng,* a white cloth inscribed with magic letters and symbols. Then the procession forms, usually led by a person carrying the lamp that has hung in front of the house. Often a man will carry a branch of the *dapdap* tree, considered magical because it grows so easily from a sprig thrust into the ground. There may be a person carrying a stuffed bird, the *manuk dewata,* symbolizing the purified soul that the still unclean spirit will soon become.

The empty sarcophaguses are snatched up by the shouting *banjar* men and spun and whirled as they are carried in a crazy melee to the cemetery. The idea is to confuse the spirit and make it lose its way so that it cannot return and haunt the family. It is said that unpopular members of the *banjar* who have died are treated to more violent handling in their cremation processions. Someone in the family generally rides on the back of the sarcophagus, and he has to hold on for dear life as it is tossed and rocked to and fro, up and down. If the procession passes near the sea, the sarcophaguses may even be taken out into the water, amid much horseplay.

After the sarcophagus comes a long procession of formally dressed women carrying the many cremation offerings on their heads. If, as is usually the case, there are other families participating in the cremation who cannot afford more elaborate preparations, effigies of their bodies, but never the recently exhumed bodies themselves, are carried in silver bowls on the heads of family members. In high caste cremations a palanquin may be carried on the shoulders of several men. In it sits a young child, dressed in elaborate traditional costume, carrying an effigy of the deceased.

Next in the procession comes a very long white cloth, the *lancingan,* attached to the tower at one end and stretched far ahead on the heads of a long train of people. Since not all of the family can actually carry the tower, carrying the cloth symbolizes this act. The tower and ramp are last in line, except for the Naga Banda that may accompany cremation processions of royal families. Members of the family may be carried along in the cremation tower, throwing rice on bystanders. If the tower is not too high it is subjected to the same rough ride to the cemetery.

The procession proceeds to the cremation grounds, located near the village Pura Dalem, the temple dedicated to God as Siwa, the dissolver and recycler of life. It may take an hour or longer, depending upon the distance and the amount of horseplay. Cremation generally takes place in a clearing in the cemetery, located in the seaward, *kelod,* or most impure direction from the village. The area is away from streets and is often well shaded by one or more huge *kepuh* trees. *Pedandas,* however, cannot be cremated in a cemetery, but instead require ground that is pure, having never been used for burial or cremation before. Upon arrival the sarcophaguses are placed in special pavilions under white sheet roofs symbolizing the sky. Everyone circles the pavilion three times counterclockwise before setting down the various items that have been carried in the procession. Those riding in the tower may release two young chickens, symbolizing the soul flying away. The direction they take is supposed to indicate the auspiciousness of the occasion. Nowadays the chickens are often deliberately thrown in a "good" direction.

Next, family members cut open the backs of the sarcophaguses with a special sacred knife. If there is an actual body in the tower it is roughly handed down or carried down the ramp, often fought over to the extent of tearing the bundle apart, and then placed into the appropriate sarcophagus. In the more usual case of previously buried bodies, the sheet-wrapped bones that have been waiting in the cemetery are placed in the sarcophagus, along with the effigy and *ukur* that has been carried in the tower. The family crowds around for a last look at whatever is left of the body as it is exposed by cutting open the wraps. The *ukur* and piles of cloth and other accessories and offerings are placed inside. Everything is then covered by the magic *rurub kajeng* cloth. Now the attending *pedanda,* senior members of the family, or the highcaste patron pour jar after jar of holy water on top of the contents, and the empty jars are smashed to the ground. The backs of the sarcophaguses are replaced. Assistants surround the base of the sarcophagus with green banana trunks to keep the fire from spreading, and firewood is packed between the logs. In recent times it has become popular to use large kerosene burners instead of wood in order to hasten the burning process.

When all is ready, the fires are ignited. This may be done by a *pedanda,* after he has blessed the torch, or it may be done by simply lighting a match. Sometimes kerosene is thrown on the logs. In mass cremations there may be small fires all over the cremation area of the cemetery. The intense heat forces all to retreat as the great fires consume the mortal remains and the expensive work of so many hours. The tower, and all of the other accessory objects, are separately burned. Sometimes the corpse falls through the bottom of the sarcophagus and has to be poked back into the main fire. Fortunately for the wife and servants of the deceased, if they are still alive, the practice of suttee, in which the widow and selected servants of the dead man were expected to jump into the pyre, is against the law and hasn't been practiced for some time.

When the fires have died down, attendants douse the ashes with water. Little boys scurry to collect the Chinese coins and family members collect scraps of ash and bone from the bodies. Some of the burned fragments are formed into a body-shaped pile in a special pavilion, the *bale selunglung,* and are wrapped in a white cloth. Other fragments are placed inside a yellow coconut that is then wrapped and decorated. Meanwhile, the *pedanda,* if present, has climbed up to an elevated platform and is ringing his bell and chanting magic mantras that will help the release of the soul and aid it on its journey to heaven.

By now it is near sunset. The *pedanda* chants his final mantras. Family members sit or kneel on the ground to pray, then rise and carry the containers of ashes on their heads in a procession to the sea. If the sea is too far distant, the ashes may be dumped into a nearby stream that will carry them to the sea. The sea itself is preferred, and sometimes the family elects to reach it by automobile nowadays. The remains may be carried out away from shore in a small boat in order to prevent their being washed up on the beach, or they may simply be tossed into the water from the shore. Now the five elements of the body have been returned to the macrocosm whence they came, and the spirit has been released to the sea where its impurities will fall as sediment, and from which its purer essence will be summoned for the next and final major series of ceremonies, the *nyekah*, wherein the soul is returned to *suarga-neraka*, just as the body's elements have been returned to the Bhuana Agung.

THE *NYEKAH* INVOLVES NO BONES OR CORPSE, but it is just as important as the *pengabenan*. Many of the activities are identical to those of the cremation ceremonies. There is a burning, a tower, a procession to the sea or to a stream, and a disposal of ashes therein. Traditionally this final ceremony took place 12 days after the cremation, and was called *ngerorasin*, from *roras*, meaning "12." Some parts of Bali specified an interval of one month plus 7 days, *bulan pitung dina* — 42 days since a Balinese month has 35 days. Today however, no particular interval is observed. Instead, an auspicious day is picked, far enough in advance to complete the preparations.

Another large tower is built, the *bukur*, decorated only in white and gold. Temporary shrines and shelters are constructed by work gangs. More holy water is fetched. More invitations are sent out. The kitchen and offering work goes on with unabated activity.

High caste offerings experts prepare special effigies for the soul, called *sekah* — the verb form of these, *nyekah*, names the ceremony. The effigy is assembled on a bamboo frame about 40 centimeters high. The conical base is covered with leaves from a sacred banyan tree, collected in a special ceremony, and symbolizing the fire that will release the *atman* from the *sekah*. The leaves must be arranged concave side down for a male effigy, the opposite for a female. The effigy is decorated with special dried flowers and a fan-shaped background, similar to the *adegan* of a cremation. It is then wrapped in white, decorated with gold leaves, and placed in a special shrine on a silver tray.

The climax of *nyekah* takes place well after midnight and is preceded by a chain of special ceremonies. First each *sekah* is unwrapped and the valuable ornaments saved. The inner framework is placed upon a round clay pedestal and set afire. Family members encourage the flames with miniature woven bamboo fans. The ashes are then ground up, each family member helping, and placed in a yellow coconut, which is then wrapped in white and decorated. This object, sometimes called *sekar*, or *puspa*, blossom, is then reverently carried on the head of a family member in a procession to various family shrines. Prayers are intoned, and the effigy is placed in the *bukur* just at dawn. In mass *nyekahs* there may be many effigies in one tower, or each effigy may have its own tower.

The tower is then carried in solemn procession to the sea or a nearby stream, prayers said, offerings dedicated, and the effigies thrown into or carried out into the water, followed by the tower itself, which is not burned this time. The soul has finally been sent on its way to God. Wealthy, high-caste families will hold more elaborate *nyekahs*, sometimes called *mamukur*. And really colossal *nyekahs*, called *maligia*, are organized on rare occasions for very important souls. These require months of preparation and involve hundreds or thousands of people and the expenditure of many thousands of dollars.

MAY THE FAMILY NOW BREATHE A SIGH OF RELIEF and be satisfied that it has done its duty for the deceased? Not at all! Those who helped with the ceremonies must be thanked by special gifts, offerings, and trips to their homes. Expeditions must be sent to various holy temples to thank God for the success of the ceremonies. And, most important of all, a whole new series of ceremonies must be conducted wherein the now purified spirit is installed in a special shrine in the family temple, as a bona fide *betara yang,* a deified ancestor awaiting rebirth. Then, and only then, can everyone who participated in all those months of work rest.

CHAPTER 13

The Supernatural

SPOOKS, DEMONS, AND UNSEEN FORCES

FROM TIME TO TIME ALONG THE ROADS IN BALI one will see a kind of small, crude tent erected from bamboo poles and covered with a net. This may actually be in the middle of a main thoroughfare or at a *tenget* — mysterious or magic — place near a principal intersection, blocked off with rocks. The police do not disturb these structures. At night a kerosene pressure lantern is kept burning inside or nearby, and one or several people spend the night there for three days in a row. This is called a *magagabag*, or *matetimbun*. An accident, probably a traffic accident, has occurred here, and blood has been spilled. If a *leyak* or other evil spirit has access to a person's blood, great harm could result, so the place is kept under guard. The net acts as a barrier — its mesh has so many entrances that a *leyak* is confused and can never find the proper one through which to reach the blood. Thus the victim of the accident is protected.

In a culture where no distinction is made between the secular and the religious or supernatural, the *sekala* and the *niskala* as the Balinese call them, the latter can enter into daily routines and beliefs in a fashion incomprehensible to one who thinks only of witches as quaint symbols of Halloween, or of magic as part of a Las Vegas stage show. *Sekala* means what you can sense — see, hear, smell, and touch. *Niskala* involves that which cannot be sensed directly, but which can only be felt within. *Niskala* plays a much more important role in Balinese culture than it does in the West. *Niskala* is a very personal matter, often difficult to articulate or, in some cases, hazardous to do so.

Most foreign visitors to Bali will hear nothing of "black magic," and not only because their skepticism is well known to the Balinese. A Balinese will usually not even mention such things to his or her fellows. One's *niskala* feelings are, if spoken, a weakness, because if a practitioner of "black magic" should be within earshot, he could use the knowledge to cause harm. People in Bali, like those in many other places, are reluctant to name something unpleasant, as though naming it — Knock wood! — would make it so. Even thinking about such things is risky.

Hindu-Balinese religious philosophy embraces the principle that for every good, positive, constructive force, there is a counterbalancing evil, negative, destructive force. The two sides are inseparable. They must necessarily coexist, but preferably in dynamic equilibrium, so that neither gets the upper hand. The principal efforts of Hindu-Balinese religion are devoted to maintaining a balance between positive and negative forces. Equilibrium and balance are the key goals.

Since both constructive and destructive forces are present in the world, an individual, should he desire, could presumably use one or the other to his own advantage. But as with all knowledge, mastery of these forces does not come easily. A great deal of study, hard work, self-sacrifice, even exposure to possible personal harm and danger is involved. The knowledge requires many years or decades of intense and dangerous study. The nature of these powers is written in the sacred palm leaf books, the *lontars,* in which all sacred Balinese writings are preserved. To command these *niskala* forces, whether to do good or foul, requires years of arduous study under the guidance of someone who is already a practitioner.

The words for black magic and for the person who practices it, the "witch" or "spook" if you want to call him or her that, are the same in Balinese: *leyak*. When speaking to a foreigner, the Balinese will use the phrase "white magic" — as close as they can come to describing the powers used to overcome, resist, and prevent black magic. The Balinese word is *pengijeng awak,* "to protect the body." Although we see these two forms of knowledge as opposites — black/white, bad/good — the Balinese consider knowledge of the ways of *niskala* something always to be respected, perhaps even feared. High priests, *pedandas,* if they are of the Brahmana caste, and lay priests, *pemangkus,* if they are of the Sudra caste, have devoted their lives to the study of the positive use of this power. *Leyaks* have studied the *lontars* perhaps just as long, with opposite ends in mind — this study, of course, a secret one. Somewhere between these two is the *balian,* a shaman and doctor, who has mastered a bit of both extremes and who is both revered and feared, lest he drift toward the negative, although his work is normally to help people rather than harm them.

A *leyak* can transform himself, or rather, his spirit, into another form — a monkey, a bird, a ghostly light, a body without a head — the variety is endless. This can only be done at night. The physical body of the *leyak*

AN AMULET TO WARD OFF LEYAKS

remains behind in bed. The transformed shape can be seen, and is regularly reported as having been seen, by those Balinese who venture out near midnight. Needless to say few do. The apparition can fly through the air — it may only scare people and disappear. But it can also kill, introduce foreign objects into the body of an intended victim, poison food, cause sickness, cause crop failure, and so on — the list varies with time and place and includes just about all the misfortunes that regularly befall people, and a few that are highly irregular.

The transformed *leyak* cannot be killed with a knife, but various other methods can be used to destroy it or ward off its evil influence and force. If it is successfully killed, the human body of the specter, back in bed, will die without any apparent injury, sickness, or cause. And this itself may be taken as an indication that such a person was, in life, a *leyak*.

Being a *leyak* is exceedingly dangerous. The Balinese consider any tampering with the forces of *niskala* to be riddled with danger and pitfalls. This is true even for a *pedanda, pemangku,* or *balian.* And to carry this practice to such extremes as to cause one's spirit to leave the body in order to harm others is unimaginably dangerous, since the body lies helpless and unprotected at home.

Leyaks most often attack members of their own family group. Stories are even told of male *leyaks* attacking and killing their wives, or vice versa, concealing themselves as, for example, a coconut that falls unexpectedly from a nearby tree, thus awakening the mate, who goes outside to investigate and meets his or her fate. It is certainly possible for a *leyak* to attack those outside the family, but this requires advanced knowledge on the part of the *leyak* and is said to be extremely difficult. Motives for intra-family *leyaks* are the usual disputes that arise in any close-knit and closely packed family group — jealousy, revenge over a real or imagined insult, desire to gain the money or possessions of the victim, and so on.

One is most vulnerable to *leyak* attack when sick, injured, or otherwise has diminished power to resist. Babies are especially vulnerable before their *nelubulanin,* their "three-month" birthday, 105 days after birth. A slice of onion is often placed on an infant's fontanel to prevent entry by a *leyak,* since they find the smell highly objectionable. All manner of talismans, amulets, offerings, and magical objects surround the baby and protect him or her from attack. After the three-month anniversary the infant wears his dried up umbilical cord in an amulet around his neck. Adults who are sick or injured prefer to remain at home, lest in going beyond the safety of the house compound they encounter a *leyak* who might take advantage of their weakened condition.

There are various degrees of control of these magical forces. To ward off a threat of black magic, one may simply go to a *balian* and obtain an amulet, a magic prayer or mantra, a ring, or some other magical object that will do the job of guarding the body or preventing intrusion of evil influences. The varieties of these objects to protect the body are endless. Another is to go to a temple, preferably the Pura Dalem, the village temple near the cemetery dedicated to Siwa, or his wife Durga. There one must meditate all night long. If one is lucky — most are not — and has the proper powers of concentration, one's mind and body will be given the power to resist evil. The precise nature of this acquisition is not always clear. Most people are too scared even to try this method. The reason is simply that this midnight meditation is also a step toward acquiring the power of *leyak.* Strong internal power or force — even if acquired to ward off evil — can be turned equally toward good or bad, depending upon the desires of the person possessing it.

SOME LOCATIONS IN BALI are more infused with black magic than others. Certain villages, Sanur among them, are known to be *angker* — unusually strange or fearful — or *tenget,* containing great supernatural power. Crossroads and graveyards are the favorite dwelling places of *leyaks* at night. Even trees of unusual shape or size, large or odd-shaped rocks or other strange objects are regarded with special care because of their possible power. You will often see offerings placed in small shrines at these places. Being out at night anywhere is a fearful experience, leaving the traveler open to evil influences, especially during the hours around midnight.

Black magic should not be confused with the ordinary evil influences that abound in the world. The personification of these negative influences are the *bhutas* and *kalas* that live in and on the earth, especially at cross-roads. They are often more bothersome rather than truly harmful — causing one to lose a valuable object, perhaps precipitating a family fight, or making the baby cry. But *bhutas* and *kalas* are not *leyaks.*

Black magic is the result of a conscious effort by an otherwise normal human being to gain control over supernatural, evil forces and use them to his or her personal advantage by causing harm to others. *Bhutas* and *kalas* are easily dealt with by placing offerings on the ground at the same time that other offerings are made to the higher, positive aspects of God's spirit. Almost every Balinese ceremony involves placating the demons with a little rice wine or palm brandy spilled upon the ground and some small offerings in triangular containers, called *segehans.* Sometimes, when these negative forces appear to be getting the upper hand in the equilibrium of forces, a major exorcism, called a *caru,* must be held, involving a great many offerings placed in a square enclosure on the ground. (See CHAPTER 20.)

Almost every Balinese has had some sort of personal night-time encounter with unexplainable noises, movements, lights, or ghostly shapes. These are generally attributable to *leyaks,* as are bad luck, sickness, crop failure, and other misfortunes. But few are able to give specific details about the identity of the person who, as a *leyak,* caused the problem or why he or she wanted to do so. Sometimes it is said that the *leyak's* apparition, if confronted by an intended victim with resistant powers, will hide behind a leaf and change from the apparition to his normal form, and then engage the observer in usual conversation as if nothing had happened. In this case, the identity of the *leyak* is known. But, normally, this is not the case. The result is seen, but the cause and identity are unknown.

UNLESS ONE LIVES IN BALI FOR QUITE A WHILE, it is just about impossible for a Westerner to understand just how much the adjustment of the Balinese people to their universe is based upon mystical powers, magical forces, and strange and unexplainable energies. I do not mean simply that the Balinese recognize the existence of these forces and attempt to cope with them. I mean that these phenomena occupy a central position in the Balinese concept of the world and that the Balinese are constantly aware of them, and that a major portion of their thinking and activities revolve around the existence of these forces and how they can best control and adjust to them.

The Balinese world is filled with *kasaktian,* a word, rarely used, that means "magical power." A Balinese might use the adjectival form — *sakti,* "magical" — but the existence of the force is not even a subject of discussion. In Bali, objects that Westerners would consider to be inanimate and wholly devoid of any ability to exert active influences on other objects may be considered the foci of concentration of a mystical force. *Leyaks* are only perhaps the most dramatic phenomena on an island charged with *kesaktian.* Even seemingly basic items, such as food and clothing, are surrounded by a vast amount of lore, ceremony, and religious procedure.

Elaborate etiquette is involved when presenting guests or elevated persons with food, and equally elaborate routines are involved in its acceptance or refusal. Offerings of food are made before each meal. Food is part of almost all offerings. Kitchens and stoves are special objects that, being involved with food, have power that must be treated properly. Culturally important food crops such as rice, coconuts, bananas, and bamboo are all especially charged with mystical power — and are ceremonially respected. Animals, too, possess mystical power. Before an animal is slaughtered as a religious sacrifice or for food, an offering is made for it and mantras are recited. On the day called Tumpek Andang, which comes every 210 days, offerings are prepared for cows and pigs. Wells and pumps are presented with daily offerings, as are streams, lakes, dams, and irrigation ditches.

Clothing, particularly that which has touched the sexual organs, is charged with dangerous power, and one must never put oneself in a position so that one is below such clothes. Certain kinds of clothing are appropriate for use when praying in a temple, and violation of the dress code is likely to result in undesirable and unforeseeable consequences. Menstrual blood is especially magically charged, to the extent that a menstruating woman is not allowed to enter a temple. Blood-stained clothing must be separated from other laundry and dried well away from any site of human activity. Jewelry, especially rings with stones set in them, have mystical power. Rare is the Balinese who does not have a ring, the stone of which has some sort of power. The same is true of amulets.

Religious paraphernalia is obviously charged with power. Holy water is an extremely important and magical substance. Masks that are used in the various religious ceremonies are great foci of power. Rangda and Barong masks are especially *angker* and must be treated with extreme care. Even the common *topeng* masks must be treated with respect. And many are the tales of the problems they have caused when not given offerings at appropriate times. Masks that are used in traditional performances must not be handled casually, even if they are not considered to be sacred. Musical instruments and dance costumes are regularly presented with offerings. Offerings are made to a *gong* before each performance.

Directions have magical powers. The *kaja-kelod/*sacred-profane axis governs everything in Bali. Colors and numbers are charged. Words and syllables are not just bearers of messages but embodiments of mystical power as well, not just in the form of mantras, but even by themselves. Books, especially *lontars,* have mystical power. Even sounds have power; not just musical sounds but certain single syllables, such as the mysterious and powerful syllables ANG, UNG, and MANG, which, combined produce OM. So do days of the week, months, and years.

Places, such as temples, cemeteries, markets, cremation grounds, mountains, lakes, and streams possess special kinds of mystic power, and only certain types of activities can be safely carried out in these areas. Automobiles and motorbikes have mystical power. A cautious driver will put a small offering in his car every day.

The Balinese are not paranoid about the dangers of the world. But they are acutely conscious of them at all times — on their guard. These forces are around all the time, and one cannot say when and where they might penetrate a weak spot and cause problems. The result is that offerings are made to just about everything imaginable.

MOST WESTERNERS TAKE QUITE FOR GRANTED Aristotle's three basic principles of logic: Identity, a term will mean the same thing in all occurrences; Contradiction, a sentence and its negative cannot both be true; and "The excluded middle," either something is true, or its opposite is true. In many circumstances, these three laws simply do not apply to Balinese lines of reasoning. This is not always the case. In immediate circumstances and for rule of thumb judgments there is little difference between Balinese logic and Western logic. But for the Balinese, Aristotelian logic does not provide a test of truth for all observed phenomena. The Balinese conceive that all things in the universe, living or not, have some connection with each other. There is no clear distinction made between oneself and some other self or between oneself and some other object. There is no clear distinction made between what we would call living things and nonliving things. There is no clear distinction made between what will happen, what has happened, and what is happening right now.

Lucien Lévy-Bruhl, a French anthropologist working in the first decade of the 20th century, called this way of thinking, the "Law of Participation."

In *Les fonctions mentales dans les sociétés inferieures,* translated as *How Natives Think,* a rather strained attempt to make the original title sound less racist, Lévy-Bruhl writes:

> ...in the collective representations of primitive mentality, objects, beings, phenomena can be, though in a way incomprehensible to us, both themselves and something other than themselves. In a fashion which is no less incomprehensible, they give forth and they receive mystic powers, virtues, qualities, influences, which make themselves felt outside, without ceasing to remain where they are. In other words, the opposition between the one and the many, the same and another, and so forth, does not impose upon this mentality the necessity of affirming one of the terms if the other be denied or vice versa.

If one is willing to forgive his self-serving use of the word "primitive" here, this seems to be a description of the Balinese concept of the cosmos.

It is not inconsistent with Balinese logic to conclude that event B could cause event A even though event B occurred at a later time than A. It is not inconsistent to attribute a cause and effect relationship between an object and event even though a Western observer would observe that there is no conceivable connection between the two. A certain kind of ring can cure a sickness. The offering made for a *gong* can help a baby to learn to speak. Climbing a tree on a certain day will result in an accident. This logical process is not unknown in the West — although it is often denigrated by a culture rooted in legalistic and scientific reason.

Under certain conditions in Bali, a person can be both dead and not dead. A man in Jimbaran was recently killed in an accident. Several days later, on an auspicious day, the men of the village collected to wash the body and carry it to the cemetery for burial. After the corpse washing, it is customary to place on the body various objects that, by association, will make the person's body fit for his next incarnation: steel on his teeth to make them strong; mirrors on the eyes to make them bright; an *intaran* leaf on each eyebrow to make them attractive, and so on. This is called the *banten paberishan.* When this had been completed, one of the men turned to me and said that now the person was dead. He had been alive till then.

CHAPTER 14

The Balian

SHAMAN AND HEALER

SICKNESS IN BALI is almost universally viewed as the result of a state of disharmony between the individual and his surroundings. In this sense, illness is no different from various other kinds of misfortunes: an accident; crop failure; the death of a family member; losing a job. Whenever one of these misfortunes occurs, a Balinese will assume that he, the sufferer, has done something inappropriate: violated a religious law or custom, perhaps by mistakenly stepping over a sacred object; allowed his hubris to exceed that allowed by his position, perhaps by calling someone by too low a name; been disrespectful of a deity, perhaps by not making the appropriate offerings on an important anniversary.

In short, when fallen ill, a Balinese will assume that he or she has been *pramada,* "insubordinate," and seeks less a cure than a kind of atonement. There is another possibility as well, that the misfortune has been deliberately caused by an enemy who found a soft spot when the sufferer's defenses were down and too weak to repel the *leyak,* "black magic," of the enemy. The enemy has open to him a very wide range of possible ways to cause harm, from the very obvious to the fiendishly clever.

When stricken by these misfortunes and ills, the Balinese see a special kind of doctor. A *balian* is often defined as "traditional healer" or "witch doctor." *Balians* very often do practice healing. But they do a great many other things as well. A better term would be "shaman," or the Indonesian equivalent, *dukun.* The point is that *balians* are not all healers, but spiritualism plays an important role in the functions of all of them.

It need not be a misfortune that leads a person to a *balian.* One common reason for a consultation is to determine the identity of the spirit that has been born into the body of a newly arrived baby. It is commonly believed that the spirit is that of one of the baby's ancestors, reborn into the same family. Just which one it is will be important in determining at which *kawitan,* or clan temple, offerings should be made, and to which spirit prayers should be directed if the baby should fall ill.

Nor need the misfortune be sickness. A *balian* may be consulted in order to determine the location of a lost object or the identity of a thief. The family of my assistant, Budi, regularly consults a *balian* who lives in Jimbaran in order to determine the proper auspicious day, *dewasa,* for carrying out some sort of project. This *balian* is seldom consulted for curing purposes. But he is in great demand for officiating at rites of passage ceremonies, such as *otons,* weddings, and other relatively small family rituals.

A *balian* owes his power to the fact that he has the ability to penetrate into the mystical world beyond the here and now — into the *niskala* plane of existence. This is a fearsome place, and only those with great knowledge and power dare venture into it. In a great many cases people become *balians* because they themselves once suffered some sort of serious sickness. They consulted a *balian,* who indicated that the sickness could only be cured if the patient learned to communicate with a particular spirit, who would then neutralize the cause of the illness. The patient did this, and having established a mystical connection with the spirit, became a *balian* himself. In cases like these, the person-spirit becomes the one to whom the *balian* owes his powers. And it is to this spirit that the *balian* directs his prayers and offerings in order to satisfy the requirements of his clients. Sometimes a suffering person may go into trance and see a spirit without the intercession of a third party — this can also lead him or her to become a *balian.* It should be added that many of the *pemangkus* (lay priests) I know in my village owe their present professions to similar circumstances — sickness and cure through the intervention of specific spirits.

Cases like the above are very rare, because most people do not venture into the spiritual world on their own. It is *pramada* and risky. And the kinds of sickness that would cause a *balian* to suggest that his client establish such a deep, and potentially dangerous, relationship with a spirit must be very serious indeed. In fact, the attitude of the average Balinese toward a *balian* is great respect mixed with a little fear. Since the activities of *balians* involve mystical forces, and since the *balian* has the power to control the flow and ebb of these forces, he is just as capable of using his power to inflict evil upon others as he is of using it to help them. This fear is not usually expressed. But one gets the impression that it is definitely not a good idea to cross these people — they are just too close to the practice of black magic.

When researching another chapter in this book, Budi and I went to a village that was new to me to collect information about the *pelelintangan* astrological chart. (See CHAPTER 18.) I had been told that the father of our prospective informant was a *balian*. When we entered the house compound, we were greeted by an elderly man who, from his manner and dress, we inferred to be the father. While we were waiting for the son to show up, I mentioned to Budi that the man who greeted us was probably the *balian*. Budi was extremely upset.

"You must not mention that out loud here!"

"Why," I said. "That man is a *balian* isn't he?"

"Yes, but you don't mention things like that. He might hear you."

"What's wrong with mentioning something if it's obviously true?"

This led to the usual impasse that results when I am being obstinate. I remember another visit to take a small gift to a *pemangku* who lives in our village. The father of the *pemangku* hinted that he would like to have a blank notebook in which to write some notes. When we had departed Budi mentioned to me that it might be a good idea if I bought a notebook and gave it to this man. I asked why. People are forever asking me for gifts. Budi pointed out that the man was known as a *balian* who was engaged in, as Budi put it, a "deep" study of various subjects — and it is just a good idea to keep people like that on your side. I bought the book.

Some years ago a Balinese friend, knowing of my interest in witchcraft, offered to take me to a *balian* who, he said, was known to be involved in this sort of activity. My friend led me straight to the informant's house and forthwith asked the man if he would please tell me what he knew about witchcraft. Of course, the *balian* denied any knowledge of the subject. When I got home and told Budi he hit the roof in dismay. One never, *ever*, mentions this subject. What a stupid thing to do. Now we have an enemy, and he probably is a *leyak* who can cause us all sorts of trouble. It was a stupid thing to do, I discovered later. And the man who offered to lead me to the witch was not very knowledgeable about such matters.

BALIANS ARE NOT USUALLY GENERAL PRACTITIONERS. There are a number of varieties, each specializing in a particular area of knowledge, including massage, finding lost objects, preparing love potions and protective amulets, delivering babies, or dispensing medicines. A *balian tulang* specializes in setting broken bones. *Balian manak* is a midwife. There is not much difference between the way some of these practitioners function and the practices of health personnel who operate the PUSKESMAS, or village clinic that is found is most small towns in Bali.

Balian tenung is the usual name for a *balian* whose specialty is divining or prophesying. The powers of such *balians*, however, are almost never directed toward foretelling the future or predicting events. Nor do clients ask for this service. Instead, the diviner is asked to do such things as locate lost objects, reveal a thief, or to find the identity of a baby. I have noticed a characteristic lack of concern for the future in many of my Balinese friends. I am an incurable planner, and I am forever asking Budi or his wife whether they are going to go to such and such an *odalan* next week, or whether they want to go to the movies next Saturday night. The reply is always that they really haven't made any plans yet, and I would just have to wait and see how they feel when the time comes.

The only instance within my experience that a *balian* was used to control future events was in connection with the planning of a large celebration to which I was invited. I expressed the hope to my hosts that it would not rain that night and spoil the decorations. I was told not to worry. The group had hired a *balian terang* to make sure that it would not rain. *Terang* means "clear" or "bright." There was a money-back guarantee, I was told. The man did his job well. It was a lovely evening.

Diviners use a variety of techniques. Some go into trance and communicate with a god who might have been involved with the theft. For example, if a *pratima* is stolen from a temple, the god who usually inhabits the *pratima* may reveal where it has been taken. Trance is generally used in divining the ancestry of a newborn baby. The goal here is to invoke the spirit of the baby or one of the closely related ancestors, who will reveal the true nature of the child's identity. Other *balians* use the local equivalent of crystal ball gazing, which involves putting some oil on the thumb of an assistant, often a young child, who then sees the act of theft or loss in the shiny surface of his thumbnail — and thus can identify the location of the lost object and perhaps the thief himself.

A *balian usada* is one whose healing powers are based upon the possession of books that deal with the subject of medicines and their uses. Authors have referred to these as "literate" *balians*. But the title only implies that the *balian* possesses the books, not that he has read them, or even can read them.

The books in question are *lontars,* their pages made from the long, narrow leaves of the *lontar* palm, a common tree in parts of Bali. The pages of the *lontars,* made from leaves that have been dried and squared off to a length of about 35 to 40 centimeters, and a width of 3 or 4 centimeters. The sheaf of leaves is threaded together, and the front and back covers are thin boards. The text is scratched into the leaves with a hard pen, and carbon black is rubbed into the etched surface to make the letters stand out. The language used is old Balinese or old Javanese (or Kawi) and the alphabet is normally Tulisan Bali, the traditional Balinese script. Only about four lines of text will fit on each of the thin leaves.

Lontars occupy a unique place in Balinese thinking. The sacred Hindu-

Balinese texts are all written in *lontars*. By association, this makes the *lontars* themselves sacred, much as the Bible and the Koran are considered sacred books. But the Balinese concept of the sanctity of the book does not refer merely to its contents. The physical book itself is sacred. Possessing a *lontar* devoted to some religious subject is like possessing a kris or a sacred and powerful mask.

Thus, although the *balian usada* may not read the *lontar*, the object itself is a receptacle of magical energy, and its energy can be conferred upon others by suitable prayers, offerings, and by using holy water that has been in contact with the *lontar*.

Lontar palm leaves, although remarkably resistant to decay, cannot be expected to last more than 50 to 100 years at the most in Bali's humid climate. And so any *lontars* in someone's possession are necessarily relatively recent acquisitions. Decaying *lontars* are regularly copied anew onto fresh *lontar* palm leaves. But, as is often the case when manuscripts are copied, the copier often inserts his own interpretations and comments and ideas. The result is that, although a *lontar* may have originated as the creation of an individual, repeated copying has resulted in many versions. And parts of these versions are often contradictory. Further, there are *lontars* with the same title that have been written by different people on different occasions, in different places. Nor is it unknown for a group simply to write its own *lontar* in order to sanctify or legitimate a practice. However, none of these factors seems to make any impression upon most Balinese. If someone questions a statement or a practice or procedure, it is quite sufficient to defend it by saying that it was taken from a *lontar*. That ends the argument. Never mind which *lontar*. If it is in a *lontar*, that is good enough.

Balian usada often are literate scholars who are consulted for their knowledge of certain *lontars* and who are able to help their clients by using the information in their libraries. This information may be of almost any variety, from advice about the use of medicines to a long list of offerings that must be made and ceremonies conducted in order to resolve the problem at hand. But this information is not ever dispensed in the same atmosphere as one might find, for example, at the reference desk of a library. The context is always spiritual.

A *BALIAN* MAY POSSESS SOME OF THE INGREDIENTS for the cures he or she prescribes, but likely as not the patient will be given a recipe that can be made up at home. Most Balinese are knowledgeable about traditional medicines. Many herbal medicines are easy to find just about everywhere. The women's organizations of many *banjars* encourage housewives to maintain what in Indonesian is called an *apotek hidup*, a "living drugstore," a small garden of medicinal herbs. Village markets are good sources of these substances. Most of them are plant substances — concoctions of leaves, bark, roots, or seeds. Those that are designed to be taken internally are boiled in water and the resulting infusion, called *loloh,* is drunk. For external use, the ingredients are mashed up in a stone mortar and pestle and smeared over the body as a *baboreh.* Some are combined with coconut oil and used to rub on the body. Every now and then Budi's little son Aris turns up looking like a man from Mars, green from head to toe. He has a skin problem and is the occasional victim of one of the local *balian's baboreh* experiments.

One need not go to a *balian* to seek traditional medicines. There are more or less stock remedies for such common diseases as colds or chills, which the Balinese call *masuk angin* — "wind enters." For a cold, one must use something hot, like a preparation with ginger or chili, or both. And something cold, such as onion, should be used if one suffers from another common malady, a "hot stomach." Medicines for these and many other illnesses may be purchased from the sellers of the traditional Javanese *jamu* found in every Balinese village.

It is not unusual for a *balian* who dispenses medicines to have some sort of magic substance. For example, it may have been found in an unusual place or in an unusual context. These substances are especially desirable and may be rubbed on a patient, or given to him to eat. Some *balians,* usually called *balian paica,* base their entire practice upon the possession of a powerful relic, divinely bestowed upon the *balian's* family. Such might be a kris, a piece of cloth, or a statue. And its magical energy can be transferred to patients by suitable prayers and offerings.

The practice of *balian apun,* sometimes called *balian uat* or *urat,* is based upon massage. *Balians* who massage should not be confused with ordinary masseurs, *tukang uut,* of whom there are a great number in Bali, many of them Javanese. As with all the activities of *balians, balian uat* combines the physical actions of massage with the *niskala* actions of the manipulation of mystical forces, through mantras and offerings. Ordinary masseurs are concerned largely with the *sekala* aspect of this profession. The usual name of this sort of *balian* stems from the widely held concept of the existence of "channels," *uat,* or *urat,* that run through and connect all parts of the body. Through these channels run various fluids that transmit the life force and that remove waste products. Blood is one of these fluids, but there are many others — some tangible, some not. A channel need not be hollow. Any stringy structure in the body, such as a tendon or nerve, could be an *uat.* The basis of massage is to straighten *uat* that have become crooked, remove lumps or other obstructions in them, and stimulate the flow of the life fluids so that the body will be healthy and perform normally. Diseases and malfunctions, pain, stiffness, sterility, constipation, and so on, are attributed to improper circulation of the life fluids to the part of the body where the problem is centered.

Balian kebal are those who specialize in magical paraphernalia such as amulets and rings, or who are powerful in spells and charms. Such *balians* are dispensers of love potions that are known to drive girls out of their minds. They can provide drawings on cloth that one should wear on his person so as to prevent spiritual attack. It is said that putting some sort of foreign object in the shrine of an intended victim can cause him great problems. Obtaining something that was once a part of the victim, such as hair or fingernail clippings is an effective way of causing him harm through magical spells. The list of the wares of such *balians* is, as one might expect, almost endless. One very common belief that I have observed is in the effect of certain stones that are usually worn in a ring on the finger. I have one that the wife of my *pedanda* gave me, and it is the source of almost universal admiration by those who see it. It is not particularly pretty, but everyone seems to see in it, even without knowing where I got it, something magically powerful. The *pedanda*'s wife told me that if I were to get sick, I should put the ring in a glass of water and drink the water.

BALIAN TAKSU ARE PRIMARILY SPIRIT MEDIUMS. They are consulted for a variety of reasons, but usually the problem relates to sickness and a desire to communicate with a god or spirit that can reveal the cause of the sickness and suggest a cure. The cause is often a curse that was placed upon the victim by an enemy because of jealousy, greed, or passion. Sometimes it is a divine curse, imposed because of failure to observe a proper ceremony or because of an improper observance or even ceremonial neglect. Sometimes a *balian taksu* is consulted so that the clients can communicate with the spirit of a recently cremated family member in order to determine if the spirit is happy, and if all the proper observances have been carried out to the spirit's satisfaction, so that the family will not be bothered or haunted, for it is known that unhappy spirits can cause great harm before the *nyekah* ceremony sends them to heaven.

People usually hear about a *balian taksu* through a friend or relation who lives in some distant village. At none of the sessions that I have attended had the clients ever met the *balian* before. This is usually not the case with *balians* that are primarily masseurs or bone setters or midwives. And of course, it is not so with those whose jobs are primarily to preside over various rites of passage ceremonies or to pick auspicious days. In those cases, the *balian* is likely to be a local person who may even come to the patient's home and whom the family has probably known for a long time.

A *balian taksu* does not make house calls. People who wish to consult with them may have to travel a long distance to the *balian*'s home. It is important to pick an auspicious day. Some *balian taksu* do not practice on certain days, such as Pasah, the first day of the three-day week. *Balian taksu* are frequently women. They attract clients by word-of-mouth recommendations. Some are in great demand, and, since no appointments are made, clients may have to wait hours before they can get a consultation.

A consultation is an unusual event to the Western observer. Clients do not volunteer information to the *balian* about why they have come or what they want. Nor does the *balian* ask for this information directly. Since the clients have come to communicate with a spirit, the mystical powers that the *balian* obtains from the spirit will shortly reveal what is wanted. But *balians* are also likely to be extremely shrewd observers of character and body language. And a little preliminary banter with the clients may reveal a great deal about their desires and intentions. A trance session begins with prayers and offerings made to the personal spirit of the *balian*. Some *balian taksu* indulge in elaborate theatrics as they go into trance. Some slip

A FAMILY CONSULTS A BALIAN TAKSU

in and out of trance so subtly that an observer scarcely knows whether the medium is speaking with his or her own voice or with the voice of the spirit.

When the *balian's* person-spirit has been summoned, a question and answer session takes place in which the purpose of the visit and the wishes of the client are divined by the spirit. The spirit, speaking through the *balian* in a voice that varies, depending upon the *balian*, asks the clients a series of leading and sometimes confusing questions which are generally answered simply "Yes," or "No." The spirit often gets irritated with what it calls the "stupidity" of the clients. And the clients readily admit their stupidity since they are in the presence of a god. These sessions gradually lead up to the point where the spirit knows that probably some other spirit is required — for example that of a dead relative. This spirit is then summoned. It often addresses the family at some length, indicating that the family's behavior has caused problems and that the spirit has not been given enough attention.

I have seen clients reduced to highly emotional states by contact with a dead family member. And I have heard spirits talk, through the *balian*, with remarkable accuracy about the intimate details of the family, even though the clients had never met the *balian* before. With some *balians* the spirit voice is scarcely different from the *balian's* normal speaking voice. With others it is a highly exaggerated, emotional sound, punctuated by laughter or growls, and often delivered in the kind of whining tone that is typical of the speech of refined characters in *wayang kulit* and other Balinese drama performances.

More often than not the responses of the spirit are quite obscure and confusing. "Delphic" is an appropriate adjective here. Some families take along tape recorders so that the information can be listened to over and over and discussed by the family elders in order to determine what it means. If the trend of the séance is away from the main point that the family wishes to investigate, family representatives may insist politely that their questions be answered. The net result may be a list of offerings that the spirit tells the family to make and a series of ceremonies that it must perform in order to right the wrong and cure the suffering or straighten out the misfortune. If the problem is harm caused by an enemy, the nature of the harm may be revealed as some sort of foreign object placed in a shrine or buried in the house compound. And often the identity of the person who is causing the trouble is revealed — or at least hints are made to enable the clients to make the identification.

When the clients are satisfied that no more useful information can be obtained, they dismiss the spirit. The *balian* comes out of trance. This may again be a theatrical performance or simply a kind of awakening. The *balian* may reinforce the idea that he or she was simply acting as the medium for the message, not as the messenger itself, by asking the clients if everything went properly. If there are obscure points to be cleared up, the *balian* may offer help and advice. But, in most cases, the *balian* will indicate that he was not aware of what was being said.

The state of mind of the client family after a trance session depends upon the degree to which what they were told meshes with what they have already found out or what they know about the problem. It is not unusual for a family that is dissatisfied by the results of consulting one *balian* to go to another, and perhaps even several more until the information obtained seems consistent with what they know about the problem themselves.

In our village one very common reaction to sickness involves the concept of *masaudan*, making a vow or promise. Faced with what is usually a serious illness, the patient, on the advice of his family, may vow in his prayers that if a particular god will make him well, he will, at the next appropriate time, provide the god with some sort of reward. This reward is usually a rather elaborate offering, taken to the god's temple at the time of a temple festival there and specially dedicated in a small ceremony with the assistance of the *pemangku*. Our Barong, Dewa Ayu, is considered to be especially powerful in this regard because of its involvement with mystical forces centered around the conflict between Barong and Rangda. And these vow-offerings are a standard feature at either the Barong's temple or Pura Ulun Siwi in our village, just before each dance performance. Sometimes a tangible reward is promised. For example, new umbrellas were provided for the Barong by one person who was seriously sick and eventually recovered.

THERE ARE PLENTY OF DOCTORS IN BALI. There are two large hospitals in Denpasar and many smaller ones elsewhere. There are clinics in almost all villages. Professional services are not expensive. What is the relationship between a sick Balinese, a doctor, and a *balian*?

I have seen a rather large number of people in our village who have birth defects, such as hare lip, or cleft palate, or an extra finger or toe. These are so easily eliminated by surgery nowadays that I wondered out loud why those so afflicted were not properly treated. The answer is that these defects are a result of past karma. If these people were born with defects, then obviously the gods wanted them to be born that way. And so the victims and their families do not want to tamper with a situation that the gods have deliberately created, for fear of upsetting the balance that has been established, which would result in even more problems for the sufferer.

I am also impressed with the fact that there are quite a few mentally unbalanced people wandering around our village, with no apparent attempt being made to restrain or treat them. There is a government hospital in

Bangli for mental patients. but families seem reluctant to send sick people to seek professional help. The people in our village just ignore these problem citizens if at all possible. There are psychiatrists, but the families of the unbalanced people do not seem to want to seek their services.

Many Balinese do go to doctors at one time or another in the course of their illnesses. But people are not as familiar with modern concepts of anatomy, physiology, and medical therapy as they are with the traditional concepts of mystical forces and the effects of imbalance. Thus many people, particularly the older Balinese, prefer *balians* to doctors. This is quite understandable. Hospital outpatient departments on the island are extremely crowded. One often has to wait for hours, perhaps days. Doctors' offices are also crowded. Private doctors' fees, although low by Western standards, are beyond the reach of many. Office hours begin late in the afternoon. Since telephones are uncommon in private homes most doctors do not take appointments. Patients are treated on a first-come, first-served basis, and that may mean a wait until late at night. At best, because of the long line of those waiting, the interaction between patient and doctor can last no more than a few minutes. There are lots of unfamiliar sights and sounds. The result of a visit is often just a handful of prescriptions that cost even more money, involve even more waiting in line, and which are often just vitamins and standard antibiotics.

Treatment by a *balian,* on the other hand, is a different affair altogether. A trance or massage session may last an hour or more, during which time the patient is the center of attention of those present. The patient is constantly in contact with a person who obviously cares and who is involved with his personal problems. There is great reinforcement and reassurance in terms that the patient understands, such as voices of dead relatives, offerings, and ceremonies. *Balians* are generally shrewd observers of human behavior and can read their patients' feelings extremely well, reinforcing where necessary, restoring self-confidence, dispelling fears.

Under these circumstances, if the illness is not an extremely serious organic one, the patient treated by a *balian* probably has better chances of recovery than if he were to run the ordeal of the impersonal treatment by a doctor or hospital. Practitioners of modern medicine know quite well that one of the reasons for their success is the human body's remarkable power to heal itself. And many patients recover and return to normal not because of, but in spite of the doctor's treatment.

CHAPTER 15

Trance

STRANGE VISITATIONS

THE GONG PLAYS EERIE, PIERCING MUSIC, the dance is clearly building to some kind of climax. Thousands crowd close, only a tiny corridor remaining for the dancers. A group of some 100 men, each dressed in traditional white Balinese garb with just a slash of red, sits on the ground. Some in the group begin rocking, shaking, moaning. Suddenly — *a shout!* — a dozen men jump up, grab kris daggers and run headlong down the aisle — toward the shrieking and ghastly figure of Rangda. Rangda wails, flicks a cloth at her assailants and they fall to the dirt, paralyzed, like logs.

Although trance is not uncommon in Bali, it is not something the short-term visitor is likely to see. The tourist dance performances such as the *barong* dance at Batubulan or the trance dance in the Bona area, do not include authentic trance. But in my village and in many parts of Bali, trance is quite common. It is an accompaniment to dance ceremonies such as the Jimbaran *barong* dance above, and is used by traditional healers, *balians*, to effect cures.

The outward appearance of an individual in trance varies greatly, from the gentle rocking of a *pemangku* lay priest in the midst of a religious ceremony to the wild self-stabbing of the Jimbaran *sekan barong* trancers. The phenomenon itself seems consistent, however: a dissociative state, daze, or stupor. The individual in trance is not completely unaware of his physical and social surroundings, he is not threatening or dangerous. But he is under a spell, swept up by some magic. There is no obvious use of drugs by the trancers, nor do they seem to be people who are mentally, physically, and emotionally other than normal. As far as I can determine, trance has nothing to do with brain disorders or epileptic seizures or any other pathology of the nervous system.

Other than the practiced trance of the *balian* shamans, trance seems often to be a group phenomenon. It may be planned, such as in the various dance ceremonies of which trance is a part, and it may even be specially induced in the dancers by *pemangkus*. It may also be spontaneous, such as often occurs in Jimbaran during an important closing ceremony of the *barong* season. Ordinary spectators at a religious ceremony or dance will occasionally go into trance. But only very rarely do individuals go into trance in the confines of their own home or in situations that are apparently unrelated to any immediately obvious provocation, generally, a ceremony.

Those who go into trance are almost invariably people who have gone into trance before under similar circumstances. In our village there are perhaps two dozen or three dozen individuals, out of a population of slightly more than 12,000, who are known as trancers. Occasionally someone else will go into trance, but this is rare. As far as I am able to determine, those who go into trance are not known to be individuals with unusual personal, economic, or social problems. Nor are they discriminated against in any way of which I am aware, or considered to be otherwise abnormal. The ones I know seem to be perfectly normal, and other than their proclivities for trance are indistinguishable from the population as a whole. Group trancers are almost always males; and they are usually fairly young, most under the age of 30. *Balians* who specialize in trance, however, seem almost always to be women.

The Balinese are drawn to exhibitions of trance and find them as interesting as the tourist. They have seen such behavior all their lives, however, and are not shocked by it. They are likely to joke about the uncontrolled behavior of one person or another, especially if he does something that they find particularly amusing. But there is a respect to this fascination, because the onlookers consider those in trance to be in the possession of a god or spirit and thus what they are seeing is not a person rolling around on the ground or uttering strange sounds, but rather a magical force making itself known through its control of the body of a fellow villager.

Villagers often squat low or sit on the ground, as they always do when a god is present nearby, so as to be on a lower level than the god, this being a typical Balinese sign of respect. Those who are in charge of the ceremony at which trance occurs are most solicitous of those who go into trance. They make no attempt to force the trancer to desist from what he is doing, unless they feel that the trance has gone on long enough. They may even provide the trancer with a kris or other object that he desires so that he may stab himself. They give comfort to the trancer when he is coming out of the trance. And they provide whatever he requires during this process.

I have no evidence to indicate that anything involved in the many trances that I have seen is "fake" in the sense of being a deliberate attempt on the part of a trancer to convey the impression that he is in trance, when, in fact, he is not. It is possible that there are malingerers, but I have no evidence or even suspicion that this is so. I have never heard villagers allude to malingering on the part of those in trance. I don't think that this would even enter their minds.

BARONG IS A GENRE OF DANCE that, although details of the staging vary, consists of a confrontation between Barong, a sacred animal- or human-like figure with an elaborate costume manipulated by dancers, and Rangda, a witch or demon. In Jimbaran the season lasts about half a year, and in that period performances are put on every 15 days. The Jimbaran Barong is of the type known as *barong ket*, a shaggy-coated beast with a mask somewhat like a Chinese lion. The Barong is sacred, and the character's mask is kept in a special shrine in a small temple in our village. Rangda, also *tenget,* full of magic, is toothy and horrific, with long, tangled hair. She speaks in Kawi, the whiney — and in this case sinister-sounding — ancient Javanese tongue. Both Barong and Rangda have attendants, whose clash warms up to the appearance of Rangda. The outcome of the battle is a draw — neither side wins or loses.

Barong, Rangda, the subsidiary masks, the costumes, the special *gong,* and all the other paraphernalia of the performance are under the control of a sort of club that is called *sekan barong.* The *seka* meets monthly and discusses various aspects of the performance, details of scheduling, finances, and other pertinent matters. There are slightly more than 100 men who are members of the group. Whenever there is a *barong* performance, called a *mapajar,* the entire membership follows the Barong and sits as close to it as possible. Among the *sekan barong* are the trancers.

A normal *mapajar* starts about 3 P.M. in the main street of Jimbaran. The movement is from the village crossroads to the Barong's temple some 100 meters north. The dense crowd of spectators leaves a tiny alley between the two points. The climax of the dance comes when Rangda first appears. The Barong is at one end of this corridor, his back to the fiend, and Rangda is at the other end, shrieking, screaming, laughing, grunting, and making threatening gestures at Barong. This point is reached by about 5 P.M., just on the verge of sunset. And it now that the trance begins.

About 75 to 100 members of the *sekan barong* are seated on the ground facing the Barong. Each wears his uniform — a clean white shirt with the emblem of the *seka* on the left breast pocket, a white waist cloth with a red "tail," a yellow *saput* covering, and a white headband. Those who own kris wear them at the belt. The *pemangku* of the *barong* and several of his assistants are in attendance. A group of about 20 men is seated somewhat closer to the Barong than the others. They are dressed for combat — waist cloths drawn up between their legs and tucked in back, T-shirts, hatless, no frills. These are the trancers. We call them *babuten* in Jimbaran. The word comes from *buta*, "blind," the idea being that they will shortly become blinded to all external stimuli, concentrating upon Rangda, and then upon themselves.

Several of the *babuten* are shivering and shaking and moaning. Some have their heads lowered between their knees. Some are weeping openly. One can see the tense muscles. Occasionally one will cry out and try to jump up. But he is restrained by the *pemangku* and his helpers. Some demand holy water, which is brought to them in a half coconut shell, some drinking the entire contents in one swallow. Others wish only to be sprinkled. The *pemangku's* assistants are kept busy fetching holy water from the temple, nearby Pura Ulun Siwi. The nervous tension becomes almost palpable, and the shivering, moaning, and weeping grow in intensity as Rangda rants and raves 100 meters down the street. The Barong's *gong*, seated under a big banyan tree, plays wild, nervous music. The huge crowd has left only a narrow aisle between the two antagonists.

Suddenly the *babuten* can stand it no longer. There is a shout. They jump up simultaneously, grab kris from whoever has one, and rush headlong down the corridor toward Rangda. The latter advances to meet them, flanked by her *lelontek*, long, magic checkered black-and-white flags on bamboo poles, and her huge ceremonial umbrella behind. Rangda brandishes her white cloth and yells menacingly at the *babuten*, most of whom stop short about 10 meters away, brandishing their kris. A few reckless ones continue their dash toward Rangda and fall senseless at her feet. Rangda advances upon the rest, who back up a bit. When she starts to retreat toward her temple, the *babuten* advance. She charges forward again, cursing and screaming, and again the *babuten* yield. One or two may again charge Rangda, and at once are overcome by her white cloth. Finally Rangda, who herself may go into trance, is subdued by the *pemangku* and led off to either Pura Ulun Siwi or to the Barong's temple.

Perhaps six or eight *babuten* lie in the street unconscious, covered with sweat and dirt. Their hands and feet are, as the local people say, "tied" — it is as if the wrists and ankles really do have ropes knotted around them and cannot be separated. The bodies are hauled out of the way by attendants and friends. The remaining *babuten* form a rough circle around the front end of the Barong, and begin stabbing themselves with kris.

Different *babuten* have different techniques. The usual is to place the tip of the blade of the kris against the pectoral muscles on one side of the chest, grasp the handle of the kris with both hands, and press the dagger against the body. Very often the *babuten* leans forward, shouts a few words to Barong, places the kris tip against his body, and then leans backward, his body forming an arc. Sometimes he leans into the blade. Some *babuten* keep up a steady pressure with the kris. Others wiggle the handle violently. None of them ever actually "stabs" himself. It is always an placement of the blade against the body, often a rather careful placement, and then exerting steady pressure against the handle. Some use two kris. Some use as many as they can hold. One man generally pushes the kris at his eye. This man rather carefully places the tip of his kris in the loose skin just above the eye, where the protective bone begins. And he then leans over almost backwards, pressing the tip of the kris in a direction toward the top of his head, parallel to rather than perpendicular to the skull. Some *babuten* fall to the ground, and lying on their backs, push at themselves with the kris. Some jump up and down in a bent-over position.

This period of violent self-stabbing varies, usually lasting for less than five minutes for a given individual. Usually it ends spontaneously. The *pemangkus* and attendants seldom try to stop a *babuten*, except when it is getting late and things must move ahead. When a trancer does stop he gives his kris to an attendant, comes up to the Barong, and often buries his head in the Barong's beard, sobbing and shouting. The black beard of the Barong is its most magic part. In our village the *babuten* usually yell "*Mapamit!*" or "*Ayah!*" The former means something like "I am going to leave now," or "Excuse me." *Ayah* means "to help with work," and it is used here to indicate that, by his actions, the *babuten* is working hard to help the Barong. Sometimes the Babuten invokes the name of one of the deified founders of our village. There is no coordination to this period of trance. There may be as many as 20 or 25 *babuten* all in trance at the same time, some stabbing themselves, some sobbing and crying at the Barong's head, some stopping their activity for a moment, other just beginning. During this time the *babuten* characteristically show a very strained, tense appearance. They are sobbing and weeping and moaning. Their words are shouted in short bursts. Some stamp their feet on the ground or lean back and beat their chests with the fists of both hands.

This may go on for 15 or 20 minutes, until the *pemangku* has succeeded in calming down the *babuten* and sprinkling them with holy water. The Barong now retires to a spot in front of its pavilion in Pura Ulun Siwi, followed by the *babuten*. After a few offerings are placed on the ground in front of the Barong, the whole sequence of events begins again. Those who passed out in the street at the feet of the Rangda are carried into the temple and laid out on the ground near the Barong. Usually they start to wake up spontaneously. If not, one of the attendants rouses them with encouragement and holy water.

Sometimes a Babuten may call *Api! Api!*, "Fire! Fire!" Nearby is a small wood fire where several helpers squat, waiting, holding dry coconut leaf

ENTRANCED BABUTEN

bundles. At the call, one of the brands is ignited and is brought over to the circle of *babuten,* and the one who called for it stamps it out with his bare feet. Sometimes a *babuten* will use his hands on the fire. When a *babuten* has calmed down, he often has a dazed, disoriented look. With some this does not last long. They may recover quickly, sit down in the circle of onlookers, and watch the trance of their fellows. Sometimes the onlookers make small jokes about the antics of one of the *babuten* and laugh nervously. Most of them view the proceedings with very serious faces.

One who sits close by the *babuten* can clearly see their straining muscles as they thrust the kris into their bodies. And one can see the tip of the kris making a depression in the flesh of those who do not have shirts on. None of the kris has a sharp point or edge, but they are not toys. I would compare the sharpness of edge and point to that of a dinner knife — not a steak knife, but an ordinary piece of dinnerware.

Often a *babuten* who had been in trance, stabbed himself, and then calmed down is aroused once again to repeat his performance. Sometimes those who are "tied" and cannot be revived become quite violent. It may take four or five men to keep such a person from thrashing around and injuring himself or others. One man in particular has a regular routine. He is usually one of those who has previously charged Rangda in the street and has passed out "tied." He is carried to the temple, revives, spends a number of minutes stabbing himself, and then acts as if he is in a daze. One of his friends stands nearby with a firm grip on the back of the *babuten's kamben* waistcloth. He bends over almost double, and suddenly cries out and jumps high into the air. His friend restrains him as best he can. The man lunges toward the crowd and falls senseless on the ground. Everyone knows that he is going to do this. And they know that he always jumps toward the south. So, they clear out a large area of the circle of onlookers well before the leap. The *pemangkus* drag him off to the side and try to awaken him. If they cannot, he is taken into the *barong's* pavilion to spend the night.

The kris are often held by several men who are sitting on the ground at the edge of the circle occupied by the *babuten*. When a *babuten* requires a kris he looks around for one who is holding them and walks over to the spot where the man is sitting. More often than not he will not simply grab a kris and start stabbing himself. Rather, he will inspect the kris carefully — especially the point. When he has found the one he wants he takes it, often gently. When he returns it, he proffers the handle toward the other person in a polite gesture. In other words, although the stabbing is certainly an occasion for detachment and dissociation from the environment, the period immediately before and immediately after the stabbing demonstrates, at least in the case of some *babuten*, that they are aware of their environment.

Sometimes a person in the crowd of onlookers will let out a yell and go into trance. In some cases this person speaks with the voice of one of the aforementioned founders of the village and makes various requests or statements about procedures to be followed in future ceremonies, offerings to be made, procedures to be followed. More often than not this terminates in a solo stabbing with a kris.

The dance ends after dark. The trance session has been going on for 30 to 45 minutes. The kris are taken away from the last *babuten* and placed in a nearby pavilion for their owners to claim. Each of the *babuten* is given one or more offerings called *ganjaran*. The head of the *sekan barong* announces the date of the next *mapajar*, and all go home.

Although Rangda clearly inspires the trance at the *mapajar*, the same trance and self-stabbing can take place without the presence of the witch. Just before the beginning of a new cycle of *mapajars*, the Barong and the *seka*, followed by a crowd of villagers, travel the 16 kilometers from Jimbaran to Pura Luhur Uluwatu on foot, spend the night at Pecatu on The Bukit, and return home the next day. The Rangda mask is taken along in its box, but it is never visible. The procession stops at every crossroads along the way, at certain bridges, and at the city limits of Pecatu. And at each of these places there is an abbreviated trance session, and stabbing with kris. Offerings are placed upon the ground, prayers are said, and the stabbing starts spontaneously in the group of *babuten*, as if upon signal. When it is over, the *babuten* recover their composure, join in the long procession, and walk along, kris in hand, chatting with each other as if nothing had happened.

Similar trance behavior may take place at the last ceremony of a temple anniversary celebration in Jimbaran. A small pile of offerings is placed on the ground, blessed by the *pemangkus*, and then two men with ceremonial spears, point up, dance around the offerings while holy water, palm brandy, and rice wine are poured on the offerings. The men then use the wooden handles of the spears to upset the offerings and stir them around. I have occasionally seen one of the spear carriers grab the loose metal point off of his spear, cast the handle aside, and engage in a self-stabbing behavior that resembles in every way that which one sees in the group of *babuten*. Usually such a person is a *babuten*, or at least one who is known to be susceptible to going into trance.

Occasionally a *babuten* will injure himself. It is seldom very serious. If he does hurt himself the *pemangku* of the *barong* causes him to be placed in the Barong's pavilion and treats him with powdered sandalwood, a red hibiscus, holy water, and mantras. It is said that there is complete recovery within about three days. These people have never been taken to a doctor, as far as I know. Villagers attribute the fact that *babuten* almost never hurt themselves to the power of their patron, Barong, which protects them from themselves by its magic. When a *babuten* does hurt himself, this is attributed to the individual's having violated one or another of the various taboos that are attendant upon one who is a member of the *sekan barong*.

I HAVE INTERVIEWED SEVERAL *BABUTEN*. They tell me that they do not enjoy the trance experience at all. They feel acutely embarrassed when it is all over, as if they had made public spectacles of themselves. They are exhausted from the experience, sometimes taking several days to recuperate. They do not like to lose control. When they are overcome, they see Rangda's face as a mass of fire, and they feel an undying hatred of her.

Their bodies itch furiously, and they feel that the only way that the itching can be overcome is by stabbing with a kris. Many of them wish that they could quit. One man whom I know well did quit, and he is so ashamed and negative about his former *babuten* activity that he will no longer even go to watch a *mapajar*, lest he fall into his old habits again. Some villagers have told me that, when young, they wanted to become *babuten*, but that, try as they could, they were never able to go into trance.

Villagers in Jimbaran have various attitudes toward the trancers. Most view them in the same way that they would view any other unexplainable phenomenon — as being caused by some mysterious power that one has no business questioning or wondering about. It is taken for granted that the *babuten* are possessed by a spirit and their actions are dictated by this spirit. While a spirit is in these people, one has to be as careful. Onlookers remain on the ground, watch with interest, and don't ask questions.

The general attitude of those who do a bit of thinking about this sort of thing is that the *babuten* are temporarily inhabited and dominated by a sort of negative force or demon that the Balinese call *kala*. *Kalas* being what they are, people do not like to be *babuten* because they do not want to be affected by these malevolent forces. Everyone is subject to good and evil influences all of the time. Some people can handle the effects of evil by virtue of study, mantras, amulets, or just by the magical force and strength of their own personalities. Some people, such as *babuten*, cannot. This does not make them inferior in the eyes of the Balinese. Everyone has *kalas* within him at one time or another. I can recall many times seeing a group of *babuten* sitting around before a *mapajar*, chatting, smoking, and obviously trying in every way to force themselves not to focus upon the coming events. But they could not. Their feelings were too strong and were directed toward one goal. And they could not keep themselves from succumbing.

A GENERAL WORD FOR TRANCE in Balinese is *rauh*, meaning "come." *Nadi* and *mijil* are also used. The idea is that a spirit has come — and entered the body of the one who is in trance. Sometimes this is unexpected or accidental. Sometimes it is deliberate. Our village sometimes holds a *marerauhang* — from *rauh* — a ceremony to determine whether a previously held important ceremony was done to the gods' satisfaction; or to see if plans and preparations for a forthcoming ceremony are satisfactory. A *marerauhang* is not usually performed for small, routine ceremonies. It is reserved for ceremonies of villagewide importance, where the effects of doing something wrong or omitting important details would affect a large number of people.

In our village there are several *pemangkus* who are well known as *sadeg*. A *sadeg* is a person who has had some sort of serious illness, usually something of a mental disturbance. Generally this is diagnosed as being caused by possession by a god or spirit. The *sadeg* has been cured, and he is now more susceptible than most to trance and possession. In some villages the low caste ceremonial leaders of the village are mostly *sadegs*. This is not the case in Jimbaran, but the four or five *sadegs* are always asked to attend a *marerauhang*. Sometimes well-known *sadegs* from other villages are invited to attend. A friend of mine from Kuta feels very close to our Barong and always attends any *marerauhang* that involves scheduling or ceremonies for the Barong.

Our *marerauhang* are always held in one of our village temples late at night. After preliminary prayers and offerings, the *sadegs* are asked to come forward and sit in the center next to a brazier of smoking sandalwood. The other village *pemangkus* sit on the ground nearby. The *gong* is playing in its pavilion. The *pemangkus* begin a prayer, asking the desired god to descend and speak. The *sadegs* sit motionless, enveloped in clouds of smoke. Suddenly one of them begins to shake uncontrollably. Then possession affects another, and another, until as many as half a dozen of the *sadegs* are in a frenzy. Their head bands fly off as they struggle. Sometimes it takes three strong men to control each one. Others are not affected by possession at all. After this induction, one or more of the *sadegs* regains his composure. But he is obviously in a detached state. He sits and sways back and forth, producing an unearthly laugh every now and then. And then he starts to speak in that peculiar whining voice — Kawi — that is used by anyone in Bali who speaks the part of a divinity.

Now one of the *pemangkus* moves over next to one of the *sadegs* who is laughing and whining. This *pemangku* is reasonably fluent in the ancient Javanese language, and he and the god in the *sadeg* now begin a sort of question and answer period. The *gong* is asked to stop playing so that the answers can be heard clearly. Everyone listens very attentively. The questions are specifically directed toward the object of the *marerauhang* — the past or forthcoming ceremony. Often as not the answers are rather Delphic in nature and can be interpreted in a variety of ways. The *pemangkus* must discuss the responses when all is over and decide precisely what was meant. Usual requests are for certain kinds of offerings to be made for a ceremony, or certain masks to be performed, or certain shrines in other villages to be visited, or holy water to be fetched from specified temples.

When the group is satisfied that all of its questions have been answered, they offer prayers to the god who took possession of the *sadeg*, and the *sadeg* himself is brought out of his trance with holy water and mantras. He appears a bit dazed, but otherwise unaffected, and is able to regain his normal functions shortly thereafter. This ceremony is sometimes called *nedunan* in other villages, from *tedun*, meaning "come down."

Although in our area this is rare, several villages in Bali sponsor dances in which the dancers are deliberately entranced before their performance, a style called *sanghyang dedari*. The dancers are commonly pre-adolescent girls who, under the influence of quantities of sandalwood smoke and prayers, become quietly possessed and then execute one or more dances while in this detached state. The several varieties of this dance differ only in the details of the dance. A small village near Kintamani used to offer a performance in which two entranced girls stand on the shoulders of two men and execute typical Balinese dance movements — this, it is said, despite that they had no previous formal dance training. The girls seemed to be somewhat aware of their surroundings because they would let some men carry them and not others. They would also only dance to certain of the *gong's* music. This particular dance is no longer given because the little girls who used to dance grew up and none were willing, or able, to take their place. In other versions of this trance dance the girls are held in the arms of men while they dance. And in still others they dance in a group on the ground.

BALIANS ARE TRADITIONAL HEALERS, or shamans, although the word is generic and there are many specific kinds. The activities of *balians* are generally directed toward healing, acting as a spirit medium, prophesy, warding off or, sometimes, causing magical spells, massage, interpreting unexplained signs and happenings, and the like. Most *balians* have had no formal medical training; some depend upon divine inspiration. Some have inherited their talents from a parent. Some have apprenticed themselves to an experience *balian* to learn their trade. Some are quite illiterate. Some are just the opposite, custodians and interpreters of large *lontar* — palm leaf book — collections. Rare is the village that does not have at least one *balian* of some sort. (See CHAPTER 14.)

Not all *balians* use trance as a regular part of their work. But the *balian taksu* specializes in trance. *Taksu* is a powerful spirit that allows one who is properly prepared to communicate with other spirits or gods, a sort of intermediary spirit. Every family temple, *sanggah*, has a shrine for the family *taksu*, called *palinggih taksu* or, more commonly, just *taksu*. Some people consider the *taksu* to be the spirit of one's profession or talent. A Balinese might go to a *balian taksu* for a variety of reasons. One common case involves sickness that cannot be cured by conventional means — a visit to a doctor or taking medicine. Another reason might be to find out something about one's lineage. For example, to a Balinese it is important to know the temple of his ancestry, called his *kawitan* temple. Most Balinese know and visit their *kawitan* temple regularly. Some do not know, and hope to find out through the services of a *balian taksu*. One might go to such a *balian*

after a ceremony, perhaps a cremation, in order to determine if the spirit of
the deceased is content and feels well treated. This is a precautionary move,
since it is felt that the spirit of a family member can cause a great deal of
trouble if there has been some inadvertent omission in the long series of
required ceremonies. These are just a few of many reasons for a visit.

Balians depend on word of mouth to find clients for their trade, and one
who has found satisfaction from a particular *balian taksu* is likely to tell
others, and the reputation of the *balian* spreads. Balinese almost always go
to *balians* in groups, bringing someone who is fluent in high Balinese, and,
preferably, Kawi, since the spirit often speaks in a higher tongue than the
average Balinese can understand. Today it is not unusual to take along a
cassette recorder so that the results can be taped and studied later.

The group will expect to speak to a spirit or a deity. In the case of a dead
person, they know who that spirit is. In other cases they do not, and they
must hope that the *balian* can summon the proper one. The *balian* is considered to be only the intermediary between the spirit and the client. The
spirit provides the information. It is not unusual for the group to be dissatisfied with the results of a visit to a *balian*. If so, they are likely to attribute
the problem to having contacted the wrong deity, rather than to any failing
on the part of the *balian*. In that case they will likely as not go to another
balian to try again. A group may go to three or four *balians* before it is satisfied that the proper spirit has been contacted and the information is valid.

Since the visit to a Balian involves contact with powerful forces, the
usual precautions are observed. An auspicious day is chosen, and no one is
brought along who is ritually impure. The proper offerings are prepared.
Payment for the *balian,* usually food and a small amount of money, is
arranged. Generally the group will pray at its own family temple and perhaps at one or more of the village temples before visiting the *balian.*
Sometimes one of the village *pemangkus* will be brought along to help
interpret the results. A *balian* may live some distance away, so the trip is
often an all-day outing. Everyone wears traditional clothing. These sessions
almost always take place during daylight hours, since there is normally no
place where the group can spend the night near the home of the *balian.*

The *balian taksu* I have seen in action were all women. All received their
clients at their homes. There was normally a pavilion arranged as a consulting place. Sometimes the *balian* and clients would sit on a kind of bed that
was elevated above the floor. Sometimes only the *balian* would sit there,
and the clients would sit on the floor. There were almost always other
groups waiting their turn. Since a session could last over an hour, the wait
was often long. One *balian* was the focal point of a kind of industry in the
little village where she lived. There were foodstalls outside her house, and
one had the feeling that the local economy profited from her profession.

A consultation with the *balian* is not a simple question and answer session. In fact, it is usual not to indicate to the *balian* where one is from or why one has come. That is not considered necessary, since the *balian* will summon a spirit who will know immediately the nature of the situation. The *balian* greets the group, makes a few casual remarks, receives the offerings that the group has brought, and proceeds to prepare for her trance. The trance here is not at all spectacular. There is usually no shrieking or moaning or tears or twitching or other acrobatics. In fact, it is sometimes difficult to tell whether the *balian* is speaking in her normal voice or whether it is the spirit that is speaking through her. There are occasional outbreaks of Kawi. And there might be an sudden outburst of demonic laughter. But, mostly, the conversations are conducted quietly and in a very dignified fashion.

The *balian* offers up prayers to her *taksu* and to the various deities that she normally consults for occasions such as this. And then her *taksu* must determine why her clients are here and what it is they seek. This is done not usually by direct questions, but, rather, in the form of a series of rapid-fire statements, which the group then responds to by simply saying "Yes" or "No." For example, the conversation may go like:

> The *balian:* "You have brought your son here to be helped."
> The group: "Yes."
> "He is being bothered by a spirit."
> "Yes."
> "You are wondering what sort of offerings you must make in order to cure him."
> "No, not exactly."
> "You need to know what temple to go to so that you may make offerings for him."
> "Yes."
> "You want to know where your *kawitan* temple is."
> "Yes." And so on.

The *balian* poses a long series of questions that are very shrewdly phrased so that the answers provides excellent clues about the nature of the visit. When this nature has been determined, the *balian* is ready to summon the proper spirit so that it can talk directly to the group. In this process the *taksu* of the *balian* often becomes upset when the information that she seeks is not immediately forthcoming or when the client does not understand what it is she is seeking. She is likely to accuse the representative of stupidity and berate him for not helping.

If all goes well, the voice of the sought-for spirit is soon heard talking through the *balian*. Likely as not the spirit will speak at some length to the group, without waiting to be asked specific questions. The clients are often very visibly emotionally affected when they hear what they take to be the spirit of a parent or child or sibling. They listen with great intensity and try to note everything that is said. They repeatedly give assent to what the spirit says, interrupting to ask questions only when it is not clear what is meant.

Typically the spirit will point out the cause of its suffering, or the cause of suffering of one of the members of the group. This may be attributed to witchcraft. And sometimes a specific person is named as the party responsible for causing the problem. Or it may be a failure to make a proper offering, or it may be simply information that the group requires. Sometimes the directions for rectifying the situation involve long lists of offerings that must be made and temples visited in order to right the wrong. Sometimes the spirit will berate the group for neglecting it and threaten reprisal if the wrongs are not made right.

When the spirit leaves, the *balian* often talks to the group at some length in her normal manner and voice, answering questions and giving suggestions. It is likely that she will say that she herself does not understand what was said. And she may not even remember the course of conversation, since she was only the vehicle for the spirit, and it was the latter that did the talking, not she.

A typical session lasts at least one hour, sometimes two. And, after a short rest, the *balian* is ready for the next group that has been patiently waiting. The clients that have just completed their session now head home, pondering the contact with the spirit and trying to decipher the often vague and puzzling information that they have received.

AN INEVITABLE QUESTION POSED BY WESTERNERS when confronting trance is: What is really happening? To the Balinese there is nothing to ponder. Trance is a supernatural phenomenon that is simply caused by a spirit of some unknown and undetermined sort entering the person in trance and causing the behaviors that have been described. That is what is "really" happening, and I have not encountered any Balinese who had any doubt at all that this was the case. A foreigner may not be satisfied with this.

To a Western psychiatrist, the trance phenomena described here are consistent with other well-known psychological phenomena. Trance states usually have an unconscious basis, but, if they are psychologically based, they often are not complete — some measure of control is usually retained by the person in trance. People who are sleepwalkers, for example, usually do not critically injure themselves by walking out of second-floor windows or walking in traffic. There are exceptions, but this is the usual rule.

Many people in Western society who go into trances that are psychologically motivated do so in a partial way without total loss of control. And these people are still able to fulfill certain patterns that are expected of them. Most of these people are not malingering. Most are in genuine disso-ciated states. But there are automatic inner limits on such states.

Technically, these are known as dissociative or hysterical phenomena. Included among them are hysterical seizures, hysterical paralyses, episodes of hysterical amnesia that may last for a long time, and probably multiple personality. People in such hysterical states may place themselves in danger-ous circumstances, but most tend to be self-protective. This is in contrast to some organically based behavior, such as epileptic seizures, brain tumors, and so on, when the behavior may not be controlled in any way.

People with hysterical fainting spells or hysterical paralyses will often recover with time and without treatment. People with hysterical paralyses will often recover in life-threatening circumstances — to flee from a fire, for example. The kind of suggestibility that leads to the trance states described is completely compatible with being, in other ways, an average person. In this respect it is very similar to the question of who or who is not hypnotiz-able. There is no way of telling without trying. Some people who are bright, decisive, and, one would think, not hypnotizable, turn out to be excellent subjects; others who seem timid or shy and, one might think, easi-ly influenced, are totally immune.

Sometimes groups go into trance on cue or at the same time. This is a socially determined phenomenon that has its base in a state of increased, dissociative suggestibility. For example, in the case of certain Pentecostal and similar religions where people go into trance and speak in tongues, the dissociation is unconscious, usually does not involve malingering, does not involve complete loss of control, and conforms to the social expectation.

Thus, the trance phenomena that have been described are not without precedent. Which explanation should one accept? Whichever one you feel fits your own ideas and makes you feel comfortable. I will not suggest the superiority of one over the other. I was trained in science, yet I have lived in Bali for a long time. I know how real the feelings of the Balinese are about these matters, and I respect them. That is as far as I care to pursue the matter.

I am indebted to my life-long friend, Dr. Jule P. Miller of St. Louis, Missouri, for the information on the psychological basis of trance phenomena.

CHAPTER 16

The Balinese Kris
CRAFT AND LORE OF THE RITUAL WEAPON

THE KRIS IS A TRADITIONAL BALINESE SHORT SWORD or dagger, sometimes wavy, usually straight, today seen only in dance performances or on days of great ceremonial importance. By 1908, when the Dutch invaded with their muskets and rifles, the kris had outlived its usefulness as a weapon. But the kris was never just a dagger — it was a *tenget,* "charged," object, full of the mysterious power of steel and the secrets of smithery. And this holds true, perhaps to a somewhat reduced extent, today.

In traditional Bali, kris were often ornately decorated and bejeweled, and, thus, expensive. The kris was one of a man's most valuable possessions, from both a *sekala* and a *niskala* point of view. It was the essence of his authority and power. As a kris passed from generation to generation it accumulated power and often acquired a personality of its own. Much like our Arthurian legends, legends abound in Bali of kris with curses or special attributes. We have a kris in Jimbaran that is considered to have been handed down directly from a god, and it is used today only to sever the cord that holds the mask on our sacred Barong, Dewa Ayu, when the time comes to separate mask and body and retire the dance troupe for a period of rest. At all other times the kris is kept hidden in a special shrine in the temple. Some kris must be stored without any sort of roof overhead; some are so powerful they must never pass under anything, even a gate. It has been reported that the occasional person who runs amok — an Indonesian word — brandishing his kris and killing people indiscriminately, is under the influence of the kris itself, without any control over his own passions.

The kris, transliterated dozens of ways from the original Malay — kriss, creese, creeze, etc. — was used all over the Indonesian islands, as far east as the Philippines, and as far west as the Malay peninsula. The earliest records of kris are 13th century relief carvings on the wall of Candi Panataran, a temple in East Java, the stronghold of the Hindu-Buddhist Majapahit empire that a century or so later came to Bali.

Pure iron is not inherently hard or tough, the characteristics we associate with steel. Raw iron ore, in various forms, consists of elemental iron combined with oxygen — essentially rust — as well as other impurities. The first task of the smith is to reduce this ore, release the oxygen, to produce a workably pure ingot of iron. The product of this reduction with the technology available to the early smiths was wrought iron, a relatively soft and impure substance. A kris made of wrought iron would be no better than a Bronze Age weapon. Thus it was the transformation of wrought iron into steel that represented the skill, the magic, of the smith's craft.

Steel making before the technological age was a very highly skilled craft whose object was achieving an almost paradoxical combination of qualities: hardness and toughness. Steel is an alloy, iron with the addition of small amounts of other metals and carbon. Today such exotic materials as molybdenum and chromium are added for strength and others, such as copper, are added for rust resistance. But the key ingredient is carbon. And a difference of a mere one-half of a percent in carbon content will produce a steel that is either much too brittle, or much too soft. Balinese smiths used the crucible process to produce working ingots of steel, melting the wrought iron in a crucible to let the waste gasses escape and pouring the slag off the top of the mix. This steel was pure enough, and contained enough carbon, to be worked on the anvil.

The smith then shaped these ingots into kris, using an incredibly laborious process of hammer welding. Hammering a hot bar of steel on an anvil produces a grain in the metal, much like wood, which gives it great strength and rigidity. The best traditional kris were made of Damascus steel, produced through a demanding process whereby the steel is hammered into ribbon-like layers, the layers then heated red-hot, folded back on one another, and laminated together with blows of the hammer. Like the edge of a piece of plywood, Damascus steel has visible layers that follow the ramp and curve of the blade. The more layers, the stronger the blade.

If a smith alternates layers of carbon steel and layers of nickel alloy steel, the pattern formed by the laminations becomes particularly distinct. An alloy of nickel produces a lighter-colored steel, which brings out the pattern of laminations, called *pamor*. At first, the only source of nickel steels was meteoric iron. Later, nickel was imported by Chinese and Buginese traders who obtained the metal in the Celebes, now known as Sulawesi, where large deposits of nickel are still mined today. Eventually Europe supplied some of this material.

A VERY FINE WAVY-BLADED KRIS

A talented smith could manipulate the *pamor* pattern. By filing cuts at intervals across the blade to reveal the layer of steel underneath, and then hammering out these cuts, he could change the longitudinal lines to a series of "islands" and "saddles" down the blade. By filing in various ways, different *pamor* patterns could be produced. Because this is a hand process, small irregularities in thickness of layer or hammering intensity would reveal other, unexpected patterns. A fine *pamor* kris is truly an original. A final treatment of citrus juice and an arsenic-containing substance was used to emphasize the pattern — the relatively corrosion-resistant nickel alloy remained silvery, whereas the ordinary carbon steel would be blackened.

Pamor designs vary widely. I have a source book that lists 116 of them. And they are not just for looks — each gives a kris a special kind of power, and a single kris may include several designs. Each traditional *pamor* design is interpreted as a magically powerful symbol. The designs are sufficiently standardized so that others who know about such things can determine the type of power of a particular kris that they have never seen before. Thus one who wishes to cause harm with a kris must conceal its *pamor* design from his intended target, lest the would-be victim is able to take precautions. In order to insure the power of the kris, the smith who makes it must observe the auspicious days and make offerings to his furnace and to the kris itself — while the work is being performed and after it is completed.

Not all kris are damasked, and some are quite plain-looking. Also, contrary to popular belief, not all kris have wavy blades. Most are straight. But some do have the curves, called *luk*. The wavy blade of a kris is symbolic of the shape of a snake, and on these kris the head of a snake is usually engraved on the top of the blade, just below the hilt. Kris hilts vary from plain wood, or string-wrapped wood, to unimaginably ornate masterpieces of goldsmithing, studded with precious stones. Some fine kris have ivory handles. Many are carved into anthropomorphic designs. Sheaths vary too, from simple cases of plain wood or bamboo to well-carved, inlaid masterpieces. A mottled wood from Java, called *pelet,* is a favorite for sheaths. I have seen the kris of many of the members of the Jimbaran *barong* group, and most are not very attractive. Some are rusty. Almost all have relatively straight blades. Some of the sheaths are simple, split-bamboo affairs. One should not think of the kris as always being the pinnacle of the smith's art.

BALINESE SOCIETY IS HEAVILY INFLUENCED by numerology and number symbolism. The kris is no exception. The magical powers of a kris are affected by the numerical relationship that exists between the proportions of its blade, and between the dimensions of the blade and those of the user's hand. To own a kris with unsuitable dimensions would be asking for trouble. I have a friend who was offered an antique kris at a bargain price.

He wanted to buy it, but when he measured it he found that it would bring him very bad luck and so refused the offer. There are three ways to measure a kris to determine its characteristics. One is simply the ratio of the length of the blade to its width. The other two relate to the width of the owner's thumb, and the distance across his palm.

The Balinese usually use a piece of *busung*, young coconut leaf, to measure the blade and width of a kris, in the same way that, with no ruler handy, we might use a piece of paper. The *busung* is first cut to match the entire length of the blade, then folded in half. This determines the half-way point in the blade's length. Then the *busung* is folded, accordion-like, each fold the width of the blade at the middle point — a length called *lumbang rai*. The nature of the kris is determined from the number of these *lumbang rai*, essentially, the ratio of length to width:

10 *rai: Kala ngamah awak* ("Kala eats his body") — If this kris is used the owner will damage himself.

11 *rai: Durga masiyung* ("Durga is with a bird") — Ownership of this kris will mean bad things for the owner and his family, and these will persist over a long time.

12 *rai: Lara muwuh* ("Poverty and grief will increase") — Bad things will result from possession of this kris, especially illness.

13 *rai: Bima kosa krana* — The person who owns this kris will be steadily peaceful and will be lucky in his trade. Soldiers will live a long time if they use this kris.

14 *rai: Darmawangsa* — This kris is good for a person who gives traditional medicine to others. It is good for a person who prays a lot. The owner will be given all that he asks for by people as well as God.

15 *rai: Arjuna sakti* ("Arjuna is powerful") — The magical power of this kris allows the owner to see his enemies even when they make themselves invisible. The kris can be owned by Ksatriya people (warrior or ruling caste). The kris is good for sellers. One who owns this kris will have many friends. Women will love him. Everything he does will be successful. He will have constant good luck.

16 *rai: Suksama angel* — The owner will find unhappiness all of his life. Magical powers will harm the owner.

17 *rai: Naga-samparna* — This kris is good to use for help. The owner can get help easily when he asks for it. It is also good for those who give traditional medicine to others.

18 *rai: Sesangkap-purna* — This kris is very useful for keeping in the house. The owner will be liked by friends and family. This kris should not be taken on a trip, nor should it be taken on a boat.

19 *rai: Durga katamu* ("Meeting Durga") — This kris is bad for traveling. It is best to keep the kris in the house because then there will be no problems. It could be used for evil purposes too, if it is taken outside the house. It will then make enemies.

This system seems to favor kris that are generally long with respect to width — all less than 13 times as long as they are wide at the middle have quite unfavorable properties. The second system determines the suitability of a kris for its owner by measuring its length in units of the owner's thumbwidth. One begins by placing his right thumb across the blade against the hilt, and then lays his left thumb against that, picks up his right and lays that against the left, working his way up the blade in this manner. He then counts the total number of thumb widths, if the last does not quite fit at the tip it is counted anyway. This total is then divided by seven. The remainder of the division becomes the key to the kris's characteristics. Suppose it takes 17 thumbwidths to reach the tip. Seventeen can be divided by seven twice, with a remainder of three. This "three" is then used in the table below:

1 The kris is *satriya;* good to be used by one of the Ksatriya caste

2 The kris is *ratna candra-masurya;* good for sellers of anything

3 The kris is *wanara cinara-cara;* good for use by subordinates of the king

4 The kris is *kala-mertyu* (the spirit who takes your soul when you die); the kris is bad for Ksatriya caste people because it can cause them to harm themselves

5 The kris is Arjuna-*pasupati,* the kris of a soldier; if the person is robbed, others will help him.

6 The kris is *kepaten twan,* very bad; not good for use by anyone

7 The kris is *dharmawangsa;* good for use by high priests

The final method is to do roughly the same thing as with the thumbs, except using the width across four fingers, close to the palm. Alternate right and left hands, starting with the right as with the thumbs. At the tip, some fingers will fit on the blade, and some will not. The fingers then serve as the remainder. Only the number of fingers remaining on the blade is significant. The characteristics of the kris are as follows:

1 This kris is *sang akarya,* which means "good behavior"; the owner will be followed by many people

2 This kris is *kalamertiyu,* meaning that it is for a person who is a good judge; the owner will have many friends and people will like him; the owner can read the character of others very easily

3 This kris is *kalajana,* it represents anger; if the owner uses it when asking something from someone, bad things will occur

4 This kris is *nagawiraksa,* meaning that it is good for people who like to fight, such as Ksatriyas; the owner will be brave in war

THE MAKERS OF KRIS were considered very important people, not only because they provided weapons of war, but also because they had the necessary skill and magical power to produce these immensely potent objects. Every raja had his own smith, always one of the Pande clan. Kris making is practiced to a small extent even today, although Pandes are more often engaged in general blacksmithing. However, they still consider themselves to be somewhat apart from ordinary mortals. Pandes theoretically do not accept holy water from a *pedanda,* and have their own temples and even their own high priests. Brahma, associated with fire, is held to be of the highest importance among the Pande, and the Pande temple at Besakih is decorated in bright red, the color of Brahma and the *kelod,* seaward, direction. (See CHAPTER 8.)

The Pande smith has to observe an elaborate series of rituals and prohibitions if he is to make a powerful kris. He must work only on auspicious days. He must make offerings for the kris every day. And he or some other priest must symbolically bring the kris to life after it has been finished. From then on the kris must be treated with great respect. One never leaves it lying around for others to handle. Especially powerful kris are kept in special shrines in the family temple and only brought out for ceremonies. Some owners will allow no one to touch their kris at all. It is bad manners to ask to see the kris belonging to someone else or to handle it unduly. My own kris is a particularly nice one — an antique with an attractive *pamor* design, nine *luk,* and a beautiful *pelet* case.

One must make a special offering for one's kris every 210 days, on a day that is called Tumpek Landep. The latter word is High Balinese, meaning "to be sharp." Visitors to Bali will doubtless see automobiles, trucks, and buses of every sort gaily decorated with offerings on Tumpek Landep. Cars, bicycles, motorcycles, guns, and kris must all have offerings for them made on this day — any steel weapon (cars being realistically classified as weapons). However, one is not likely to see the ceremony for the kris because it is conducted within the family temple or inside the house.

I own a kris, and every Tumpek Landep, Wathi, Budi's wife, makes an offering for my kris of an *ayam biing,* a chicken with rust-colored feathers and yellow feet and beak. Usually such a chicken has a green tail, but the tail color doesn't matter. I hang my kris up on my porch, and Wathi brings over a whole table of offerings, sprinkles the kris with holy water, and wafts the essence of the offerings toward it.

It should be noted that *taji,* the sharp steel blades that are affixed to the legs of fighting cocks, are considered magically powerful also. All sorts of special precautions have to be made when these are forged by Pande. They are treated with care and respect, and they too are given offerings at the time of Tumpek Landep.

I bought my kris because I had become a member of the *barong* group in our village, and members were encouraged, but not required, to own kris. If the kris one owns is physically strong enough it is frequently used by those who go into trance at the time of a Barong performance. Weak kris that bend easily or may snap are not allowed. Mine classified as a strong one, and so I had to give it to Sopir, the *pemangku* of the *barong,* the day before it was first used. His wife made a special *prayascita* offering for it, and it was kept in the *barong's* pavilion overnight. Only then could it be used in connection with the performance.

In our village the word "kris" is not often used. Villagers instead use euphemisms, *kakadutan,* from the word for "belt," and *saselet* — "to have a kris in one's hand or sheath." This indirect nomination is another sign of the respect the Balinese have for the power of the kris. For example, the Barong, which is very powerful, is usually called *pelawatan,* which means roughly "dance costume." Disregarding this politesse is considered *pramada,* "insubordinate" and one who does this risks endangerment.

Today one does not often see Balinese people wearing kris. But even well into this century, some villages, especially the more remote Bali Aga villages, had strict rules requiring anyone who left town to wear his kris. This is no longer enforced. But one almost always sees males wearing kris when they are involved in important ceremonies connected with rites of passage, such as tooth filing. Most male dancers wear a kris. And the members of a *barong* group may also wear them. When used in one of the rites of passage or in a dance, the kris is normally slung across the back of the man, handle on the right, held in place by a long cloth belt that is wrapped over his shoulders and under his arms.

A symbolic act occasionally seen at a wedding involves the husband-to-be piercing a small plaque, placed amid offerings, with his kris. Sometimes this is arranged to cause red *brem*, rice wine, to spill out — this has been considered to symbolize the man piercing his wife's hymen with his penis, attributing yet another magical power to his kris. In fact, there are a number of comments in the literature about the kris being a phallic symbol, although I have never heard this explicitly stated by Balinese people.

Our *barong* performances usually involve a dozen or more people who go into trance, then "stab" themselves with kris. Sometimes as many as 20 or more do this. And every member of the group of attendants, the *sekan barong*, who has a kris wears it stuck in his belt. As I have mentioned earlier, almost all of these kris are rather ordinary, with no decoration and plain, undecorated blades. Of the more than 100 members of the Barong group, there are perhaps 40 who own kris. Of these, there are maybe 25 that are deemed strong enough to be used by those who stab themselves. These kris usually have a thick blade with a reinforcing rib down its length.

The people who go into trance and engage in this self-stabbing ritual are called, in Jimbaran, the *babuten*. They become enraged at the Barong's antagonist, Rangda, and work themselves into a frenzy. Their faces are drawn with strain and hatred. Just when Rangda is berating Barong most actively, they jump up from where they have been seated, sobbing on the ground by their Barong, and, grabbing a kris from the nearest member of the group, rush headlong down a narrow aisle left by onlookers in the middle of the main street and confront Rangda with their kris ready for attack. In our village no *babuten* actually strikes Rangda with his kris. I have seen villages where they do. But the Rangda is so powerful that she can withstand the thrust and is unscathed. In Jimbaran, the *babuten*, frustrated at their inability to defend their Barong, go back into the temple and usually spend half an hour or so in a frenzy of self-stabbing. Muscles strain as the kris blade is directed against their chests. But the power of the Barong is greater than the power of the kris, and few ever wound themselves.

Sometimes there is a wound, and if this occurs it is always attributed to a violation by the wounded *babuten* of one of the various taboos that he, as a member of the *sekan barong*, must observe. The *pemangku* then orders that the wounded man be taken into the *barong's* pavilion, where he treats him with holy water, a red hibiscus, sandalwood powder, *arak*, and prayers. It is said that the wounds so treated heal completely within a couple of days.

During the self-stabbing various helpers keep the *babuten* supplied with kris as these are required. Some of these helpers sit on the ground next to the *babuten,* and when a *babuten* is finished with a kris he hands it to the helper, who often ends up with quite a handful. One must never hold the kris with its point down. And one should always put the thumb and fingers of the left hand over the point of the kris that is being held point up in the right hand. This is mainly for protection, lest someone fall down and injure himself. Having held most of the Jimbaran kris at one time or another, I observe that none is really very sharp. In fact, none, including my own, would be useful for any cutting purpose. Certainly the kris is not designed for anything but stabbing. But there is no such thing as a kris in our village with a razor edge. After all, no one would dare attempt to sharpen his kris.

After the melee, the couple of dozen kris that have been used by the *babuten* are collected and placed upon a table in one of the *bales* in the temple. The owners, who may not have seen their own kris for an hour or more, come to the table. Usually there is someone there in charge. Everyone knows everyone else's kris by sight, and they are quickly returned to their rightful owners, taken home, treated with coconut oil, and hung up until the next *barong* performance.

WHERE MIGHT THE INTERESTED VISITOR go to buy a kris? There are innumerable cheap souvenir kris made exclusively for tourists in the Celuk area, but these are not really kris. You could have one made by a Pande, but it would be difficult to find one in the Denpasar area who could do the job. Better to buy one from an antique shop. I can personally recommend the man from whom I bought my own kris, I Wayan Ritug, who lives in Banjar Jeleka in the village of Batuan. His card states that he is a "Tukang Sarung Kris Pusaka, Spesial Kris Antik" — a maker of kris sheaths, specializing in antique kris. That is an accurate description. Ritug's house compound is overflowing with kris. My kris was medium priced. It cost Rp 200,000 — about U.S. $120. There are some that are much cheaper. There are many that are a great deal more expensive. Before I found Rutig I spent weeks searching in vain for a good kris dealer.

PART III

Anniversaries and Temples

CHAPTER 17

Balinese Calendars

A DAY HAS A DOZEN NAMES

THE "INCREDIBLE BUSYNESS" OF BALI, in Margaret Mead's apt phrase, produces an endless stream of festivals, anniversaries, celebrations, dances, dramas, and offerings. And none of these myriad events takes place without an auspicious date first being picked for it. There are good days — *dewasa luwung* — and bad days — *dewasa jelek* — for doing any of these things. Even seemingly ordinary activities, such as chopping wood or building a house, can only be undertaken when the day is right. And keeping track of all these good and bad, proper and dangerous dates are no less than three independent calendar systems.

Like most of the world, the nation of Indonesia has standardized itself around the Gregorian calendar. Government offices are closed on Sundays, and Indonesia observes most of the holidays celebrated in industrial countries, such as New Year's day. Religious holidays of many different faiths — Hindu, Buddhist, Christian, and Muslim — which are tracked according to the familiar calendar, are also celebrated throughout Indonesia. But in Bali, two very different systems are overlaid on the familiar Western calendar — the 210-day Pawukon calendar, and the Saka lunar calendar.

THE PAWUKON, ALSO CALLED THE UKU OR WUKU, was brought to Bali in the 14th century with the fleeing Hindu Majapahits of Java. Although vestiges of this system can still be found in Java, it flourishes in Bali. The Pawukon calendar provides the reference system for most of the religious ceremonies in Bali, as well as market days, personal anniversaries, good and bad luck days, and days for doing special things. A Pawukon "year," which lasts 210 days, should really be thought of as a cycle, since no record is kept of successive "years," nor are they numbered or named. They just pass by.

The Pawukon cycle appears extremely complex to a Westerner because its 210 days are subdivided not according to a simple system of months and weeks, but into ten separate week systems. There is a week that is only one day long, one with two days, one with three, and so on, up to the ten-day week. And they all run concurrently. Each week has been given a Sanskrit-derived name, according to the number of days it has. The three-day week is called Triwara, the five-day week Pancawara, the seven-day week Saptawara, and so on.

And each of the days of each of the ten different weeks has a unique name. Thus any given calendar date may have ten different weekday names, one for each of the ten weeks that are going on simultaneously. The number of day names is 1+2+3+4...+10, a staggering total of 55. Not all these weeks are equally important, however, and most Balinese pay attention to only the three-, five-, and seven-day weeks. The first two are based on the Balinese and Javanese market weeks, in which the village market day rotates among neighboring villages, returning to any given village every three or five days. Three is the common market system in Bali, five in Java. Three and five are also important numbers in Hindu-Balinese theology, representing, to offer just two examples, the Hindu triad and the five directions in space — the four compass points, plus center. The seven-day week is our familiar one, except the Balinese use different weekday names. The sequence of seven is based upon the sun, moon, and the five planets (that is, the five that can be seen with the naked eye). The day names of these three week systems are:

TRIWARA (3-day week)	SAPTAWARA (7-day week)
Pasah (also Busaya)	Redite (falls on our Sunday)
Beteng (also Galang Tegeh or Pekenan)	Coma (Monday)
Kajeng	Anggara (Tuesday)
	Buda or Budha (Wednesday)
PANCAWARA (5-day week)	Wraspati (Thursday)
Umanis	Sukra (Friday)
Paing (also Pahing)	Saniscara (Saturday)
Pon	
Wage	
Keliwon (also Kliwon)	

Further, each of the 30 seven-day weeks in one complete Pawukon cycle has a unique name:

1. Sinta	11. Dunggulan	21. Matal
2. Landep	12. Kuningan	22. Uye
3. Ukir	13. Langkir	23. Menail
4. Kulantir	14. Medangsia	24. Perangbakat
5. Taulu	15. Pujut	25. Bala
6. Gumbreg	16. Pahang	26. Ugu
7. Wariga	17. Krulut	27. Wayang
8. Warigadian	18. Merakih	28. Kelawu
9. Julungwangi	19. Tambir	29. Dukut
10. Sungsang	20. Medangkungan	30. Watugunung

A SPECIAL CALENDAR, CALLED A *TIKA*, keeps track of the most important of the weeks and days in the Pawukon cycle. (See page 175). The *tika* is laid out like a chart, the vertical axis consisting of nine rows, a heading and footing row, and seven rows, each corresponding to one of the days of the seven-day week, with the days listed at the left and Redite (Sunday) at the top. Across the horizontal axis are 30 vertical columns, each representing one of the thirty seven-day weeks with the week name at the top, from Sinta at the left to Watugunung at the far right. The *tika* is read vertically downward rather than across, beginning at Redite of week Sinta and reading down, until past Sanisara of Sinta, when one goes back to the top — Redite of week Landep — then back on down.

Tikas are either carved of wood or painted on cloth. The wood *tikas*, which are hard to find these days, contain no writing. Geometric figures — dots, triangles, dashes, and circles — symbolize the various auspicious days. They are quite small, and there would be no room to fit all 55 day names. The larger cloth *tikas* are more common, and they usually feature abbreviated week and day names inscribed in Balinese script. Small pictures, instead of symbols, illustrate the auspiciousness of any given day.

The paper wall calendar in Bali has a page for each of the 12 months, just as with a Western calendar, but the Balinese calendar also shows the Pawukon cycle and the Saka. The names of the 12 months are very similar to the English names except for those which are altered a little to fit the habits of Indonesian speakers — for example, February turns out to be "Pebruari," since the letter "F" is rarely used in the Indonesian language (I am called "Pred" by everybody).

The paper Balinese calendar reads something like a *tika*, however, from top to bottom as you move from Redite (Sunday) to Saniscara (Saturday) and then to the right for the next week. The calendar lists the weekday names first in Indonesian, then Balinese, English, Japanese, and finally in Chinese. The Pawukon weeks, with their corresponding number, are printed in red ink at the top of each column. Thus the Pawukon cycle is cross-

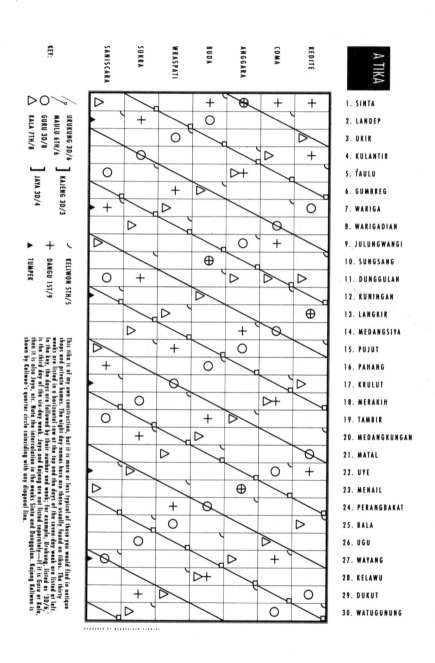

A TIKA

REDITE
COMA
ANGGARA
BUDA
WRASPATI
SUKRA
SANISCARA

KEY:

1. SINTA
2. LANDEP
3. UKIR
4. KULANTIR
5. TAULU
6. GUMBREG
7. WARIGA
8. WARIGADIAN
9. JULUNGWANGI
10. SUNGSANG
11. DUNGGULAN
12. KUNINGAN
13. LANGKIR
14. MEDANGSIYA
15. PUJUT
16. PAHANG
17. KRULUT
18. MERAKIH
19. TAMBIR
20. MEDANGKUNGAN
21. MATAL
22. UYE
23. MENAIL
24. PERANGBAKAT
25. BALA
26. UGU
27. WAYANG
28. KELAWU
29. DUKUT
30. WATUGUNUNG

URUKUNG 30/6   KAJENG 30/3
MAULU 6TH/6
GURU 30/8   JAYA 30/4
KALA 7TH/8

KELIWON 5TH/5
DANGU 1ST/9

TUMPEK

This tika is of my own construction, but it is more or less typical of those you would find in antique shops and private homes. The eight day names here are those usually found on tikas. The thirty weeks are listed in a horizontal row at the top and the days of the seven-day week are listed at left. In the key, the days are followed by their number and week; for example, Urukung, listed as '30/6,' is the third day of the six-day week. Jaya and Kajeng are not listed separately—if it is Jaya, then it is also Jaya, etc. Note the intercalation in the weeks Sinta and Dunggulan. Kajeng Keliwon is shown by Keliwon's quarter circle coinciding with any diagonal line.

RENDERED BY WOODPECKER STUDIOS

referenced with the Gregorian day and date. Armed wiith a *tika,* a Western calendar, and the knowledge of a single date in both, one could pretty easily synchronize them — find the Pawukon week and day for a given Gregorian date, or vice versa. But a Balinese calendar has this worked out.

On the calendar all of the day names for all of the weeks except the one-day week (which can be determined by a simple rule that will be explained below) are printed for every day of the year. The name of the seven-day week, of course, is given in the left hand column. The other eight day names for each calendar date are printed around the number that represents the date, in this pattern:

Three-day week name   Five-day week name
Six-day week name   Four-day week name

DAY
NUMBER

Ten-day week name   Two-day week name
Eight-day week name   Nine-day week name

THE IMPORTANT THREE-, FIVE-, AND SEVEN-DAY WEEKS are fairly easy to follow using a *tika* or Balinese calendar. The chart is based on the seven-day week, but one can pretty easily trace a given day of, say, the five-day week — it will just repeat more frequently than one of the seven-day week days, thus falling diagonally across the chart instead of horizontally. The days of the three-, five-, and seven-day weeks are sequential. So are those for the less important four-, eight-, and nine-day weeks.

But the days of the one-, two-, and ten-day weeks are not sequential. Weekdays for these three seem to pop up just randomly. For example, the days of the two-day week are Menga and Pepet. Abbreviating the two days M and P, over five seven-day weeks, the following pattern emerges for the two-day week:

MMPMPPP
PPMMMMM
MPPPPPM
PMMMPMP
MPMPMPM

Each line represents one 7-day week, Redite to Saniscara; after five weeks, 35 days, the cycle repeats.

The reason for this seemingly strange pattern is that the days of the two-day week are derived from the combined *urips*, or ritual numbers, of the five-day weekday and the seven-day weekday. Each day in the five-day week has a special number associated with it, as does each day in the seven-day week. Determining which day it is in the two-day week requires adding these two numbers — if the sum is even, the day is Menga; if odd, Pepet.

The *urips* of the five- and seven-day weekdays are:

PANCAWARA (*urip*)	SAPTAWARA (*urip*)
Umanis (5)	Redite (5)
Paing (9)	Coma (4)
Pon (7)	Anggara (3)
Wage (4)	Budha (7)
Keliwon (8)	Wraspati (8)
	Sukra (6)
	Saniscara (9)

The *urips* come from the several sacred *lontars*, palm-leaf scriptures, devoted to the calendar system. The formula results in a repetition after 35 days, because the *urips* of the 5- and 7-day weeks will be identical after a period of 5 times 7 or 35 days — then the pattern repeats again.

The formula to determine the name of the one-day week is: add the *urip* of the Saptawara to the *urip* of the Pancawara, as above. If the result is odd, the day is Luang. If the sum is even there is no one-day week that day. The day is vacant. One might reasonably think that every day would be the same day of the week for a week that has only one day, but the formula says no — on some days there just isn't any one-day week. That is why it was carefully specified that a given calendar day *may* have ten different day names. It may have only nine. The pattern of the day name for the one-day week is the same as that for the two-day week, repeating its cycle every 35 days. Since the day names of the one- and two-day weeks are determined by the same *urip* formula, there is a correlation between the two. The one-day week is always Luang on Pepet of the two-day week; it is vacant on Menga of the two-day week.

Determining the day name of the Dasawara, the ten-day week, is a bit more complex: add the *urip* of the Pancawara to that of the Saptawara, as above. Then add 1, and divide the total by 10. The day of the ten-day week is determined by the remainder of this division. For example, if the Pancawara day is Umanis and the Saptawara day is Redite, the sum of their *urips* is 10 (5 plus 5). Adding 1 makes 11 which, divided by 10, gives 1 and a remainder of 1. A remainder of one, andthe ten-day week name is Pandita. A remainder of two, Pati, and so on, according to the list below:

DASAWARA (*urip*)
Pandita (1)
Pati (2)
Suka (3)
Duka (4)
Sri (5)
Manuh (6)
Manusa (7)
Raja (8)
Dewa (9)
Raksasa (none)

The number of days in the Pawukon cycle, 210, is not divisible by four, eight, or nine; thus the four-, eight-, and nine-day weeks require adjustment to keep the cycles even. This kind of adjustment to a calendar, like the addition of a February 29 every leap year, is called intercalation. Dividing 210 by 9 leaves a remainder of 3, and the 3 days are added to the Pawukon at the very beginning of the cycle. Dangu, the first day of the nine-day week, occurs on Redite (Sunday) of Sinta, the first week of the Pawukon. Because of intercalation, the next three days of Sinta are also Dangu of the nine-day week. This period, coinciding with the important religious festival called Pagerwesi, is sometimes called Dangupat (*empat* meaning "four"). The succession continues normally on the fifth day of Sinta, which is Jangur, the second day of the nine-day week.

SANGAWARA (9-day)
Dangu
Jangur
Gigis
Nohan
Ogan
Erangan
Urungan
Tulus
Dadi

Dividing 210 by either four or eight leaves the same remainder, two. Therefore, two extra days must be added to both the four- and eight-day weeks. The intercalation for these weeks is a little more complicated. Both intercalations take place the first three days of the 11th seven-day week, Dunggulan. The first day of Dunggulan is also Jaya, the third day of the four-day week, as well as Kala, the seventh day of the eight-day week. The following two days of Dunggulan, Coma (Monday) and Anggara (Tuesday), are also Jaya and Kala. Then the regular succession of day names picks up again. Buda (Wednesday) of Dunggulan is Menala, the last day of the four-day week, and Uma, the last day of the eight-day week.

CATURWARA (4-day)	ASATAWARA (8-day)
Sri	Sri
Laba	Indra
Jaya	Guru
Menala	Yama
	Ludra
	Brahma
	Kala
	Uma

THE MOST IMPORTANT DAYS IN THE PAWUKON CYCLE occur when special days in one of the week systems intersect with important days in one of the other week systems, that is, when cycles overlap. The closest thing to this in our Gregorian system is "Friday the 13th," when a particular date lands on a particular day of the week. But this coincidence date occurs at irregular intervals, since our months have irregular numbers of days. The intervals between coincidence dates in the Balinese calendar are regular because there is no variation in the lengths of the various weeks and all of the important conjunctions involve the three-, five-, and seven-day weeks, which have orderly progressions of day names.

To determine the interval between the repetition of coincidence days you multiply the number of days in one of the sets by the number of days in the other set. For example, suppose that we have two sets of weeks, a two-day week and a three-day week. Suppose that some event occurs when the first day of the two-day week coincides with the first day of the three-day week. The interval between these events is every 6 (2 times 3) days.

KAJENG KELIWON. The most important of these conjunction days takes place when the last days of the three- and five-day weeks coincide. It is named after the two days, Kajeng and Keliwon, and occurs every 15 days. Kajeng Keliwon is a good day for prayers, and many temple anniversary festivals and other religious ceremonies are held on Kajeng Keliwon. But the day is also especially dangerous because evil spirits are about. Every family makes special offerings to guard against the spirits doing any harm. Late in the afternoon of every Kajeng Keliwon one will see women placing offerings on the ground outside the gates of the house compound. Kajeng

Keliwon is also an important day for making offerings to any objects that possess some sort of magical spirit, such as dance masks and *wayang kulit* shadow puppets.

Kajeng Keliwon is usually shown on the *tika*. Since it occurs every two (seven-day) weeks plus one day, the symbols for Kajeng Keliwon on the *tika* will show up on every other vertical column, and each successive symbol will be one horizontal line down from the previous one. There are five other important conjunction days, all of which involve coincidences between one of the days of the seven-day week and one of the days of the five-day week.

SAPTAWARA DAY	PANCAWARA DAY	CONJUNCTION DAY
Buda	Keliwon	*no special name*
Saniscara	Keliwon	Tumpek
Buda	Wage	Buda Cemeng
Anggara	Keliwon	Anggara Kasih
Redite	Keliwon	Pengembang

Each of these conjunction dates repeats at 35-day intervals, since all are specified by coincidences between days of the five- and seven-day weeks. And they go in regular cycles. Starting with the first, there may be a Buda Keliwon in one week. This, of course, occurs on a Wednesday, because Buda is Wednesday. Ten days later, Saturday of the following week, there will be a Tumpek, since this occurs on Saniscara, which is Saturday. Four days later, Wednesday of the next week, there will be a Buda Cemeng. Six days later, Tuesday of the next week, there will be an Anggara Kasih. And five days later, on Sunday of the next week, there will be a Pengembang. Ten days later, on Wednesday of the next week, there will be a Buda Keliwon, and the cycle has started all over again, because this is exactly 35 days after the first Buda Keliwon where we began.

Kajeng Keliwon, a 3- and 5-day week conjunction, lands on one of these 5- and 7-day week coincidence dates every 105 days (5 times 7 times 3) — or twice every Pawukon cycle. Since the 5-7 coincidence days are on a 35-day cycle, there are 6 (210 divided by 35) of them every Pawukon. And at intervals of 105 days, these will also be Kajeng Keliwon days, when the three-, five-, and seven-day weeks all coincide with respect to a particular set of three days.

The five important five-day/seven-day coincidences require special offerings and prayers, just like Kajeng Keliwon. Some are considered good days, some bad. Special events, such as temple anniversary ceremonies, are often scheduled for these days. And most personal events, such as rites of passage — marriage, tooth filing, cremation, and so on — are timed to occur on one of these dates. Thus a visitor to Bali seeking some sort of ceremony to attend should consult the calendar to find one or another of these coincidence dates, since his or her luck will be best on one of them.

TUMPEK. Tumpek is one of the most interesting of the coincidence dates. As mentioned above, Tumpek occurs six times in every Pawukon and each of these dates is separately important. The first Tumpek to take place every cycle is Tumpek Landep, the Saturday of Landep, the second week of the Pawukon. This is a day of offerings to weapons of war, particularly the sacred kris short swords, but also guns or other weapons. If a family owns such a weapon, on Tumpek Landep it is reverently unsheathed in the family temple, sprinkled with holy water, and presented with offerings of woven coconut leaves, flowers, and fruits. Incense and sandalwood are burned, and family members, a lay priest, or a *balian* — a kind of shaman — offer prayers. The *balian* will know the proper mantras for the weapon.

Although originally specified for weapons of war, the chief recipients of attention on Tumpek Landep today are motorcycles, trucks, and automobiles which, though certainly lethal weapons, seem hardly to be what the founders of Balinese Hinduism had imagined. No matter to the Balinese however, and plaited coconut leaves are hung from the bars and mirrors of motorcycles, and holy water and grains of rice are sprinkled on the machine. Ceremonial cloths are wrapped around the seat. The hoods of cars, trucks, and buses are always dressed with cloth, batik or brocade, to approximate the *kambens* worn by people at ceremonial occasions. A woven ceremonial mat called a *lamak* is hung from the radiator grill. And special little offering baskets are placed on the dashboard. (My computer, made of "iron," gets offerings on Tumpek Landep as well.) A priest or lay priest may be called upon to minister prayers. This practice has become so widespread that some Balinese jokingly refer to the day as Tumpek Jepang, after the country of origin of most of the island's vehicles.

Tumpek Uduh falls five weeks later on Saturday of Wariga, the seventh week. This day has many alternate names, including Tumpek Nyuh ("coconut"). This is a day to offer respect to trees, particularly the coconut palm, that are important to the livelihood of the Balinese. In South Bali the trees are dressed in traditional Balinese clothes, complete with a headband, the *udeng,* a kilt-like *kamben,* and a special scarf, *saput,* as a belt. Then the tree is hit ceremonially with a hammer to notify it that offerings are nearby and to ask it to produce abundant fruit. Rice porridge offerings are hung on the trees and placed on large altars in front of them, and prayers and holy water are offered. The prayers and offerings take place throughout Bali, but dressing up the trees seems to be unique to the southern part of the island.

The third Tumpek is the most important, partially because it is also a Kajeng Keliwon and partly because it marks the end of the most important of the regular religious ceremonies, called Galungan. Tumpek Kuningan, usually called just Kuningan, takes place on the Saturday of the 12th week of the Pawukon cycle, which is the Tumpek's namesake. The activities of Kuningan — which comes from the word for "yellow," *kuning,* because the turmeric in rice offerings gives them this color — is part of the elaborate Galungan ceremony which will be described below.

On the 17th week Tumpek Krulut takes place, taking its name, like Kuningan, from the week of its occurrence. On this day offerings are made to the musical instruments, masks, and dance costumes used in many of the religious ceremonies in Bali. The instruments and other paraphernalia are decorated with coconut leaf offerings, and holy water is sprinkled over them. Sometimes the members of the group that uses the instruments and the costumes and masks gather to pray and be blessed also. There is some variation to this practice. In some parts of Bali Tumpek Krulut is ignored, and homage is paid to these objects on the last Tumpek of the Pawukon.

Tumpek Kandang, sometimes called Tumpek Andang, falls five weeks later, on Saturday of Uye, the 22d week of the Pawukon cycle. The name comes from *kandang,* the Balinese word for the household animal pen, because this is the day to honor domestic animals, especially cows and pigs, which are highly valued by the Balinese. The cows are washed, *kambens,* just like those humans wear, are thrown over their backs, and special cone-shaped spirals of coconut leaf are placed on their horns. The pigs are usually just decorated by wrapping a white cloth about their bellies. The animals are given special foods, prayers are offered, and they are sprinkled with rice and holy water.

The sixth and last of the series, Tumpek Ringgit, or Tumpek Wayang, is again a Kajeng Keliwon, and thus particularly important. Some areas of Bali use this date for making offerings to musical instruments and dance equipment. But this day is always the most important for the shadow play puppets, the *wayang kulit.* Many families have inherited puppets from an ancestor who performed them, a *dalang.* Of course, all *dalangs* have sets of them. The puppets are taken from their box, placed in position just as if an actual performance were being given, and blessed by the owner. A *dalang* will remove all his puppets from storage — as many as 100 of them — and set them all up to receive the offerings. It is considered very unlucky if a baby is born on this date, and if such an event should take place on this inopportune day, a special ceremony has to be performed in order to purify the child and protect it from harm.

GALUNGAN DAYS. The ten days between Wednesday of Dunggulan, the

11th week, and Saturday of Kuningan, the 12th week, are a period called Galungan, or the Galungan Days, starting on the day Galungan and ending on the day Kuningan. During this period the most important regular religious celebration in the Pawukon cycle is held. The deified ancestors of the family descend to their former homes during Galungan, and they must be entertained, and welcomed with prayers and offerings. Families with deceased relatives who are buried and have not yet been cremated — thus not yet deified — must make offerings at the graves.

Everyone gets to work. *Penjors*, long bamboo poles hung with offerings, are erected everywhere. The tops of the *penjors* arching over the narrow roads look for all the world like the top of a gothic cathedral. Commerce practically ceases during the Galungan Days. Schools are closed, and the normal life of the village concentrates exclusively upon the events surrounding this very sacred period. On the Sunday before Galungan, called Penyekeban, from *sekeb*, "to cover up," green bananas are sealed in huge clay pots upon which a small coconut husk fire burns. Lots of bananas are required for Galungan offerings, and this heat treatment ripens them quickly. The next day, Penyajaan, is devoted to making the many colored cakes of fried rice dough, *jaja*, that are so loved by the Balinese and used in many ceremonies as offerings. The village markets are full of *jaja* of every description in case a busy housewife has no time to make them herself. On the day before Galungan, called Penampahan — from *nampah*, "to slaughter an animal" — pigs or turtles are killed for the traditional Galungan morning feasts. Featured at these feasts is the traditional *lawar*, a spicy hash made of finely ground turtle meat or pork and dozens of spices. Five different kinds of hash are prepared, as are sticks of *saté*.

Galungan day is a time for prayer, family get-togethers, and offerings. Almost no work is accomplished between then and Kuningan day. The day after Galungan — called Manis Galungan because it falls on the day Umanis of the five-day week — is a time for visiting friends, and the roads are jammed with cars and motorcycles. Kuningan marks the end of the Galungan celebration. It is a time for family groups, prayers, and still more offerings, as the ancestors return to heaven. (Actually this return is supposed to be five days after Galungan, and the arrival of the ancestors is five days before Galungan, but not many people know that, and it really makes little difference.) The day after Kuningan is usually called Manis Kuningan (even though it falls in the next week, Langkir), and is a time for a holiday, visiting, and fun.

There are two interpretations of the three Sugian days. Some people accept both. Many know of neither. One is that this period is symbolic of the Mayadenawa story (See CHAPTER 4). Sugian Tenten, from *enten* "remember," or "wake up," should bring to mind the triumph of dharma

over adharma. Sugian Jawa commemorates the help of the Majapahit
Javanese in defeating Mayadenawa. And Sugian Bali celebrates the victory
of the Balinese and of dharma. The other interpretation is that the latter
two days symbolize the spiritual cleansings of the *bhuana agung*, the
macrocosmos, and of the *bhuana alit*, the microcosmos. In some parts of
Bali it is traditional on this day for the wife or mother of male members of
the family to make offerings to them and symbolically wash their feet.

In earlier times the 35 days following Galungan were a period during
which it was not permitted to marry, pay debts, or buy animals. The period
is known by some as Buncal Balung meaning, loosely translated, "throw
away a large bone." These prohibitions are seldom enforced in modern-day
Bali, although the day following this period, Buda Keliwon Pahang, is still a
popular one for weddings. The date is sometimes called Pegat Uwakan, or
Pegat Wakan, meaning, roughly, "to be given permission." There is some
controversy among experts as to whether the 35-day period of prohibition
traditionally began on Galungan day, in which case it would end on Pegat
Uwakan, or whether it began on Kuningan Day, in which case it would end
on Tumpek Krulut.

An indication of the importance of Galungan can be found in a theory
offered by Dutch-Indonesian anthropologist Roelof Goris. Noting that the
first seven-day week of the Pawukon, Redite-Sinta, does not have weekday
names that correspond to the first days of each of the ten weeks, Goris
speculated that the cycle used to begin on what is now the 13th week,
Langkir. On this day, the first to follow the Galungan-Kuningan ceremonies, the first days of the important weeks fall together. This would
make the Galungan days a climactic year-end ceremony, which made sense
to Goris. Note that the intercalation for the eight- and four-day weeks takes
place at the beginning of the Galungan days. There is no confirmation to
be found for this theory, however, and it must remain conjecture.

PAWUKON BEGINNING/END CELEBRATION. The end and beginning of the
the current Pawukon cycle is punctuated with ceremony, although the celebration is not as grand as Galungan. The very last day of the Pawukon,
Saturday of the 30th week, Watugunung, is a special day for Saraswati,
goddess of learning and wife of Brahma. Her festival day is a time for making offerings for books, especially the sacred *lontar* palm leaf books. All
books are the subject of devotion on this day. One is not supposed to read
on Hari Raya Saraswati, however. Schools have special ceremonies, and students jam the big temple, Pura Jagat Natha, in Denpasar, for a special early-
morning ceremony in which they pray for success in their studies.

The next four days, the first four of the new Pawukon cycle, are special
religious days. They are most fervently celebrated in North Bali, where

some people put up *penjors* just as for Galungan, and where special offerings are made for the uncremated dead in the cemeteries. The climax of
these four days is on Wednesday of the first week of the Pawukon, a day
called Pagerwesi, coming from two words meaning "iron fence." The suggestion is that one should surround oneself with a strong fortification
against the forces of evil. Pagerwesi is also a day upon which an ancient battle between good and evil is celebrated. The three days preceding
Pagerwesi have special names and are for special activities. Sunday, the first
day of the Pawukon, is called Banyu Penaruh. Many people who live near
the sea go to the beach at dawn and symbolically purify themselves by
bathing. This is a special day for fishermen, who make offerings for their
boats and nets. Monday is called Comaribek, a day that is not widely celebrated. Tuesday is Sabuh-Emas, when one is supposed to make offerings
for jewelry, especially that of gold, and for the Chinese coins that are often
used in offerings.

ANNIVERSARIES. Many Balinese anniversaries are observed according to the
Pawukon cycle. The Balinese refer to a period of five seven-day weeks as
one month. There are no "months" on the Pawukon calendar, but a division of the 210 days into six 35-day periods conveniently approximates the
lunar month of a little over 29 days. The first really big ceremony for a
newborn child occurs after three of these "months," or 105 days. The ceremony is called *ngelubulanin*, from *telu*, "three," and *bulan*, "month." A
child's first birthday, called an *oton*, takes place six "months" after birth. At
this ceremony the baby is allowed to touch the ground for the first time.
The Balinese consider it base for a baby to crawl around on the ground,
animal-like, so young babies are always carried. When they touch the
ground at their *oton*, a colorful ceremony is held. In some areas they are
covered by a cage like those used for fighting cocks. In fishing areas a circular throwing net is flung over mother and child. Lots of offerings are made,
and many prayers are said for the health and wealth of the baby. From this
oton comes the oft-heard saying that a Balinese has two "birthdays" a year.
He doesn't really. Many people do celebrate their *otons* after growing up,
but it is a rather private affair, with only prayers and an offering. And it
doesn't come twice a year, but rather once every Pawukon cycle — six
Balinese "months," or 210 days.

Often the calendar date of a birthday is forgotten. It is only the
Pawukon date and the year that is remembered. For example, my friend
Budi knows that he was born in 1953 on Redite-Menail — Sunday of the
23d week. But he doesn't know what Gregorian calendar day that was. And
it is impossible to determine this date because there were two Redite-
Menails in 1953. If there had been only one, it would be easy, with a calcu-

lator, to figure out the calendar date.

Most, but not all, Balinese temple anniversary celebrations are observed once every 210 days. And practically all of the activities concerned with planting, growing, and harvesting rice are connected with auspicious Pawukon days.

ANOTHER, EQUALLY IMPORTANT, BALINESE CALENDAR system is the Saka calendar, sometimes spelled, in Romanized Sanskrit, Çaka. This Hindu calendar had its origins in South India during the reign of a ruler by that name. The Saka calendar is a lunar calendar. Each of the 12 lunar months ends on a new moon, called Tilem. The calendar begins the day after the new moon that ends the ninth lunar month — almost always in Gregorian March. New Year's Day, the first day of the 10th lunar month, is called Nyepi and is an important religious day.

Unlike the Pawukon, the Saka is formally a calendar, with numbered years. The sequence begins with the commencement of the Saka era of rule in India. Because this tribe, considered to be Scythian, came to power in the Gregorian year A.D. 78, the Saka year numbering system is 78 years behind the Gregorian system. Thus Bali entered the 20th Saka century on Nyepi of 1901 — March 29, 1979. This date also marked the climax of the greatest series of religious ceremonies ever held in Bali, Eka Dasa Rudra, a grand exorcism of evil and a bringing back into harmony of the microcosm and the macrocosm. Eka Dasa Rudra — though extremely rare — is scheduled according to the Saka calendar. (See CHAPTER 21.)

It is not unusual for calendar systems to begin in March, around the time of the vernal equinox, the first day of spring, and the general re-awakening from the cold and dreariness of winter. Although Bali has no winter, parts of India do, and the Saka calendar came from India. Even Gregorian calendar month names reflect this: although October is our tenth month, November the eleventh, and December the twelfth, the names of the months are derived from the Latin words for eight, nine, and ten, because the year originally began in what we now call March.

The day before Nyepi is a time for casting out evil. Animals are sacrificed and the *pratimas*, the small statues that serve as receptacles for gods and deified ancestors, are carried to the holy springs or to the sea for symbolic washing in a rite called *melasti*. A big enclosure of woven coconut leaf mats is assembled at the village crossroads and filled with offerings to the *bhutas* and *kalas*, the evil spirits that always try to interfere with human activities. Late in the afternoon, everyone — especially little boys — bangs on anything bangable, including petroleum drums, pots and pans, and pieces of metal roofing. In addition to raising this ruckus, they all wave flaming torches. General pandemonium takes over the village, as the people scare away the evil spirits with shouts and din and flame.

Nyepi, New Year's Day itself, is supposed to be a day of silence, prayer, and meditation. Nobody is to eat, drink, drive, smoke, or go outside the house compound. The purpose for this is to make each village, in fact all of Bali, appear abandoned to the evil spirits — or at least those few who remain after the previous day's activities. Thinking everyone has left, they will leave too. These once-strict requirements are no longer uniformly observed in the urban areas. But some rural villages do observe the day of silence and station guards to make sure nobody violates the prohibitions.

This explanation for Nyepi is the one most commonly heard from guides and read in books. But according to my *pedanda* and Hindu scholars, the noise on New Year's Eve is not designed to scare the demons away. The noise is in fact intended to wake them up so they will see the offerings that have been laid for them. The quietude on the day after is not intended to trick the *bhutas* and *kalas* into thinking that everyone has left, rather it is a matter of showing contentment that the forces of evil are satisfied and will not bother us — for a while, anyway.

Each lunar month has 30 lunar days — 15 days of waxing moon, called *tanggal,* and 15 days of waning moon, called *panglong.* Sometimes these are spelled *penanggal* and *pengelong.* The waxing and waning days are numbered 1 to 15. On the widely used Balinese paper calendar, the waxing and waning day numbers are displayed immediately to the right of the date number for each day, in between the day names of the four- and two-day Pawukon weeks. Waxing days are printed in red, waning days in black. Waxing day number 15 is full moon, Purnama, indicated by a large red circle immediately to the left of the number representing the Gregorian date. Waning day number 15 is new moon, Tilem, and is indicated by a black circle in the same position. The name of the month occupies the bottom line of each date square. The Balinese word for lunar month is *sasih,* and the names of the months are just the Sanskrit words from 1 to 12:

THE SASIH

1. Kasa	7. Kepitu
2. Karo	8. Kaulu
3. Ketiga	9. Kesanga
4. Kapat	10. Kedasa
5. Kelima	11. Jiyestha
6. Kenem	12. Sadha

The actual lunar cycle, from one new moon to the next, takes slightly more than 29-1/2 lunar days, not the 30 specified by the Saka calendar. If 30 solar days corresponded to 30 lunar days every month the observed full and new moons would not coincide with the calendric full and new moons — the phases would appear half a day earlier every month, an error that would quickly throw the calendar noticeably off. Yet the calendar prescribes 30 lunar days in a lunar month.

To keep this error from accumulating, the Saka calendar incorporates an adjustment. Every 9 weeks — 63 days — 2 lunar days are made to fall upon a single solar day. Such a day is called *ngunalatri,* from the Sanskrit for "minus one night." The paper calendar indicates this day by printing 2 lunar day numbers, separated by a slash, to the right of the date number. Currently this double lunar day is set always to fall on a Wednesday. If you look at the calendar and run horizontally along a Buda/Wednesday line, you will find such a *ngunalatri* every 9 weeks. In the past, the *ngunalatri* did not always fall on a Wednesday, and it may not do so in the future. According to the officials at the Department of Religion in Denpasar, and according to those at the Central Hindu Dharma Committee, the *ngunalatri* day of the week should change every century. It did not change at the end of the Saka 19th century in 1979, but serious consideration is being given to changing it now.

Determining past practices in the formulation of Balinese calendars is extremely difficult. Only one reasonably complete collection of old calendars exists in all of Bali, at the Gedong Kertya *lontar* library in Singaraja. The collection dates back to 1935, but there are several gaps, and most of the early calendars contain unintelligible symbols, omissions, and abbreviations with no standards of nomenclature. From these records I found that the *ngunalatri* was observed in the past sometimes on Wednesday, sometimes on Sunday or Tuesday, and sometimes on several different days of the week in one year. (An aside: Strangely enough, the year 1963 is missing. That was the year that Gunung Agung, Bali's sacred and highest volcano, erupted during the Eka Dasa Rudra ceremony, killed hundreds, and nearly destroyed the most important temple in Bali.) In any case, it is obvious that until recently there was no standardization. For example, according to these old calendars, North Bali had its full and new moons a day earlier than South Bali.

The calendars become more or less decipherable in the year 1955. This is the first year that the calendar was compiled by I Ketut Bangbang Gede Rawi. This is the man whose photograph, taken some years ago, adorns every page of the most common calendar. But when I visited him in Celuk, I could not extract any useful information from him. He is quite secretive about his work. For some years, he was individually in complete control of formulating the calendar. Only in recent years has the Department of Religion codified the calendar systems. The rules are spelled out now, but they were not as recently as 1980. The result is inconsistencies and errors of various magnitudes almost up to the present.

There is a complete cycle of *ngunalatri* days relative to moon phases every 32 months. That is, if a double lunar day date occurs on a new moon on a particular date, it will next fall on a new moon 32 months later. The 32-month cycle contains 19 29-day months and 17 30-day months, for a total of 945 days. This averages out to 29.53125 days a month. According to modern astronomical observation, this figure is in error by only 0.002 percent — not bad for a rule of thumb intercalation.

The lunar year may contain either 354 or 355 solar days, depending upon where in the 32-month cycle it begins. After the completion of one year, if no compensation were made, Nyepi would slip backward through the Gregorian calendar anywhere from 10 to 12 days. This would mean Nyepi would fall back about one month every three years and would soon take place nowhere near the vernal equinox. This happens to any lunar calendar that is not adjusted to take into account the differences between the lunar month and the solar year. The Islamic calendar is a good example. Such religious periods and days as Ramadan slip backwards through the Gregorian calendar year after year, and one cannot expect them to fall at any particular season or in any particular month of the year.

The Saka is adjusted by inserting an intercalary month every so often. Precisely when and where to do this has been a source of confusion for years. The old calendars reveal a total lack of pattern or regularity. Recently, the Department of Religion has decided that the guiding principle for intercalation should be that the new moon — the last day — of the seventh lunar month, Sasih Kepitu, must occur in January. If it does not so fall, then an extra month must be added ahead of time to keep Tilem Kepitu from slipping back into December. If left to itself, Tilem Kepitu, and all other lunar dates, would slip back 10 to 12 days a year. Sooner or later it would fall in December.

The department picked Tilem Kepitu because it is a special day in the Saka calendar called Siwa Latri, the night of the Hindu god Siwa, dissolver of life. The new moon is always associated with fear, darkness, and death. Many Pura Dalems — temples to Siwa — in Bali hold their anniversaries on a Tilem. And, being nearest the December solstice, the new moon night of January, Tilem Kepitu, should be the darkest night of the year. Thus it would naturally be associated with Siwa.

On the night of Siwa Latri one is supposed to stay up all night and meditate about Siwa, perhaps the most emphasized and important manifestation of God in Bali. Schools, especially, encourage this practice. And there is an all-night meditation ceremony held at Pura Jagat Natha, the big temple in Denpasar. There is a long legend about the origin of Siwa Latri. It has many variations, but basically it involves a hunter who was caught in the forest on Tilem Kepitu at nightfall. To avoid wild animals, he climbed a tree. To keep himself awake, so that he wouldn't slip, he picked leaves off the tree, which happened to be a sacred *bodhi* tree. Unknown to the hunter, there was a *linggam,* a shrine to Siwa, just below the tree, and the leaves fell on it. Siwa assumed that the hunter was showering him with offerings and granted him safety and protection.

The curious thing is that Tilem Kepitu is *not* the darkest night of the year. Bali is some 8 to 9 degrees south of the equator and thus its period of highest sun comes during the winter, the opposite of the Northern Hemisphere. The December solstice is the longest, not the shortest, day of the year, and Siwa Latri is the shortest new moon night, not the longest. The Saka calendar had its origin in India, however, and in India the sun is lowest at the December solstice. No Balinese to whom I spoke was aware that Siwa Latri is not the darkest new moon night of the year. In any case, Bali is so close to the equator that there is very little variation in the length of the day or night from season to season anyway — at most, about one hour — so the difference would be hard to notice.

In non-leap years the intercalary month is added after the 12th month, Sasih Sadha, and is called Sasih Mala Sadha. In leap years the intercalary month is added after the 11th month, Sasih Jiyestha, and is called Sasih Mala Jiyestha. The intercalary month may be either 29 or 30 days long, according to where it comes in the normal sequence.

On the average, there is a year containing an intercalary month every third or fourth year, more often every fourth. Some Balinese say that during intercalary months one may not observe the usual good, bad, dangerous, lucky, and unlucky days that are normal during regular months. The calendar still shows these auspicious and inauspicious days, so one wonders.

Some temples and villages use the Saka calendar instead of the Pawukon cycle to determine their religious celebrations. Of the 66 major temple anniversary festivals listed by the Department of Religion, 40 are keyed to the Pawukon cycle and 26 to the Saka calendar. The Saka ceremonies are usually held at Purnama rather than at Tilem, although, as previously mentioned, Pura Dalem anniversary celebrations are often held at Tilem.

NOT ALL ANNIVERSARIES FALL ON PAWUKON OR SAKA dates. The island has its share of civil festivals as well. Independence Day, August 17, is celebrated throughout Indonesia by parades of marchers, foot races, band concerts, military displays, and public entertainments. On this date in 1945 President Sukarno proclaimed Indonesia's independence from the Dutch — an independence that was not actually won for another five bloody years of war.

September 20 is a special day in Bali because it commemorates the end of the Denpasar raja. On this date, in 1906, a Dutch army that landed at

Sanur advanced upon Denpasar. The royal family, dressed in its ceremonial best, confronted the Dutch on the Denpasar-Sanur road and dared the Dutch to advance farther. The Dutch fired on the crowd. Faced with certain defeat — kris are no match for rifles — the raja stepped out of his palanquin and signaled his priest to stab him with the sacred kris. His wives and the rest of the palace inhabitants turned their kris upon themselves. In Balinese, the word *puputan* means "conclusion," or "bringing to an end." The event is known to all as Puputan Badung, the end of Denpasar nobility, and it is commemorated each year by a sort of fair on the large public field near the four-faced statue in Denpasar, sometimes called Puputan Badung Square. The field has a huge statue portraying the Balinese who met the Dutch. At the fair there are many refreshment booths, various kinds of public entertainment, including *wayang kulit* shadow puppets, and a long drama given in a temporary outdoor theater, depicting the battle with the Dutch.

November 10 is Indonesia's National Heroes' Day, and November 20 is Heroes' Day in Bali, the anniversary of the 1946 battle of a small army of 96 Balinese troops under the leadership of Lt. Col. I Gusti Ngurah Rai against a vastly superior Dutch army. The battle symbolizes the Balinese part in the war of Independence. Every last man in Ngurah Rai's small force died in the battle at the village of Marga, 27 kilometers north of Denpasar. Ngurah Rai's name is given to Bali's International Airport, and there is a statue of him at the east end of the runway.

THE BALINESE PAPER CALENDAR CONTAINS much more information than just cross-references between the Pawukon, Gregorian, and Saka calendars. At the bottom of each column, printed in large red capitals, is the *ingkel* for the week. This is a schedule of forbidden activities. If the week is *ingkel sato* one may not cut, kill, or make offerings to four-legged animals. *Mina* applies the prohibition to fish, *manuk* to birds, *taru* to wood, and *buku* to any jointed object, such as bamboo.

The first section on the left, below the *ingkel*, is a list of the important Hindu dates for the month, with a brief description of the most important. Tilems and Purnamas are listed, important coincidence dates, and special days, such as those involved with Galungan and Pagerwesi. Next are listed the *odalans* — temple anniversaries — for some of the more important temples, not only in Bali, but also Balinese temples in other parts of Indonesia. This is only a partial list of *odalans,* but it should be useful to anyone who is interested in attending one or more. The next section is titled: "Dewasa Ayu untuk melakukan s.b.b." This is a list of auspicious days for certain activities. A Balinese, glancing at this list, can determine the best days for planting, for holding a cremation, making a fishing net, getting married, and so on. Such lists are frequently consulted.

The last sections of this lower part of the calendar contain lists of religious holidays other than Hindu, by category. Here is such miscellaneous information as eclipses, government holidays, and so on. The right-hand vertical column of the calendar lists, for every day of the month, three classes of what might be called determiners of auspicious and inauspicious days. These three are named Ekajala Resi, Pertiti, and Kala. For one who is unschooled in interpretation, these lists are meaningless — hence the brief note above. But someone with the *lontars* or other publications that tell about Ekajala Resi, Pertiti, and Kala, can obtain detailed information about the activities that are appropriate or inappropriate for each day.

If, for example, the Kala for a given day were Mangap, the day would be a bad one for facing east — if it also happens to be the day Buda Pon. If the Pertiti of a particular day is Upadana, then you should be very careful if you are nine days old, two months old, or nine years old. If you are born on that day, you will be a rather sleepy person, and you will like people very much. The information fills pages and pages of text and is so detailed that hardly anyone could abide by all the prohibitions and encouragements that are offered. Because of the complexity of the matters, most people just go to an authority and let him figure it all out.

The day squares on the calendar also contain information beyond that outlined here. For example, the top line of each square lists the Muslim month and its number. The second line indicates the Chinese month and its number. A truly complete description of the calendar would require again as much space as has already been devoted to it.

CHAPTER 18

Balinese Astrology

BROKEN HOES, CRABS, HEADLESS BODIES

NO BALINESE IN HIS OR HER RIGHT MIND would plan a major event without consulting several calendars, carefully examining the upcoming dates of proven auspiciousness, and picking the exact day that shows all the signs of luck and success. Usually, because the various calendrical systems are so complex and the knowledge of inauspicious and auspicious days so esoteric, one leaves the decision to an expert — perhaps a *pedanda* (priest), and at least a high caste scholar or a *balian*.

Given this belief in the inherent portentiousness of dates, it should come as no surprise that the Balinese attach a similar degree of importance to the date of a particularly important *un*planned event: a birth.

The *pelelintangan* is a chart that enables one to determine the characteristics one will display as a result of having been born on a particular day. It functions something like an astrological chart, but the *pelelintangan* is not based on what we think of as astrology in the West, or even on the seasonal appearance of various constellations. "Having one's chart done" in Bali does not mean looking for "moons" or determining "rising signs." The *pelelintangan* merely cross-references one's birthdate with two of the most important week cycles of the Pawukon calendar.

The Pawukon "year" is an undated, 210-day repeating cycle on which are overlayed ten distinct "weeks." One-day weeks, two-day weeks, three-day weeks, and so on up to ten-day weeks all run concurrently. When determining auspicious days for festivals and ceremonies, the Balinese look for coincidence days, such as those days when the last day of the three-day week falls on the last day of the five-day week — this particular example, an important one, is called Kajeng Keliwon, and the coincidence takes place every 15 days. Although there are ten distinct week cycles in the Pawukon, only three of them — the three-, five-, and seven-day weeks — are really important. The Balinese names for these are, respectively, Triwara, Pancawara, and Saptawara. Each of these has unique names for its week-days:

TRIWARA	PANCAWARA	SAPTAWARA
Pasah (*also* Busaya)	Umanis	Redite (Sunday)
Beteng	Paing (*also* Pahing)	Coma (Monday)
(*also* Galang Tegeh,	Pon	Anggara (Tuesday)
or Pekenan)	Wage	Buda (Wednesday)
Kajeng	Keliwon (*also* Kliwon)	Wraspati (Thursday)
		Sukra (Friday)
		Saniscara (Saturday)

The Kajeng Keliwon coincidence is a day of important religious signifi-cance. But there are hundreds of days, of varying auspiciousness, for all kinds of activities. Important occasions — temple anniversaries, festivals, ceremonies, trips, and so forth — are planned for these days. A special anniversary for the patron deity of our *barong* group in Jimbaran is held every Sukra Pon — when the sixth day of the Saptawara coincides with the third day of the Pancawara. Sukra Pon happens every 35 days. Anggar Kasih, an important Hindu-Balinese religious day, takes place when Anggara of the seven-day week falls on Keliwon, the last day of the five-day week, again, every 35 days. A simple mathematical formula predicts the fre-quency of these coincidence days: multiply the number of days in the two relevant weeks. For any Saptawara-Pancawara coincidence, the time between consecutive occurrences will be 35 days.

The *pelelintangan* is based only on the coincidence of the five- and seven-day weeks. The days of these weeks are laid out as axes of a grid, with five rows and seven columns, each square of which represents one of the 35 possible coincidences of Saptawara and Pancawara days. (See the charts on pages 198 and 199.) The horizontal axis, left to right, lists Redite to Saniscara of the seven-day week. The vertical axis, after the heading row, lists Umanis to Keliwon of the five-day week, then a footing row of general characteristics. The coincidence days run from Redite Umanis in the top left corner to Saniscara Keliwon in the bottom right corner. These 35 possi-bilities are comprehensive; no matter on what day someone is born, it will fall somewhere on the chart.

THE HEADER ROW IN THE *PELELINTANGAN* offers some general attributes for those born on that day of the Saptawara. These attributes apply equally to any of the five Pancawara days listed directly underneath. Each of the seven days has associated with it a god, a *wayang kulit* shadow puppet character, a tree, a bird, and an animal. A syllable — the first in the relevant Saptawara day name — is also an attribute, and the Balinese ascribe certain magical properties to syllables when used, for example, in mantras. A list of these seven groups of attributes, with an explanation of each, is given later in this chapter.

Each of the 35 rectangles of the Saptawara–Pancawara grid represents what is called a "*bintang*." And each of the 35 days bears a *bintang* name. "*pelelintangan*," in fact, is derived from *lintang*, an alternative spelling of *bintang*, meaning "star." The Balinese are not sticklers for spelling.

Almost all the *bintang* names are taken from everyday, tangible objects or animals: plow, coconut tree, rice barn, dog, and so on. Some are supernatural occurrences, such as the demon's head — Sungsang Kala. Some are exotic or mythological animals — elephant, *naga* ("dragon-snake"), *gajah mina* ("elephant fish"), and so on. And each of the 35 pictures on the chart depicts some aspect of the object or idea with which the *bintang* name is associated. For tangible objects or animals, the pictures are obvious. Intangibles are represented by a simple scene. The nature of a person's *bintang* is the nature of the person — someone with a *bintang* of *kelapa*, the coconut tree, would be expected to be good, useful, and honored.

In addition to the picture of the *bintang*, each of the 35 squares contains two short character descriptions. These are taken directly from the sacred *lontar*, or palm leaf book, that specifies *pelelintangan* characteristics. The lontar offers two lists, one with seven and one with 10 descriptions. Each day takes a character description from each of these two lists. (These lists are given later in the chapter.) These 17 character descriptions are accompanied by a descriptive name. One of them, for example, is Laku Api, which means "like fire" and a person with this characteristic would be expected to be volatile and hot-tempered. Some are contradictory, and are thus never paired. For example one could not pair Laku Air, "as water," a person who has very correct behavior, with Tunggak Semi, "flower stem," from the second list, which portends a person who is conceited, arrogant, and belligerent.

To use the *pelelintangan*, the two character descriptions must be combined with the *bintang* to form the final judgement of the personal characteristics of a person born on that day. Some days will have the same pair of character descriptions, but they will differ in bintang. For example, *bintang* Lembu, the bull, which falls on Coma Wage, and *bintang* Kuda, the horse, which falls on Anggara Umanis, both have Laku Api and Wisesa Segara as their character descriptions. Both tend to get angry and have terrible tempers — dictated by their "as fire" and "powerful sea" personality characteristics. But the *bintang* Lembu makes for a person who, though he or she angers quickly, also cools down quickly. And the inherent calmness of *bintang* Kuda attenuates these fiery personality characteristics — once angry, however, the *bintang* Kuda is difficult to calm.

The bottom row of the *pelelintangan*, like the top row, shows characteristics that apply to anyone born on that Saptawara day, regardless of the day of the five-day week. For each day, this row shows one of the seven aspects of the multiheaded demon Kala Maulu, also called Buta Ulu — from *ulu*, "head." *Kalas* and *butas* are generic names for demons. The particular head shown in the bottom row is the aspect that a person born on that day should be most wary of, or on guard against.

SEVEN SHAPES OF BUTA ULU

Redite	*gajah*	elephant
Coma	*asu*	dog
Anggara	*kuda*	horse
Buda	*gagak*	crow
Wraspati	*jadma*	human being
Sukra	*sampi*	cow
Saniscara	*kebo*	water buffalo

The aspect of Buta Ulu listed at the bottom is not the same as the animal given in the general descriptions at the top of the *pelelintangan*. But on one popular version of the *pelelintangan* the seven shapes of Buta Ulu are omitted, instead picturing these animals in the squares along the bottom row. And on another widely available *pelelintangan*, the animals replace the heads in the above list, and are shown attached in each case to the same two-legged figure of a man.

WHAT THEN IS THE SIGNIFICANCE of all these animals, gods, birds, *wayang kulit* puppets, trees, and so on? These various factors influence the character and behavior of a person born on the day associated with any one or group of them, but the relationship goes beyond that. One should give preference and preferential treatment to whichever animals, birds, and gods are his or her own. For example, if a Balinese is going to have a bird around the house, it should be the bird of his or her Saptawara day. Similarly a shrine, or picture, or statue of a god should be of one's Saptawara god. These choices should influence even such decisions as which tree to plant near the house. The proper choice will bring luck, and the wrong choice may bring trouble.

Although essentially stuck with these characteristics for life, a Balinese has a number of options for lessening the influence of the negative ones, and encouraging the positive. By knowing just what the characteristics are, one can pick appropriate days with them in mind, avoid situations where some of the more negative characteristics might come out, and make prayers and offerings to the various gods and demons who could affect one's situation. This in order, respectively, to encourage and discourage their interference.

Most of the specifics of the information given by the *pelelintangan* is quite esoteric to the average Balinese. A *pedanda* will use it when deciding upon a date for a ceremony for that person — say a tooth filing, or wedding — but it is not something that one is always aware of. In fact, it might even be considered presumptuous for a Balinese to imagine that he understood these things. Most people feel they are best left to the experts, the *pedandas* and other religious authorities. In fact, gathering information for this chapter was rather difficult because most of my usual informants had no information about the *pelelintangan*. Several mentioned that this is information studied only by those who are *leyak,* "witches."

FIRST LIST OF CHARACTERISTICS

ARAS KEMBANG: "A Flower Close to Something"
Solves problems easily
Has difficulty producing children
Has many friends
Ignores the well-being of his family
Pays attention to the well-being of the public

ARAS TUDING: "Point to Something"
Courageous
Resolute
Social, friendly
Has many desires
Lustful and passionate

LAKU AIR: "As Water"
Gentle disposition
Correct in behavior; good manners
Many ambitions for leadership
Strong mind; not easily influenced by others
Often quarrels with spouse

SAPTAWARA:	REDITE (Re)	COMA (Co)	ANGGARA (A)	BUDA (Bu)	WRASPATI (Wre)	SUKRA (Su)	SANISCARA (Sa)
DAY:	Sunday	Monday	Tuesday	Wednesday	Thursday	Friday	Saturday
GOD:	Indra	Sri	Brahma	Wisnu	Siwa	Uma	Durga
WAYANG:	Mamri	Galuh	Yaksa-Yaksi	Mentah	Tualen	Sangut	Delem
TREE:	ambaha (banni)	pule	loreş (tungtul)	cincik	bingin banyan	koyo putih	kepuh
BIRD:	siung myna bird	titiran turtle dove	gagak crow	dara pigeon	merta peacock	bango egret	cangak owl
ANIMAL:	garuda	singha lion	sambaha tiger	raja snake	meong cat	kambing goat	kambo bull
PANCAWARA: UMANIS	KALA SUNGSANG / upside down demon / Laku Pandito Sakti / Sumur Sinabo	KELAPA / coconut tree / Laku Angin / Tunggak Semi	KUDA / horse / Laku Api / Wisesa Segara	TANGIS / tears, crying / Laku Bintang / Satrio Wibowo	SANGKATIKEL / broken hoe / Laku Bintang / Satrio Wibowo	BANYAK ANGREM / brooding goose / Aros Tuding / Satrio Wirang	BEGOONG / demon hood / Laku Bulan / Bumi Kapetuk
PAHING	GAJAH / elephant / Laku Bulan / Wisesa Segara	KUKUS (DUPA) / smoke / Laku Bintang / Bumi Kapetuk	YUYU / crab / Laku Api / Wisesa Segara	LUMBUNG / rice granary / Laku Air / Wisesa Segara	SALAH UKUR / wrong size / Laku Suryo / Satrio Wirang	BUBU BOLONG / leaky fish trap / Laku Suryo / Tunggak Semi	RU / arrow / Laku Api / Wisesa Segara
PON	PATREM / stabbing kris / Aros Kembang / Bumi Kapetuk	KIRIMAN / package, gift / Aros Tuding / Sumur Sinabo	ASU / dog / Laku Pandito Sakti / Satrio Wibowo	KARTIKA / Pleiades / Laku Bulan / Bumi Kapetuk	BADE / cremation tower / Laku Bintang / Satrio Wibowo	PRAHU PEGAT / broken boat / Laku Suryo / Laku Kutiop Angin	SUNGENGE / sunflower / Laku Air / Wisesa Segara
WAGE	ULUKU / plow / Laku Angin / Satrio Wibowo	LEMBU / bull / Laku Api / Wisesa Segara	JONG SARAT / full ship / Laku Bumi / Laku Kutiop Angin	TIWA-TIWA / death ceremonies / Laku Suryo / Laku Kutiop Angin	KUMBA / vessel, container / Aros Kembang / Tunggak Semi	MAGELUT / two people embracing / Laku Pandito Sakti / Sumur Sinabo	PUWUH ATARUNG / fighting quails / Laku Bintang / Satrio Wibowo
KELIWON	LAWEYAN / headless body / Laku Bintang / Laku Kutiop Angin	PEDATI / empty cart / Aros Kembang / Satrio Wirang	KALA RAU or SIDAMALUNG / eclipse demon or pig / Aros Tuding / Sumur Sinabo	NAGA / dragon / Laku Air / Bumi Kapetuk		UDANG / shrimp / Laku Bulan / Wisesa Segara	PAGELANGAN / starving / Laku Bumi / Tunggak Semi
BUTA ULU or KALA MAULU	gajah / elephant	cou / dog	kudo / horse	gagak / crow	jadma / human being	sampi / cow	kebo / water buffalo

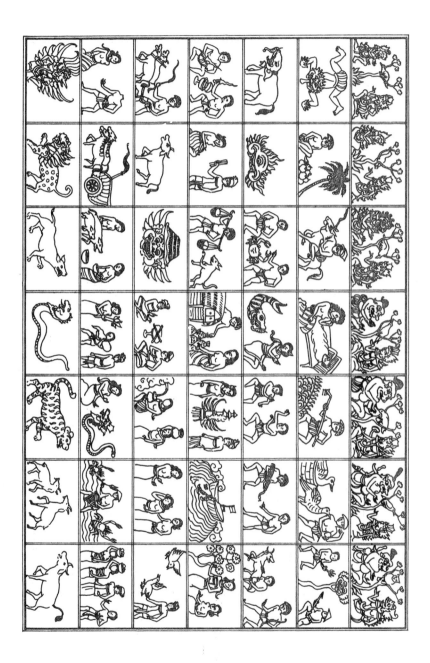

LAKU ANGIN: "As Wind"
    Likes to be flattered
    Likes to behave like a shrewd person
    Cannot be silent
    Likes to brag
    Does not have deep-rooted feelings

LAKU API: "As Fire"
    Radical
    Angry
    Maliciously jealous
    Immodest
    If a woman, she creates problems for others

LAKU BINTANG: "As a Star"
    Quiet, calm
    Gentle disposition
    Does not like to stay awake late at night
    Has talent for selling
    Has strong opinions

LAKU BULAN: "As the Moon"
    Capable worker
    Clever, skilled
    Has wide knowledge
    Knows how to associate with others
    Often takes it easy
    Has a contented life

LAKU BUMI: "As the Earth"
    Taciturn
    Makes decisions too quickly
    Likes to associate with women
    Has difficulty making friends
    Rather lazy

LAKU MATAHARI: (Laku Surya) "As the Sun"
    Intelligent
    Correct in behavior; good manners
    Responsible
    Likes to give information and explanations

LAKU PANDITA SAKTI: "As a Powerful Priest"
    Always believes his problems are easy to solve
    Intelligent, but conceited
    Likes to be praised
    Likes mysticism
    Well-known person

SECOND LIST OF CHARACTERISTICS

BUMI KAPETAK: "Clear Earth"
    Doesn't like to travel
    Diligent in performing his duty
    Likes to meditate

LEBU KETIUP ANGIN: "Dust Blown by Wind"
    Unsteady
    Uncertain position
    Rarely satisfied

SATRIA WIBAWA: "Ruler with Authority"
    Gallant, brave, courageous
    Extravagant and happy life
    Frank and open person; hides nothing

SATRIA WIRANG: "Angry Ruler"
    Angry and hot-tempered
    Defiant

SUMUR SINABA: "Full Well"
    Hot-tempered
    Often disappointed

TUNGGAK SEMI: "Stem of a Flower bud"
    Conceited, arrogant
    Likes to fight
    Likes to maintain his position, even when in error

WISESA SEGARA: "Magically Powerful Sea"
    Very influential
    Willing to forgive others

SUMMARY OF EACH DAY

THE FOLLOWING LIST begins in the top left corner of the *pelelintangan* chart (See pages 198 and 199) at Redite Umanis, and proceeds down the five-day week, then back up to Coma Umanis, and so on in this fashion. It should be pointed out that there is some variation in the subject matter scenes in the Bintangs, and so *pelelintangan* will vary somewhat from maker to maker. The descriptions that follow are based upon the *pelelintangan* charts that are made by I Gusti Putu Kebiar in Bedahulu.

1. Redite Umanis
Bintang — kala sungsang
Laku Pendita Sakti
Sumur Sinaba

Kala sungsang is the demon who stands on his head. This person will be like a *kala* — a demon or evil spirit. He will be against things, such as the opinions of other people. He will be clever, but insensitive to the feelings and ideas of others. He is quiet, intelligent, and likes to study mystical things. He often does not reach his goals. He is well known. He promises to do many things, but often does not keep his promises. He gives in to the desires of others. Physically, he is attractive. He is clever at hiding his true feelings.

2. Redite Pahing
Bintang — gajah
Laku Bulan
Wisesa Segara

Gajah is an elephant. This person has strong, but inflexible opinions. When angered he cannot control himself and often releases his anger physically. When he has calmed down, he realizes his errors and apologizes. He is good at all kinds of work. He makes people happy. People like him. He is clever at hiding his real feelings. He is unlucky. He does not care about the ideas or suggestions of others.

3. Redite Pon
Bintang — patrem
Aras Kembang
Bumi Kapetak

Patrem is a kris, or sword. This person is likely to commit suicide. There may be a drawing of a container of food in this rectangle. The food symbolizes all of man's needs. The needs of this person are good. But he has a quiet anger that is not readily apparent. And if he cannot hit or kill another person, he will destroy himself. This person is likely to be emotional, and he has an aimless, undirected approach to problems. He likes to show off his possessions and talk in an artificially complex manner.

4. Redite Wage
Bintang — uluku
Laku Angin
Satria Wibawa

Uluku is a plow being pulled by animals. The name is sometimes spelled and pronounced *waluku*. But the usual word for plow in Balinese is *tenggala*. This person likes to work hard. This is not confined to physical labor — he plows through ideas as well. He can give comfort and cheer to those who are sad and have problems. He has the authority of a leader. He is charitable and generous, but he does not like those who disagree with him. This person likes to gamble, and he may end up losing the results of his hard work.

5. Redite Keliwon
Bintang — laweyan
Laku *bintang*
Labu Katiup Angin

Laweyan is a headless body because the man's head is in his heart. He is an important man. He realizes his importance, as do others, who defer to him. In the drawing, a woman who is sitting down looks at the man's capabilities and gives him respect. This is a quiet person with good manners. He wants to achieve his goals quickly. He is diplomatic and good at expressing himself. His feelings and behavior are difficult to predict. He usually does not stay very long in one place.

6. Coma Umanis
Bintang — kelapa
Laku Angin
Tunggak Semi

Kelapa is the coconut tree. And just as this tree is useful, helpful and good, so is the one born on this day. He is generous and charitable, courteous, polite, and has good manners. He likes to be involved with the problems of others — sometimes to excess. He likes to debate. He is often inflexible in his thinking. He likes to travel from place to place.

7. Coma Pahing
Bintang — *kukus*
Laku *bintang*
Bumi Kapetak

Kukus is smoke or steam. This *bintang* is sometimes called *dupa,* "incense." The symbol is a fire emanating from a weird-looking kind of head. *Kukus* is also the word for comet, since this object looks like smoke. This person will have strong thoughts about everything. He works hard, charging straight ahead to achieve his goals — uninfluenced by the feelings of other people. This person talks a great deal. He has good feelings and manner and is honest. He has high ideals, is thrifty, does what he promises to do, but is stubborn. He has what the Balinese call "thin ears," meaning that he is sensitive to criticism.

8. Coma Pon
Bintang — *kiriman*
Aras Tuding
Sumur Sinaba

Kiriman is something given to others through an intermediary, like a parcel. In the drawing a man is giving an object to a woman. This person likes to give things to others, especially to his family. He likes to be praised. He enjoys showing off his wealth and possessions in a pretentious way. He likes to exhibit his cleverness. He is likely to give the wrong impression of himself to others, because, although he has good intentions, they are not usually apparent because he has difficulty expressing them to others. He has a strong desire to possess material things. Sometimes he takes an opinion against what is considered right and correct. This makes him brave and reckless, and by studying his position carefully, he can often turn it to his own advantage, at the expense of others.

9. Coma Wage
Bintang — *lembu*
Laku Api
Wisesa Segara

Lembu is a bull. He is easily angered, but he does not stay angry very long, and is easily calmed down. It is hard for this person to do something.

He does not work very hard to help others or himself. He is not lazy, but rather, just a procrastinator. This person is not impatient, rash, or hasty. He investigates problems with an honest, balanced judgment. He understands and is sympathetic to the problems of others. His talk tends to be coarse.

10. Coma Keliwon
Bintang — pedati
Aras Kembang
Satria Wirang

Pedati is an empty cart. The symbolism is a bit obscure. People sit on him, as on a cart. That makes him unhappy. However, people also pull him, as with a cart. That makes him happy. This person finds good and bad easily, and quickly changes his mood from sadness to happiness. This person easily gets love and affection from others. He is clever, and he works diligently. He is easily offended and annoyed. He gets angry quickly, but he quickly forgives. He is self-sacrificing and quickly forgets grudges.

11. Anggara Umanis
Bintang — kuda
Laku Api
Wisesa Segara

Kuda is a horse. In constrast to a bull, he does not get angry easily, but, when he does, he is difficult to appease and stays angry for a long time. He works very hard, has enormous stamina, and does not tire easily. He is honest. He strives to develop his high ideals. He works skillfully. He has a strong character and is not easily influenced by others. He is jealous and dislikes those who disagree with him.

12. Anggara Pahing
Bintang — yuyu
Aras Kembang
Satria Wirang

Yuyu is a crab, as shown in the drawing. This person is said to be "light handed" by the Balinese, meaning that he likes to help others. He easily gets love and affection from others. He enjoys helping only those whom he likes. He often has good luck, but this luck sometimes makes him greedy and causes others to distrust him. He gets angry easily and is sometimes blinded by his anger. After the anger subsides he becomes repentant.

13. Anggara Pon
Bintang — asu
Laku Pandita Sakti
Satria Wibawa

Asu is a dog, depicted here trying to steal eggs from a man who is carrying them using a pole. This person is greedy. He likes to steal the possessions of others. He enjoys fighting. He is stubborn, quiet, and smart. He often is led by irrational thoughts. He has strong desires. He is always cautious, wary, alert, and suspicious. He is capable and willing to do all the work that is required of him and never gives up. He enjoys material possessions. He is not concerned with the well-being of others.

14. Anggara Wage
Bintang — jong sarat
Laku Bumi
Lebu Katiup Angin

Jong sarat is a full boat, although the drawing does not look like one. Actually it depicts the bow of the boat that has a head, like that of the *bhoma* that is seen over entrance gates. Some *pelelintangan* show a side view of the overladen boat. The idea here is that the boat is so heavy that it grounds easily in shallow water and cannot continue. This means that the person who is born on this day gets sick often and easily. He does not talk very much. He sometimes gets angry in a group and leaves quickly. He likes to improve himself and to investigate matters that he thinks are important. He likes to shelter and help others who are less fortunate than he. He is firm and persevering. But he is jealous and easily offended.

15. Anggara Keliwon
Bintang — (see below)
Aras Tuding
Sumur Sinaba

There are two versions of the *bintang* of this date which involve name only. The interpretations of character are more or less the same. Some give the *bintang* as Depat or Dpat, another name for Kala Rau. Kala Rau is a demon who stole the holy water of immortality from the gods and started to drink it. The Sun and Moon saw him and told Wisnu, who hurled his discus at Kala Rau and cut off his head. By that time, however, Kala Rau had started to swallow the holy water. And so his head was immortal. The water had not reached his body, which was killed. Kala Rau was so mad at the Sun and Moon that, even today, he chases them through the skies, and, occasionally, when he catches them, eats them, causing eclipses.

The other version of this *bintang* gives its name as Sidamalung, or Si Damalung, or Sudamalung. This is a female pig, mentioned in the epic Adiparwa stories. A person born on this day is nice unless attacked, in which case he will turn and fight his aggressor viciously, like a sow. This person does not follow the suggestions of others. His mind and behavior are not at all clear or easily understood. He likes to receive, but not to give. In the Sidamalung version, the pig is shown being given something by one of two women. He does not generally trust others. He likes to correct the faults of others, and, as a result, suffers restless feelings. He likes to gamble.

16. Buda Umanis
Bintang — tangis
Aras Kembang
Sumur Sinaba

Tangis means "crying." The drawing shows a person who is very sick in bed. A woman is crying over him. A person born on this date is often sad. He does not have a straight mind. He is hesitant and confused and dubious. He does not have strong motivation. He is afraid to start something new and thinks long and hard before he begins a new undertaking. His manner and behavior are correct. He makes friends easily. He likes to help others and be involved in their problems without thinking of himself. He is likely to harm himself.

17. Buda Pahing
Bintang — gajah mina
Laku Air
Wisesa Segara

Gajah mina is a mythical creature with the body of a fish and the head of an elephant. In the drawing a person is depicted looking at the *gajah mina* and considering what to do. A person born on this date is careful before he does something. He thinks carefully about something before he undertakes it. He likes to help others and has an open mind toward them. But he is sometimes stiff and hard. He tends to follow his passions and desires. Sometimes he is apathetic.

18. Buda Pon
Bintang — lumbung
Laku Bulan
Bumi Kapetak

Lumbung is a rice granary. This person has good luck. If he is a seller, he makes good profits and has luck at making money. The weather is always good for his activities. He gets insulted very easily. He is correct in behavior, careful, alert, and cautious. He associates well with others and makes friends easily. He can do all kinds of work. He does not easily lose hope. He perseveres through all obstacles. He likes to show off his cleverness and riches to others. He likes to be praised.

19. Buda Wage
Bintang — Kartika
Aras Tuding
Satria Wibawa

Kartika is the name for the fourth lunar month in India. It is also the name of the constellation known in the West as the Pleiades. This constellation, sometimes known as Muung in Bali, is important to some Balinese because its appearance low in the eastern sky signals the beginning of the rainy season. In some areas it is traditional for people to read a great deal during the month Kartika. The drawing represents two people about to consult two sacred *lontars* about the lunar months. The books lie crossed upon a clay *dulang*, a round stand upon which offerings are usually placed. The symbolism here is that these people are scholars who wish to determine the meaning of important ideas. There are five stars at the top center of the picture, probably representing the Pleiades. Thus the person born on this day is one who weighs matters carefully, makes wise decisions, and has good judgment. This person is just and fair when mediating the problems of others. He understands the value of money, and, as a result, is often considered to be stingy by others. However, his thrift eventually is proved to be simply good judgment. This person is inclined toward harsh and awkward talk.

20. Buda Keliwon
Bintang — tiwa tiwa
Laku Surya
Lebu Katiup Angin

Tiwa tiwa refers to the ceremonies that are performed at the time of death and afterwards, including cremation. The drawing is that of a corpse wrapped in white. One person is carrying a torch, the symbol of light, that leads the spirit of the deceased to the graveyard, as is actually done in some Balinese funeral processions. The symbolism in this case is not particularly clear. The person who is born on this date is sensitive to criticism. He likes to be praised, but is easily offended. He fits well into society, and he expresses himself well, especially in writing. He acts in bad character when involved in a dispute.

21. Wraspati Umanis
Bintang — sangkatikel
Laku *bintang*
Satria Wibawa

Sangka is the bottom part of a wooden plow that is sheathed with iron. By extension, this can refer to a hoe. *Tikel* means "broken." Hence *sangkatikel* means "broken hoe," which is clearly seen in the drawing. This person is likely to encounter problems and have accidents. He is often sad about his bad luck. He talks very little but has many desires. He seldom succeeds at what he tries to do. He has high ideals and is good at finding friends. He is a wise person. He likes to interfere in the affairs of others, without being invited to do so.

22. Wraspati Pahing
Bintang — salah ukur
Laku Bumi
Lebu Katiup Angin

Salah ukur means "wrong measurements." The two people in the drawing look as if they are fighting. But actually, each person is measuring the sizes of the various parts of his own body — arms, hands, and so on, to see if they are properly proportioned. At the same time, each person is guessing about the proportions of his companion, without actually measuring them. And he is not able to do this accurately. Such a person is not able to predict the outcome of an event accurately since he is prone to over- or underestimating the result. He is unable to tell what is right and what is wrong. This person has high ideals. He eagerly pursues self-development. He likes to shelter his relatives from suffering. When he expresses his innermost thoughts it is likely to offend others. He is prone to be loud and cantankerous. He has the ability to answer questions of all varieties.

23. Wraspati Pon
Bintang — bade
Laku Surya
Satria Wirang

Bade is a cremation tower, shown in the drawing. The symbolism here is that a cremation tower is a temporary structure that requires a lot of work to make, but that is totally consumed by fire in a few minutes. A person born on this day may accumulate a lot of wealth quickly, but he is likely to lose it quickly. This person is friendly, and has high ideals and good capabilities. He is always interested in new ideas. He is determined to further his development. But he likes to show off his possessions. He is likely to suffer misfortunes after he has attained his goals.

24. Wraspati Wage
Bintang — kumba
Aras Kembang
Tunggak Semi

A *kumba* is a large clay container for water. People are shown carrying them in the drawing. Like a water container, a person born on this date likes to be full. He must have his share of whatever he desires, and he does not give in to those who want more than their fair share. In other words, he stands up for his own rights. A water jar should be full. This person should have what he wants. A full water jar is steady and cannot be easily tipped over. An empty jar is unsteady. Thus, if someone born on this day insists that he be given something that he desires, there will be problems if it is not given to him. This person easily finds friends who love him. He is idealistic, cautious, and alert. He solves problems quickly and easily. He likes to be flattered, and he hates criticism. He does not give up easily.

25. Wraspati Keliwon
Bintang — naga
Laku Air
Bumi Kapetak

A *naga* is a snake. This is taken to be a very large, lazy snake, perhaps like a python. This person does not feel like working hard. He is sleepy and lazy. But his anger is dangerous if he is aroused. This person does not easily surrender. He has strong faith and high ideals. He has a noble mind and good intentions. He is liked by his subordinates, and he is influential. But, he has "thin ears," and is easily offended by criticism.

26. Sukra Umanis
Bintang — banyak angrem (angerem)
Aras Tuding
Satria Wirang

Banyak angrem is a goose sitting on her eggs. The drawing shows a man stealing eggs from the nest. The idea is that people will steal things from this person. He himself is very honest and well behaved. He seldom tries to hide his feelings. He customarily helps others. He likes to be involved with the problems of others. If something does not fit in with his wishes, it makes him persevere, and this may have fatal consequences. He does not think before he speaks. He says what he thinks.

27. Sukra Pahing
Bintang — bubu bolong
Laku Surya
Tunggak Semi

A *bubu* is a long, thin, tapering fish trap that has an inward-pointing cone at the open end, so that a fish can get in easily, but not out. The other end is sealed. The word *bolong* means that there is a hole in the trap — hence this is a leaky fish trap. The drawing shows one of these, with a *lindung*, a rice paddy eel, poking its head out. This person is leaky like a fish trap with a hole in it. He gets money quickly, but he spends it just as quickly. This person is friendly and talks in a pleasant manner, so that he is liked by wise and sensible people. He is clever at expressing himself. He is stubborn and persevering. He does not like to give up his bad habits. He is easily offended.

28. Sukra Pon
Bintang — prahu pegat
Lake *bintang*
Lebu Katiup Angin

Prahu pegat is a broken boat, as shown in the drawing. The boat constantly breaks down, requiring repairs. But, as soon as it is underway, it breaks again. It cannot continue regularly and consistently. A person born on this day is irregular in his work habits. He constantly starts and stops. His ideals are inconsistent and irregular. His thoughts are unsteady, and he is often sad. On the other hand, he is kind and gentle, and his behavior is always quite correct. He has a tendency to be a gambler. He likes to show off his possessions. He is worried and anxious and hesitant.

29. Sukra Wage
Bintang — magelut
Laku Pandita Sakti
Sumur Sinaba

Magelut means to embrace, in the sense of being held or bound by something. In this case it is being bound by problems of all sorts. This person is tied up by problems, which causes sadness and suffering. The drawing shows a woman in tears, being comforted by two others. This person is quiet, but intelligent. He is pure in heart and honest in character. He often makes sacrifices to help his relatives. He is firm and persistent in his opinions, and this is often the cause of his unhappiness.

30. Sukra Keliwon
Bintang — udang
Laku Bulan
Wisesa Segara

Udang is a prawn. Prawns are considered to be pretty and to be clean. They are not bothered by fish, it is said, because they live in the crevices of rocks. Prawns are also said to be mysterious and secret. The drawing shows a person spearing prawns. This person has a pleasing appearance. He is clever at expressing himself, both in his art and in his writing. He promises to lead and fulfills these promises. He is a diplomatic person. When young he has many shortcomings, but he overcomes them and is successful as an adult. He is very clever at all kinds of work. He is liked by others and has a great influence over them. He is inclined toward laziness.

31. Saniscara Umanis
Bintang — begoong
Laku Bulan
Bumi Kapetak

There is some difference of opinion about the nature of this bintang. If Anggara Keliwon, day number 15, is bintang Sidamalung, as in some *pelelintangan*, then Begoong is identified with Kala Rau, who is described under a previous entry.

Otherwise, there is no connection expressed between *begoong* and Kala Rau. In either case, *begoong* is a headless apparition, shown in the drawing at the top of a tree, being accosted by two men. These two men think that *begoong* is bad. One is trying to kill him with a spear, the other with a torch. Actually *begoong* is not a bad spirit. People only think he is bad. So it is with a person born on this day. Others slander him because they do not know him very well. He may look or act frightening, and he may scare others, but he is not a bad person. This person is clever at every kind of work. He is open-minded, and he thinks out his problems from every possible angle. He likes luxury. He can appreciate and evaluate the opinions of others. He has great perseverence. His desires are hard to restrict. He speaks with a sharp tongue. He likes to interfere in the problems of others.

32. Saniscara Pahing
Bintang — *ru*
Laku Api
Satria Wibawa

Ru is an arrow. The drawing shows a man with a bow, having shot an arrow into a deer. A person born on this date is like an arrow. An arrow has no intelligence. It is sent on its way by another person and does its damage quickly. But it cannot direct its own aim and has no control over what it does. A person born on this day gets angry quickly. He is not in a great hurry to do anything. He frequently makes excuses for himself. He weighs problems carefully before solving them. He understands money and is careful in financial matters. He is fond of praise. He does not like to be surpassed by someone else or to be treated as an inferior.

33. Saniscara Pon
Bintang — *sungenge*
Laku Air
Wisesa Segara

Sungenge is a sunflower, an object that attracts attention and is admired. The drawing shows people admiring the flowers. This person has high ideals and good intentions. He likes to show off. He gets attention from important people. He likes luxury. He is influential. He forgives those who acknowledge their mistakes.

34. Saniscara Wage
Bintang — *puwuh atarung*
Laku bintang
Satria Wirang

Puwuh atarung means "fighting quails." These are shown in the drawing. This person likes to argue, debate, and fight. When he becomes angry he is likely not to be able to control his anger and may become sick. He is charitable to those who do favors for him. But he is jealous and sticks to his opinions.

35. Saniscara Keliwon
Bintang — *pagelangan*
Laku Bumi
Tunggak Semi

There are two interpretations of the word *pegelangan*. One shows the word derived from *gelang,* meaning "bracelet" or "wrist." The other indicates that the word comes from *angelangen,* meaning "to stare at something that is very interesting." This is the case in the drawing here. The man in the drawing is staring intently at the girls who are carrying fruit on their heads. This person is self-deprecating and ashamed. For example, he does not like to go out in public with his inferior clothes. He admires things that he thinks are good. He is careful in what he does. He uses careful grammar, especially in his writing. He does not like to take risks, and, as a result, is likely to be apathetic. If he cannot solve a problem or accomplish his goals quickly, he quickly loses hope.

THERE IS AN EASY WAY to find out your Saptawara and Pancawara birthdays. Go to almost any bookstore in Bali and buy a copy of the *Kalender 301 Tahun,* by Sudharta, Dhermawan, and Winawan. This is a paperback, published in 1984 by PN Balai Pustaka in Jakarta, and it contains 301 years worth of calendars, listing the 30 weeks of the Pawukon, the Saptawara, and the Pancawara, for every date. It is not expensive, and, from my experience, is widely available in Bali. It is written in Bahasa Indonesia, but the tables of dates use standard Latin numbers and, if you are reasonably perceptive, you can find the year and month and date of your birth and determine the Pancawara date from the listings. The only alternative is to find a *balian* or other practitioner who knows how to determine such things. Or, you can write to me, since I have a computer program that will determine Pancawara days, given the Gregorian calendar date.

If you are interested in the *pelelintangan,* visit I Gusti Putu Kebiar in Bedahulu, just north of the Y where the roads from the Elephant Cave, Gianyar, and Kintamani come together. This is just a bit south of the village of Pejeng. Kebiar also makes *tikas,* the calendars that list the Pawukon cycle. You can buy them directly from him, if he has some on hand. It takes him about 15 days to make a *pelelintangan* of good quality, and perhaps a day and a half for a *tika.* He is a fountain of information, and I am indebted to him, and to my friend I Ketut Guweng, calendar expert extraordinaire, now retired from the Department of Religion, for much of the information in this chapter.

pelelintangan are available at many art shops, especially in the Ubud-Mas area. The Rudana Painters Community in Mas usually has a number of them for sale. They make very attractive wall hangings.

The *pelelintangan* that you will find in shops are made specifically for tourists. You never see one in a Balinese home — a function not of their authenticity, but of the Balinese reluctance to consult such sources themselves. Kebiar's work is done precisely as dictated by the *lontars*, and his drawings are somewhat more realistic than those used on some of the *pelelintangan* you may see. The latter are Kamasan-style drawings, done in the more ancient and traditional manner of the *wayang kulit* puppets. The portrayal of living creatures in anything approaching a realistic style was not common in Bali until the influence of European artists became evident in the 1930s.

CHAPTER 19

Offerings

GIFTS TO THE GODS

ONE OF THE BEST-KNOWN BOOKS IN THE WORLD is virtually unheard of outside of Asia except by scholars — but in Bali almost everyone knows the Mahabharata. Several times the length of the Bible, with more than 100,000 verses, this great Hindu epic spins an enormously long and complex tale revolving around two families, the Pandawas and the Korawas, who engage in a series of adventures, battles, and trials of strength and courage. The tale reaches a climax, the two armies poised to do final battle, when Arjuna, the leader of the Pandawas, hesitates to fight against his own cousins. Arjuna's charioteer, Krishna, then reveals himself as Wisnu and narrates the Mahabaharata's most famous passage, the Bhagavad-Gita. In one of the most celebrated moments of this long philosophical exposition on hesitation, action, passivity, and the worship of God, Krishna tells Arjuna what God expects and requires of an offering:

> Whosoever offers to me with devotion a leaf, a flower, a fruit, or water, that offering of love, of the pure heart I accept (ix: 26)

This passage lies at the heart of the tradition of preparing offerings in Bali. And although they range from modest to extravagant, most offerings contain just what Krishna specified — leaves, flowers, fruit, and holy water — and all are presented with devotion.

Offerings can be seen everywhere in Bali. Tiny coconut leaf baskets of rice, fruit, and flowers are presented in front of every home and business, the smoke from a stick of incense lifting the essence skyward. Even the dashboards of cars and trucks are often not without their *banten* ("offerings"). In the temples and shrines, the more elaborate *daksina*, consisting of rice, fruit, and a carefully shaved coconut, serve to demonstrate devotion. During special ceremonies, huge *banten tegeh* — "high-offerings" — are constructed, with fruits, rice cakes, and even roasted ducks and pigs skewered to a three-meter banana trunk.

Offerings in Bali are always made of natural things — objects of everyday use and life. They may be purchased, but they are never made of anything other than items that the Balinese use or consume themselves. They may be articles of food. They may be objects "sewed" together from palm leaves. They may be flowers. They may be leaves. They may be food adjuncts, such as the ingredients of the betel chew that is such a popular masticatory in Asia. And, with minor exceptions, an offering cannot be presented to God more than once. An offering is something tangible, presented to God (in some manifestation or another) at the time of prayer.

Offerings to the higher aspects of God, those manifestations that the Balinese called *betara-betari*, must be beautiful — not necessarily elaborate (although often so), but nicely made, appealing objects that would delight the senses. Offerings made to the negative forces, the *bhutas* and *kalas*, are often less carefully made. These demons are known to be greedy and will voraciously consume almost anything. Thus many offerings to them are objects that have been made or cooked some time ago and may be partially decayed by the time they are offered. Offerings to the *betara-betari* are always presented on a platform, raised well above the ground. Those made to the earth demons are just placed on the ground.

Philosophically, an offering is a kind of self-sacrifice. One spends time and money making an offering, putting something of oneself into it. And, as such, the individual making the offering is making a small personal sacrifice to give thanks to God. Most Balinese would probably not express the idea this way. They make offerings because that is what they were taught to do. They know God enjoys them, and that is why they are made.

Included in almost all offerings in Bali are the three ingredients of the masticatory called "betel" by English-speaking people: the leaf of the betel pepper tree, a bit of lime, and a sliver of *areca* nut, the fruit of a tall, slender palm that grows all over lowland Asia. The Balinese words for these three ingredients, *areca* nut, betel leaf, and lime, are *buah, base,* and *pamor.* Originally, no doubt, they were merely ingredients of a pleasant and stimulating chew. They are still widely used for that, especially by older Balinese. But *buah, base,* and *pamor* also have a deep religious significance. Their colors are the same as the colors associated with the Hindu *trimurthi:* Brahma, Wisnu, and Siwa — creator, preserver, and dissolver of life. *Areca* nut is red, the color of Brahma; betel leaf is green, the color of Wisnu (also black); and lime is white, the color of Siwa. And so a tiny bit of each of these three substances is placed in all offerings in order to provide a place for the presence of these three most important aspects of God. Usually the three are present in the form of *porosan,* a little dab of lime paste plus a tiny sliver of *areca* nut, wrapped up in a betel leaf.

Simple daily offerings are the most common. Almost every Balinese housewife puts a little of the food she has just cooked in a small, triangular container made out of a coconut leaf and presents it to God in appreciation for the food about to be eaten. These modest offerings are called *segehan* (See CHAPTER 20). Many Balinese will pour a few drops of their first cup of coffee or tea on the ground before they drink any themselves, as a small expression of thanks as well as an offering to placate the demons. In many households *segehans* are placed daily in all the shrines, in the family temple, in the kitchen, by the well, and on the family motorbike. A truck driver stops at a roadside shrine and offers a prayer with a flower or two.

In every case the offering is not just put in its place and left, but, rather, a simple gesture — the *ngayab* — is made three times, waving with the right hand the essence, *sari,* of the offering toward God. In both large and small ceremonies, even when the main subjects of attention are the *betara-betari,* the *bhutas* and *kalas* are not forgotten. If he can, each worshiper obtains a bottle of *brem,* rice wine, and a bottle of *arak,* palm brandy. These are generally provided by the temple religious leader, the *pemangku,* for anyone who wishes to make such an offering. A bit of the *brem* is poured into a *tapan,* a ladle-shaped container made of banana leaf, and held aloft in the left hand. The right hand performs a *ngayab* to waft the *sari* aloft, and then, switching hands, the *tapan* is held in the right hand, the right elbow is grasped with the left hand in a gesture of respect, and a bit of the *brem* is poured on the ground as an offering to the negative spirits. This procedure may be repeated with the *arak.* This is called *matabuh.*

Perhaps the most common offering of all is a bit more elaborate than these. It belongs to a large class of offerings called *jajahitan,* meaning "sewed" objects. The general word for offering in Balinese is *banten.* A *banten jahitan* is made from leaves that are actually not sewed in the usual sense, but rather skewered together with a sliver of bamboo or the central spine of a coconut leaf. The most common type of leaf used is the young, yellowish-white leaf of the coconut, called *busung.* The huge coconut tree leaf consists of a long, large central stem from which the leaves branch out, featherlike. But before the leaf opens it is folded in half near the center of the tree, sticking almost vertically upwards. In the folded immature leaf, the individual "feathers" have not yet separated, and the two halves of the leaf each form a flat sheet. It is these that are used in sewed offerings, although *selepan,* the mature leaves of the coconut, are used in the base of offerings. Sometimes the leaves of the *lontar* palm are used, but coconut is most common. *Lontar* leaves have the advantage of staying the same color more or less indefinitely. Coconut leaves turn brown after a few days. But this hardly matters, since sewed offerings are generally used immediately after they are made. *Busung* may be collected by the woman making the offerings. But many coconut trees are high, and it takes some effort to get to the young leaves, which are at the very top. Most people buy them in the village markets. The central spine, or *lidi*, is cut off and the two halves are cut and sewed into various shapes.

The most widely used of the sewed offerings is the *canang*. There are a great many varieties of *canangs* but, basically, each consists of a square frame, about ten centimeters on a side, made by folding the leaf. A flat bottom is fitted and skewered in. Then the little basket is filled with the *porosan*, a slice of banana or sugar cane, a colored leaf or two, and then filled with flowers of various colors, but generally containing red and white ones, and green in the form of shredded *pandanus* leaves — the colors of the Hindu triad. A dash of perfumed oil completes the little offering. You can see thousands upon thousands of them for sale at almost any market in Bali. Almost all truck and taxi drivers put *canangs* on the dashboards of their vehicles every day.

After putting such an offering as a *canang* in place, its *sari* must be wafted to God. This is always done, if possible, using some sort of smoke to carry the essence of the offering upward. The most convenient way to do this is to use incense, *dupa*, and you will see *canang* sellers with a large selection of *dupa* as well. The proper way to accomplish this is to take a flower from the *canang*, place it between the fingers of the right hand, and make three waves of the palm forward over the burning incense. *Canangs* are always placed on top of the high offerings that ladies carry to the temples at the time of the temple anniversary festival, or *odalan*. The *canang* is taken to the high platform in front of the worshipers, sprinkled with holy water, and blessed. Then, when someone comes, sits down, and asks to pray, one of the attendants gives him a *canang* and a stick of incense. They are used for a whole host of purposes — too many to enumerate here. The smoke need not be from incense. Every Kajeng Keliwon, an important Balinese calendar cycle day that comes around every 15 days, and on the days of full and new moon, Purnama and Tilem, each housewife places *segehans* and *canangs* in the various house shrines, and then puts some offerings outside the front entrance gate on the ground, usually using a burning coconut husk to provide the smoke. When *pemangkus* dedicate a large number of offerings inside a temple, they place sandalwood chips upon a brazier of coconut charcoal, and the fragrant smoke wafts the *sari* toward God.

The *lamak* is another common sewed offering. Usually made of *lontar*

A CANANG OFFERING

leaf, a *lamak* is a large hanging, like a mat, that is decorated with many colored leaves, or today, sometimes even plastic. *Lamaks* are usually hung outside on one of the temporary shrines that are erected for a special occasion, such as the Galungan festival. Some of them are very long — up to ten meters. A *lamak*, although an offering, is used more like a decoration.

Sampian is another common type of sewed decoration, not an offering in and of itself, but a decoration that is often found on other offerings. A *sampian* may be in the shape of a triangle or a circle, or it may have a basically cylindrical shape. It is the decorative piece upon which the flowers are placed in a *canang*. It is the decoration at the very top of a high offering, with its skirt hanging down over the edge. A *sampian* may be hung from some sort of a pole or other support.

The variety of sewed offerings is almost endless. Little girls are taught practically from the time that they can safely wield a knife to cut and sew the intricate patterns that are required in so many ceremonies. Making them is almost invariably women's work, and groups of women may work all day in preparation for the larger ceremonies, chatting and gossiping as they cut and pin the leaves — their hands move almost automatically, since they have been doing it for so long. It is not an exaggeration to say that the average Balinese housewife spends one-third of her waking hours making offerings. There is a special knack in making the cut varieties. A group of coconut leaves is held together and a few cutouts made in just the right place. And when unfolded, sewed together, and arranged in whirls or flowers or curlicues, they make the most beautiful sight imaginable.

One of the most important offerings is the *daksina,* again inspired by Krisna's instruction to Arjuna. The maker first makes a cylindrical basket of coconut leaves about 20 centimeters high and about as big in diameter as a coconut. Then a coconut is prepared. It is husked and the hard nut inside shaved so that none of the fibers remain. A special kind of plane is sometimes used for this, its bottom rounded to match the curvature of the coconut. The women place uncooked rice, banana, a dab of *porosan,* several different kinds of leaves, colored seeds, a green banana, a raw egg, and a *canang* on the bottom of the basket, then place the shaved coconut inside. This is sometimes called the basic Balinese offering, containing the leaves, flowers, fruit, and water (inside the coconut) prescribed by Krishna. *Daksinas* are used for all major ceremonies. One is usually kept in each of the major shrines of the family temple, and perhaps one in the kitchen shrine, dedicated to Brahma, controller of fire.

Daksinas are not used in all ceremonies. Most kinds of religious ceremonies in Bali can be classified according to three levels of extravagance. *Utama* ceremonies are the largest, and *nista* ceremonies the smallest, with *madia* being the medium variety. *Daksinas* are usually not used in *nista* ceremonies, *canangs* are substituted instead. Unlike most other offerings, when you take a *daksina* to a temple, you cannot take it home after the *sari* has been presented to God. Generally the *pemangku* will take it home and eat the materials inside. If they are made in the home, usually at least two are made — one for God and one for the humans. The former cannot be used for food, but the latter can.

THE MOST SPECTACULAR OFFERINGS are the high offerings, or *banten tegeh.* This is the type that most people make and then carry to the public temples for such occasions as the *odalan,* the anniversary celebration for the local temple. These high offerings are sometimes made right in the temple, because they are often so tall and so heavy that they can be carried only with great difficulty. First the maker — usually, but not always, a woman — secures a special base. It looks like the regular round base that is used for many of the larger offerings, except that from the center extends upwards a long spike, firmly embedded in the wood. Next, the stem of a banana plant, a *gedebong*, is cut to a length that is a bit larger than the final offering and impaled with some force upon this spike. The various materials of the offerings are assembled nearby, together with a number of long bamboo skewers, which are used to attach the offerings to the banana trunk.

The materials skewered to the banana stem vary from village to village and person to person. Fruits are almost always used, depending upon what is in season. And there are always *jaja*. *Jaja* are cakes made out of rice. Usually the rice is reduced to flour by pounding, then mixed with water and seasonings, and cooked by boiling, steaming, or frying. The cakes may be colored or left white. There are a great many different varieties of *jaja*, some unique to Bali, some found everywhere in Indonesia. I have a list of more than 60. And on the *banten tegeh*, one is likely to see almost every imaginable variety. Some are thin and crispy cakes, usually colored. Some are doughy, like cupcakes. Still others, though not often used for offerings, are wrapped in a banana leaf and steamed. The thin, crispy kind are favorites on offerings, but they cannot be impaled or else they would break. The maker has to make shelflike arrangements with the skewers and wedge the fragile cakes between the shelves. Some villages include large cylinders of sticky rice that have been molded by rolling or placed in a cylindrical banana leaf. In other villages one sees cooked eggs impaled on the banana stem. Some places include a sort of decorative plaque among the fruits. In certain areas a grilled duck or chicken may be placed at the top front. (I have even seen these with cigarettes in their mouths.) Over the top is generally placed a very fancy cut coconut leaf decoration, the *sampian*, with its decorative outer border draping over the top edge like a lacy skirt. And on top of the whole thing is the *canang* itself, often covered with a silver bowl. When skillfully made neither the skewers nor the banana stem show through the surrounding cluster of fruits, cakes, and other objects.

The village markets on the several days before a large temple festival or before an important day in the Balinese religious calendar are bulging with colored *jaja* of every size, color, and description. A trip to any of these is well worth the effort. It is quite a chore for a housewife to make a suitable assortment of *jaja*, and most women buy what they need in the market. It is not unusual to spend the equivalent of U.S. $20 for the materials used in a high offering — not an inconsiderable sum for a family that may count on an income of this much for several weeks of living. Market prices, especially of fruit, rise about 20 percent at festival time.

These towers of food may be two or three meters high, or they may be relatively short — say one meter. The really tall ones require some skill to carry. The most difficult part is entering the gate to the inner temple, which always has a lintel. The woman who carries the *banten* must stoop very low so that the top will clear, not an easy job with such a heavy load. There is always someone around to help the carrier lift the offering off of her head and put in on the ground. Then the *banten* is placed in front of the people who are praying while the maker makes her devotions. In some temples the offerings are placed in *bales,* open pavilions, for a long period of time during the ceremony. In others, the offerings are taken home immediately after prayers are said. There is always much checking around to see how friends and neighbors made their offerings — to see if there are any new techniques.

In some villages, the high offerings are carried to the temple in a procession. Usually each neighborhood association, *banjar,* has its own group, each lady dressed identically, with offerings generally rather alike. In other villages, the ladies simply make whatever they feel like making and go when they are ready. The processions are a sight to behold, led by little girls dressed in lovely brocades, as many as 100 women filing along with the high offerings on their heads, all dressed alike, followed by the marching band of gongs and cymbals. Sometimes a person will promise God to have a high offering made for a ceremony if some wish that he has can be made to come true. This may be hope for success on an examination, a wish that a family member will recover from a sickness, or the like.

When the prayers have been said and the offerings made, the high offering is carried home, and those who wish may eat any of the food. There is no prohibition about this except for some *pemangkus* and for high priests. God has partaken of the *sari* of the offering, and it can now no longer be used for religious purposes. There is nothing bad about eating an offering. In fact, sometimes a skewered banana or orange is eaten right in the temple after prayers have been said.

Another variety of offerings, especially for large and important ceremonies of the *madia* or *utama* class, consists almost entirely of highly colored, fried cakes of rice dough shaped into animal, plant, and human forms, according to prescribed rules. These too are called *jaja,* just like their more humble relatives. Since these are not common offerings, very often an individual or even a whole team of offering specialists is called in to prepare the offerings specified for the particular ceremony. Often these specialists are high caste women, and for a really big ceremony, as many as a dozen women may work for a week or several weeks to prepare the rice cakes. When the cakes are finished, they are usually tied onto a big bamboo frame that may be several meters tall. The resulting offering is called a *babangkit* and is usually made to represent, symbolically, the Balinese concept of the universe. On the bottom is the turtle, Bedawang Nala, that supports the world, with his two attendant dragon-snakes entwined around him. Above this representation of the underworld is the world of man, populated by humans, dogs, and other rice cake animals. And above all is heaven, complete with gods and goddesses. These *babangkit* offerings are usually placed in the inner courtyard of a temple and left there for the entire ceremony, usually protected from rain by plastic sheets. They are wonderful examples of miniature art. Some of the realistic dough figures are only an inch or two in length. The *babangkit* is similar in design to the stone shrine, *padmasana,* found in all temples, and to the cremation towers. These two are also representations of the three divisions of the universe, *bhur, buwah,* and *swah,* a favorite theme of Hindu-Balinese thought and practice. One occasionally sees a similar representation of the Balinese universe, except it is executed entirely in pig fat. These are best admired when fresh, since they do not age well in the sun.

Ceremonies are invariably accompanied by feasts. And, except where turtles are plentiful, as in my village, Jimbaran, feasts mean rotisseried pig, *b e guling.* Part of the food is cut up into various shapes similar to the cakes described above and arranged into a recognizable *bhur-buwah-swah* form. The name for this is *saté renteng,* or *saté gembal.*

Selat, a community near Gunung Agung, Bali's most sacred mountain, specializes in an offering called *barong salaran,* assembled from all of the fruits of the earth and made into the shape of a *barong,* a mythic beast, often a shaggy, lion-like creature, whose representation is used in many villages to protect the people from evil. The *barong* dance, featuring a confrontation between Barong and the witch Rangda, is a staple of many village *odalans.* Here is a *barong* made entirely of fruits, roots, vegetables, and rice. Such an offering may be so large as to require 20 men to lift it.

One often sees offerings of cloth. These are small piles of neatly folded material, usually placed upon a tray or upon a *dulang,* the usual clay or wood support that the Balinese use to carry offerings. A *dulang* is a round tray upon a pedestal, the bottom of which flares out so that it fits on top of the head. The cloth offering, called *rantasan,* must consist of material that has never been worn. Usually it is just piece goods, not sewed into clothes.

Many visitors to Bali don't realize it, but even cockfights are, in a way, offerings. Gambling is now officially illegal in Indonesia, and cockfights are theoretically extinct. (There are still plenty, however, if you know where to look.) But at every temple ceremony, large or small, and even at family temple celebrations, there is bound to be a cockfight, because the evil spirits are appeased by the blood of the loser being spilled on the ground. There is not supposed to be any betting at these ceremonial cockfights, but telling a Balinese not to bet on a lovely fighting cock is like telling an American male not to bet on his football team.

The *caru* is not exactly an offering, but rather a ceremony that involves a set of offerings especially made for the earth demons. Since it is intended to placate negative forces, it often contains a great many rather foul-smelling, partially decayed offerings that were made days beforehand. But there are some beautiful offerings too. Some involve large circular plates with sectors of colored rice that represent the nine directions and the aspect of God that dominates each. Other less savory parts of a *caru* may involve animals, especially chickens, and sometimes dogs or even water buffaloes that have been sacrificed as offerings. Before each animal is killed, however, an offering is made to it, its pardon asked, and it is reassured that it will be reincarnated into a better form. (See CHAPTER 20.)

FROM CASUAL OBSERVATION, it would appear that the art of making offerings is not likely to die out soon in Bali. Girls in designer jeans and modern hair styles still sit in the *bales,* their nimble fingers effortlessly producing the intricately folded and cut masterpieces. There is even a weekly television program, originating in Denpasar, during which a specialist illustrates the techniques of making offerings and explains their meanings and purposes.

Though beautiful, offerings are never monuments to their makers. They are made of the most ephemeral materials imaginable, and within a few hours of their presentation to God as things of beauty and devotion, they are either eaten or wither to an ugly brown that scarcely hints of their former majesty and beauty.

CHAPTER 20

Blood Sacrifice

PLACATING THE DEMONS

NOT ALL BALINESE OFFERINGS ARE THINGS OF BEAUTY — delicate frangipani blossoms, folded and cut coconut leaves, and dabs of bright yellow and red rice. In the Hindu faith, one must take the bad with the good, and while the gods must be worshiped, the demons — in respect for their great power — must be placated. And the demons, the leering and fanged *bhutas* and *kalas,* have great and gross appetites. Therefore at many ceremonies, one might see a decidedly unaesthetic arrangement of offerings — a huge enclosure heaped full of rotted and rotting fruit and flowers, shriveled palm and coconut leaves, and chunks of fly-covered meat. Although the *bhutas* are clearly not picky eaters, to truly satisfy their hunger they must be provided with the fresh blood of a slaughtered animal. If properly fed, they will not only not bother people, but will actually help them.

Caru is the name for a class of blood sacrifice that is made to the demons, *bhutas* and *kalas* or, more philosophically, to the negative aspects of the universe. The various *caru* offerings accompany the series of rites known as *bhuta yadnya,* one of the five divisions of Hindu-Balinese ritual. *Caru* range from a fairly simple offering requiring the sacrifice of a single chicken, to elaborate ceremonies involving the slaughter of dozens of animals and great stinking piles of coarsely made vegetable offerings. All *caru* seek to "satisfy" the *bhutas* or *kalas,* though the larger ones are intended to do so for a longer period of time. But this explanation is something of an oversimplification.

Bhuta yadnya is said to be a set of rituals for purifying the world from the disturbing influences of *bhuta kala.* But what exactly is, or are, *bhuta kala?* The average Balinese would reply that *bhutas* and *kalas,* or *bhuta kala,* are evil spirits that cause a great many of the small and large problems of mankind, from a lost watch to a crippling disease. They are powerful, but can be controlled by various rituals and offerings. Their shapes? These can be seen everywhere, leering from the gates and walls of temples, with bulging eyes and fiendish fangs.

But *bhuta* and *kala* are Sanskrit words, with shades of meaning beyond mere "demons." *Bhuta* means "the gross elements of which the body is composed," as well as "uncanny being," or "goblin." *Kala* means "time," as well as "fate," and "god of death." The point here is that *bhutas* and *kalas* (the two, by the way, are never really distinguished from each other by the Balinese) are supernatural demons, as they are portrayed in the leering carvings, but they are also more generally the dark side, the animal side, of man and of the Hindu universe. In the world, they represent the physical, the ugly, the temporal. In man, they represent greed, passion, and hunger.

Bhutas and *kalas,* to the Balinese, are monsters, spooks, somehow tangible and existing in rather specific places at specific times. They are considered to frequent village crossroads, which are the sites of yearly *caru* offerings; and they are said to be unable to go around corners, hence the screening wall, *aling-aling,* that is built just inside the entrance to Balinese house compounds. A Balinese is liable to think of an offering to the *bhutas* as cheaply purchased peace of mind, like now and then throwing a scrap of meat to the neighbor's drooling and fierce-looking dog.

Hindu *pedandas* and theologians consider *bhutas* and *kalas* to be manifestations, like gods — *dewas* — of locally competing mystical forces. That is, a *bhuta* is not so much a monster as a pocket of destructive force, an imbalance, a ripple, which, in order to maintain balance, must be smoothed, annulled, with an offering — thus restoring order. Man, as an analog of the universe, contains identical forces. A *bhuta* within the Hindu microcosm of man might be best considered as an illness, or a foul temper. The Hindu cosmos is continuous, and it makes no sense in Hindu theology to suggest that evil, or evil forces, are "driven out" or "permanently destroyed." The concept of the coexistence of good and evil is called *rwa bhineda* by the Balinese and is summed up in the expression: Bhuta ia; dewa ia ("He is an evil spirit; he is a god"). Thus the proper language to describe the goal of a *caru* is appeasement, satiety — not eradication, or driving out evil.

Because offerings to *bhutas* and *kalas,* including *caru,* are placed on the ground, one will constantly hear it said that these demons live "in" the ground. This is not true. The offerings are placed on the ground because it is a "low" place, which is distinguished from the "high" places reserved for sacred offerings to the *dewas. Bhutas* and *kalas* could be anywhere —

depending on one's philosophical approach, as discussed above — but as befits their role, their offerings are presented in a low and profane manner. In fact, in some parts of India people say the best way to get away from *bhutas* is to lie flat on the ground because *bhutas* are known to hover at some distance above ground level. I have not heard this mentioned in Bali.

CARU SACRIFICES, WITH ONE MINOR EXCEPTION, are blood sacrifices — an animal, or animals, must be killed. Killing an animal in this way is not considered a cruelty. When an animal is killed in a sacrifice, it acquires karma, enough, perhaps, to allow it to be reincarnated at a higher level. The body is not important to the Hindu faithful. It is a shell. Any animal that is killed for a sacrifice is always treated with great reverence. Offerings are made to it. Mantras are recited, asking for an improved status in the next life. An animal cannot be sacrificed without these prayers and offerings.

Hindu philosophers believe in a chain of existence, a circle from human to animal and back. Animals and humans honor and respect one another. In a sense, when a human sacrifices an animals he is sacrificing himself, particularly his passions. It is an attempt to kill one's evil characteristics. One cannot properly pray, *sembahyang,* unless one's mind is first cleared of negative thoughts. It is quite common among Balinese I know to avoid going to a temple and praying, even at an important ceremony, if their minds are occupied with negative feelings. To clear the mind of these evil thoughts that obstruct the pathway toward the *dewas,* one should make a sacrifice to appease the negative forces that are providing the opposition. This is why *caru* usually precedes the main part of the ceremony. Such a ceremony may be quite minor, such as a tooth filing or other rite of passage. Or it may be much larger — the purification of a new building or a new temple complex. The size of the *caru* is adjusted accordingly.

The very smallest *caru* is the *segehan.* There are several varieties of *segehan* offerings, but the most common is the *ituk-ituk,* built on a triangular cup of folded coconut leaf, each side no more than about five centimeters in length. The *segehan* is the only kind of *caru* that need not necessarily have blood or meat in it. The tray must always contain a small slice of onion, *bawang,* and ginger, *jahe.* The onion is "cold" and the ginger "hot." They are opposites, reminding the *bhutas* and *kalas* that a balance is sought. The simplest *segehan* also contains at least two lumps of cooked white rice, and salt. *Segehans* are very commonly placed on the ground in front of the gate to the house compound so that *bhutas* and *kalas* will feel no urge to venture further inside. Several of these may be laid out, usually accompanied by a small *canang* offering. Normally the woman who puts them there wafts their essence with her hand and then pours three dollops of rice wine on the ground, the while reciting the magic syllables *rang, ring, tah,* meaning "born," "living," "dead," or the law of the cosmos, the rising and setting of the sun, or any of a number of other analogous series. In some households *segehans* are offered daily; at the very minimum they must be put out every 15 days, on Kajeng Keliwon of the Pawukon cycle.

A *segehan* is normally offered by a housewife as part of her daily chores. Larger *caru* may be offered by individuals, but more often the services of a religious man, a *pemangku* lay priest or a *balian* are requested. For really large *caru* a *pedanda* or a *rsi,* a Bujangga Wesnawe priest, is called in. (See CHAPTER 7.) Anything larger than a small *caru* requires a staggering amount of preparation. Normally an enclosure is fenced off in the house compound or temple to receive the offerings, and for even a medium *caru* this enclosure may be several meters along each side and half a meter or more high. When completed this area is heaped full of offerings. It is not unusual for a medium-sized *caru* to require the services of a team of offering specialists. There is one such team in our village, and they are constantly busy. It may take several of these people weeks to assemble all of the offerings for a *caru.* The cost may run to well over one million rupiah. Since the offerings are for *bhutas* and *kalas* it doesn't matter if the meat is spoiled and the coconut leaves are withered. The offerings may be prepared well in advance and kept for considerable periods of time until needed. There is nothing fresh or delicate or beautiful about *caru* offerings. The odor of rotting meat is sometimes extremely strong, and the offerings are normally covered with flies.

There is always some color symbolism in offerings, but this is especially noticeable in those made for *caru.* The symbol of the orderly Balinese universe is an eight-pointed figure, at the center is Siwa, with his eight manifestations distributed over the four cardinal and four intercardinal directions. With each god in his proper place, each with his own weapon, color, magic number, vehicle, day of the week, and all of the other attributes, the macrocosm and microcosm are in order. Since this is the goal of a *caru,* the offerings mimic the color symbolism of the nine (eight plus center) directions, the *nawa sanga.* The colors and gods are:

N: Wisnu, *black*

NW: Sangkara, *green*   NE: Sambu, *blue*

W: Mahadewa, *yellow*   CENTER: Siwa, *all colors*   E: Iswara, *white*

SW: Rudra, *orange*   SE: Mahesora, *pink*

S: Brahma, *red*

To be perfectly accurate we should substitute *kaja* and *kelod* for north and south above, which mean "mountainward" and "seaward," respectively. In South Bali the above chart is accurate, but in North Bali, "north" and "south" would be reversed. (East and west, *kangin* and *kauh*, are the same everywhere on the island.) "Mountainward" in Bali means toward Gunung Agung, the island's highest and most sacred mountain, which is in the east-central part of Bali. (See CHAPTER 1.)

White, red, and black rice grow naturally. Yellow rice is made with *kun-yit*, turmeric. The other colors are usually commercial food dyes. Large *caru* require many offerings with piles of rice of the different colors spread out in the eight different directions. In the center is a circle of a mixture of all the colors. The Balinese call this mixture of all colors *brunbun*. The offering, when placed in the *caru* enclosure, is oriented so that the colors line up in the proper compass directions.

Although this may be self-evident from some of the descriptions given, unlike the offerings made for the other *yadnyas*, *caru* offerings are never eaten by people after the completion of the ceremony. In most cases a hole is dug next to the place where the offerings are dedicated and as many of the offerings as will fit are piled into the hole and covered up. In some cases there are so many offerings that they will not fit. In that case, the left-overs are gathered up and taken to the sea or a nearby river and thrown in.

Most *caru* ceremonies involve the use of temporary shrines in which small offerings may be placed. The most common of these is called the *sanggah cucuk*, made out of a low, split-bamboo platform with something like an open, triangular tent on top. This sort of shrine is almost always also used at the base of a *penjor*, the graceful poles that extend out over the streets during ceremonies, and in death rites.

Many people consider that the purifying and ordering effect of a *caru* is proportional to its size. That of a *segehan* lasts but a day. A small *caru* might be effective for six months. Still larger ones would be good for a year, or five or ten years. And the very largest of all, such as Eka Dasa Rudra, is effective for 100 years.

OTHER THAN THE BASIC *SEGEHAN*, the smallest *caru* is the *eka sata*, which requires one *brunbun* chicken, placed at a base of a *sanggah cucuk*. The offering includes a number of other ingredients, but only one animal need be sacrificed. This *caru* is usually used in the dedication-purification cere-mony for a new building, called *melaspas*. *Eka sata* is also commonly per-formed the day before a tooth filing.

Next in scale is the *panca sata*, which requires five chickens of different colors, representing the four cardinal points — white, red, yellow, and black — with a *brunbun* chicken for the center. There must also be a *sang-*

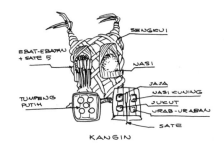

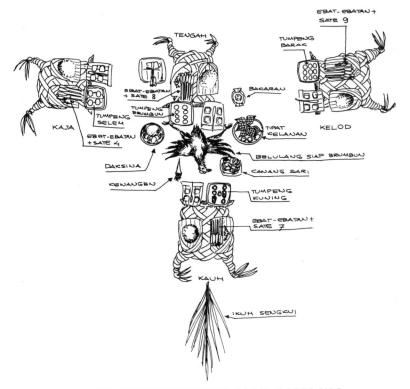

A RELATIVELY MODEST CARU *OFFERING*

gah cucuk for each chicken, in each corner. This size of *caru* is normally used for the ceremony held at the village crossroads just before Nyepi, New Year's Day. The temple festivals for some of the larger village temples will also include a *panca sata*.

Next is the *panca kalud*, which includes the five chickens plus a dog of the color the Balinese call *blang bungkem*, or *bangbungkem*. These dogs have a black snout and a red or brown body. Such a color is symbolic of

Rudra, the wild and stormy aspect of Siwa, and thus the dog is always put in the southwestern corner of the *caru* enclosure, Rudra's direction. We had a *panca kalud caru* at my friend and assistant Budi's house a few years ago at the time of the dedication of the renovation of his family temple. Budi's house is located on a spot said to have been used as a camp during the Japanese occupation, which was deemed to have caused various kinds of sickness within the family. And so this major *caru* purification was carried out just before the *melaspas* for his *sanggah*.

Larger still is the *rsi gana*, requiring the same animals as the *panca kalud* plus one white duck. As the number of animals sacrificed increases, so does the number of other offerings and trappings. The next in scale is the *warespati* kalpa, which involves all of the above plus one goose. (Cats never seem to be sacrificed in *caru*, and I'm not sure why. There are plenty around. But they are never eaten, and they are not symbols of anything as far as I know. They do not receive offerings at the traditional time for animals, Tumpek Andang. But if a cat is killed by an automobile, the driver must pick up the body, bring it home, and bury it in front of where he normally parks his car, and he must make an offering for it. I have no idea why this is done. The roads in Bali are littered with dog bodies, and nobody gives them a second thought. But if you do not treat a cat corpse as indicated above, it is said you will shortly have an accident with your car.)

The most elaborate *caru* of all is called the *taur* or *tawur*, which literally means "pay," perhaps in the sense of an extortion payment to the *bhutas* and *kalas*. A *caru taur* is truly a titanic undertaking and is reserved for only the most important occasions. These include the yearly ceremony called *taur kesanga*, at Besakih, the large ceremony held on the day before Nyepi on the date of new moon in the ninth lunar month, Tilem Kesanga. In addition to the above animals these *taur* require a water buffalo, a goat, a cow, a black pig, and a goose with black-and-white coloring.

Once every hundred years comes the great series of ceremonies called Eka Dasa Rudra, last held in March 1979. The scale of the *caru-taur* on March 28 of that year was truly staggering. (See CHAPTER 21.) An effort was made to get an example of every sort of animal native to Bali, and that including everything from insects on up. One of the stars was a *garuda*-eagle, which was said to have flown into an open window voluntarily, and another was a small tiger, actually a Bengal cat. (Neither of these species is, by the way, native to the island.) The count eventually reached about 60 varieties of animals.

On the day before the *taur* the animals were paraded three times around the temple area, and then most, but not all, were ceremonially killed by a very sacred kris wielded by a member of the Pande clan. This took place amid the chanting of the *pedandas*, their mantras consigning the souls of the animals to heaven and a more favorable reincarnation next time. The animals were physically killed in another area of the temple after the ritual killing occurred. Those that were spared were assembled to witness the proceedings.

NOT ALL OFFERINGS TO THE *BHUTAS* AND *KALAS* are *caru* although they still may require blood. A normal part of the conclusion of a variety of ceremonies involves a *pemangku* removing a small chick, *pitik*, from a bamboo box and twisting its head off, throwing the head and body on the ground so that the blood will flow. Sometimes a small male pig, a *celeng butuhan*, is used for the same purpose, in which case its throat is cut. In the very largest ceremonies a water buffalo, *kebo*, may be used. This action is called *penyamblehan*, from *sambleh*, meaning "to kill an animal as part of a rite against demons." This act is something like that of a *caru* except that no offerings are made along with the letting of blood. And the act of *penyamblehan* is usually performed in connection with a ceremony that is not a *bhuta yadnya* ceremony at all. The Rangda in our village always twists (or pulls) the head off a chick and drinks the blood as the first act performed after removal of the mask at the end of a *barong* dance performance.

The cockfight, *tajen*, provides another opportunity to appease the *bhutas* with the spilling of blood. Cockfights, and indeed, all forms of gambling, have at least theoretically been illegal in Indonesia for some years now. But the cockfight is a very old pastime in Bali and, if you know where to look, there is one going on every day. It is legal, however, to stage public cockfights in connection with temple ceremonies and other religious occasions. This way of spilling blood is considered essential. The law allows for only three rounds of a cockfight, however, and no betting is allowed. I have seen cockfights at *odalans* in our village start at dawn and continue until mid-afternoon, by which time worshipers have begun arriving with their offerings. The first three rounds are usually held in front of the main shrine of the temple. But after that the aficionados adjourn to a less public part of the temple grounds and continue all day long.

This sort of blood spilling is called *tabuh rah*. *Tabuh* in this case means pouring a liquid on the ground for the *bhutas* and *kalas*. In performing a *tabuh*, one executes a series of actions called *matabuh*. One first holds the container of liquid up to the *dewas*. The container is in the left hand. The right palm, fingers together, is used to waft the essence of the liquid to the *dewas*, in an action called *ngayab*, as if fanning the liquid's essence away from oneself toward the front. Usually the worshiper holds a flower between his first and second fingers. The container is then placed in the right hand. The right elbow is grasped with the left hand, and the contents of the container are spilled on the ground. Although the offering is directed toward the *dewas* or, depending on how one wants to look at it, the *dewas* are "informed" of the offering, the *tabuh* is really for the *bhutas* and *kalas*. A devout person, commoner or high caste, will pour a little of his drink and place a little of his food on the ground before eating.

A container for a *tabuh* may be almost anything. In the case of a bleeding cock, there is no container. The loser is just allowed to shed his blood on the ground. In most temple ceremonies many of the worshipers *matabuh* a little *brem*, or rice wine. The container is a banana leaf folded into the shape of a crude ladle, called a *tapan*. A bottle of *brem* and several *tapan* are generally close at hand for anyone wishing to use them. *Pemangkus* and *pedandas* generally *matabuh* using a *caratan*, a type of drinking bottle with an extended neck on one side. This may be made out of clay or metal, it makes little difference.

Theoretically a *tabuh* should consist of five different kinds of liquid, but one usually only sees all five used in the larger *caru* ceremonies. They are:

> *Tuak,* palm wine — white
> *Arak,* palm brandy — yellow
> *Brem,* rice wine — black
> *Toya anyar,* plain water — colorless
> *Darah,* blood — red

These five liquids symbolize the five liquids in the body: lymph, gastric juice, bile, serum, and blood. Their use in a *tabuh* gives hope that the five liquids in the body, the microcosmos, will be balanced and in harmony with the macrocosmos. In practice, only *brem* and *arak* are commonly used in ordinary temple ceremonies. And *tabuh* using blood, *tabuh rah,* is only the consequence of a cockfight.

CHAPTER 21

Eka Dasa Rudra

CENTENNIAL PURIFICATION OF THE UNIVERSE

"*BANGUN, LENGAR NYABLAR*" (rough translation: "Get up, bald man"). The voice of Budi, my brash young Balinese assistant, filters through the steady state background noise of dog howls. "You gotta have bright eye and bushy tills." Budi is proud of the American slang I have almost taught him. He already has my cameras and tripod on his shoulders, and drags me, still half-asleep, out into the chilly night.

Then I remember. Full moon tonight. When I checked earlier in the evening the usual hat of clouds obscured Gunung Agung, Bali's highest and most sacred mountain. So I decided to turn in early. Budi went off in search of entertainment because, on this most special of all special religious occasions, dances and musical performances were given every night. But with an eye always for a good photo, he left the dances and came to get me as soon as the clouds lifted.

"Look," he says, "*purnama*" (full moon).

And I behold one of the most chillingly beautiful sights I have ever seen on this island, where magnificent spectacles are routine. Before us lies Besakih, the mother temple complex and most sacred spot in Bali. At 1,000 meters above sea level the air is clear now, and the temporary electric lights shimmer in the midnight coolness. Above the pagodalike *merus* of the almost-deserted temples towers the hulk of Bali's Mount Olympus, a 3,142-meter silhouette against the bright, moonlit sky. Above it floats that brilliant time keeper. "Lovely" is somehow too benign an adjective — I feel in the presence of primordial, elemental forces. I think to myself that this is what Jawaharlal Nehru must have meant when he called Bali "the morning of the world."

EKA DASA RUDRA is Bali's most elaborate ceremony, held only on extremely rare occasions, in this case, 1979. The ceremony, which takes months to enact, intends to pacify "evil" represented as Rudra, the stormy side of Siwa. Rudra, loosely translated as "howler," is a god who represents wildness and can be traced back to pre-Hindu Vedic days. The ceremony is often represented as an exorcism, in which evil, incarnate as Rudra, is driven to the 11 (*eka dasa*) directions of space — the four cardinal points of the compass, the four intercardinal points, and up, down, and center. But the effort is really to achieve a balance between Siwa and Rudra, good and evil, throughout the 11 directions of space. In any case the ceremony is extremely rare. David Stuart-Fox, an Australian student of Balinese religion and foremost authority on Besakih, said there is no record of Eka Dasa Rudra being held more than twice since the 16th century. Once was in 1979. And once — an event shrouded in portent — was in 1963.

The 1963 Eka Dasa Rudra is still somewhat controversial. As it was held, in March of that year, Gunung Agung erupted, showering the area with ash, pouring down lava, and unleashing earthquakes. The event left thousands dead, and hundreds of thousands homeless. Bali still wears scars of ash and scorched earth where fertile rice fields once lay.

Two interpretations are offered for the disastrous 1963 ceremony. Some say the year was wrong, that it was chosen for reasons more political than religious and god showed his wrath by bringing the lava down. Religious leaders, however, say that to declare 1963 the wrong year questions the wisdom of the holy priest who set the date. The sacred texts, they say, provide for the ceremony to be held at nonstandard times if it seems urgent to restore harmony. This kind of ceremony is called Eka Dasa Rudra Peneregteg. Proponents of this viewpoint do not choose to interpret the meaning of the volcanic event.

I ask my friend of many years, Njoman Oka, whether 1979 is the correct year. After all, my wife, Maggie, Budi, and I are going to live here at Besakih, just six kilometers from Agung's crater, for three months. We don't want to experience the consequences of another miscalculation. Njoman, the most knowlegeable guide I know, replies that Eka Dasa Rudra should be held every century. And, according to the sacred palm leaf books, the *lontars*, it must be held whenever the year number ends in two zeros. This year is, indeed, 1979, which ends in no zeros at all. But the calendar in question here is the Hindu-Balinese lunar calendar, the Saka.

This calendar was named for a South Indian king from the Saka tribe, and it began when he ascended to the throne, in A.D. 78 according to our calendar. So the Saka year 1900 began in March of the Gregorian year 1978. And the climax of Eka Dasa Rudra will occur on the last day of the Saka year 1900, which is March 28, 1979 by the Gregorian calendar. The day after that Bali will join the 20th century. Saka years always end on the day of new moon, Tilem, of the ninth month, Kesanga, of the Saka calendar. And that date almost invariably occurs some time in March.

The ceremony involves elaborate preparation of offerings, animals for sacrifice, prayer, and performance, all culminating in a vast *taur* ceremony in which some 200,000 people, including the President of Indonesia, watch two dozen priests, attending tons of slaughtered animals and offerings, pacify the evil forces. The great *taur* took place on March 28, 1979, but the Eka Dasa Rudra ceremonies continued for another 42 days.

The article here takes the form of a journal, beginning with the description of the preparations, and then a day-by-day record through the important events of these three historic months.

EARLY MARCH. Preparations. The full moon that makes me wax so ecstatic marks half a month until the spectacular climax of Eka Dasa Rudra. Budi and I have been living at Besakih for almost three weeks, watching the complex preparations. Suci, the holy kitchen of Besakih, is busy day and night with high caste offering specialists, almost all of them women, making intricate and colorful *jaja,* special cookies of rice dough. The cookies are fried in large woks in hot coconut oil, fished out, drained, and then stacked up in the storeroom in huge piles. Outside of this sacred area, food is prepared for the hundreds of workers from all over the island who come to volunteer their time and talents.

Two weeks ago, at new moon, a ceremony to announce to God the beginning of Eka Dasa Rudra took place. It was cold, wet, and miserable. One could hardly see across the main temple of Besakih, the Pura Panataran Agung. The workers had to take shelter under the several *bales,* (pavilions). Offerings were placed in the *padma capah,* an open throne shrine dedicated to Ida Ratu Sila Majemuh, lord over the weather. It was always nice and sunny thereafter.

I Gusti Agung Gede Putra, the head of Bali's Department of Religion, and his wife, Ibu Putra, organized and directed many of the Eka Dasa Rudra ceremonies. Putra is a dignified, soft-spoken, scholarly man, and his wife is a human dynamo. She is never without a list in her hand and never more than a step away from the center of action. As I enter Suci one day, sprinkling myself with holy water from an earthenware pot as required, I am at once reprimanded by Ibu Putra: "Not with your left hand." I was to be reminded quite often thereafter that I had to curb my natural southpaw tendencies. The left hand is considered to be unclean.

Besakih is the principal state temple of Bali. Tourists are kept away for the several months of Eka Dasa Rudra, but thousands of Balinese pilgrims arrive daily to place offerings in one or more of the many temples and shrines of the complex. They are ministered to by one of the *pemangkus,* the lay priests who are in immediate charge of all the temples of Bali. Always clad in white, the *pemangkus* are the real workers — they take care of the routines of day-to-day ceremonies, receive the offerings, sprinkle the throngs with holy water, and look after the maintenance of the temple properties. The *pedandas* show up only for the most important ceremonies, and then only to chant their powerful mantras, ring their bells, waft their incense, and communicate directly with God. They are deeply revered, but they do no physical labor in the temple. Their lives are entirely occupied with spiritual matters.

One day Ibu Putra called Budi over and hastily filled him in on an imminent event. "The white cow is here," said Budi, "and it's going to be milked. Come on." In Bali a white cow is holy. Every cow I had ever seen in Bali was tan, with a white rump. There just isn't any other color. But this one is albino. The cow is ceremonially washed, covered with a white cloth, and led into Suci, where a *pedanda* waits to bless it. The holy milk from the cow is to be used in making *madu parka,* a kind of special cookie that will be used in making sacred offerings. From the size of the cow's udder, I can immediately see there are going to be problems. A *pemangku* tries valiantly, but no milk. Fortunately another holy cow was present, this one black and white, and her udder bulged encouragingly. But with one more try the milker of the albino triumphantly held up his finger with one drop on it. That was deemed sufficient — it is quality, not quantity. These two cows of unusual color generated a remarkable amount of interest, and one would think that they were two-headed cows from the throngs of Balinese who crowd around.

Early in the celebration, the rice that will be used in making the many offerings is washed with holy water in a ceremony called *ngingsah.* Once blessed, the rice is stored in large woven bamboo baskets, the lids bearing inscriptions of Dewi Sri, the Rice Mother, a favorite of the Balinese. As one of the high caste ladies walked by these baskets of rice she noticed that the rice grains were jumping around like popping corn. Others hurry over and they corroborate her observations. News of this unusual event aroused much excitement. A few days earlier another portentious event took place. A women went into Suci to get the large frying pan offerings are cooked in and she found a large red snake coiled inside. It slithered out, headed in the direction of Gunung Agung. When she poured coconut oil into the pan it turned bright red. Again, others saw the same phenomenon.

A meeting of the Eka Dasa Rudra Committee is called. The two strange events are discussed, and the members decide they are "miracles." Obviously Dewi Sri is manifesting her satisfaction with the proceedings, as she herself jumped into the rice basket. And the red snake was surely one of the two great dragon-snakes, Naga Basuki and Naga Anantaboga, who rest upon the back of Bedawang, the world-turtle who supports the island of Bali. The omens are good for a successful ceremony. And the committee decides to commemorate the two miracles by distributing samples of the rice and oil to every village in Bali, to be installed in suitable shrines.

Finally the various manifestations of God are invited to come down from heaven to witness the ceremonies from the shrines of Besakih. *Pratimas,* small woodcarvings usually in the shape of small statues, are made ready as temporary homes for the visitors. *Pemangkus* and members of the committee carry the *pratimas* on their heads down the main steps of the Pura Panataran Agung which have been draped with a white sheet for the occasion. At the bottom of the steps is a water buffalo offering, the *titi mahmah* — head, hide, and hooves laid on the ground, covered with many offerings, with a sugar palm leaf figure on each side of the buffalo's head. *Titi* is the word for bridge, and the offering becomes a bridge between the world of man, *buwah,* and the world of God, *swah. Pedandas* offer mantras, and the *pratimas* are carried one at a time over the bridge and up to the pavilion where they will reside until the end of Eka Dasa Rudra.

Like people, the manifestations need to be sheltered, fed, and entertained with music and dance. The temple and offerings take care of the room and board, and the entertainment is provided by the music and dance that accompanies any Balinese ceremony, and Eka Dasa Rudra is no exception. Seldom was there a night during the many weeks that we lived at Besakih when entertainment was absent. Budi didn't miss a single one.

There is really no major distinction made between traditional Balinese music intended for pleasure and that for the entertainment of God — all music is sacred. The most common form of musical accompaniment to Balinese dance is provided by an orchestra that the Balinese call a *gong* and foreigners usually call a *gamelan.* The instruments played include bronze-keyed xylophones, double-ended drums, gongs and cymbals. The *gong* is limited to five-tone melodies, and rhythm and time changes provide the backbone of the music. The sound is metallic, bright, and exciting.

During the most important ceremonies of the festival, a very unusual musical group, called *selonding,* offered accompaniment. The instruments have iron instead of bronze keys, and are sacred and almost never exhibited to the public. Few people know how to play the *selonding,* and nobody is even allowed to touch it unless he is specifically given permission.

MARCH 24, 1979. My wife has arrived, and we get set for one of the more spectacular parts of Eka Dasa Rudra, when the *pratimas* are carried to the nearest beach — in this case, 30 kilometers away — for symbolic purification with holy water. All preparations for the procession to the sea, called *melasti,* have been completed.

Gigantic offerings of holy cookies are placed before the *padma tiga.* These *sarad* offerings depict the Balinese interpretation of the universe. At the bottom are the turtle and the two dragon-snakes. In the middle is the word of man, complete with trees, mountains, and fields. On top is heaven, populated with various aspects of God. One of these offerings, called a *gayah,* is made entirely of pig fat, omentum, and other connective tissue. It doesn't smell very good after a couple of days in the hot sun.

One of the most necessary preparations for going on such a trip is to get in sync with the Balinese sense of time. One thing you quickly learn in Bali is that time is most decidedly not of the essence. Indonesians half-jokingly refer to this as *jam karet* — "rubber time." True. Our quartz LCD watches, accurate to within 15 seconds a month, could just as well be replaced with sundials or hourglasses. We want to be up and away early so as not to miss the beginning of the procession. Budi takes it easy. "Remember," he says, "*jam karet.*" He is right as usual. We wait.

Instead of a stately procession of *pratimas* carried on the heads of their bearers, the *melasti* turns out to be more of a mad 30 kilometer dash. The goal is Batu Klotok, a black sand beach not far from the area's largest town, Klungkung. Budi and I have chartered a *bemo,* a truck with seats in the back, in order to stay ahead of the parade to get pictures. My wife Maggie and Njoman Oka go off in another car to another beach to watch a *ngeed* ceremony, a sacrifice of a water buffalo to the sea demons. They will meet us later at Klotok.

An electric power line stretches across the road on the way out of Besakih village. Just as they are about to pass under it, the bearers of one of the *pratimas* come to a halt, unable to move their legs. The manifestation within the *pratima* refuses to pass beneath the power cable. It is taken down, and the procession continues. Our *bemo* dashes madly ahead, stopping at predetermined locations to take telephoto shots of the procession twisting down the many hills and through the terraced rice fields.

All along the route villagers have erected tall *penjors* of bamboo, whose graceful arching tops roof the entire narrow street in places. And each village's entire population is turned out to pay homage. Tables full of offerings are displayed, and most villages provide a table of colored punch or young coconuts to quench the thirst of the marchers.

At Klungkung our *bemo* driver stops for a bite to eat. Budi tries to persuade him to stay ahead of the parade. No luck. The procession passes right through town. I am still ahead of it, but no *bemo* and no Budi. I have to walk the remaining four kilometers to Klotok lugging my camera gear.

An immense crowd has gathered at Batu Klotok. The *pratimas* are placed on raised platforms, *pedandas* intone their mantras, and the symbol-

THE PURA PENATARAN AGUNG AT BESAKI

ic washing occurs. Miraculously, Maggie and Njoman find us. They saw the buffalo sacrifice at a beach near Amlapura. There is to be another one here. A water buffalo calf, its horns gilded and its legs decorated with silver bracelets, is lugged into a Balinese double outrigger boat. Its legs are bound and a large stone hung around its neck. It is rowed out a few hundred meters from shore and the rock is thrown overboard. One of the officials told me that 58 buffaloes were used in Eka Dasa Rudra. Similar ceremonies occur today all over Bali, including one all-important one made right at the crater of Gunung Agung.

That night the procession returns to Klungkung and, early the next morning, proceeds to the temple at Sidemen, on a different road back to Besakih, where once again the entire village turns out for the welcome. The *pratimas* are enshrined, and they and the crowd are entertained by a performance of *topeng* — three men, singly or in a group, put on a series of fanciful masks and assume the identity of whatever character the mask portrays, an idiot, a gossip, an old man, a king, a servant, or even a tourist. The audience finds the conversation side-splitting. It is usually topical, often coarse, and occasionally downright bawdy. The crowd loves it.

On the third day the procession returns to Besakih. The *pratimas* receive a royal welcome at the foot of the main steps leading up to the Pura

Panataran Agung. A group of costumed girls performs a welcoming dance. Two *pedandas* in their tall and impressive miters, each hat topped with a quartz crystal ball, chant their mantras, wave their incense burners, and tinkle their bells. As when the *pratimas* were called down five days before, there is a buffalo sacrifice on the ground. The *pratimas* are carried over the buffalo bridge and on up to their shrines.

MARCH 27. Today is Mapepada, the day that animals, gathered for sacrifice in tomorrow's *taur* ceremony, are purified. Animals have been arriving in Suci for some weeks now, and the place is looking like a regular zoo. The *lontars* specify that certain species of animals native to Bali should, if possible, be sacrificed. I don't know how many species are required, but the committee did a pretty fair job, by their own count rounding up 85 species. The animals arrived during the days of preparation and were put in cages and boxes and left in the outer, less sacred, part of Suci. The pilgrims always stopped by to have a look. Some of the less-familiar species attracted considerable attention.

One of the stars of the growing zoo is a *garuda,* an eagle. This particular *garuda* was said to have flown right through an open window and into a house, allowing itself to be captured. All considered that to be an excellent omen. The zoo also boasts a tiger. According to Nature Reserve officials, although tigers are supposed to be extinct in Bali, there may still be some alive in the wild western part of the island. Looking very much like a striped house cat, the "tiger" was later identified from my photograph by a zoologist at the Smithsonian Institution as a leopard cat, *Felis bengalensis,* a small cat native to India.

There are turtles, deer, crocodiles, anteaters, bats, monkeys, centipedes, mice, rats, and the usual barnyard collection of ducks, goats, cows, water buffaloes, dogs, cats, and so on. My wife, who is quite an animal lover, expresses distaste at the thought of all these creatures being killed. "Well," says Njoman, "you must agree that they are being sacrificed for a good cause. And all are assured of reincarnation in a better form."

Each of the animals is covered with a cloth of an appropriate symbolic color and led or carried to the Pura Panataran Agung. All are sprinkled with holy water, and the *pedandas* pray over them. Then the entire procession parades three times clockwise around the outside of the temple enclosure, thousands of spectators crowding to get a good view. At the bottom of the stairs a member of the important clan of smiths, the Pande, symbolically kills each creature by laying his holy sword on its neck. The animals are actually sacrificed later on that day.

MARCH 28. Tilem Kesanga — new moon of the 9th Balinese lunar month;

the end of the Saka year 1900. Tonight is New Year's Eve. Tomorrow, Nyepi, New Year's Day, everything will be silent. No activities are allowed except those essential to safety and health. Everyone stays indoors and meditates. But that is tomorrow. Today is the emotional and physical climax of Eka Dasa Rudra, the day of the *taur*, the enormous sacrifice to the demons. A huge crowd is on hand. I estimate it at around 200,000. The president of the Republic of Indonesia, Suharto, is to arrive at noon. Everything is ready.

A large enclosure fenced with bamboo stakes has been set up near the foot of the main stairway. Within the enclosure are 11 shrines, one for each of the 11 directions. Each shrine is a high tripartite tower on bamboo poles with an adjoining pavilion for the *pedandas*. A 12th shrine stands in the center, not so high as the others. This will be used by the Bujangga Wesnawe, a priest specializing in *bhurta yadnya*. Because he is not of the Brahmana caste, as are all *pedandas*, his platform is lower.

Two *pedandas*, one of each of the two sects, Siwa and Buddha, attend each shrine. There are, therefore, 23 high priests in attendance this day — a most unusual concentration of them. The *taur* enclosure is literally spilling over with offerings, many of them heaped on the ground (these for the demons). All of the animals that were killed the day before are here, and all of the sacred cookies and other offerings that have been made during the many weeks of preparation in Suci are stacked here and there, the whole area bulging at the seams with offerings.

Near the *taur* enclosure, from which the public is excluded, a sacred and seldom-performed Gambuh dance begins, accompanied by a special orchestra featuring very long bamboo flutes. Near the pavilion where President Suharto will be seated a ceremonial *baris*, a warrior dance, is going on. A double line of young men and women from two of the remote and secretive Bali Aga villages of northeast Bali form an aisle down which Suharto will pass. Many are dressed in their traditional *geringsing* cloth, a double *ikat* material that is made and worn by no other group of Balinese.

The president arrives on schedule and sits next to Dr. Ida Bagus Mantra, governor of Bali. Suharto gives a short speech, stressing freedom of religion in Indonesia. He is a Muslim, and he is dressed in his traditional Central Javanese costume, with a tight-fitting black hat.

Then the *taur* begins and the priests present the offerings to the 11 directions. Each of the 23 priests prays independently. In a separate enclosure outside the *taur* area, still another priest performs the *mapedanan*, a ceremony directed toward the purification of humanity, an analog of the *taur* world-purification ceremonies. The immense crowd, seated on the ground, prays too, and *pemangkus* and high caste women sprinkle everyone they can reach with holy water.

Then the praying stops and pandemonium breaks out within the *taur* enclosure as hordes of Balinese pour in and grab anything and everything in sight. The celebrants paw over offerings in search of a holy part to be taken home to disperse more local demons. Here one stumbles over a horse's head, there a buffalo hoof, an eagle wing, or a monkey skin. The ornate *sarad* offerings are ripped asunder. Since God has absorbed their *sari*, "essence," the physical remains are now up for grabs. The most sought-after item is the holy water used in the purification ceremony. Eager villagers thrust bamboo containers at the *pedandas* who obligingly fill them up. It is an hour of chaos, incongruously following the solemn and stately purification rites. Almost everyone goes home now. The narrow road back to civilization is impossibly jammed.

Those who are in a hurry to leave miss another impressive and stately ceremony up in the Pura Panataran Agung, the *mapeselang*. The *pratimas* are once again taken from their pavilion. Officials carry them on their heads over a white ground cloth three times around the temple, each time stepping over yet another *titi mahmah* buffalo "bridge" sacrifice on the ground. A group of young girls performs the *pendet* welcoming dance. A *pedanda* requests God to bless and accept the prayers of the devotees with His love and involvement. The *pratimas* are returned to their pavilion. And with this the long day of March 28, 1979 comes to a close as does the climax of the biggest and most important ritual conducted in Bali within the memory of man.

But it is not the end of Eka Dasa Rudra. The climax, yes. Eka Dasa Rudra doesn't come to an end until May 9, 42 days from today. As we descend the long slope to the sea in our car we pass through village after village where little boys are beating on pans, drums, and barrels, anything that makes a noise, all waving kerosene torches and yelling. They are awakening the demons on New Year's Eve.

MARCH 29. Nyepi. New Year's Day. The first day of Bali's 20th century. Everything is abnormally quiet. The beach at Sanur is empty. We ponder the enormous sight we witnessed yesterday.

Budi and I continue our residence at Besakih. Maggie stays in Sanur photographing the Balinese as they prepare to make their pilgrimages to Besakih. We are at the other end, photographing the people as they arrive and pray. It is almost impossible to get into or out of Besakih village. The crowds are overwhelming.

Everyone in Bali is supposed to come to Besakih during the 42 days between the *taur* and the end of Eka Dasa Rudra, the first week of May. At the very least each family is supposed to send a representative if the entire group cannot make it. It appears that just about all 2.5 million Balinese do come. The place is mobbed every day and doubly so on weekends. Neighborhood village organizations, *banjars,* throughout Bali hire huge cargo trucks to take their members to Besakih for the day. Some ride their motor bikes. Some come on busses or *bemos.* A near tragedy occurs when an ancient bus, coming down the twisting mountain road from Besakih, cannot negotiate a hairpin turn. It rolls over onto its top, stopped from tumbling down the mountain by a large coconut tree — nobody is injured. This doesn't surprise anyone. After all, the pilgrims within had just been to Besakih to pray.

Those paying their respects at the temple dress in their finest traditional clothing. The sight is a feast of color. The women carry the offerings in woven bamboo baskets on their heads. The members of the crowd are of all ages. The parking lot is jammed with pilgrims, hustlers of refreshments, and police. It is a two-kilometer walk, steeply uphill, to the foot of the temple steps. The first half of the route is lined with food, drink, and souvenir stalls, selling delicious-looking skewers of *saté,* peanuts, fluorescent soft drinks, plastic toys, Eka Dasa Rudra T-shirts, film, rice, and pennants. The crowd is orderly, but not solemn.

You can tell who in the crowd has been to the temple and who is yet to go because those coming from prayer have rice grains stuck to their foreheads and temples. Homage is paid in a simple ceremony. Each man sits, each woman kneels, before the *padma tiga.* The men sit on their sandals. Hands are extended as the *pemangku* in charge asperges everyone with holy water. He then gives each supplicant a small square coconut leaf basket called a *canang,* in which there are flowers and other small essentials for prayer. He lays a stick of smoking incense on top to carry the prayers to God. Each person takes a blossom and holds it between his fingertips, pressing his thumbs to his forehead. At the end of each prayer, the flower is flipped forward toward the *padma tiga* with the fingers. Another is taken up, and the process is repeated three times. An attendant comes around with holy water. The worshiper holds out his hands, takes the holy water into his right palm three times and sips it. The fourth pouring is spread over face and hair. The *pemangku* passes around some sticky rice, and each presses a few grains onto forehead and temples. The whole takes but a few minutes, and no formal prayers are said.

The groups of villagers often take photos of themselves or their friends before they leave, and many stop for a picnic lunch on the grass strip dividing the access road. There they eat the offerings that they brought to the temple — God having consumed the essence and the nonedible parts left back at the temple.

Sometimes a whole village will bring a particularly elaborate or unusual offering. One day Budi heard through his intelligence network, by now well established, that the members of the nearby village of Selat were bringing an unusual *barong* offering. The Balinese *barong* is a holy beast that takes many forms. The usual is that of the *barong ket*, the lion, which is featured in the famous *barong* dance. Two men, under a shaggy coat of palm fiber, manipulate the bright and bearded mask of the Barong, clacking the jaws loudly during the performance. What arrived in Besakih was a full-sized Barong, perhaps 15 feet long, made entirely of various kinds of fruits, edible roots, vegetables, and rice, all tied to a wooden frame. The villagers lugged it up the steps and left under a canopy near the temple. This is a *salaran* offering, the fruits of the earth in the shape of a *barong* — itself a sign of prosperity. I want to show it to my wife, but by the time she returns the next day, all that remains is the wooden frame, the fruits having been picked off by hungry pilgrims.

APRIL 12. Purnama Kedasa, the full moon of the 10th lunar month. Today is the date of what is normally the most important ceremony of the Balinese lunar year, *bhatara turun kabeh* — "the gods descend all together." This year, dwarfed in size and importance by the great purification, the ceremony has become part of Eka Dasa Rudra. It is none the less impressive. Five water buffaloes are sacrificed, their hides, heads, and hooves laid out in still other bridges linking the world of man with heaven in the Pura Panataran Agung. Three *pedandas* officiate. In a large circular frying pan, attendants whip up an offering to the demons out of eggs, coconut, rice, and blood. They pour the mixture on the ground around the buffalo sacrifices. Then the *pratimas* are taken down, as on the evening of the *taur* sacrifice, carried three times around the temple over a white cloth, welcomed by a *pendet* dance, three *baris* dances, and a *rejang* dance. The *pedandas* pray over them once again, and the *pratimas* are returned to their pavilion.

APRIL 23. We are in the temple at 7 A.M. It is going to be a very busy day. The first ceremony, conduced in front of the *padma tiga*, is the distribution of the "miracle" oil and rice to representatives of all the villages of Bali. The oil is packed in little bottles wrapped in white cloth. The rice has been placed in brown pottery containers and also wrapped in white. Although some confusion slows down the distribution, each village representative eventually is on his way home from Pura Panataran Agung with his two treasures placed securely in a silver bowl.

All of the *pedandas* of Bali have been invited to the temple to share the thanks from the Eka Dasa Rudra Committee for making the ceremony successful. About 125 of them show up, more *pedandas* in one place than anyone has ever seen. A place is prepared for each one in front of the *padma tiga*. Every spot has the ingredients for making holy water, as well as suitable gifts. As they chant their mantras, each in his own pitch and at his own tempo, the overall sound is eerie and impressive.

Budi's informants have told him that there is now to be a cockfight, so we walk over to the pavilion where Governor Mantra is sitting. Cockfighting is, or used to be before gambling was prohibited, the national pastime of Bali. The man who didn't own a fighting cock and who didn't make considerable wagers on it at every opportunity was the exception. Today cockfights are usually held in an arena outside a temple in connection with festivals — the spilling of blood is considered an important way to placate the demons. This is the first cockfight I've ever seen that is actually in a temple. Despite loud warnings that the contest is purely a religious event and betting not allowed, those in attendance cannot refrain from a friendly wager or two.

Months ago, the Eka Dasa Rudra Committee had vowed to sacrifice a water buffalo if the proceedings went flawlessly. They certainly did. So today the promised sacrifice is made in a ceremony called *megat sot,* which refers to "cutting" an obligation. Cutting this tie involves seven *pedandas* — two are *pedandas* Buddha, five Siwa. By the time the chanting and praying begin, it is already dark. They dedicate a commemorative plaque, which announces the successful completion of the 1900 Eka Dasa Rudra. In a little pavilion at the top of the main stairs the governor and members of the Committee place offerings, coconut and white thread on the backs of their left hands. They are sprinkled with holy water. With a sudden toss, the offerings are thrown into the air and a large basket of offerings is torn open inside the pavilion. All present walk back to the Pura Panataran Agung across the debris of offerings.

Finally the bamboo containers of holy water from the mountains of Java, Lombok, and from all over Bali are taken down from the bamboo tower-shrines where they have hung for several weeks. The waters are mixed, sprinkled over the shrines of Besakih and over all those present. The ceremony is called *panyimpenan,* heralding the return of God to heaven. The *pratimas* are carried down, led by a woman carrying a tall basket of offerings. When all reach the bottom of the steps the woman turns to face the *pratimas.* She tips the basket over, spilling the offerings on the ground. The *pratimas* are carried to their home shrines in the other parts of the Besakih complex, away from the Pura Panataran Agung.

High caste offering specialists take some of the leftover offerings, burn them in a small fire, and place the ashes in two small, green coconuts which are then wrapped in white cloth and buried in the ground of the main temple. This is a request for fertility of the soil and prosperity for humanity.

MAY 9. Today is the final ceremony of Eka Dasa Rudra, 42 days after the *taur* sacrifice. During the past several days groups from the committee have gone to temples and shrines all over Bali and to Gunung Semeru on Java and Gunung Rinjani on Lombok to give notice that Eka Dasa Rudra has succeeded and that the ceremonies are coming to a close.

The final ceremony is to take place at a temple called Pura Pasar Agung, halfway up the slopes of Gunung Agung. The 1963 eruption destroyed this temple and it has only recently been rebuilt. Budi and I spend the night in a villager's house in the tiny village of Sebudi. This hamlet was totally wiped out in 1963. The scene on each side is still almost total desolation — nothing but black lava and debris. Early the next morning, we start out on foot. Although there is no road, several hundred people make the three-hour climb. (A new road now leads to within two kilometers of Pura Pasar Agung.) Vapor and clouds give an air of mystery to the small temple.

A *pedanda* leads the prayers that ask the forgiveness of God for inadvertent mistakes and shortcomings during the course of the last three months. A *pemangku* brings holy water from a holy spring near the crater of the sacred mountain. Everyone prays. Eka Dasa Rudra is over.

It is a solemn and joyful moment — solemn because all realize that they have taken a part in a historic event; joyful because that part and that event have been successful and have been accompanied by good omens. Here, a couple of kilometers from sacred Agung's fog-shrouded summit, is a fitting place for Eka Dasa Rudra to end. Wayan Surpha calls Budi and me over to lunch. I remember to eat the *lawar*, Bali's favorite ceremonial feast, with my right hand. There is relief, laughter, joking, and joy. The walk back to Sebudi and our vehicles is light-hearted and pleasurable. Good and evil have been brought back into balance for another 100 years.

CHAPTER 22

The Odalan

VISITING A TEMPLE FESTIVAL

IT IS MID-AFTERNOON, and the heat of the day has broken, the air finally growing more comfortable. Approaching the temple by road you pass streams of villagers moving in both directions. All are dressed in their very best traditional clothes, frangipani or hibiscus blossoms woven into their hair or thrust behind their ears. Batiks, and brocades woven with gold, shimmer in the afternoon sunlight, and all walk with utmost grace and poise. The women carry offerings on their heads. Some may be great towers of fruits, colored rice cakes, and meats. Others may be relatively simple, square leaf baskets containing multicolored flowers.

As you get out of your vehicle your senses are overwhelmed. The shimmering, staccato sounds of the village *gong*, the percussion orchestra, greet your ears from within the temple. In a tower near the temple entrance, two small boys energetically beat the hollow log *kulkul*, the summoning drum. Food sellers hawk their wares outside the gate. The smell of sweet hair oils mixes with clouds of incense and sandalwood smoke, and sizzling *saté* competes with the shouts of card players squatting on the ground nearby. Sellers of patent medicines vie with displays of T-shirts, sunglasses, knives, batik, colored pictures, and with sellers of violently colored beverages.

EVERY TEMPLE IN BALI has a regularly scheduled festival, an *odalan*, to celebrate the anniversary of its dedication. There are so many temples in Bali that there is an excellent chance that any visitor who stays more than a day or two can witness one of these colorful, lovely, moving religious celebrations. Every village has at least three temples, the Pura Desa, Pura Puseh, and Pura Dalem, and most villages of any size have many more public temples than the minimum. There are, in addition, regional temples, state temples, irrigation societies' *subak* temples, neighborhood associations' *banjar* temples, and even modest temples in individual house compounds called *sanggah*. (See CHAPTER 24.) Someone once estimated that there are 20,000 temples in Bali. My guess is that there are many more than that. And every one of these temples has an *odalan*. The ceremonies range in size from simple family affairs to enormous celebrations that last for days and attract worshipers from all over the island.

The Balinese use three different calendar systems. One is the standard Gregorian calendar — but that is not the calendar by which *odalans* are set. *Odalans* are scheduled by either the lunar calendar, the Saka, or by the 210-day ceremonial cycle, the Pawukon. The latter consists of 30 weeks, each seven days long. Most *odalans* are set by the Pawukon, which makes things difficult for the visitor. Fortunately, however, just about every house on the island has a Balinese calendar, and it is easy to determine the calendar date of a particular *odalan* if you know its day on the Pawukon.

Some temples fix their *odalans* according to the lunar calendar. Usually an *odalan* occurs at either full or new moon, more likely full than new. The date will be specified by indicating the name of the lunar month and whether the date lands on full moon, Purnama, or new moon, Tilem. The month name will be the number of the month according to the Saka system. The first month of the Saka calendar, Kasa, begins sometime in June, which confuses matters for the Westerner. But again, a Balinese calendar will display the dates of new and full moon — they are marked with large black dots for new and large red dots for full moon — and the month names are printed under the dates for each day of the month.

When visiting a temple, dress is important. Shorts and bathing suits are no more appropriate in a Balinese place of worship than in a church or temple or mosque anywhere in the world. And the Balinese are very sensitive about tourists' costumes. They feel that it is sacrilegious to enter a temple without some sort of sash or scarf tied around the waist.

Most *odalans* last for three days, although some go on for more than a week and a few last only one day. Further, the elaborateness of a given temple's *odalan* varies from one year to the next, every other *odalan* usually being larger. Although many days of preparation are involved in staging the ceremonies, the part that intrigues most visitors begins at 3 or 4 in the afternoon when women carry offerings to the temple and villagers gather to pray. *Odalans* go on until very late at night or even into the morning hours. The ceremonies vary so much from village to village that it is impossible to state exactly what the visitor will see. But there are many common features, and it is possible to draw a useful composite picture.

AS YOU ENTER THE MIDDLE TEMPLE area through a huge split gate you sense a change of spirit. Here commerce is prohibited, but people do sit, chat, and relax. You now see the *gong,* the *gamelan* club, many of them mere children, hammering gaily away at their tinkling, bronze-keyed instruments. When the trained musicians rest, a horde of little boys descend upon the instruments and start improvising, often rather well. Fortunately it is almost impossible to harm a *gamelan.* During the musical performance you are likely to see a child sitting in the lap of his father as he plays. As soon as father takes a break for a cigarette, the child takes up where daddy left off. Just a short way off from the *gong,* a group of older men recite from palm leaf books in an ancient language. This recitation is called *kakawin.* The alphabet and language are ancient Balinese, related to the Sanskrit-derived Kawi of Central Java. After one man reads a phrase in a sing-song fashion, another translates into the vernacular so interested bystanders can understand. Few Balinese can read or understand Kawi. The women set down their offerings in a pavilion and put last-minute touches on them just before entering the inner temple.

You follow some women carrying offerings through a gigantic gate graced with the leering visage of a fanged monster. This is Bhoma, son of the earth. You are entering the inner sanctum, the most sacred part of the three temple courtyards. Evil spirits are discouraged from entering by this scary face as well as by a short, free-standing wall that partially blocks the entrance. Evil spirits cannot readily turn sharp corners. You stand quietly behind the worshipers, never moving in front of them. You are welcome to take photos (there is no roof), even using a flash, and to talk, ask questions, and move around unobtrusively. This is not a solemn event. No Balinese ceremonies are solemn. Everyone chats, jokes, and laughs. It is a joyous occasion. It is not a time to humble oneself, but to welcome the village gods to the temple, to make them happy with beautiful sights, sounds, and smells. Gay flags, banners, and umbrellas decorate the small buildings and shrines within. Long, decorated bamboo poles, *penjors,* sprout from the entrances to the shrines. The atmosphere is charged, at once with magic, festivity, and prayer.

The men remove their sandals and then sit cross-legged on them on the ground. The children sit alongside. The women put down their offerings in a small open *bale* (pavilion) and make last-minute adjustments. The offerings are then carried to a temporary table next to the principal shrine. Here the women have the small bottles that they have carried from home filled with holy water by the temple priest or one of his assistants. These will be carried home and placed in a shrine in the family temple. And each woman accepts from the priest several small square or round trays. These trays are made of coconut leaf and contain, among other things, flowers, a bit of fruit, and a small package that contains *areca* nut, betel leaf, and lime. This is the *canang,* the most common form of Balinese offering. The *canangs* are brought by every worshiper, usually atop a larger offering, and the small baskets are then blessed by a priest and returned to be used by each individual who offers prayers. One doesn't necessarily use the same *canang* she brings — after blessing them, the priest or lay priest usually just sets them out in a line, the worshipers picking one up from the front. The women then rejoin their families on the ground, kneeling rather than sitting. Each worshiper dips his right hand into a coconut shell bowl of holy water to purify himself before praying, puts a *canang* on the ground in front of where he or she is seated, and then places a stick of smoking incense on top of the *canang* or sticks it into the ground nearby.

The act of prayer consists of grasping a flower from the *canang* between the middle fingers, palms together, thumbs against the forehead. A prayer is recited and the flower is flipped forward. A second, then a third prayer is offered in this same way. If a priest leads the praying there may be as many as five separate prayers, the first and fifth offered without flowers and the second, third, and fourth each offered with a differently colored flower to symbolize the color associated with that aspect of God toward which the prayers are directed. At some of the larger ceremonies a kind of fan-shaped offering, called *kewangen,* is held to the forehead in one of the prayers.

After the prayers, the attendants offer holy water. First the attendant dips a flower into a dipper of holy water and uses it to flip water onto the worshiper. Then the worshiper holds his hands palms up, right on top of left, and the attendant pours some holy water into the right palm of the worshiper, who sips a bit. The attendant holds the dipper in his right hand, clasping the right elbow with his left hand, a gesture symbolic of reverence. The worshiper sips three times from the holy water, and rubs the fourth and fifth portions on his or her face and hair. After a final sprinkling from the attendant, the prayers are over. The attendant offers a dab of damp rice, and the worshiper presses a bit of it onto each temple, the forehead, and the chest just below the throat. A small amount of this rice is also eaten.

Meanwhile, seated in the center on a mat, one or several men clad all in white are praying fervently, each ringing a bronze bell with his left hand and occasionally flipping flowers toward the offerings piled in front of them. Sandalwood smolders in a brazier nearby, and its fragrant smoke mixes with the incense that fills the air above the worshipers. Periodically each man takes a small basket and wafts the essence of the offerings and the smoke toward the deities. These are the lay priests, the *pemangkus,* who have direct charge of temple affairs. Their prayers present the offerings themselves to the focus of the ceremony, the visiting gods. In contrast to the high caste *pedandas,* who are often regal and very conscious of their exalted position, *pemangkus* are humble, often very poor people who

FAMILY PRAYING AT AN ODALAN

devote a large portion of their lives to taking care of their temples, seeing to it that they are kept clean and in good repair, and presiding over any ceremonies that are held within. They are not necessarily well-educated, but are intensely religious and undergo considerable personal hardship in order to fulfill their functions. Most *pemangkus* are men, but there is no gender restriction, and one sometimes sees a woman in this role.

The worshipers now arise, put on their shoes, take up their offerings, and leave to go home. If the high offerings are heavy, there is always someone nearby to help a woman lift the tall, unwieldy column to her head. There is much socializing in the middle and outer courtyards of the temple as neighbors visit, admire each other's children, and discuss village affairs. An *odalan* is also a social event, and the Balinese are not immune to gossip. When an offering is returned home the fruits and cakes and meats can be eaten freely by the family. The essence, *sari*, of the offerings has been given to God, and the remains can be consumed. For most people, there are no prohibitions against eating an offering, but *pemangkus* generally do not, and *pedandas* never do. But most people do, and quite willingly, because no expense is spared to buy the finest fruits, to make the most delicious cakes, and to cook the best meats — luxuries the average family is forced to deny itself under ordinary circumstances.

A constant, two-way stream of those who have prayed and those who are about to do so passes through the narrow temple gate. Those women who carry very high offerings are forced to stoop low so that their loads will pass under the lintel of the entrance gate. It is a truly unforgettable sight, as the afternoon shadows start to lean, and the sun shimmers in the gold hair decorations of the women and the gold brocades of the men. The little children, clean as a whistle and, for once, behaving themselves, are proudly led by father or uncle. The grace of the women balancing their offerings is matched only by the lovely gestures of their flowered prayers.

At the *odalans* of some of the larger and more important temples, the women of each neighborhood association, *banjar,* come with their offer-ings in a group — a long procession of identically dressed women, followed by an abbreviated version of the *gong,* a sort of marching band that has only the drums, cymbals, and a large gong. These processions are especially spectacular and photogenic. There may be two or three in a single after-noon, each led by several little girls, dressed in the finest traditional cloth-ing that money can buy. The members enter the temple as a group, and their offerings, all stacked in the area in front of where prayers are said, make a lovely sight.

Some *odalans* may feature one or more visiting *barong* dance troups. I have seen *odalans* at which as many as 50 guest *barongs* and their retinues regularly attend. Chances are that you have seen one of the *barong* perfor-mances at Batubulan. But there are many varieties other than the lion *barong ket* that performs there. A *barong* is a creature possessing great magic powers whose principal task is to guard the village and protect it from evil influences. Most *barongs* are animals, usually lions, but there are other varieties, such as boars. The animal-like *barong* characters wear elabo-rate masks with movable jaws and very fancy headdresses, with shaggy bod-ies usually of palm fiber. Inside the *barong* are two men who support the heavy costume, walk with it when it has to be transported, and dance when the occasion presents itself.

Certain *barongs* have ties to certain temples and to certain other *barongs.* This may come about for any of several reasons. One is that the magical mask of a *barong* may have been made from the wood of a tree that grows or grew in the temple courtyard. If that is so, the *barong* is obliged to visit this temple at *odalan* time, no matter how far away the members of the troupe live. It may be a considerable distance, in which case the *barong* may have to be taken to the temple by truck. Whatever the reason, the dancers arrive amid much ceremony. The *barong* is powerful, and people squat or kneel in its presence. There may be several visiting *barongs*. Some temples have dozens — each with its followers, *pemangkus, gong,* and special worshipers. In the dance, Barong is often accompanied by its counterpart, Rangda. Rangda is a complex figure. She is generally regarded as a very magical witch, the personification of all that is bad. She certainly is a fearsome sight, with great fangs, a long tongue, pendulous breasts, a hairy body, and threatening gestures.

Most visitors to *odalans* are content to spend only an hour or two watching the parade of worshipers coming and going, the color, and the spectacle. If one stays into the evening hours other equally interesting events occur, but these may not even begin until well after 10 or 11 P.M. and often last until dawn. Before the *odalan* begins, the gods are invited to descend to the temple (this is one reason Balinese temples do not have roofs). Most public temples, and some large family temples, own elaborate carved and painted wooden statues, usually in the forms of a fantastic and fanciful animals. Always associated with these carvings are much smaller, rather inconspicuous humanlike figures that the gods are invited to inhabit while visiting. Each pair of figures is called a *pratima*. The larger, animal-like figure is the vehicle upon which the god symbolically rides. The *pratima* are normally kept locked up in the several temple shrines, but at *odalan* time they are taken out, decorated, and left exposed for the duration of the ceremonies. At most *odalans,* usually at night, these *pratima* are taken down from their pavilions and paraded with reverence around the temple on the heads of women, blessed with holy water and greeted with mass prayers. They may be taken to a nearby holy spring or well, or to the sea, where they are symbolically cleansed with holy water. The Balinese do not worship the *pratima* themselves. After the *odalan,* when the spirits return to heaven, the *pratima,* although treated with respect, are put away, locked up, and forgotten about until the next *odalan*.

During the evening there are almost always very sacred dances held in the inner temple courtyard to welcome and entertain the visiting deities. These are usually stately and graceful performances that have no narrative function. And there is almost always a performance of some sort of dance drama, with music. These are of a more secular nature than the inner temple dances and usually have some sort of story. They are never held in the inner courtyard, but rather, in the middle or outer areas of the temple. The famous *wayang kulit,* or shadow puppet play, is a very popular adjunct to many *odalans*. The principal function of all of these performances is to entertain the visiting deities, but the villagers crowd the temple, standing or squatting on the ground for hours on end to share in the ancient tales that they know by heart.

A BALINESE VILLAGE IS VERY MUCH A LIVING ORGANISM. Its many temples and its inhabitants must be fed a regular series of ceremonies, just as a human being must consume food, in order to keep the negative, impure forces of destruction in balance with the positive, holy, pure forces of construction. Hindu-Balinese philosophy conceives of the universe, and all within it, as an equilibrium between good and bad forces. Neither can be eliminated, but ugly things can occur when nothing is done to maintain balance so that the negative influences get the upper hand. Religious ceremonies maintain the balance. The lovely offerings that you see are for the positive forces, but just as much effort and attention is given to their negative counterparts, though this is not apparent to the casual visitor.

About 95 percent of the time a temple stands empty, unused and uninhabited by gods or people, except for the *pemangku* who comes to clean up occasionally. Simple rites may be held at full or new moon, or on other minor religious days. But, the *odalan* is the only really major event. The occasion of an *odalan* is not just one for worship. The temple has to be repaired and cleaned. It is a major cooperative social event and, as such, is a time when disparate groups can get together and work on a single project for the common good. Hundreds of villagers work together to prepare offerings, food, decorations, and to attend to the thousand and one details involved in any big occasion such as this. But the major theme, of course, is religious. The gods are invited to descend and occupy the special shrines reserved for them alone. A "ladder" of prayers and incense is provided for their descent by the *pemangku*.

Once the invited gods are present they must be suitably fed and entertained and catered to just as any honored human guest would expect to be treated, except in this case more so because the guests are divine. The perfumed air, the colors and decorations, the music and dance and entertainments, the chanting of the sacred texts, and the essence of the many offerings are provided only to satisfy all of the sensory perceptions of these holy visitors and to welcome them to their former earthly home and family.

So an *odalan* is a multifaceted event. It is basically a religious rite, but it has important social functions in the life of the village. It provides entertainment in areas where TV is still an expensive luxury. It is a county fair, a night market, and a place to chat with friends from out of town. It provides an occasion for repairing and renewing the local temples. And it is an essential force in restoring that most important of all requirements in the Balinese concept of the universe — balance between opposing forces.

Since *odalans* are regularly scheduled events they are actually the easiest of all Balinese ceremonies to visit. There is always some sort of ceremony or another going on some place or another in Bali, but there is normally no predictable pattern to the scheduling. The Badung Government Tourist Promotion Board publishes annually a leaflet titled: "Bali Calendar of Events." It doesn't list all of the *odalans* — that would be impossible. But it does list the important ones and the ones near the Denpasar-Sanur-Kuta-Ubud areas, in one of which you are likely to be staying. The Badung Tourist Promotion Board is located at Jalan Surapati Number 7, Denpasar. This is the large, new building on the main road between Denpasar and Sanur, two blocks east of the big four-faced statue that marks Denpasar's main intersection. The tourist board is open every day except Sunday. All services are free, including the calendar of events. You may also be able to get information about other interesting events here. But you will at least be able to get accurate and helpful information about the dates of *odalans,* their locations, how to get to them — and how to get back.

If you have time, and if, in the course of your travels around the island, you see something going on that looks like a festival of some sort, then by all means stop and have a look. Always carry a sash to wear around your waist. If you are wearing long pants or a skirt, and if you put on the sash, you will always be welcome. The Balinese are extremely friendly people and welcome foreigners to their ceremonies — if the guests dress properly and observe elementary good manners. Remember that what you are seeing are sacred ceremonies, not public shows, and behave accordingly.

HERE IS A LIST of some of the island's many *odalans,* with a brief description of each and the day of the Pawukon or Saka calendar on which they occur. (For more on the calendars, see CHAPTER 17.) First a list of the dates, for the next decade, of the first day of the Pawukon according to the Gregorian calendar.

June 18, 1989
January 14, 1990
August 12, 1990
March 10, 1991
October 6, 1991
May 3, 1992
November 29, 1992
June 27, 1993
January 23, 1994
August 21, 1994

March 19, 1995
October 15, 1995
May 12, 1996
December 8, 1996
July 6, 1997
February 1, 1998
August 30, 1998
March 28, 1999
October 24, 1999

LIST OF *ODALANS*

WEEK 1, SINTA

WEDNESDAY: Pura Kehen, Bangli. An hour's drive from Denpasar, this is a lovely old terraced temple on the side of a hill. High offerings are carried up the long stairs, starting in the afternoon. Usually entertainment at night.

Pura Agung Intaran, Sanur. Not especially distinguished except that it is near the Sanur hotels.

Pura Gunung Lebah in Ubud. Again, only mentioned for its proximity to a tourist center.

WEEK 2, LANDEP

SATURDAY: Pura Mutering Dalem Jagat Sidakarya. An important temple in South Sesetan.

WEEK 4, KULANTIR

TUESDAY: Pura Penataran-Tangkas in Sukawati. There is a long and colorful parade of young girls wearing long dresses that trail on the ground. They go to a holy spring nearby.

WEEK 6, GUMBREG

WEDNESDAY: Pura Desa and Pura Puseh Guang in Sukawati. Has a procession of young girls wearing long dresses. Procession goes to a nearby holy spring.

WEEK 7, WARIGA

SATURDAY: Pura Puseh-Pura Desa, Batuan. A very colorful *odalan*, often with daytime entertainment and always some at night. Batuan is the home of a famous *gambuh* dance group that usually performs during the day.

WEEK 9, JULUNGWANGI

TUESDAY: Pura Ulun Danau Beratan near Bedugul and Baturiti. This temple, on the shores of Lake Beratan, is especially important to the irrigation societies, since the lake is supposed to be the source of all irrigation water in South Bali. It is about an hour's drive north of Denpasar.

Pura Batu Klotok. A small but spectacularly located temple right by the sea. Take the road from Klungkung straight south, past Gelgel, as far as you can go. It takes at least 1-1/2 hours to get there from Denpasar, but it is worth the trouble.

WEDNESDAY: Pura Bukit Sari. This is the temple at the famous Monkey Forest in Sangeh, about a 45-minute drive north of Denpasar.

WEEK 11, DUNGGULAN

THURSDAY: Pura Batukaru in Tabanan Kabupaten. High up on the slopes of Mount Batukaru, this is a very holy temple, though not large, and people from all over Bali come to pray. It is often cool and rainy.

Pura Puseh, Sempidi, a 15-minute drive north of Denpasar on the Tabanan road. This is a very colorful *odalan*. There are several processions, starting at about 4 P.M., in which groups of ladies from the different *banjars* carry high offerings to the temple. Within, the temple is beautifully decorated, and the attendants are particularly nicely attired.

Pura Dalem, Beringkit. This is located near Mengwi, about a 20-minute drive north of Denpasar, right next to the big cattle market. It features exceptionally high offerings.

FRIDAY: Pura Ulunsiwi, Jimbaran, just south of the airport, about a 10-minute drive from Kuta. A beautiful old temple with a multiroofed tower or *meru*. Crowded with worshipers at about 4 P.M. and on into the night. Usually no entertainment. Lasts only one day, but there is some indication that this will be extended to the usual three.

WEEK 12, KUNINGAN

SUNDAY: Pura Tameng, Sukawati, next to the Kantor Camat. The actual date of the *odalan* is the preceding Wednesday, but there is a procession to a holy spring on this day of young girls wearing long dresses. Otherwise not especially noteworthy.

SATURDAY: Pura Taman Pule, Mas. About half an hour's drive from Denpasar. This is a three-day *odalan*. It has everything: a huge outdoor fair, day and night-time entertainment, colorful processions with high offerings just at sunset, and a lovely interior decorated with hundreds of umbrellas.

Pura Desa, Sempidi. Exactly the same as the *odalan* of the Pura Puseh, described under Thursday of week 11, above.

Pura Sadha, Kapal, about a 20-minute drive north of Denpasar. A very colorful, nicely decorated temple, jam-packed with worshipers. It always has a nice *gong*.

Pura Timbrah, Paksabali. This small temple is located north of Klungkung, about an hour's drive from Denpasar. Cross the bridge east of Klungkung and take the first paved road to the north. The temple is just a few kilometers north of Klungkung on the west side. In mid-afternoon a long trough of white rice is placed on the ground and children eat their fill. The *pratimas* are then carried on litters to a holy spring away from the temple. When the *pratima* bearers return, they find that the *pratimas* "don't want to go back" into the temple. There follows a wild melee in which a chorus of women tries to coax the spirits to return, but they resist. The bearers go into trance, and there is some self-stabbing. Be sure to stand well clear of the free-for-all. Sometimes called a "God fight."

Pura Sakenan, on Serangan, Turtle Island, lying about one kilometer off the coast, between Sanur and Benoa. The *odalan* starts on this day, but the big day is the following day, Sunday.

WEEK 13, LANGKIR

SUNDAY: This is the big day at Pura Sakenan, on Turtle Island, see previous entry. At low tide you can walk across from the beach. But, most people take boats from an area along the Nusa Dua by-pass highway between Benoa and Sanur. There is always a very colorful and confused traffic jam of boats of all sizes and descriptions. Pura Sakenan is a very sacred temple, and people from all over Bali come here to pray. It has one of the biggest outside fairs.

WEDNESDAY: Pura Tanah Lot. This famous little temple is perched on a huge rock just off the coast of Tabanan. Drive toward Tabanan and turn left at the stop light in Kediri. It takes about an hour to get there from Denpasar. Big crowds come to pray. Many booths of food sellers. Stay to watch the sunset.

Pura Dalem Waturenggong, Mengwi Tani. This is an interesting and colorful ceremony at a temple just north of the main Denpasar-Tabanan road, on the main road to Mengwi and Sangeh.

WEEK 14, MEDANGSIYA

SUNDAY: Pura Petilan, Pengerebongan, Kesiman, just northeast of Denpasar, on the main road toward Batubulan. Only a 10-minute drive from Sanur or central Denpasar. Big processions of *barongs* and *rangdas,* parading in all afternoon. After praying in the inner temple, with a sudden shout, many boys and men go into trance and try to stab themselves with kris. The entire procession of struggling men, *barongs,* and *rangdas* passes through the gate to the outer temple in a wild melee and parades around in a circle before returning. Here another interesting drama occurs, after those in trance are calmed. There is a reenactment of a historical account of a battle that took place here, featuring old men and women dressed in ancient costumes. Tourists are not allowed in the inner temple, but you can watch the strange procession on the outside.

TUESDAY: Pura Taman Ayun, Mengwi. This is a lovely royal temple, partly surrounded by a lake and with many multistoried *merus.* Processions of women from different *banjars* begin arriving with high offerings about 4 P.M. The *odalan* goes on for three days.

Pura Luhur, Uluwatu. This is one of Bali's most holy temples, located on a rocky cliff overlooking the sea on the Bukit, the southern extension of Bali. It is half an hour's drive south of Kuta. People from all over Bali come to pray here. It is crowded, as the temple is very small. (See CHAPTER 23.)

Pura Alas Kedaton. This lovely temple is set in a small forest full of monkeys. The processions of ladies with high and colorful offerings are especially nice, as is the gong music. To get there head toward Tabanan from Kediri on the main road, but, instead of taking the 90-degree turn left toward Tabanan, continue on straight about five kilometers. The temple is on the east side of the road, and some little distance back, on a dirt path.

Pura Dalem, Tanjung Bungkak. This is a small and colorful temple very close to where the Kecak dance is held at Ayodya, on the main road from Denpasar to Sanur. A very colorful and unusual ceremony takes place here at night.

WEDNESDAY: Pura Dalem, Sempidi. The same as the *odalan* of Sempidi's Pura Puseh, described under Thursday, Week 2, above.

Pura Desa-Puseh, Sanur. Notable only because of its proximity to the Sanur hotels.

WEEK 16, PAHANG

MONDAY: Pura Penataran Agung, Sukawati. A procession of girls with long dresses to a holy spring is the only interest here.

WEDNESDAY: Pura Maspahit, Singgi, Sanur. Important only because it is in the Sanur area.

WEEK 17, KRULUT

WEDNESDAY: Pura Desa, Ubud.

WEEK 19, TAMBIR

TUESDAY: Pura Dalem Kangin, Sukawati. A procession of girls in long dresses to a nearby holy spring. There are processions for four days, sometimes two or three a day. A *rejang* dance is held in the temple every night.
   Pura Dalem Singa Kerta, Ubud. Near a tourist center.
SATURDAY: Pura Puseh, Ubud.

WEEK 21, MATAL

WEDNESDAY: Pura Puseh, Sukawati. The girl's procession to the holy spring occurs two or three times a day. *Odalan* lasts for four days. *Rejang* dance every night.
   Pura Desa, Batuan.

WEEK 27, WAYANG

SATURDAY: Pura Ratu Alit Dan Ratu Lingsir, Desa Singakerta, Ubud. Important only because near a tourist center.

WEEK 28, KELAWU

WEDNESDAY: Pura Gaduh Jagat, Desa Singakerta, Ubud. Important only because near a tourist center.

THIS SECOND GROUP OF *ODALANS* consists of those that are determined by the Saka, lunar, calendar. Almost all fall on full moon, Purnama. You can find the Gregorian dates for yourself if you have a Balinese calendar. The name of the month for each day of the year is the last printed line below the number for the Gregorian date.

BALINESE	GREGORIAN	BALINESE	GREGORIAN
1. Kasa	June, Jul.	7. Kepitu	Dec., Jan.
2. Karo	Jul., Aug.	8. Kaulu	Jan., Feb.
3. Ketiga	Aug., Sept.	9. Kesanga	Feb., Mar.
4. Kapat	Sept., Oct.	10. Kedasa	Mar., Apr.
5. Kelima	Oct., Nov.	11. Jiyestha	Apr., May
6. Kenem	Nov., Dec.	12. Sadha	May, June

MONTH 1, KASA
(note: all are on Purnama)

Pura Penataran Agung, Sukawati. Three days after this opening date of the *odalan*, at about 2 P.M., there is a procession of girls in long trailing dresses to a holy spring

Pura Gunung Kawi, between Pujung and Sebatu. This is not the archaeological site of the same name at Tampak Siring, but rather a lovely little temple with a lake and a cave in a little valley below the village of Sebatu. Notable for its beauty and simplicity and the nice setting. Note that this date is not absolutely fixed. Some years it occurs a month before Purnama Kasa, some years a month later.

MONTH 4, KAPAT

Pura Panataran Agung, Pura Besakih. This is the principal temple in the Besakih complex and perhaps the most important in all of Bali, to which people come from all over the island. Besakih is a complex of many temples. Pura Panataran Agung is just inside the main gate of the first temple at the top of the long flight of stairs. This is a two-hour drive from Denpasar.

Pura Tirtha Empul, Tampak Siring. This is the famous temple with the holy spring that is on every tour group's itinerary. It is located just below the palace built by Indonesia's first president, Sukarno.

MONTH 5, KELIMA

Pura Kehen, Bangli. This is not the *odalan,* which is on Wednesday of Week 1, but rather a ceremony called *ngusaba*. If anything, it is bigger than the *odalan*. There are processions of ladies with high offerings up the long flights of stairs to this old and famous temple on a hillside. It is about 1-1/2 hours from Denpasar. There is entertainment at night, starting late.

Pura Jagat Natha, Denpasar. This is a state temple, just east of the big public field, next to the museum and southeast of the big four-faced statue at Denpasar's main crossroads. Everybody in the surrounding area comes to pray here late in the afternoon.

MONTH 9, KESANGA

Pura Penataran Sasih, Pejeng. This is just north of Bedulu, on the road from Gianyar and Ubud north to Tampak Siring and Kintamani. It is famous for the huge drum, the "Moon of Pejeng." This is a large and colorful *odalan* with entertainment and music.

MONTH 10, KEDASA

Bhatara turun kabeh, one of the most important ceremonies at Pura Besakih, Bali's most important temple. This ceremony is attended by people from all over Bali. Every fifth year it is bigger than usual, every tenth year bigger still, and every hundred years it is Eka Dasa Rudra, the largest ceremony held in Bali.

Pura Batur, Kintamani. This ceremony, a *ngusaba*, lasts over a week. Batur is one of the most important temples in Bali, and people come from all over to pray here. It is located on the rim of the spectacular Batur caldera. The grand old *gong gede*, a classical *gamelan* orchestra, plays for the ceremony.

Pura Dalem Tangsub, Sukawati. Not especially noteworthy except for the procession of girls with long trains to a holy spring.

Pura Samuan Tiga, Bedahulu. *Ngusaba*.

THERE SHOULD BE ADDED to the list of *odalan*s above that of Pura Dalem Sanur, almost opposite the main gate of the Bali Beach Hotel. It is noteworthy not just because it is in Sanur, but because of the interesting and unusual ceremony. First there is a long procession of girls with high offerings in the late afternoon. Then there is a procession of *baris gede* dancers and the temple's *pratimas* to the nearby beach for cleansing and ritual purification. Returning to the outer temple, the *baris gede* dance is given, and immediately thereafter the dancers go into violent trance. The date of this *odalan* is difficult to explain. It occurs on the third day of the three-day week, called Kajeng, that is the first one to follow the first new moon after the day called Kuningan, which is the Saturday of Week 12. So, this *odalan* varies considerably in the Gregorian calendar, since Kuningan is fixed according to the Pawukon and Tilem is fixed according to the Saka calendar.

Pura Uluwatu

THE SPECTACULAR TEMPLE OF RUDRA

ONE OF BALI'S MOST IMPORTANT TEMPLES is located on the far southwestern tip of Bukit Badung, the peninsula that dangles from the south of the
island. The main road from Kuta leads south, past the Ngurah Rai Airport,
past Jimbaran, up over the hilly, desolate Bukit and ends, on a high cliff 50
meters above the ocean, at Pura Luhur Uluwatu. This temple is one of the
sad kahyangan, the six temples of the world — the most important temples
in Bali. The other five are Pura Besakih, Pura Lempuyang Luhur, Pura Gua
Lawah, Pura Batukaru, and Pura Pusering Jagat in Pejeng. Pura Luhur
Uluwatu, the most southwestern of the six, is dedicated to that aspect of
Sanghyang Widhi known as Siwa Mahakala, or Rudra, the dissolver of life.

Actually the name Rudra (sometimes Ludra) was given to one of the
very important Aryan gods of the Rig Veda, the oldest religious text in the
world. The hymns of the Rig Veda, composed between 1500 and 900 B.C.,
are still considered sacred. They were used at the sacrifices of the Aryans
who invaded northern India during that period, and their nature gods and
religion evolved into modern Hinduism. "Rudra" is thought to mean "the
howler." He was an archer, and his arrows carried disease. Rudra was associated with storms. He was remote — an object of fear, and offerings were
made to him to prevent plague and disaster. But Rudra was also the god of
healing and medicines, revealing a beneficent aspect to an otherwise fearful
nature. As Hinduism developed, a single god, *brahman,* came to the fore
and Rudra, the patron of Pura Uluwatu, is considered a   manifestation of
brahman. In Bali, *brahman* is called Ida Sanghyang Widhi. Violent interac-
tions, such as storms and plagues, are Sanghyang Widhi acting as Rudra.

THE HISTORY OF PURA ULUWATU is not well recorded. But it is known that two of the most famous figures in Hindu-Balinese religious history were involved with the development of the temple: Empu Kuturan (also known as Empu Rajakerta) and Danghyang Nirartha (also known as Pedanda Sakti Wawu Rauh and Dwijendra). Empu Kuturan — *empu* means "sage" — came to Bali from Java in the 10th century of the common era, according to legend riding on a deer. He landed on the island at a point near Padang Bai, and in commemoration of this event the well-known Pura Silayukti temple was built on the spot. Kuturan was a Siwaist priest, but he was also strongly influenced by the teachings of Buddha. He is famous for renewing the customs and manners of religious ceremonies and ethics, which, at the time of his arrival, had suffered decline. He is known as the great *meru* builder. A *meru* is a tiered shrine, something like a Chinese pagoda, constructed of an odd number — up to 11 — thatched tiers. When Empu Kuturan came to the area of Pura Uluwatu there was probably already a small temple there. But he added a number of shrines and built the *meru* , making the temple more complete.

Danghyang Nirartha, another Siwaist priest, came to Bali in A.D. 1546 from Daha in Java, according to legend crossing the water on the leaf of a *keluwih* tree. He landed near Negara, in Jembrana Kabupaten, and rested under an *ancak* tree, a species related to the banyan. To commemorate his arrival, his followers built Pura Ancak, later called Pura Purancak, a splendid temple of white coral. Danghyang Nirartha had such magical powers, it is said, that the people with whom he came into contact began calling him Pedanda Sakti Wawu (or Bawu) Rauh, meaning "The Holy Priest Who Recently Arrived." Wawu Rauh journeyed all over Bali, building temples and shrines. Many of them are quite famous, including Pura Tanah Lot and Pura Rambut Siwi. Wawu Rauh's teachings helped incorporate some of the principles of Buddhism into Balinese Hinduism. He is well known for adding *padmasana* shrines to the temples that he visited, believing that there should be shrines not only to the manifestations of Sanghyang Widhi, but to the one God himself. A *padmasana* is an empty chair, generally made of stone. It is a feature of almost all large temples, and you will see such shrines in many temples all over Bali. The shrine is now considered to be for Sanghyang Widhi only, although some say it is for Surya, the sun.

Wawu Rauh built a *padmasana* at Pura Uluwatu. And from this spot he achieved liberation, *moksa*. Only the purest spirits can achieve *moksa*, which means they have been freed from the cycle of reincarnation and joined with God. When Wawu Rauh achieved *moksa* from Pura Uluwatu, it is said, the name "Luhur" was added to the temple's name. *Luhur* comes from the verb *ngeluhur*, literally meaning "going up," or more figuratively, reaching *moksa*. A more prosaic etymology for *luhur* is "above." *Ulu* means "end," and *watu* means "stone." Hence Pura Luhur Uluwatu also means "the temple above the stone at the end." And indeed it is.

Until the end of the 19th century, Pura Luhur Uluwatu was the chief sanctuary of the Kingdom of Mengwi. Now it belongs to all the Balinese people, but is administered by the estate of Puri Jerokuta in Denpasar, the former raja of the area. Uluwatu is the chief temple of a whole complex that includes Pura Dalem Jurit — located inside Pura Luhur Uluwatu — as well as Pura Pererepan in Pecatu, Pura Dalem Kulat, east of the Suluban surfing beach, and several other minor temples in the vicinity. Worshipers going to Pura Luhur Uluwatu will also stop and pray at Pura Ulunsiwi in Jimbaran, as there is a connection between the two temples.

THE ROAD FROM THE MAIN PART OF THE ISLAND ends at the Pura Uluwatu parking lot. The walk from there to the temple follows a paved road, about 300 meters down a gentle grade. The temple faces northeast so that, when facing the entrance, one is looking southwest, not west, as one might assume from the drive out to the temple. The peninsula upon which Pura Luhur Uluwatu is located juts out from the main cliff in an almost precisely southwesterly direction. The first view is of the northeastern part of the temple perched on a steep hill. There is a new *pasanakan* where you will be asked to make a small contribution to the upkeep of the temple and where you must get a sash to put around your waist and a *kamben*, or cloth, to put around yourself if you are in shorts. The Balinese are very sensitive about foreigners dressing improperly when visiting a sacred place. The word *pasanakan* comes from the verb *masanakan,* meaning "to take a rest." Local Jimbaran rules strictly prohibit anyone entering Pura Uluwatu carrying or wearing a red hibiscus or any article of black-and-white checkered *poleng* cloth when accompanying the Jimbaran *barong* on its visit to Pura Uluwatu. The rule applies to the Balinese as well as tourists.

An brief ascent of four steps takes you to the platform at the base of the main stairway, which has wide steps, with a low wall on each side. Most of the way up one comes to a new *candi bentar,* or split gate, made of white coral with a wall of rough limestone blocks on each side. The gate is not carved, but the coral blocks are set in a decorative pattern. The top of the gate has the unusual "winged" appearance of the other two *candi bentars* in the temple. The gate curves away from the center in a graceful arc, then curves back again and ends in a point like the tip of a bird's wing. The Balinese called this style *bersayap,* meaning winged. This is a very rare style of *candi bentar.*

Passing through this gate and ascending a few more steps, one comes upon the outer courtyard of the temple, the *jaba* or secular area, a rectangular enclosure about 10 meters wide and perhaps half as long. To the left is a building occupied by visiting priests or officials. To the right is the *bale*

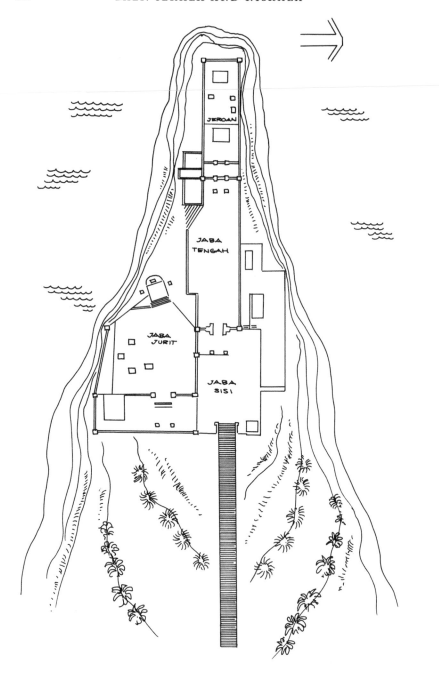

LAYOUT OF PURA ULUWATU

kulkul, the tower for the *kulkul* signal drum. To the right is a *bale agung* with a corrugated roof, and farther to the right are steps leading down to a lower level where there is a building in which worshipers can sleep or rest.

Beyond them is the entrance to the middle courtyard, or *jaba tengah,* which is marked by another *candi bentar,* an old one that has been restored considerably. It, like the rest of the temple, is made of a hard, white, coral limestone. On each side of this gate is a statue of Ganesha, one hand on his head, a favorite Hindu god, the remover of obstacles. Whenever some undertaking is considered, Ganesha's aid is sought in removing hindrances, especially in literary and educational matters. He has come to symbolize wisdom. Traditionally Ganesha had one broken tusk, and his vehicle was a rat. Such gate-guarding statues are common in Bali and are called *dwara-pala.* On each side of this gate is a wall with windows made of pierced, decorated coral blocks. One ascends a few steps through the gate and then descends again to the middle courtyard, an area about 40 meters long and 10 meters wide. It is paved in places near the southwest end with white stone blocks, but part of the floor is just the natural limestone outcrop. This courtyard is entirely surrounded by stepped, undecorated walls. In the middle of the northwest wall a small gate leads to a spot that offers a nice view of the cliffs and sea to the northwest.

A large cistern adorns the southeast wall of the *jaba tengah.* A tower leads to this cistern and beyond it is a stairway leading to a visitor observation platform that affords a view of the inner courtyard. Visitors are not allowed inside this most sacred part of the temple. The middle courtyard is dominated by the great gate, the *kori agung,* a massive, largely unrestored structure of white coral with a design unique to Bali. This gate is distinguished by a *gapura,* or arch, an architectural device almost never used in Bali. The entire arch protrudes from the gate, as if the gate were built on top of it. The arch has no keystone; instead two interlocking horizontal blocks hold the stones together. Above the arch is the leering face of Bhoma, "Son of the Forest," who guards the inner, sacred courtyard from evil spirits — a usual feature of such gates. Above Bhoma, at the very top, is a large carving of the *kamandalu,* the bowl in which the Tirtha Amerta, the elixir of eternal life, was carried from the sea when it was generated by the churning of Mount Mandara (See CHAPTER 6).

On the walls to each side of the gate are two *kasar,* coarse-looking, heads. Other parts of the gate are decorated with one- and two-eyed faces of *kalas,* or evil spirits. On each side of the gate are even larger *dwarapala* Ganesha statues.

Access to the *jeroan,* the sacred inner courtyard, is limited to those who have come to pray, but the view from the observation post shows the general architecture. After passing through the *kori agung,* celebrants must turn either left or right to avoid a large wall, the *aling-aling*. This is to bar access to evil spirits which, it is said, can travel only in a straight line. The *jeroan* is paved in white squares, and the light can be blinding on a sunny day. The courtyard is 8 meters wide and 40 long. Near the far end is the most important shrine in the temple, the *meru matumpang tiga*, three-tiered, which is guarded on either side by smaller thatch-roofed shrines. A few years back, lightning struck and burned the *meru*. This, as one might imagine, was taken as a very bad sign and resulted in extensive repairs and a rededication and purification of the entire temple.

From the *jeroan's* undecorated, stepped wall the cliff drops almost straight down to the sea, some 50 meters below. On a clear day from Pura Uluwatu you can see the tip of Java (more than 50 kilometers). A troop of monkeys makes itself at home here, snatching anything in sight and dining on the scraps of food that are left behind in the offerings. One can see sea turtles coming up for air, especially to the southeast. It is a magnificent, spectacular sight.

Returning to the outer courtyard, turn to the right immediately after passing through the first *candi bentar*. Passing one of the square columns, one enters the separate temple known as Pura Dalem Jurit. This temple is dedicated to Ida Ratu Bagus Jurit, loyal general and minister of Bhatara Mahajaya. The entrance here is another new, white coral *candi bentar*. There is only one courtyard in Pura Jurit. There are four new shrines with white coral bases and *duk* (palm fiber) thatched roofs with varnished wooden frames. Three have single roofs, but the one nearest the entrance is double. In it are kept the three sacred statues — Ratu Bagus Jurit, to whom the temple is dedicated, Brahma, and Wisnu — which are brought out and dressed in their appropriate colors for *odalan* day, Anggarkasih Medangsiya. The *odalan* lasts for only one day.

On the southwest side of Pura Jurit is a tall square stone shrine with a stone roof. Inside is a very weathered statue said by some to be of Danghyang Nirartha. (Scholars deny this.) A rectangular platform with stepped and decorated sides leads up to the shrine. In front of the platform are two white coral statues, apparently old, each about one meter high. On each side of the shrine of Danghyang Nirartha there is a stone "boat" made of black rock. The boats, it is said, symbolize the peninsula upon which Pura Luhur Uluwatu is located — which is boat-shaped — as well as Dalem Jurit's defenses against enemies who might come from the sea.

CHAPTER 24

Household Shrines

TENDING THE DOMESTIC SPIRITS

BALI IS AN ISLAND OF TEMPLES, the Department of Religion cataloging at least 11,000 — small and large, local and regional. But the integration of Hindu-Balinese religious belief into the daily lives of the Balinese is even more thorough than these numbers indicate. Every house compound is organized around at least five, and often more, shrines — ranging in importance and size from the three-section *kemulan* to the inconspicuous *sanggah paon* kitchen shrine.

The Balinese call a shrine *palinggih,* which simply means "place," or "seat." This refers to any sort of permanent or temporary place toward which devotions and offerings are made. In fact, although specific types of shrines are required in every compound, it is often not clear — even to the Balinese who set offerings there every day — exactly to whom and for what purpose the shrine has been erected. In no case is the shrine itself considered sacred, rather the shrine exists or is built as a residence for sacred, or holy, spirits — either ancestors or Hindu deities.

Ancestors are very important to the Balinese. They are deified as spirits who have a special affinity for the family, and can be counted upon to protect and help the family in time of disaster or need. The ancestors can help ward off evil forces and insure prosperity and happiness and peace. Alternately — like most forces in Hindu Bali — they can cause no end of trouble, causing just the opposite of the above benevolence. Which of the two they do depends upon the respect the family accords them. If the family directs good feelings toward them, if the family invites them to religious ceremonies, if the family makes regular offerings to them, and if the family maintains the shrines to the limit of their financial ability, then their powers will be turned to aiding the family. If the family neglects these courtesies, then sickness, death, and all sorts of unimaginably bad things may result.

It seems curious to Westerners, with our emphasis on genealogy, that nobody in the family that worships at the ancestor shrines has any knowledge whatever of the names of any of his or her forebears. There are several reasons for this, not the least being the way the Balinese take names. A person generally has just one unique name. And very often people with whom the person comes into contact daily have no idea what it is, instead calling him or her by a nickname or birth order name — Wayan, Ketut, etc.

For example, my long-time friend and assistant I Wayan Budiasa, whom I call Budi, was called when he was young by either of two nicknames, Sela or Termos, because he looked like a *sela* (sweet potato) or a Thermos bottle when he was born. His mother called him Yasa, as did the rest of his family and neighbors. When he was older, he added to Yasa the prefix Budi, producing Budiasa. People who are not terribly close to him call him Wayan, or Yan, a birth order name that means nothing more than that he was the first-born. Budi now has a son, Aris. And Budi now finds himself being called Gurun Aris — "Aris's father." When Aris has his own first child, Budi will again change names and be called the grandfather of Aris's child — Kak plus the name of the grandchild. By the time Budi dies it will come as no surprise if nobody has a clue to what his unique name was. And when his spirit is installed in the family shrine, perhaps many years after his death, his real name, not even well known now (and he is a young man) will have disappeared into the dim past.

Not only is it well-nigh impossible to keep straight all the names of one's ancestors, it is also not considered important to do so. (In fact, it is even considered impolite to call someone by his or her "true" name, even if it is known.) The deified ancestors are lumped together, known variously as Nenek Moyong, Dewa Hyang, Pitara Hyang, or Bhatara Hyang. Often the Hyang part is spelled Yang. No attempt is made to single out one of the deified ancestors over the others. In death, just as in life, names are not that important. The feeling and the treatment one directs toward them is. One hears the word *kawitan* ("beginning" or "origin") in this connection. An extended family group is spoken of as having a common *kawitan*.

A TYPICAL FAMILY HOUSE COMPOUND contains several obligatory shrines. Each has a family temple in the *kaja–kangin* corner — *kaja* being in the direction of the holy Gunung Agung, *kangin* being east. In low caste families this temple is called a *sanggah*. Higher caste families have more elaborate family temples, called *merajan* or *pemerajan*. Although the family temple may contain shrines dedicated to manifestations of the Hindu god Sanghyang Widhi, the main focus is upon the deified ancestors of the family. Shrines for the gods are more prominent in public temples. The family temple may be small or large, but it is almost always well maintained, and the family is careful to place offerings in the shrines whenever appropriate, often daily.

A roofed shrine with three side-by-side compartments, called a *kemulan* or *kemulan taksu*, is found in every family temple. Many people say the three sections are for Brahma, Wisnu, and Siwa — the Hindu triad. The shrine is generally on the *kangin* side of the family temple, facing the interior of the compound. Thus, as one faces the shrine, Wisnu is to the left, Siwa in the middle, and Brahma to the right. Sometimes the *kemulan* is described as having a center section for Bhatara Guru, an epithet for Sanghyang Widhi, with the left compartment for the female characteristics, and the right for male. The *kemulan* is sometimes called the shrine of origin, and is a shrine for the deified ancestors.

The *kemulan* generally has a thatched roof, made of *duk*, a tough, black fiber from the sugar palm tree or, since *duk* is expensive, it might be woven of grass with just a little *duk* on the peak. A coconut, in a basket and wrapped in a white cloth, forms a kind of statue called a *prerai*, which stands in the center section. The *prerai* is a symbol of the spirit, Sanghyang Atma. The *kemulan* itself is a symbol of the body.

Another shrine found in all house compounds is the *sanggah pengijeng*. The name comes from *ijeng*, "to guard," or "to stay at home." The *pengijeng* is a roofed shrine with one compartment, the spirit of which acts as a guardian or caretaker of the property. It is located more or less in the middle of the house compound, and not in the family temple. Some say it is dedicated to Bhatara Surya, the sun. Others claim it has a connection with the *kanda empat* — the four spiritual siblings of every Balinese. This shrine is sometimes described as being for the family, just as the *kemulan* is for the deified ancestors. This can be either the actual, physical family that lives within the walls of the house compound or for the *niskala* family of the *kanda empat*.

The *palinggih taksu*, the "place for the *taksu*" is another obligatory shrine. The *taksu* is the god of one's profession, or talent. Everyone is born with a *guna* (talent) of some sort, and his or her specific *taksu* will reside in the *palinggih taksu*. It is also a roofed shrine, usually with a single compartment, and is located on the *kaja* side of the family temple.

House compounds also have a shrine called a *tugu* or *penunggun karang*, or *tugun karang*. The ordinary *tugu* is a low, roofless shrine, found in the *kaja–kauh* (*kauh* is 90 degrees counterclockwise from *kaja*, mountainward) corner of the property. The spirit of the *tugu* watches the property. The shrine is to Kala Raksa, or Bhatara Kala — a demon/deity. One must place offerings to Bhatara Kala in the *tugu* to have peace.

Tugu shrines are found in many places, not just in house compounds. The Balinese feel that any object, animate or inanimate, that has an unusual shape or is peculiar or very large may well be the home of a spirit of some sort. And to placate the *kala* that may live therein a *tugu* shrine will be erected nearby — or in or on the object itself — and offerings placed in it regularly. One can see these next to or in big banyan or *kepuh* trees, or near particularly large or strange rock formations.

The main entrance gate always has a shrine, called *apit lawang* — *lawang* meaning "gate." A properly constructed gate will have a niche on each side in which to place offerings; failing this, they are placed on top of the stone wall next to the main entrance. The purpose of the *apit lawang* shrine is to welcome those who come with good intentions and discourage those who come with bad intentions. The shrine acts as a guardian to the main entrance to the house compound. People do not pray at this pair of shrines, but do keep them filled with offerings. Sometimes the *apit lawang* is considered to be a place where the *bhutas* and *kalas* can get what they need without having to enter the compound and bother the people within.

The house compound always has a small shrine in the kitchen called *sanggah paon*, for Bhatara Brahma, who is associated with fire, and one by the well, *sanggah sukan*, dedicated to Bhatara Wisnu, god of water. These are usually quite inconspicuous, hanging up high and out of the way on the kitchen wall, or attached to a tree near the well. The name for the well shrine varies considerably, since the word for "well" varies among villages.

The family temple may have a shrine called a *padmasana*, but does not necessarily have to. For example, if a member of a family builds a house compound of his own, away from his traditional, ancestral *sanggah*, he will build his own temple, but he need not put a *padmasana* shrine in it. He simply uses the one that is still in the original family temple. *Padmasana* is one of a class of shrines, all of which are called *padma*, the name of the leaf of the lotus — traditionally the seat of God. The word *sana* means "seat." The ordinary *padmasana* is an eight-leafed lotus, with the gods of the eight directions seated on the eight leaves. There is an empty chair on top, the seat of Sanghyang Widhi. A swan or eagle frequently decorates the back of the shrine — the swan being Brahma's vehicle, the eagle Wisnu's.

The *padmasana* is divided into three sections — the familiar Tri Loka: *bhur* (the world of demons), *buwah* (the world of man), and *swah* (the world of gods). At the base of a *padmasana*, in Bhur Loka, is Bedawang Nala, the world-supporting turtle, and the two snakes, Anantaboga, and Basuki, symbolic of man's earthly needs. In the center part of the Padmasana, in Buwah Loka, man's daily activities are sometimes displayed in carvings. Near the throne, below the top, various manifestations of God may be depicted in Swah Loka.

The *padmasana* is normally located in the extreme *kaja-kangin* corner of the temple, often placed at an angle so that the open chair faces *kelod-kauh*. In the large Pura Jagat Natha in downtown Denpasar there is an enormous and elaborate *padmasana* directly in the center of the temple. At the other extreme are small *padmasana* shrines made of pre-cast concrete that one can buy quite cheaply in Kapal.

Whether modest or grand, erecting a *padmasana* is never a task to be taken lightly. This, to be sure, is true for any shrine. Whether it is of cheap or dear materials, once dedicated and purified the temple becomes the home of God, and must be maintained and cared for in a careful, pre-scribed manner.

There are nine kinds of *padmasanas*, one for each of the nine directions. Each has a slightly different name and type of construction, and each faces in a different direction. Although these are outwardly different, they all basically serve the same purpose. The most famous *padmasana* in Bali is the triple shrine located in the most important courtyard of the Pura Penataran Agung at Pura Besakih. There three *padmasanas* are arranged side by side, the group together called the Padma Tiga. Although it is often said that the three shrines are for Brahma, Wisnu, and Siwa, actually all three are for aspects of Siwa. The red shrine on the right is dedicated to Sadhasiwa; the black shrine on the left, Siwa; and the middle white shrine, Paramasiwa.

The elaborate tiered shrine called a *meru* is not often found in ordinary family temples, because it is very expensive to build and maintain. But some of the larger *pamerajans* have them, as do many public temples. The shrine symbolizes the world mountain, Gunung Maha Meru, and has one to eleven tiers or, as they are called, *tumpang*, or "levels." There must always be an odd number, although one *meru* at Pura Taman Ayun in Mengwi has two. The *tumpang* are square and diminish in size toward the top, so that the effect is that of a Chinese pagoda, except the colors are somber — each *tumpang* being thatched with black *duk*.

The laws of traditional Balinese architecture carefully specify the dimensions of a *meru*, the way it must be constructed, the types of wood appropriate for each part, and the ceremonies involved in its dedication. Some *sanggahs* and *pamerajans* have five-tiered *merus, meru matumpang lima*, dedicated to the god of Gunung Agung, Bhatara Mahajaya. A *meru* with three levels is often dedicated to the god of Gunung Lebah, Bhatara Danu. The one in Mengwi with just two *tumpangs* is for Datu Ngurah. The most spectacular *merus* are to be found at Pura Besakih, at Pura Taman Ayun in Mengwi, at Pura Kehen in Bangli, and at Pura Danu Batur in Kintamani.

Throughout the island one will see a type of small roofless shrine called a *bedugul*. These shrines serve several purposes. One often finds them out in

A LARGE MERU

the rice fields — put there by the *subak*, the local irrigation society, as a
kind of branch of the principal rice temple in Pura Ulun Siwi. Some people
say that *beduguls* are dedicated to the spirits that guard the area where they
are built. *Bedugul* shrines are sometimes erected to the spirits of people
who have died in battle in a particular place, for example soldiers and villagers who died fighting the Japanese during World War II, and those who
died fighting the Dutch after the end of the war.

EVERY PERMANENT SHRINE, no matter how simple or complex, must be initiated in a special purification ceremony, called a *melaspas,* before it can be used. Special *padasaran* offerings must be placed under the foundation, often in the shape of bricks, wrapped in white cloth and accompanied by many other offerings. More *padagingan* must be placed inside the stone, brick, or concrete structure itself by digging or chipping a hole in the structure, placing the proper offering inside, and then filling the space with stone or mortar. The ceremony is expensive, and not taken lightly. If a shrine must be moved to another locality, the spirit of the shrine is first transferred to a *daksina,* a special offering, which is then placed nearby in a temporary shrine. Then the original shrine is completely destroyed. None of its components may be reused for any purpose. Often the materials are dumped into the sea to insure that they are not unwittingly used again.

Into and upon these permanent family shrines offerings of food, *banten jotan,* are placed every day after the meal has been prepared and before it is eaten. The shrines also receive offerings on Kajeng Keliwon and other important dates, including Tilem and Purnama, all the Tumpeks, Galungan, and the host of *rarahinan* or festival days that every Balinese family observes. Normally these are not large offerings. Usually a small triangular container of coconut leaf filled with bits of rice and other prescribed materials is sufficient.

The housewife prepares enough of these small *segehan* offerings to satisfy all the shrines, puts a sash around her waist, places the offerings on a round tray with a stick of burning incense, and makes the rounds of the shrines, setting one offering in each and wafting its essence toward the shrine. It is a simple daily routine that quickly becomes a habit. Often one of the older children, usually a girl, is entrusted with the task if the mother is busy. A *daksina* is often kept in the most important shrines because this is considered to be the most important of all offerings.

In addition to the permanent shrines mentioned above, temporary shrines are often built for various purposes. When someone dies, a shrine must be brought with the corpse to the cemetery. Five shrines are needed for a *caru* — animal sacrifice — offering. Every large ceremony needs many shrines to serve as receptacles for special offerings.

The most common temporary shrine is called *sanggah cucuk.* The base consists of a single stalk of bamboo, its top segment split into four to support a simple woven base. The roof of the *sanggah cucuk* is open and triangular, and its general appearance is that of a small, open tent sitting on top of a pole. Such a shrine can be fashioned in just a few minutes by almost any Balinese man, thrust into the ground, blessed briefly, and be ready for the offerings. A *sanggah cucuk* is usually associated with ceremonies dealing with the *pancamahabhuta,* the five elements of which man is constructed and which must be returned to the universe when he dies.

Some temporary shrines are simply square or rectangular platforms supported by four bamboo poles. The smallest is called *sanggah laapan.* Somewhat larger is the *sanggah panggungan,* and the biggest is the *sanggar agung.* One can see these, laden with offerings, set up on the street outside of house compounds. This is a sure sign that some sort of ceremony is taking place in the family temple. The larger *sanggar agung* shrine serves as the temporary receptacle for the spirit when a shrine is moved. These temporary shrines are considered important when they are in use, but having fulfilled their function, the offerings are removed and the shrine discarded without much ceremony.

PART IV

The Performing Arts

CHAPTER 25

Dance in Bali

TOPENG, LEGONG, KECAK, AND MORE

THE NUMBER AND VARIETY OF DANCE PERFORMANCES in Bali is dizzying. From modest "social" dances to the elaborate performance of the *barong ket* to the sacred and mysterious *sanghyang* temple dances, somewhere on the island a dance goes on every day. In varieties of entertainment, dance in particular, Bali is an embarrassment of riches. It may not always appear so to the visitor however, because finding out about a dance, perhaps to be given at a temple *odalan* celebration, can be very difficult. And even if one knows the whereabouts and time of a given performance, getting there can be expensive or impossible.

One solution can be the tourist shows. The advantages to seeing a tourist performance are that the shows are regular, start on time, are short enough to sit through easily, and are held in central locations at convenient times. The dancers and musicians are almost always very talented and the shows are quite enjoyable. The dances themselves, though often abbreviated, are usually stories or genres rooted in tradition. But what is missing from the tourist shows is the "scene" — the crowds, the atmosphere, the smells, sounds, and excitement of a real village or temple dance. And the experience of these is worth digging around for.

Travel agents try to keep abreast of the various ceremonies and dances going on, but they may be unwilling to provide such information unless their services are hired. The Badung Tourist Promotion Board (Jalan Surapati No. 7, Denpasar) offers a "Bali Calendar of Events" that lists major *odalans* — where there are likely to be dance performances — as well as other entertainments. The board's services are free and a visit to the office can yield much valuable information.

At almost any Balinese Hindu religious celebration, from an *odalan* to a tooth filing, there is likely to be entertainment of some sort, usually dance. Although the entertainment is intended for the gods and ancestral spirits who are being honored at the ceremony, the events are equally entertaining to the Balinese. If the show is of any size at all, a great crowd of people will be there, no matter how many times they have seen the same performance, standing or squatting or sitting on the ground, the little boys in the front row chattering excitedly. If you go to a village ceremony try to find out about the type of entertainment that will be offered. Some dances are commonly performed in the daytime, but the majority don't begin until quite late in the evening.

A tourist is almost always welcome at a traditional dance performance — provided he or she observes a few simple rules of etiquette. These festivals are sacred. Although the Balinese usually dress quite casually, they consider formal, traditional Balinese dress to be an absolute necessity at sacred ceremonies. They do not necessarily expect foreigners to wear such attire, but if one did it would be greatly appreciated. The essentials are few: no casual or beach clothing; a long skirt, not pants, for a woman, and long pants for a man, with suitable tops in both cases; some sort of material tied around the waist like a sash. For this last, in a pinch, even a towel will do. You may take pictures, flash included. You may make tape recordings. Just remember that you are witnessing a sacred and important religious festival and behave accordingly. Stay in the background. Never stand in front of people who are praying. And expect to pay a small fee, perhaps Rp 100, to enter a temple. This goes toward upkeep.

THE *BARONG* IS ONE OF THE MOST POPULAR and important dances in Bali. Although there is wide variation from village to village, the dance usual revolves around a conflict between Rangda, the witch, and Barong, a powerful, mythic beast. Chapters 26 and 27 in this volume describe the *barong* at Jimbaran in detail, but it is just one of many troupes on the island. *Barongs* are most common during the Galungan Days festival, although they can be seen other times. There are *barong ket,* lions, *barong macan,* tigers, as well as boar, deer, and even humanlike figures. The *barong landung* — *landung,* "tall" — is particularly distinctive. There are two characters, the male, Jero Gede, and his wife, Jero Luh. Jero Gede is dressed all in black with ferocious teeth; his wife has a white face and large ear lobes. There may even be two or three *barong landung* children. The costumes are constructed on huge frames carried by a single man underneath.

There is an interesting *barong landung* family at Padang Sambian, halfway between Denpasar and Krobokan, about a 15-minute drive from Denpasar. Head east on the eastern extension of Denpasar's main street,

Jalan Gajah Mada, and, instead of turning right to go to Tabanan, keep straight ahead on Jalan Gunung Agung. Where the road makes a 90-degree turn to the north, turn south, and follow the road about two kilometers to the small temple on the left. The performance starts about 4:30 P.M. on Kajeng Keliwon, although the season ends periodically. There are regular *barong ket* performances on Kajeng Keliwon in Kuta, one at Banjar Seminyak, Legian, the other slightly farther to the south at Pura Agung.

A variety of more or less common dances accompany temple anniversaries and religious festivals. These dances range from sacred and stately religious dances, always held in the innermost part of the temple, to more or less secular dances held in the outer courtyard. Balinese temples are always divided into three areas or courtyards. The inner temple is called the *jeroan,* the less sacred middle part is the *jaba tengah,* and the outer compound is the *jaba,* really a secular space. Only very sacred dances may be performed in the *jeroan,* slightly less sacred ones in the *jaba tengah,* and secular performances are given in the *jaba.*

The *mendet* or *pendet* is a common inner-temple dance used to welcome the honored gods. As with so many things, characteristics of dances and practices vary from village to village. *Pendet* is usually danced by a group of women — sometimes even elderly, gray-haired women. Anyone who wishes may join, and occasionally one sees a man participating in this stylized welcome to the visiting spirits. Dancers wear ordinary traditional clothes, and each carries an offering in his or her right hand. The dance is quite technically demanding, but almost every little girl in Bali learns the rudiments of *pendet* in school or from an older sibling. A *gong* always accompanies the dance, and any dancer can perform with any *gong,* since the movements are very controlled. In the last round of the dance, the offering may be replaced with a stick of incense.

Rejang is a very ancient inner-temple dance. It, too, is performed to delight and entertain the visiting spirits. *Rejang* consists of little more than a slow procession, but the participants conduct themselves with extreme grace and delicacy. It is a dignified and elegant affair. Women of all ages participate. All wear traditional temple dress, but with elaborate semicircular headdresses of gold, decorated with flowers. Some villages perform *rejang* in the daytime, some at night. Night *rejang* is common in the major *odalans* in Sukawati. Day *rejangs* are given in the Bali Aga villages such as Tenganan, Bungaya, and Asak.

Although sometimes seen at cremations and other ceremonies held outside the temple, *baris gede* is basically an inner-temple dance. This ancient and commonly performed dance is enacted by groups of men, often middle-aged, dressed in distinctive triangular helmets. The helmets are covered with pieces of pointed shell that quiver when the dancers move. The men are the soldiers, the personal guard, of the visiting spirits. They carry spears or guns or kris — but usually very long spears. The *baris gede* dancers may go through various military maneuvers, including a mock battle, shouting occasionally in unison. At the *odalan* of Pura Dalem Sanur the *baris gede* ends in a melee of entrancement.

Sanghyang dances, which involve young girls who often go into trance, are not often seen except in the more remote parts of North and East Bali, and then usually only when needed to help ward off danger or disaster. It is by no means uncommon to encounter trance in the inner temple — a lay priest, *pemangku*, or sometimes just an ordinary person may become possessed by a spirit and speak in a peculiar and unintelligible voice, not his or her own. But formal dances involving trance are not often performed in areas accessible to visitors. Some *"sanghyang"* dances are performed for tourists and these will be described below. Some *sanghyang* ceremonies have as an accompaniment a chorus of men who chant precisely like the monkey circle in the common tourist *kecak* dance. The reason, of course, is that the choreographers of the modern *kecak* drew their inspiration from the *sanghyang* performances of old.

The dances held in the courtyard of the middle temple are less sacred, and most narrate some sort of a story. As with inner-temple performances, their purpose is to welcome and entertain the visiting spirits. The most basic of all Balinese dances, from which it is said that all other dances and movements derive, is the *gambuh*, a dance that is at least 400 years old. The story of the *gambuh* is usually part of a long romantic poem, the *Malat*, in which a prince, Panji, and his eventual princess, Candra, have a variety of adventures. The principal characters speak in the ancient Javanese Kawi, so few in the audience can understand them. But like in the shadow puppet performances, attendants and comedians provide a running translation in common Balinese for the benefit of the audience. *Gambuh* is accompanied by a distinctive orchestra, featuring low-pitched flutes that are so long that a man can barely reach the bottom holes with his fingers. Also present is an ancient ancestor of the violin, the *rebab*, held vertically, one end on the ground, and played with a very loosely strung bow. *Gambuh* can be a very long story, a complete performance lasting some six hours. Today excerpts are usually all that are performed. The village of Batuan has an active *gambuh* group that usually performs at ceremonies in that area.

Gambuh is not a masked dance, but there are two masked dances that are performed in the middle temple courtyard. One of these is the famous *topeng pajegan*. In this dance a single dancer/actor tells the entire story, constantly changing masks and characters. He is, by turns, the prince, the princess, the old man, the servant, the king, the king's minister, and the clown. It is truly a virtuoso performance, with a different voice, mode, and

A BARIS DANCER

style for each character. The last mask to be performed in a *topeng pajegan* is always Sida Karya, by far the most important and sacred. The words mean, roughly, "he who can get the work done," and the purpose of the mask is to ensure that the work — the ceremony — is brought to a success-ful conclusion. This performance is sometimes given in the inner temple courtyard. While the main ceremony is in progress, the dancer dresses and changes masks in full sight of the audience.

Balinese *wayang wong*, another middle temple masked dance, is quite different from the Javanese dance of the same name. The basis of the drama is the well known Hindu epic, the Ramayana. The dance often accompanies purification rites, as it tells the story of the defeat of an evil king by Rama and the monkey army. Most of the monkeys are not exactly purebred, looking rather as if at least one parent was some sort of other animal. All have long tails and wear heavy masks. Many of the characters speak Kawi, but the same four interpreter/clowns from the *wayang kulit* puppet show, the *panasars*, help the audience understand. Only a small part of the exceedingly long story is ever presented, and a small *gong* provides accompaniment.

Outer courtyard dances may have religious significance in the context of a ceremony, but they are also performed on nonreligious occasions in purely secular venues. The *legong* dance, a staple of tourist shows, is a common *jaba* performance. When given at an *odalan* or other ceremony, *legong* is much longer and more complete than the brief excerpt that tourists see. The three young girl dancers, a servant and her two mistresses, enact a drama, each girl assuming several different roles. It is not obvious to the untrained observer at which point a given dancer assumes a new role, and so the foreigner has difficulty following the story. No matter. The graceful movements of the dancers are the main attraction. *Legong* is considered to be the fundamental female dance style, and it is taught to all beginning dance students.

The Ramayana ballet is occasionally seen at a temple ceremony. This pantomime is done to the accompaniment of a flashy *gamelan* with quick changes of tempo and sudden stops and starts — the *gong kebyar*. There is always a comic scene in which Hanuman, the white monkey, a special favorite of the Balinese, fights with the forces of evil. This dance is a recent invention, copied from the performances given monthly in Central Java at Prambanan. It has become popular with the Balinese, and so it is occasionally performed for their own purposes, apart from tourist shows.

Arja, sometimes called "Balinese Opera," is a common sort of entertainment at temple festivals. This art form is somewhat different from the other dances or dramas in that the dancers sing and dance at the same time, with the vocal line being more important than the dance itself and more important than the musical accompaniment. *Arja* is a technically difficult undertaking because the four leading women — who play men — must sing well and dance well at the same time. The words are Balinese, not Kawi, and the style strikes the foreign ear as a high-pitched, nasal whining. There is the usual clowning by the many servants of the main characters. The attendants of the hero, Punta and Kartala, are a wonderful vaudeville team. Punta, self-important and pompous, is the straight man for the clever Kartala.

The solo *baris* dance, similar to that fragment given at tourist shows, has become a standard feature of some religious ceremonies. The dance is just a character study of a warrior as he prepares for and engages in combat. Solo *baris* is considered to be the basic male dance and is taught to all male dance students, since it incorporates the fundamental movements of the entire spectrum of Balinese dance. Solo *baris* is often performed by young boys, in contrast to the *baris gede* groups, which are largely older men.

There is also an outer courtyard version of *topeng*, which is extremely popular. This is performed by a troupe of usually five dancers and is thus called *topeng panca* ("five"). The various parts in the drama are distributed to all of the dancers, rather than being undertaken one a time by a single dancer, and the non-Balinese visitor can follow the story much more easily. Before the drama itself begins, several short dances introduce the characters. The dancers emerge from a little enclosure, the entrance of which is covered by a curtain. Before emerging the dancer vibrates the curtain to signal the audience and the *gong*. Canang Sari, near Sangeh, hosts the most famous *topeng panca* group in South Bali.

THERE IS A GROUP OF POPULAR VILLAGE DANCES that can best be called "social" since they have really no connection at all with any religious ceremony and are never seen under anything other than secular circumstances. These dances are sometimes performed in the village movie house or in an improvised outdoor arena by visiting troupes, and admission is charged. Travel agents or hotels will often book these troupes as entertainment for their guests. These are not "tourist" shows, however — they are for the entertainment of the Balinese. Most performances start about 8 P.M. Many are advertised in the villages, especially if they are profit-making enterprises.

Popular among these social dances is the *joged bungbung*. The word *bungbung* refers to a length of hollow bamboo. Unlike the bronze-keyed, xylophone-like instruments of musical groups that accompany most of the performances described above, the keys of this ensemble are tuned lengths of bamboo, struck with rubber-covered mallets held in both hands. The music is very soft and mellow. One may hear it played by a soloist as background music at restaurants. But the *joged bunbung* group consists of half a dozen or more of these instruments, some very large bass xylophones, several of medium size, and tiny ones to ornament the melody. There are also drums and cymbal-like *ceng-cengs*. Since it has no religious connection, *joged* is now a popular lobby entertainment at many of the larger hotels.

Joged bungbung is always performed by a paid troupe. The five or six young female dancers dance one at a time, each for perhaps 20 minutes. Costumes vary, but they almost always feature a mass of fresh flowers tied in the hair. The *joged* is a sort of flirtation dance. After a brief solo, a dancer pulls a man out of the audience, puts a sash around his waist, and makes him dance with her. The victim always makes a pretense of protest. But almost all Balinese men know the basic dance steps and styles, and often the result is a remarkably artistic duet. Traditionally, the male dancer makes passes at the Joged, trying to poke her or grab her good-naturedly as she deftly parries the thrusts. She may even pretend to beat the man with a small leafy branch that someone will toss into the arena. After the man tires, he thanks the Joged, takes off the sash, and the girl goes after another partner in the audience. Tourists are favorite targets if available. After three or four pairings, the Joged retires, and a second takes her place. The village of Luwus, on the road between Mengwi and Bedugul, is famous for its several *joged* troupes who travel all over the island.

Janger is a social dance that is waning somewhat in popularity. But one finds it still given for pure entertainment in the villages. A *janger* troupe consists of about a dozen male and a dozen female dancers. The men are dressed in rather startling, non-Balinese costumes, sometimes with fake mustaches, short pants, and jogging shoes. The girls are more traditionally attired. After an initial group dance in which the audience is welcomed, the dancers form a rectangle, two lines of girls facing each other, and two lines of boys perpendicular to them. The next part consists of several set pieces, girls and boys singing alternately in chorus. The boys sing a *"c(h)ak-cak-cak"* chant at times, obviously copied from the *kecak/sanghyang* performances. They make characteristic shrugging shoulder movements as they sit on the ground, swaying. The girls also sing and dance slowly. The performance ends with a drama, performed in the middle of the square of dancers. This generally has nothing to do with the rest of the performance and is sometimes left out.

Balinese drama, sometimes called "Drama Gong," is still a very popular form of village entertainment. The performances, which are held in the local movie house, are invariably very long and would probably be unintelligible to the outsider. A simple *gong* accompanies the performance. For a large part of the show the only accompaniment is the steady beat of a single pot-like instrument. Serious episodes, often declaimed in the peculiar whining, high-pitched style described before, are interrupted frequently by the usual slapstick comic routines that are so beloved by the Balinese. There is a Drama Gong on TV every Sunday evening, and it is the most popular program on the Denpasar station.

A TOURIST DANCE PERFORMANCE does not offer the same sense of setting and mood that a village or temple dance does. But the tourist shows are convenient to tourist centers, and are presented regularly, and frequently. Few of these shows last more than an hour. Most foreigners get bored with regular village festivals, which may go on all night long and which are always jammed with spectators who have to stand or sit on the ground. In the tourist shows comfortable seats are provided, the view is good, and shelter from the sun and rain is provided. These shows are also professionally choreographed and executed. Everything is done well.

By far the most popular of the tourist shows is the *barong* dance. Batubulan, on the main road from Denpasar to the northeast, has a virtual monopoly on tourist *barong* performances. In fact, it is the village's major industry, with three or four active groups. In the past, the shows were separate, but a new pavilion has been constructed off the road to relieve parking congestion, and the the groups alternate performing at this new area.

The *barong* dance, as it has now been standardized, is a kind of collection of bits and pieces of traditional Balinese dances, woven into some sort of simple story that tourists can follow. The story is more or less based on a tale from the Hindu epic, the Mahabharata, called "Sudamala" or "Kunti Sraya." Most of the masks and the general format of the show are taken from the *calonarang*, a sacred exorcism story. But he masks used in the tourist show are not sacred, nor are any other sacred objects employed. Tidbits of the *legong* dance, *topeng*, and other traditional dances are woven into the plot. A synopsis of the story, printed in several languages, is available to the audience. There are also *barong* dance shows given in Kuta, Singapadu, and at the Pura Dalem in Banjar Medaan, Sumampan village, near Blahbatuh. These are not so regular, so inquire before making a trip.

The *barongs* in the shows are all *barong ket*, the magical lion. The Barong is given a somewhat more lovable and humorous character in the tourist shows. The show centers around a simple drama which the Barong always begins with a long solo. There follow various bits and pieces from other traditional Balinese ceremonies — a pair of girl dancers, a lot of clowns who engage in rather typical crude humor, a monkey to taunt Barong, a king and his servants. Finally Rangda appears and threatens one and all. The followers of Barong rush in, confront Rangda, and attempt to defeat her. But her magic is too powerful for them and, instead, they turn their swords upon themselves and attempt to commit suicide. This "trance" is feigned in the tourist show. The whole performance is accompanied by a regular *gamelan* orchestra, a modified version of the *gong kebyar*, the most popular ensemble in Bali. As mentioned before, this is a show. It is not something that you would see anywhere else. The Balinese, with direction, have set it up specifically for tourists. It is nonetheless quite entertaining.

A second popular tourist show is the *kecak*, or monkey dance. This is a performance conceived and choreographed specifically for tourists, and the Balinese never put one on for their own purposes. But just as in the case of the *barong* dance, *kecak* has its roots in traditional Balinese dance and music. The most dramatic feature of *kecak* is a chorus of up to 100 chant-

A LEGONG *DANCER*

ing men who sit in concentric circles around a large oil lamp. Their chant is not a monotonous, repetitive one, but rather a highly structured piece of choral music, following ideas from modern Balinese music, with great and sudden variations of pitch and rhythm. At times the chant is melodic, with rising and falling cadences. More often the chorus assumes the identity of the monkey army that is a popular part of the famous Ramayana epic, and chants in nonsense syllables: "c(h)ak, cak, cak," like a band of chattering simians. Part of the Ramayana story is acted out by dancers within the circle, while the monkey chorus alternately stands, lies supine, waves its arms, and helps the hero overcome the evil demon. It is a very engaging performance and well worth an hour's time. There is a *kecak* every night at the Art Centre, Jalan Nusa Indah, and one at Ayodya, in Tanjung Bungkak, on the main road between Denpasar and Sanur. In Kuta there are *kecak* shows at Banjar Buni and Banjar Pande Mas, but these are given somewhat irregularly, seldom more than once a week.

The very popular *legong* dance is offered twice each weekend at two different localities in Peliatan, near Ubud, about a 45-minute drive from Denpasar. The show that is now generally called *legong* is really no such thing. It is a kind of dance revue that consists of five or six separate dance routines, each unconnected to the others by story or style. One of these, indeed, may be a fragment of the much longer, traditional *legong keraton* dance described above. In the tourist shows the *legong* dancers tend to be considerably older than was traditionally the case. And I have seen shows billed as "Legong Dances" that have no *legong* in them at all, just the rest of the revue. Before the *legong* fragment, if there is one, there is always an opening dance given by a group of half a dozen or more girls who greet the audience, and wind up by showering the guests with flowers. This opening dance is called *panyembrama*, a purely secular dance, adapted in the late 1960s from the ancient and sacred *rejang*. You will hear it incorrectly called *pendet*.

The remainder of the show usually features a segment of a solo *baris* dance in which a young male warrior prepares himself for battle, beautifully dressed in ribbons and with a peculiar miterlike helmet. This is the same dance described above that is sometimes given in the villages. There are dozens of varieties of *baris*. Another popular part of the *legong* show is a single *topeng* performer, usually the Topeng Tua, or old man mask, in which the dancer emulates the action of a white-haired man attempting to dance, with stiff joints and uneasy balance. There is often a *trompong duduk*, in which a young man squats behind the musical instrument called *trompong*, a series of inverted bronze pots played with two sticks. The dancer alternately hops about and plays the *trompong*, twirling his sticks like batons, and managing his long skirt with great skill. There may be either or both of two other dances. *Panji semirang*, or *bebancihan*, is a type of *kebyar duduk* — a sitting dance for a solo female dancer without *trompong*. This is a rather recent genre of dance. And there is likely to be an *oleg tumulilingan*, or "bumblebee dance," created in 1953 specifically for a Balinese dance group's international tour. This is a courtship dance for a pair of performers, male and female. *Legong* shows are scheduled at many of the larger hotels in Sanur, Kuta, and Nusa Dua at regular intervals.

There are also performances in Kuta at Banjar Buni, usually once a week, and at Banjar Pekandegan and Banjar Pengabetan at irregular intervals.

Sanghyang means "possessed by a spirit." There are several traditional Balinese *sanghyang* dances, named differently, depending upon what sort of spirit possesses the performers. At Bona, near Blahbatuh, *sanghyang dedari* and *sanghyang jaran* are regularly performed. In the former, two young girl dancers go into trance, possessed by celestial nymphs. In the latter a male dancer is possessed by a horse. The tourist shows at Bona are not sacred, like the *sanghyang* given in the temple. There is a regular show at Bona Sari, including these two dances, plus a *kecak*. The same show is given at Ganda Wisma in Bona. Travel agents sponsor trips to the dances, and, unless you have your own transportation, it is a good idea to book through an agent. Bona is a half hour's drive from Denpasar and night-time public transportation is infrequent or nonexistent.

The Ramayana Ballet was created at the KOKAR dance institute in 1965. It was heavily influenced by the very successful Javanese tourist show of the same name first performed at Prambanan, near Yogyakarta, in 1961. It has become a very popular dance in Bali, not only for tourists, but also as entertainment in the villages. It is, of course, a modern adaptation of the beloved Hindu epic in which the hero, Rama, assisted by a monkey army, defeats the wicked monster, Rawana, and rescues his wife, Sita. It is a tremendously long story, and only a small fragment is ever performed. Banjar Pengabeton and Banjar Tegel in Kuta have Ramayana Ballets, but their schedules are uncertain. Another is given irregularly at Banjar Pekandegan in Legian. The dance is an occasional feature at the big hotels.

In addition to the above shows, you may find occasional performances of the *godogan*, or "Frog Dance" at some of the hotels. This is also a dance created for tourists — the old story of the princess who married a frog. Featured in the musical accompaniment is the ancient instrument, the *genggong*, a kind of Jew's harp made from palm leaf that produces a frog-like, croaking sound. Many of the above dance groups can be chartered for private performances, either at one's hotel or in the troupe's home village. Prices are not excessive if shared by a group.

A WAY TO BE SURE TO SEE AS MUCH DANCE as possible in a visit to Bali is to arrange one's trip to coincide with the annual Bali Arts Festival. The government always schedules the arts festival well in advance, and it is held between the middle of June and the end of July. All programs except the opening ceremony and procession are held at the Werdi Budaya Art Centre on Jalan Nusa Indah (formerly Jalan Bayusuta). There are usually about 25 programs scheduled throughout the period of approximately six weeks. Most of them are at night, beginning around 8 P.M. They include all sorts

of traditional and modern dances with musical accompaniment, contests
and competitions for musicians, dancers, decorators, flower arrangers, and
even a fashion show. There are displays of offerings, food, clothing, and
crafts. And there is an exhibit and sale of Balinese crafts under the main
grandstand at the Art Centre, open throughout the six weeks of the festival.
Printed programs are available from hotels and travel agents, as well as from
the various tourist promotion bureaus. Tickets are on sale at the Art Centre
and at most hotels.

Other more or less regular activities that are worth visiting are music and
dance lessons. There are two special government-run schools for musicians
and dancers in Denpasar. The equivalent of high school training is given at
Sekolah Menengah Karawitan Indonesia, SMKI, commonly called KOKAR.
The school is in Batubulan, near the place where the *barong* shows are
given. The equivalent of university training is given at Sekolah Tinggi Seni
Indonesia, commonly called STSI, on Jalan Nusa Indah, just north of the
Art Centre. If you go to the office of either of these two schools and get
permission, you are welcome to watch and photograph the great variety of
dance and music lessons and rehearsals that take place all week long. The
offices can provide class schedules. These schools often put on special dance
and music shows for visiting dignitaries or special events, and you are
always welcome to attend.

Another real treat is to watch the regular Sunday afternoon dance
lessons given for young children at Khursus dan Sanggar Tari Bali/Jawa.
These take place at Abian Tuwung, just north of Mengwi, on the main
road between Denpasar and Tabanan, about a 20-minute drive from
Denpasar. After leaving Mengwi you wind through some rice fields, go
down a hill, and then up a long hill. On your right, north, you will see a
huge banyan tree. Below it is a sign pointing to the right, with the name of
the school on it. The lessons take place in the mid-afternoon in a pavilion
about 200 meters north of the main road.

CHAPTER 26

The Barong (PART I)
SEKALA – THE PERFORMANCE

THE *BARONG* IS THE PROTAGONIST of one of Bali's most famous and popular dances, usually described as a contest between good and evil, the good
Barong and the evil witch Rangda. But it is not really accurate to say that
the mythic beast Barong is the hero and that Rangda, hissing and fierce,
her coarse locks and poisonous tongue flailing, is the villain. The real story
is much more involved. The *barong* performance is the expression, through
theater, entrancement, and celebration, of the whole complex of the
Balinese mythic and religious world — the choreography involves not just a
troupe of dancers and musicians, but a whole village.

Instead of trying to describe the *barong* dance in general which would
be sketchy and incomplete because practices vary so widely in Bali, I have
tried to describe the performance of the Jimbaran *barong* in particular. I
think our Dewa Ayu, and the role it plays in our village, is representative of
other *barongs* throughout the island. Not that it resembles exactly, or even
very closely, the *barong* performances in other parts of Bali. But the way
Dewa Ayu, a kind of beneficent patron deity of Jimbaran, fits into the life
of the village I think reflects *barongs* elsewhere. In this chapter I will
describe the performance and the preparations for the season (*sekala*), leaving the religious and mythical implications (*niskala*) for the next.

THE CAST OF CHARACTERS

DEWA AYU. Barong. Jimbaran owns two *barong* masks, an older one,
duuran, and a younger one, *alitan.* The two masks look alike, are used

interchangeably, and share a common body. According to tradition the mothers of both came from Pura Sarin Buana, a few kilometers south of Jimbaran on the Bukit, and their fathers came from Pura Ulun Siwi. The older Barong is said to *duwen,* "belong to," the Pura Dalem, called Kahyangan, in Jimbaran, and the younger one to Pura Ulun Siwi. Both masks, however, are kept permanently in their own temple, Pura Pererepan. Dewa Ayu is a *barong ket,* the lion. There are *barongs* of all kinds in Bali, including tigers, boar, elephants, deer, dogs, goats, and horses. There are also *barongs* that represent more or less human figures. The *barong ket* of Jimbaran is exceptionally well kept up, with fresh paint and refurbished dress for each cycle of performances. Its coat, like most, but not all, *barong ket,* is made of the shredded leaves of the *peraksok,* a kind of agave. The leaves are stored underground for a while to soften them and then shredded and combed into hair to make Barong's shaggy coat. The body decorations are carved of leather, painted gold, and ornamented with mirrors and bells.

"Dewa Ayu" is gendered in a contradictory way — although *dewa* is the male form of "god," *ayu* means "beautiful woman." There is some confusion about this even among the people of Jimbaran. No particular significance is attached to Barong's sex, however. Dewa Ayu is always attended by

BARONG KET

a large white umbrella and two *lelontek,* the long, thin, pointed flags commonly used as decorations in hotels. Dewa Ayu the older has *lelontek* made of a black-and-white checkered cloth called *kain poleng.* The younger Barong has two white *lelontek,* and two of *kain poleng.* The terminology can be confusing: Barong is a character in the *barong* dance performance as well as a god, Dewa Ayu. The two dancers who animate Barong are members of the *barong* club, or *seka.*

AUBAN. Our Rangda. She is in no important way different in appearance from the *rangdas* in other villages. She has a long mane with strands of different colors and textures and the usual ferocious-looking, gold-painted mask — gaping mouth, long tusks, bulging eyes, and a pendulous red tongue reaching almost to her knees. Gold-painted leather projections, like tongues of fire, protrude from her headdress. She wears white gloves with long fingernails, red-white-and-black striped pants, a white waistcloth, and a shirt sporting fringes of black hair. One can hardly imagine a more horrible-looking creature. She speaks in the ancient Javanese Kawi, with its peculiar whining tones, and between speeches she issues loud grunts. Her gestures and demeanor are threatening and hostile, and she periodically throws her head back and lets loose a great, shaking cry of laughter.

Attendants always shade Rangda with a large, green-fringed umbrella, which she occasionally leans on for support. Two tall *lelontek* flags of balck-and-white checkered *poleng* guard her sides, and during a performance she will grab them, each in a hand, and cross their points to "fly." Rangda carries a white cloth, *kakudung,* or *kekereb* in high Balinese, her principal weapon. By putting this over her face she becomes invisible. Barong has such a cloth also.

SANDAR. Six Sandars participate in the Jimbaran *barong,* all outfitted alike, and one Rajan Sandar performs occasionally. The role is sometimes called "Telek" in other parts of Bali. The Sandar mask, a refined or *alus* type, is white with delicate eyes and red lips. Its closed mouth traces a faint smile. A black band with seven gold, four-lobed symbols decorates the forehead. The characteristic hat resembles a pagoda and is made of gold-painted leather, cut through with ornamentation, the lowest step hung with shiny pendants. A small white flag adorns the left side of the pagoda, and a single peacock feather dangles from the left side of the mask. The Sandar dancer wears a short-sleeved jacket and a white cloth, tied much like a pair of pants. Over these is draped a sash pinned with many long ribbons, a broad, green apron, brocaded with gold, and green-and-gold leggings. As with all dancers, the Sandars are barefoot. Each carries a constantly fluttering fan in his right hand, and over the back of each dancer is slung a kris. The

Sandar's movements are graceful and feminine, although the dancers in Jimbaran are always young men. In other villages girls dance these parts.

The Rajan Sandar appears only briefly. His mask is similar to the others, but more wide-eyed, and his forehead band is gold, instead of black, and displays green and red stars. His leggings are purple brocade with red cuffs, and his shirt is black with red cuffs. Instead of the green brocaded apron, he wears a broad bib around his neck, painted gold, black, and red, with gold tassels. He wears a few wide ribbons on top of this clothing, instead of the many thinner ribbons of the other Sandars, and he carries no fan. This part is usually danced by an older man.

OMANG. A group of usually six Omang dances in Jimbaran, their masks and demeanor *keras*, meaning "coarse," or "hard." Eight masks are available to the group, and the dancers switch wigs, masks, and functions from performance to performance. There are, however, always at least the following three characters among the set of Omangs:

TELEK. The raja or leader of the Omang, sometimes called Ratun Omang. He wears a black shirt and pants, and a tall *jauk* hat with a white flag, just like the Sandars. His mask is black, with a long, sharp nose, a white mustache, and a serious, commanding expression. He wears ribbons like the rest, but his apron and leggings are red brocade. His gestures are forceful and kingly rather than brash and sudden, like the other Omangs. He wears a red hibiscus flower over each ear.

CEMUNG. The Jimbaran *barong* has the only Cemung Omang I have ever seen in Bali. He looks for all the world like a ham actor playing Rigoletto, because his grotesque costume is a caricature of that of a court jester. He wears a white conical cap of goat skin, its tip pointing forward. His mask is a tannish-yellow, with big, bulging eyes and bushy white eyebrows, a mustache, and a goatee. Each ear wears a big red hibiscus. His clothing is all red, except for a garland of ribbons, a round red-and-gold bib, and layered aprons — a blue, then a yellow, and finally a purple. His leggings are red. Cemung dances with a rolling, froglike hop, arms extended in a circle, his body bent over. He acts as a clown, occasionally picking up and pretending to scare small children in the audience. He stares members of the audience in the face, pushes them back, hops to and fro with his ridiculous motion, and then pauses, standing erect in the characteristic Omang posture — right hand on hip, left arm ahead.

JAUK. Also mandatory is at least one Omang dressed exactly like the conventional Jauk that dances solo before a *topeng* or *calonarang*. Jimbaran has four Jauk masks, each slightly different in expression, but all of them white with black mustache, bulging eyes, and open mouth with teeth showing. The Jauk wears the same tall, pagoda-like, gold hat as do the

Sandars, plus the circle of ribbons. His shirt may be either black or white. His legs are covered with a white *kamben,* and his leggings and large apron are red brocade. There may be as many as four Jauks, since four masks are available, but usually there are no more than three. One of the Omangs wears a black bushy wig, conferring on him the name Sobrat. He wears a red mask with no hat. He dances in a violent, athletic way, with exaggerated gestures and sudden stops and starts. His music is different from that of the other Jauks.

The other two Omang masks are purple and red. Both are quite coarse-looking, with bulging, wide-open eyes and fierce tusks. The red Omang mask is a bit less terrifying, with a smaller mouth and eyes that are not as protuberant. Any of the Omangs except Cemung and Telek can wear whatever mask he wishes and can wear either a Sobrat wig or a Jauk hat.

Other than Cemung and Telek, the Omangs are named not according to their costumes, but according to the specifics of their dance. In a typical performance, one Omang — other than Telek or Cemung — stops and dances in front of the drum of the *gong* and claps his hands to make it stop. Any one, but only one, of the other Omangs can do this, and he is called Omang Ngiuking Kendang, "The Omang Who Says 'Ngiuk' to the Drum." One of the Omangs "kills" a Sandar during the dance, and he is called Omang Ngematiang Sandar, "The Omang Who Kills the Sandar."

RARUNG. A pupil of Rangda — quite subservient to her mistress — who, in the course of the performance, tries to do Rangda's bidding, but fails and is roundly scolded. Rarung is dressed entirely in red, including her magic cloth, and is sometimes referred to in Balinese as Sane Barak, "The Red One," in the typical elliptical Balinese way of avoiding the real name of a sacred person. Rarung has a great, tousled head of completely black hair that dangles almost to the ground. Her gold mask has prominent, bulging eyes, large fangs, a red nose, and a long, red tongue with gold decorations. She wears a leather apron painted gold and decorated. She wears a bird in the back of her hair, and leather flames extend from her head.

JERO LUH. Another one of Rangda's attendants, sometimes called Anak Lingsir, "The Old One," as a term of respect. Jero Luh has a shorter mane than does Rarung, and it is a mixture of hairs of different colors, some rather light. She has a purple mask, with prominent eyes and large fangs. Unlike Rangda and Rarung, her red and purple tongue protrudes only a short distance. Jero Luh wears the same golden leather apron as does Rarung, but she wears a white cloth wrapped around her legs and her shirt has red-and-white banded sleeves, with circles of hair attached. The demeanor of Jero Luh is quite different from that of Rangda and Rarung.

She often acts as a kind of teaser, frightening the children, pushing the crowd back, hitting Barong from behind with her white cloth, and generally seeming to have a good time. Unlike Rangda and Rarung, Jero Luh never speaks.

THE *PEMANGKU*. Sopir, or Pan Bingkil, is the *pemangku*, the priest, of the Pura Pererepan, the temple of the Jimbaran *barong*. His father was *pemangku*, and he has inherited the job. When the *barong* is active, Sopir, like other *pemangkus*, must stay with it night and day — in this case in a special pavilion in Pura Ulun Siwi. The Sandar and Omang masks are kept in Pura Pererepan during periods when the performance is dormant. Even then, people come to pray every Kajeng Keliwon, Sukra Pon, and often at other times. And, because the Dewa Ayu is known to have special magical powers, Sopir, as *pemangku*, must be available to help those who come as supplicants to Pura Pererepan, as they pray for the help of Dewa Ayu and set out their offerings. When the *barong* is active, it performs every Kajeng Keliwon, every 15 days, and often more frequently. It must perform at the *odalans* of all of the major temples in the Jimbaran area. This keeps Sopir very busy, because he must not only act as *pemangku* of a regular temple, but also attend to the needs of the entire *sekan barong*.

SEKAN BARONG. This is a group (*seka* or *sekehe*) of about 100 men who are followers of Barong and who participate actively in every performance. They meet once a month, every Sukra Pon, outside of Barong's temple. The *sekan barong* has an organization, with a president, but members pay no dues. Membership qualifications vary, although every member should have a kris. Most members join because a father or uncle was once a member, and the feeling is that the membership should continue through the male line. Some people are members because of illness in their families. It is not unusual for a family to promise that one of its members will join the *sekan barong* if the illness is cured. Most of the members are rather young, and not all really enjoy the service. It is not easy. Great demands are made on their time because of frequent performances. The performers of the dances are taken from this group, as are the flag and umbrella holders, those who help Sopir control the activities, and those who go into trance. During the performances, members of the *sekan barong* dress all in white, but for the red end of their *kambens* showing in front and a yellow *saput*.

THE *GONG*. Pura Pererepan has its own special *gong* — an instrumental ensemble — that is used for the *barong* performances. It is kept in Pura Pererepan. The *gong* is allowed to play for other ceremonies, but never for any connected with death. Nor can it be used for any *manusa yadnya* cere-

BARONG, TWO OMANGS, AND A SANDAR

mony — one connected with a living person — such as a baby's *oton*. But it can be used for *odalans* and other temple activities, and it can even be rented out for suitable occasions. The *gong* is somewhat smaller than the Jimbaran village *gong* headquartered at Banjar Teba, and its instruments are undecorated. The roster of musicians changes throughout any given performance.

THE VILLAGERS. Since Dewa Ayu is an extremely important part of the religious life of the community of Jimbaran, the 12,000 people who live there form an important part of the *barong*. It is they who bring offerings for Dewa Ayu to Pura Pererepan and to Pura Ulun Siwi. It is they who jam the streets to watch the performances. It is they who walk the 16 kilometers each way to Pecatu and on to Pura Uluwatu to accompany Dewa Ayu on its required journey at the start of each cycle of performances. And it is they who are the beneficiaries of Dewa Ayu's beneficence, or wrath.

THE SETTING

PURA PEREREPAN IS THE "HOME" of Dewa Ayu, and the temple houses the equipment when the *barong* is not assembled and performing. It is not a large or imposing, or even a pretty temple. There is no decoration of any sort. The temple has only one courtyard, and that is not large. The name of the temple comes from the Balinese word *sirep*, "to spend the night." The masks are kept in shrines at the east end of the temple. The *odalan* of Pura Pererepan is on Sukra Pon of the 14th week, Medangsiya.

Pura Ulun Siwi, where the *barong* is kept once it is assembled, is across the street from Pura Pererepan, and just a short distance south. Pura Ulun Siwi is an extremely important temple in Bali, since it is the mother of the Subak rice temples. Even though no rice is grown in the Jimbaran area, farmers from all over Bali who have insect pests on their rice must come to Pura Ulun Siwi to get holy water to sprinkle on their fields. Pura Ulun Siwi has a close connection with the famous Pura Uluwatu, and theoretically, anyone going to pray at Uluwatu should also pray at Ulun Siwi.

Barong's pavilion is to the north and a little east of the *meru* in Ulun Siwi. A temporary building still farther to the northeast holds the various Sandar and Omang masks while the *barong* is put together. The performers use it as a dressing room. Many of the ceremonies connected with the *barong* take place in Pura Ulun Siwi. Sometimes the *barong* performance is held in the *jaba tengah;* the ceremonies of putting together and taking apart the *barong* take place in that same area. And at *odalan* time, the *barong* occupies a prominent spot in the ceremony. The *odalan* of Pura Ulun Siwi is on Paing Galungan, the Friday after Galungan Day.

Pura Kahyangan, the Pura Dalem of Jimbaran, is southwest of the main part of town, due west of the *sema* (cemetery) and not far from the beach. When Barong is put together or taken apart, important ceremonies are held in Pura Kahyangan. And the adjacent cemetery is the actual scene, at midnight, of the ceremony at the start of each performance cycle to "re-awaken" Rangda and her two attendants. The *odalan* of Kahyangan is on Pon Galungan, the Saturday after Galungan Day.

Pura Pererepan in Pecatu and Pura Luhur Uluwatu figure prominently in the Dewa Ayu story. Whenever Barong is assembled, the *sekan barong*, all those who participate in the ceremony, and a fair percent of the villagers of Jimbaran walk the 16 kilometers to Pura Uluwatu, and then walk home, stopping for quite some time to rest and pray at Pura Pererepan in Pecatu, because of the close connection between the three temples. It is quite an important event in the religious life of the area, for Pura Uluwatu is one of the most holy temples in Bali.

The *barong* performance is called *mapajar,* derived from the Balinese *pajar,* "to speak" and referring to the conversation between Rangda and Barong at the end of the show. The setting for the *mapajar* itself is rather unglamorous, simply the main north-south street through Jimbaran. For the dance, the street is blocked off for a 300-meter stretch beginning at the entrance to Pura Pererepan, and including Pura Ulun Siwi. The big banyan tree next to the east wall in the middle courtyard of Pura Ulun Siwi provides shade for the *gong* and some members of the audience on hot days. The main street of the village is where the action takes place — not inside the temples.

THE PERFORMANCE

IT IS ABOUT 2:30 P.M. ON A KAJENG KELIWON as you approach the Candi Bentar of Pura Ulun Siwi. The roads to the north and south have already been blocked off, and only an occasional motorbike passes by. The *gong* is being assembled in the shade of the big banyan tree to the north of the entrance to the temple. Outside, the usual collection of food sellers, hawkers of awful squeaking toys, sellers of pictures, clothing, peanuts, batik, *rujak,* and vendors of fragrant skewers of *saté* have already begun to set up their booths and carts. As you pass through the Candi Bentar into the outer courtyard of the temple you see hardly anyone at all, but crowd noises drift from within.

Once through the side gate, you discover the source of the sound — a cockfight. Although gambling is officially illegal in Indonesia, three rounds of a cockfight are tolerated to spill blood in sacrifice for a ceremony. To your right, dancers get ready for the ceremony, helped into their elaborate

ribbons and decorations by the older men who taught them the dances.
The dancers are all young men, most in their late teens and early 20s. The
day is hot and sticky, and the dancers sweat profusely as the costumes are
layered on. A batik *udeng,* tied backwards, goes around the head before the
headdress is put on. The masks, taken from bamboo baskets kept in the
temporary pavilion north of the temple, are hung around the necks of each
performer, there covered with a cloth. They will be revealed and put on
only at the last moment.

Sopir and his wife and family are busy over by Barong's pavilion, sprinkling holy water upon the many villagers who have come to pray — some
have brought high offerings to make good a promise made to Dewa Ayu.
Members of the *sekan barong* trickle in, each clad in shining white, with a
bright red *kancut,* a kris sheathed in its wooden case at the belt. A last
cockfight is held for blood-spilling purposes in front of Barong's pavilion.

Now ready, the dancers gather to pray at the pavilion. Sopir sprinkles
them liberally with holy water. Three members of the *sekan barong* come
forward to bear, on their heads, the three large bamboo boxes with the
Rangda, Rarung, and Jero Luh masks. Sopir sprinkles them and they carry
the masks across the street to the Pura Pererepan, where Rangda and her
ghastly cohorts will be dressed. Barong's umbrella, flags, and spears are carried from the pavilion to the east side of the Kori Agung, and you hurry to
see Barong exit from the main gate. This he does with difficulty, because
the two-man Barong is just about the same width as the opening. Offerings
are placed in its path, and the *pemangku* waves incense. The entourage
leaves the temple and heads toward Pura Pererepan. Passing the *gong,*
Barong, head covered in cloth, stops just north of the temple entrance. The
members of the *sekan barong* who have followed fan out in a large group
and sit on the ground in front of Barong, facing it. Two umbrellas are
opened and held behind it. The four spear carriers take their positions,
forming a rectangle enclosing the street in front of the *gong.* While this
positioning takes place, the *gong* plays a kind of overture, the musicians
chatting noisily with each other as they play the familiar music. It is 3 P.M.
The performance almost always starts on time.

A few surfers from Kuta, diverted from their usual route, stop to gawk at
the proceedings, take a few quick photos, and pass on their way. The villagers stand two or three deep along the blocked-off stretch of road, little
boys, as usual, sitting on the street in the front row. Not too many spectators have arrived as yet. Their main interest is the encounter between
Rangda and the entranced members of the *sekan barong,* which is still an
hour or so away.

The *gong* strikes up a new melody and, glancing south along the alley
between the two lines of spectators, you see that the six Sandars have come

onto the street and are dancing in a line toward the gong. Fans twirling vigorously, they advance slowly northward. The music pauses for a moment, switches to a new melody, and the Sandars pair up to form two parallel columns. At first they dance in place, alternately crouching and rising, the left hand always extended in a graceful posture, the fans fluttering ceaselessly. Then the lines begin circling, the two columns changing position with mincing, graceful steps. The sun is low in the west, and in its yellowing light the headdresses glitter and glisten as if they were real gold.

Once the group reaches the *gong*, two Sandars kneel and the other four encircle them, fans always fluttering. Then all six kneel, and just as quickly rise. The music halts, and all six sit on the ground in front of the *gong*. The two umbrellas that had been placed just north of the gong are now advanced to the south, and the Rajan Sandar comes out. He is an older and more experienced dancer, and you can tell. What he lacks in youthful suppleness he more than makes up for with his grace and deliberateness. His dance starts off slow, cautious, then speeds up, his feet and hands tracing intricate patterns, the movements graceful. He grasps the poles of the two umbrellas, poses briefly, and continues. Now the six seated Sandars rise, and all seven dance together. It ends quickly, and the raja departs to the south. The original six take up positions in two lines of three, just south of Barong, but facing south — away from Barong, towards the *gong*. Their dance has lasted about 20 minutes.

Back down the street to the south, the growing crowd jostles for position and is pushed back by members of the *sekan barong* who try to keep the view of the dancers clear for the drummer. The line of Omangs strides on to the street, their hands gesticulating and their movements wild and coarse — a contrast to the gentle Sandars. They advance quickly in a line to a position about 20 meters south of the *gong*, and all but Cemung sit down in the street, facing the Sandars.

Cemung advances northward toward the Sandars with his strange rolling gait, to the accompaniment of peculiar and dissonant four-beat music. He stops — right hand on hip — and surveys the crowd, then grabs an umbrella pole and pulls it toward himself. He hops ahead again, gently grabbing a young child, then letting him back down to the street. Suddenly he spots the Sandars, who have been dancing in place. He advances menacingly, claps his hands, and points the index and middle finger of his right hand at them — the Balinese equivalent of the thumb-and-forefinger pistol. Nothing happens. The Sandars ignore him, and keep dancing. He doesn't seem to mind, turns, and with a rolling hop joins his group.

An Omang with the Sobrat mask has arisen and, dancing wildly, advances toward Cemung. As they pass they face each other and each lifts his apron to his chin. They grasp each other's shoulders briefly, and

Cemung pantomimes telling Sobrat about the Sandars. Sobrat's music now plays, and he advances vigorously toward the Sandars, drives them back, slaps his hands, two-fingers them, and retreats. No result. He repeats his aggression. Nothing. He retreats, meeting the very coarse-looking, brown-masked Omang on the way. As they pass they face each other and raise aprons. Brown-face taunts and leers, and receives the same indifference from the Sandars. The procedure is repeated, with variations, by several more Omang dancers.

The next Jauk to advance passes his predecessor with the usual apron raising. But this one is Omang Ngiuking Kendang. His music is wild. He strides rapidly to just opposite the *gong*, clears an area in the crowd, and kneels on one knee, facing the musicians. He slaps his hands together and cries out — "*Ngiuk!*" — the drum stops, then begins once more. He advances toward the *gong* and leans over it, screaming in unintelligible bursts. All his attention is focused upon the music until, at last, he too retreats to the south, not bothering at all with the Sandars.

Now Omang Ngematiang Sandar rises. He often wears a red shirt, but is otherwise indistinguishable from the other Jauk. Cemung stands and follows him. The Omang advances quickly to the Sandar group, penetrates it, threatens and drives the group northward, whereupon they surround him. He slaps his hands several times, and two-fingers one of the Sandars. The Sandar drops to one knee, head down, and the Omang lays one hand on the tip of the Sandar's hat and dances a few steps. Cemung comes up to exult in the victory. But as they are celebrating their victory, the Sandar nearest his stricken fellow comes forward, hits the Omang with his fan, and kills him. He revives the dead Sandar, and the two switch places. The Sandars resume their stationary dance. Pandemonium reigns in the Omang camp as the black-masked Telek rushes to his fallen comrade. Cemung and another Jauk lift the dead Omang, and drag him back to Telek, who revives him and scolds him. They haul the Omang who killed the Sandar back to where their fellows are sitting and put him on the ground. Then Telek advances into the Sandar group, dances among them briefly, slaps his hands and two-fingers them, and finally all Omangs retreat to the south and sit down in the road. The Sandars sit down to one side of the road. It is a little after 4 P.M.

While the *mapajar* has been going on in the street, village women have been bringing a steady stream of offerings into Pura Ulun Siwi and praying. The *mapajar* is usually held on Kajeng Keliwon, an especially important day for offerings for the demon-gods, *bhutas* and *kalas*. On ordinary days the offerings are more modest, the usual being a basket of small coconut-leaf and rice *canangs*.

The first of the two pairs of Barong dancers don their striped red-and-white pants and slip in under the heavy *barong* costume, replacing two men within who have been holding it stationary all this time. Sopir takes the white cloth off Barong's head and ties it to one of the umbrellas. The Barong is now visible, dancing in place, its head tossing and hindquarters wiggling. Finally it turns, faces the swelling crowd, and just stands there — mouth agape, head turned quizzically to one side. The fast-sinking sun casts a few last rays on the mirrors of Barong's headdress, which glows orange. The music switches once again. Then Barong advances slowly southward, the two dancers within coordinating their movements. Little children rush forward to grab the *capaka* flowers that spill from Barong's black beard, and others grasp the hair and pull off a tuft. These souvenirs are magic.

Barong advances toward the *gong*, to which it pays great attention. Sometimes it rests its great head on the big gong for a moment. Then it clacks its jaws loudly at the drummer. It repeatedly backs into the crowd of people who rush to get away. Bystanders gently nudge it away when it is about to collide with a power pole. It is a graceful, even humorous performance, Barong acts like a huge and amiable lion — at once a beast, and a pussycat. Then Barong advances to the south a bit, Sandars at its heels. One of the Omangs rises and rushes at Barong, tweaking its head on alternate sides. All the Omangs rise to assist, but one of the Sandars comes forward, takes Barong by the head, and guides it to its former position, facing north toward the *sekan barong*.

Then the second pair of dancers, in black-and-white pants, climbs into the *barong*, and the same routine is repeated. If there is time, yet a third Barong dance may occur, with the red pants performers again. When Sopir decides it is time to quit, the Sandars and Omangs all rise, dance toward each other until they meet, and stop dancing. They then file out to the south, enter Pura Ulun Siwi, and shed their costumes. The *gong* takes a break. Sopir leads Barong to the south, stationing it near the crossroads, with the *sekan barong* sitting facing it. It is about 4:30 P.M.

The *gong* begins again, this time taking up a haunting, ethereal tune. The *gangsa* players sometimes damp their keys with their hands, allowing the metal instruments to produce sounds like a wooden xylophone. Rarung and Jero Luh enter from the gate of Pura Pererepan, each with her head covered with a magic cloth. They advance slowly southward, Jero Luh walking with a short hopping step, Rarung wailing in Kawi. Jero Luh pushes back the crowd, which retreats willingly. Both have pulled off their cloths and hold them in their right hands. Rarung moves south of the *gong*, and cradles her red cloth, talking to it like a baby. She puts it on the ground, then takes it in her arms again. Barong, with the original pair of dancers, spins and comes up behind Rarung unnoticed. Barong grabs the red cloth, turns and runs to the south, Rarung in pursuit. They face each other, Jero Luh joining in the fray, but always from safely behind Barong, hitting Barong with her cloth. Rarung grabs her red cloth back, and Barong chases them partway north before retreating to its resting place in front of the *seka*. It is 5 P.M.

Rangda has come out of the temple with her great umbrella and *lelontek* flags. With her white cloth over her face, grasping the umbrella pole for support, she screeches and screams in the most unearthly way imaginable. She issues loud grunts, sometimes leaning over backwards in a weird arc, sometimes gesturing wildly at nothing in particular. She then takes off the cloth, turns, and sees Jero Luh and Rarung advancing. She moves a little to the south as Jero Luh and Rarung kneel in front of her. Rangda then initiates a long dialogue in Kawi with Rarung, accompanied by groaning, screaming, and moaning. As the speech degenerates into moans, the *gong*'s accompaniment grows loud and wild, slowing and quieting again when speech resumes.

At the other end of the 200-meter corridor, near the crossroads, some members of the *sekan barong* seem taken by fits. These are the *babuten*, those who are prone to entrancement. Some shake violently. Others moan and rock back and forth. Some sit, heads on knees, muscles taut as guy wires, sweating and shivering. Sopir and his assistants fetch coconut shell after coconut shell full of holy water from Pura Ulun Siwi. After Barong's beard is dipped into the water, some members of the *seka* drink down the whole containerful. Others pour it over themselves. Some dozen or so of the *seka* members are thus affected. Their friends try to restrain them. Some are thrown into almost uncontrollable convulsions and have to be physically restrained. As the dialogue at the other end progresses, the agitation among the *babuten* grows.

One of the assistants comes to get Jero Luh, who rises from her kneeling position and goes off to Pura Pererepan, leaving Rarung and Rangda still screaming at each other. When Rarung has finished, she too goes back to her temple. The crowd has now swollen to pack the entire street and every available doorway and wall. All are bursting with anticipation and keep glancing expectantly toward the south. Helpers keep pushing them back to leave a wide, clear space. Rangda now assumes the most threatening of attitudes, waving her white cloth and taunting Barong. The *gong* plays wildly. It is 5:20 P.M. — just getting dark.

Suddenly a great shout arises. Fifteen or twenty of the *babuten*, in trance, have leapt to their feet. Each grabs the nearest kris, throws off its scabbard, and the armed group dashes headlong up the street to face Rangda. One rash *babuten* throws himself at Rangda, who flips her cloth at him, and he crumbles, immobilized at her feet. The others halt at a safe distance, their kris held at the waist, in attack position, blades pointed toward Rangda. Rangda keeps taunting them, waving her cloth and advancing slowly. The *babuten* retreat a bit, then advance a bit. The sweating, shaking members have unmitigated hatred on their faces. A fearless one rushes forward toward Rangda, slips as if on mud, and falls senseless at her feet. Sopir and his assistants come up to Rangda from behind and try to restrain her. She pushes them back, laughs wildly, and continues to attack and threaten. Finally Sopir and his helpers gain control of Rangda and, still screaming and growling, she is led back north to her temple. The performer doffs his costume in the temple — he grabs a tiny chick, wrings off its head, and drinks the blood.

The fallen *babuten* are at once hauled out of the way by their friends. They are rigid and unconscious, unable to move. Their hands and feet are held together tightly, as if tied with a rope. Those who did not fall, perhaps a dozen or so, burst into tears of frustration and anger. Barong comes up, turns around and faces the group on the south. The *gong* has now stopped, and Barong and the *babuten* are in the center of a great crowd of onlookers, completely surrounded. The men in trance then turn their kris upon themselves. Some roll on the ground, pressing, but never jabbing, the swords to their breasts. Some try to stab themselves in a standing position, all muscles taught, straining and sweating. There are wild cries of "*Ayah!*" After several minutes of stabbing, a man in trance comes up to Barong, grabs its beard with both hands, puts it to his face and screams: "*Mapamit! Mapamit!*" Sopir sprinkles holy water liberally. Some of those in trance are brought to their senses, drink the holy water from the coconut container, and wait quietly, each with a very dazed expression. Others go back into trance, call for another kris, or sometimes even two, and resume their destructive urges. I have seen men, muscles straining, a kris in each hand, one being pushed onto each eye. Old men and young men participate. The crowd watches, fascinated. Those who have fallen remain attended by their friends.

When the last person in trance has come out, Barong is led back into Pura Ulun Siwi to a spot in front of its pavilion. The "tied" *babuten* are carried in like so many logs and laid down at the feet of Barong. Trance resumes, more "*Ayah!*" and "*Mapamit!*" Old, dry coconut leaves are lit on fire and the burning branches brought up are promptly stamped out by the bare feet of those in trance. A large crowd of villagers throngs to watch. It is now dark — well past 6 P.M. Lanterns and burning coconut leaves glow. Eventually it is all over — perhaps by 7 P.M.

The crowd disperses. Sopir turns his attention to reviving those who were tied, by administration of holy water and mantras. This is usually successful, unless the condition has been brought about by a violation of a serious taboo by the *babuten*, in which case he may have to spend the night in the temple. The empty Barong costume is put back into the pavilion and hung up. And then Sopir ministers to anyone who might have cut himself. This rarely happens. But it if does, either to a *babuten* or accidentally to a member of the audience, Sopir puts powdered sandalwood and *arak* (palm brandy) in the cut, places a red hibiscus flower over it, and requires the wounded person to spend the night in the temple, where the *pemangku* offers mantras. By morning the cure is almost always successful, and in two or three days the person is well again. He is never taken to a doctor.

THE *BARONG* IS NOT ALWAYS ACTIVE, and the staging of the dance follows a complex calendar based on religious (and financial) dictates. Dewa Ayu is one of the more active Barongs in South Bali, and it is *matangi*, "awake," for longer than the those in most villages. *Matangi* does not mean Barong is performing, it means that it has has been brought to life through the proper ceremonies, and is ready to perform. The *barong* is *masimpen*, "stored," only when it is necessary to refurbish the costumes.

Dewa Ayu is *matangi* for a period of just under one Pawukon cycle of 210 days. The start of a cycle of *matangi* is always Panampahan, the day before Galungan, Tuesday of Week 11, Dunggulan. The *masimpen* ceremony is almost always held on Sukra Pon Julungwangi, Friday of the ninth week, one week before Sugian Bali and 12 days before Galungan. Thus, the *barong* is *matangi* for a period of 199 days. In some cases the performances will immediately continue for another 199-day cycle, but even so the *masimpen* ceremony takes place, and the *matangi* ceremony 11 days later. For a period of eight years, ending in 1982, Dewa Ayu remained *masimpen* and did not perform at all. Since then, it has alternated, resting for one Pawukon cycle, active for the next. Ideally, if there were enough money, it would perform all the time. The activity of the *barong* is important to village of Jimbaran, since when it is *masimpen* its spirit remains in Pura Pererepan, and thus so does the full power of Dewa Ayu. The *barong* does not perform every 15 days, skipping those that are ill-omened for one reason or another, and skipping days of rain, which would quickly ruin the costumes. If important members of the *sekan barong* are *sebel* ("ceremonially impure") — for example, because of a death in the family — no *barong* can be held. A patron can hire the *barong* to give a free-lance performance, although the cost can be quite high.

It rarely happens, but occasionally one or more of the masks have to be repainted. I was lucky enough to witness this in 1985, when five days were spent stripping and repainting all but the one *barong* mask. (The youngest *barong* mask had been last repainted in 1961 and was not thought to require repainting.) The others had been repainted about 1980, as far as anyone could remember, and these were the ones that had to be refinished.

Scraping the paint off of the masks had started a couple of days before, and much of that work had already been completed when the painter arrived on Buda Manis Julungwangi, a week and two days before Sugian Bali. Such *tenget* (magically charged) objects as holy masks cannot be painted by just anyone. A good deal of knowledge and power is required. One of the renowned Brahmana painters from Sanur had been asked to come to do the work. Not content with the paint scraping, he spent most of the first day removing every trace of undercoat. It was easy to see the antiquity of the *barong* mask. It had cracked here and there and was wired together in places. The painter said it was made of *kayu mundeh,* a wood unknown to me, taken from the Pura Dalem. The mask of the younger *barong* is made of *kayu pule,* the usual wood used for traditional masks. Its wood came from Tinja Pula, on the west side of the Bukit south of Jimbaran.

The pigments were bought as powders, and ground on a plate with *ancur,* a varnishlike material made of fish paste. The paints were applied a little at a time, with great care, by the Brahmana man. After each coat, the masks were placed on a table out in the sun to dry. Sopir, the leader of the *sekan barong,* and several others sat and watched all day long, making sure that the painter had everything he needed and, of course, always sitting at a lower level than he.

I should add, by way of interest, that when the painter was finished with the *rangda* mask, he made the mistake of holding it up to his face and looking through it. Sopir was shocked. And sure enough, some days later this man became sick. He tried many doctors over a period of several weeks and only recovered when treated with holy water from Pura Pererepan.

An important part of the preparations for a new *barong* cycle is the training of new dancers for the Omangs and Sandars. The *seka* likes to have at least twice as many dancers available as are needed, so that they can be replaced quickly had in case of illness. For at least a month before the first *barong* performance, a group of young men gathers in the small space on the street, just south of the entrance to Pura Pererepan and practices for an hour or so just after sundown. The *gong* sits facing at the temple entrance. There is only one small electric lamp bulb. Older men who once danced the parts themselves are the teachers, and they shout at the dancers, laugh at their mistakes, forcibly twist their bodies into the proper positions, and seem to be intensely absorbed in this important job of transmitting their knowledge to the younger generation. The latter sweat and strain, sometimes losing their way, sometimes showing surprising grace and skill in spite of inexperience.

WHEN THE *SEKAN BARONG* DECIDES that another *matangi* will occur, they consult the calendar to pinpoint the dates. Activities formally begin with a ceremony called *pamakuh bulu,* meaning "to install the *bulu* (body hair)" of Barong, Rangda, Jero Luh, and Rarung. Before this, however, a ceremony is held in Pura Pererepan called a *marerauhang — rauh* means "come," and the name of the ceremony refers to the fact that the gods are invited to come and take possession of one of those present. The *pemangkus* do this by asking questions of a person who goes into trance and is possessed by a god. This is by no means a ceremony unique to Jimbaran, or to Dewa Ayu, or to *barongs.* It is widely used whenever it is necessary to communicate directly with the supernatural world.

The *marerauhang* for Dewa Ayu is held on Sukra Pon Kulantir, Week four, enough in advance of the commencement of the season that, should any changes be necessary, there is time for adjustment. The ceremony begins in the evening, about 7 P.M., in Pura Pererepan. First come the usual prayers of many villagers. Dewa Ayu's *gong* plays in the south pavilion. Then the village *pemangkus,* led by Rembon, *pemangku* of the Pura Dalem and acknowledged leader of the *pemangku* group, pray in front of the shrines. A chorus of men keeps up a steady chant. Great scoops of sandalwood chips are heaped upon burning braziers, producing almost suffocating smoke in the small, cramped temple. Hundreds of villagers come to watch, filling every available nook and cranny.

Suddenly one of the *pemangkus* utters a cry and starts to shake violently, his hair whipping about as his *udeng* comes flying off. He, and then several others, have to be physically restrained as they moan. When released, they rock back and forth. The *pemangkus* who are liable to trance are known as *sadegs.* Eyes turn to one of the older *pemangkus* who also goes into trance. He is not nearly as violent as the others, but obviously in trance, rocking and talking quietly to himself. Sopir questions him at some length, sprinkling him with holy water now and then. Finally, when all of the necessary information has been obtained, the group of four or five entranced men is sprinkled with holy water, whereupon they recover.

Installing the hair, the *pamakuh bulu* ceremony, is always held on Sugian Bali, Kajeng Keliwon of the week Sungsang — the Friday before Galungan. This is a day of hard work. The main job is to get the dance paraphernalia for Barong and its two companions repaired and in good shape. For a month or so prior to the ceremony, leaves of the *peraksok* have been soaking in mud and water. They are removed, dried, and combed, making the long hair for Barong's coat, which is patched and repaired on this day. Starting early in the morning, the entire *sekan barong* works very hard in Pura Pererepan to make sure that the leather is freshly gilded, and that all the decorations — such as flags, umbrellas, and spears — are in top shape. The *barong* costume is propped up on poles out in the sun, and the back pieces, tail, and so on are tied to the body with stout rope. A short ceremony, at about 3 P.M., ends the process.

The series of ceremonies which govern the procedure of attaching the masks of Barong, Rangda, Rarung, and Jero Luh to their headdresses and bodies is called *ngatep*, from the stem *atep*, "connect." These are held on Panampahan, one day before Galungan. Events commence at about 3:30 in Pura Pererepan, with the *sekan barong* and the *gong* outside on the street. The *pemangkus* are inside the temple, and they lead a crowd of people in prayer. The *barong* mask sits on an elevated platform facing west and the worshipers. After the offerings have been made, Sopir, assisted by other members of the Seka, attaches the mask to the rest of the elaborate head-dress with stout cord. The old *peraksok* hair that was removed from the *barong* costume when it was refurbished is gathered, packaged, and taken in procession to Kahyangan, the Pura Dalem, Barong's "home," where it is buried in a special little plot just to the north of the main shrine.

Everybody now goes in procession to the Pura Dalem, where the *pemangkus* pray once more. Now maskless, Barong sits in their midst, fac-ing the main shrine. Sopir and his assistants attach the headdress to the body of the *barong*, sprinkle it with holy water several times, and pray. Barong comes to life, clacks its jaws, and executes a very short dance. The *babuten* go into trance, with great vigor. This phase lasts until dark, and when the stabbing is over everyone goes home to rest and have a bit of supper before the long events of the evening.

At about 7 P.M. the eeriest part begins. The Kahyangan temple is totally dark. The *gamelan* plays soft, ethereal music, usually a single *gangsa* sound-ing the melody that floats quietly out to the huge crowd of people. Sopir and his assistants remove the three Rangda masks from their boxes and attach them to the headdresses in total darkness. When finished, the cos-tumes are replaced in their boxes and carried to the cemetery where they are put near each other under the giant *kepuh* trees. Now the three dancers who are to take the parts of Rangda and her attendants dance quietly into the *jeroan* of Kahyangan, fully dressed except for masks. It is still totally dark. They move to the front of the temple and then out again in the direc-tion of the cemetery. The crowd follows, making a large circle enclosing the three dancers and the mask boxes. As we watch in near-total darkness, the dancers put on their masks. There is a human skull under each. The first sound heard is a blood-chilling scream from Rangda. (Mind you, it is near midnight in the village cemetery. One gets a little edgy under such cir-cumstances.) A series of grunts and a long conversation in Kawi between Rarung and Rangda, both now fully masked, follows. Suddenly cries and running feet — the *babuten*. From their positions in the Pura Dalem with Barong they have heard Rangda screaming in the cemetery and are now tearing after her, kris in hand. The entranced men are forcibly restrained and carried back to the Pura Dalem, and the three Rangdas are led off to Pura Pererepan. Back in the Pura Dalem, the self-stabbing begins and goes on until well past midnight.

AFTER BARONG BECOMES *MATANGI*, it can and does perform for the various Jimbaran temple *odalans*. Generally, however, there is no showing of Rangda, although there is plenty of trance. Just before the *odalan* of Pura Pererepan Barong has to go to Pura Luhur Uluwatu in order to receive a recharge of magical power so that the *babuten* can thenceforth be allowed to stab themselves. New members are restrained from doing this before their first trip to Uluwatu. This trip is generally held on Redite, Sunday, of Medangsiya, Week 14, just before the Friday when the *odalan* of Pura Pererepan — and the *barong* — is held.

Locally, this trip is called *mapinton*, although some feel that the word is not used correctly in this context. The ceremonies involve a fair share of the village of Jimbaran. The last time I went along, in 1988, at least 3,000 people followed Barong, and the procession stretched out for well over a kilometer along the road, several people abreast. Many of the *pemangkus*, the offering specialists, and most of the offerings are hauled to Pecatu on the Bukit by truck. But most of the people walk the 16 kilometers to Pura Luhur Uluwatu and back, stopping both going and returning at Pura Pererepan Pecatu, some 10 kilometers from Jimbaran. The procession begins at Pura Ulun Siwi about 7 A.M. The pace set is a very brisk walk, and some of the older people have difficulty keeping up. The three Rangda masks are carried on the heads of members of the *sekan barong*. Barong walks too, as do members of Barong's *gong*, carrying and playing their "marching music" with drums, cymbals, and gong only. As a member of the *sekan barong*, I carry the umbrella shading Rangda's mask. It gets very heavy after three hours, and three of us trade off the task along the way. The heavier instruments go to Pecatu by truck.

Pecatu is jammed with carts, foodstalls set up for the occasions, hawkers of all sorts, and many curious people. We buy plates of *nasi campur* ("mixed rice") and some soda for lunch, stop to rest, and then pray in the *jeroan* of Pura Pererepan, where Barong stops and where permission is asked for us to go on to Pura Luhur Uluwatu. The procession forms up again about mid-afternoon and walks the remaining six kilometers to Pura Uluwatu — most of this part of the trip being flat or downhill. The small *jeroan* of Pura Uluwatu can hold only a fraction of those who have come along, so there must be several shifts of praying. Barong does a brief dance in the *jeroan*. There is the usual self-stabbing, the necessary holy water is obtained, and we make our way back to Pecatu just at dark.

After a break for dinner, ceremonies resume in the *jeroan* of Pura

Pererepan in Pecatu. The *gong* plays quietly in a separate pavilion. The *pemangkus* assemble in the *jeroan*, and another *marerauhang* takes place — clouds of smoke, violent thrashing about by those possessed, and the characteristic rocking back and forth exhibited by people whom the god has entered. Throughout all of this women from Jimbaran dance *pendet* — the last dance being a spectacular symbolic fight with glowing sticks of incense. Then everyone adjourns to the nearby cemetery where the corridor and stages have been set up for the *calonarang*.

The *calonarang* is a reenactment of the story of how a wicked witch of East Java, Rangda, tried to marry off her daughter. She was unsuccessful because there was a distinct shortage of young men who wanted a witch for a mother-in-law. Rangda unleashed her hostility, causing plagues of illness and various disasters, which finally motivated a nearby ruler to try to depose her by sending his son to marry the daughter. He did, learned Rangda's secrets, and transmitted them to his father who was then able to attack Rangda and, if not defeat her, at least maintain some sort of balance. The play is an all-night-long event, beginning after midnight and lasting until dawn. But nobody leaves until mighty Rangda emerges from her hiding place inside an elevated stage at one end of the small performing area and roars off into the cemetery, shrieking and shouting at her intended killer. Quite a lot of performers take part in the *calonarang*, and rehearsals go on for four days before the dance.

Another prayer in the temple at Pecatu, and we are off for home at about 6:30 A.M., a bit groggy from staying up all night. Along the way, especially at bridges and crossroads, the leaders of the procession stop, and some of the *babuten* go into trance and stab themselves. Trance and stabbing occur even though the Rangda masks are still in their boxes and Rangda is not present, at least physically.

THE LAST REGULAR *MAPAJAR* IN ANY CYCLE is held on Kajeng Keliwon of Kulantir, the fourth week, which is an Anggar Kasih also. This is exactly 50 days before Galungan. The last public showing of Barong is at the time of its becoming *masimpen*. These ceremonies are held on Sukra Pon Julungwangi, Friday of Week 9, 12 days before Galungan. These are tremendously powerful ceremonies, packed with emotion and tense with drama as the mask of Barong, *angker* and *tenget* as it is, the subject of so much veneration, fear, and respect, is severed from its body and stored.

A large bamboo platform with a long ramp leading up to the top has been built in the outer courtyard of Pura Ulun Siwi, facing south. By 2 P.M. the platform is already loaded with high offerings and the temple jammed with people going to pray and coming from prayer with their offerings. At about 4 P.M. the group of *pemangkus* prays in front of this platform, Barong in their midst. There is the usual stabbing. The procession then goes to the main crossroads, where there is more prayer and stabbing, and thence to the Pura Dalem, where the prayers and trance are repeated. There follows a procession to Pura Gaing Mas, and finally to the Pura Puseh–Pura Desa in the middle of town, returning to Pura Ulun Siwi just after dark.

Barong is seated in the *jaba tengah*, facing the platform. There is a long period of trance, perhaps a half hour or more, with much stabbing, walking on fire, and all the accompaniments. The *gong* is sitting just north of the Kori Agung, facing east. Barong gets up and dances briefly. It is then led up the ramp to the top of the platform, where the group of *pemangkus* is sitting. Barong then turns to face the crowd below, and all pray long and fervently to it for the last time. The entire village is assembled. There is not an open square centimeter in the large courtyard. Offerings are everywhere. The smell of incense is overpowering, the crush of bodies irresistible.

Finally Barong turns north for the last time. The *pemangkus* sit in two rows facing each other looking east and west. Sopir sits directly in front of Barong's head. He takes up a special kris, holds it high in the air as if to kill Barong, then plunges it into the string holding the mask on — and faints dead away into the lap of a nearby *pemangku*. The assistants quickly cut the mask away from the headdress and body and put it in its basket. The maskless Barong heads quickly toward Pura Pererepan. Sopir has regained consciousness. It is 8 P.M. There is a break for dinner.

The last act commences about 9 P.M. in Pura Ulun Siwi. The masks of Rangda, Rarung, and Jero Luh are sitting in front of their boxes on the platform. The group of *pemangkus* prays in front of the masks. The lights go out. The three dancers silently enter the courtyard from the inner temple, maskless and dancing slowly and deliberately. They ascend the ramp to the platform and don their masks. They hold a short conversation in Kawi. The *sekan barong* takes up burning torches and gasoline pressure lanterns and heads for the cemetery, the three mask box bearers in the lead, most of the villagers following. The three dancers stop briefly at the main crossroads, then proceed to the center of a large circle that the villagers have formed in the cemetery, with the three mask boxes in the center. Again there is a long conversation between Rangda and Rarung in Kawi. All three masks are removed, and the entire group moves to the *jeroan* of the Pura Dalem. Here Sopir and his assistants cut the masks off the headdresses and put everything away. The dancers put on their regular clothes. All pray.

It is midnight, and another cycle has been completed. The masks are carried to their shrines in Pura Pererepan, not to be seen until Barong once again becomes *matangi*.

CHAPTER 27

The Barong (PART II)

NISKALA - THE MEANING

THE SOURCE OF THE MOVEMENTS AND PLOTS of particular Balinese dances is often extremely hard to trace; scraps of myth, Hindu theology, and bits and pieces of the great epics are often assembled in a quite eclectic way into the dance. And the variety from village to village is considerable. The Jimbaran *barong* is no exception. In this dance, the Barong-Rangda confrontation is a fairly straightforward enactment of a fragment of a longer story, the *calonarang*, which describes the conflict between a powerful widow — *rangda* in high Balinese means "widow" — and an East Java ruler. But no such clear-cut source can be found for the Sandar-Omang standoff that precedes the climactic entrance of Barong and Rangda. After watching some three dozen different village *barongs*, reading several texts, and talking to Department of Religion sources, a score of *pemangkus*, and other knowledgeable observers, the best I can report is a handful of theories. Some of which, in the best Balinese tradition, contradict one another.

There is little argument about the Barong-Rangda story. Jimbaran's play, and those of most other traditional villages in Bali, follow the basic outline of the *calonarang*. Some diverge from this story, particularly those put on for tourists, who are unfamiliar with the somewhat complicated tale. The tourist show in Batubulan, for example, is based on the story of Kunti Seraya — probably an adaptation from the Ramayana — which is more dramatic, and includes comic relief and action. The tourist show also does not begin in the middle of the night and last till dawn, as some of the full *calonarangs* do. There is no particular rule as to what story is used as a framework for the Barong-Rangda confrontation, nor is one or another necessarily superior in any way.

The *calonarang* takes place during the reign of Erlangga, king of Java in the 11th century. Erlangga's mother was Mahendradatta, a princess from Java and her husband was Dharmodayana, a Balinese ruler. Because Mahendradatta practiced witchcraft, her husband exiled her to the forest and married another woman. When Dharmodayana died, Mahendradatta, by definition, became a widow, *rangda*.

She carried a grudge against Erlangga, because he had refused to urge his father not to remarry after exiling Mahendradatta. She had accumulated a group of students, and she turned their talents to the destruction of Erlangga's East Javanese kingdom. But what bothered Mahendradatta most was that although her daughter Ratna Menggali was lovely, nobody would marry her — the thought of having a witch for a mother-in-law was just too powerful a deterrent. And Ratna, as a woman of high caste, had to marry a man of high caste. Thus Rangda-Mahendradatta and her students went on a rampage, raining down disease, destruction, and death on East Java. For her magic Rangda often required the body of a dead baby, and her daughter and students would be sent to the cemetery on grisly errands. Erlangga tried to destroy Rangda, but her magic was too strong. Accordingly, he sent for a holy man, Empu Pradah, and asked for help.

Empu Pradah sent his son or assistant (it is not clear which), a man named Bahula, to marry Ratna Menggali. The two lived happily together. But Bahula's real mission was to learn his mother-in-law's secrets. He finally found an opportunity to steal her magic book and turned it over to Empu Pradah. The Empu used her secrets to restore life to Rangda's victims and, finally, to confront Rangda herself. Pradah first killed Rangda by turning her own black magic against her, then revived her and killed her again when she was in human form.

Only a small part of this legend is used in the Barong-Rangda *mapajar*. When a *calonarang* performance (rather than a *mapajar*) is given in Jimbaran, most of the story is performed — including, as is usual with Balinese drama, many diversions and extraneous subplots. Mahendradatta is also called "The Widow of Girah," after the area in which she lived, and sometimes "Calonarang." Tourist *calonarang* shows are regularly presented, but these bear very little resemblance to the original. A true *calonarang*, including the full story described above, is generally given only in the more remote villages in connection with sacred religious ceremonies.

The only fragment of the *calonarang* story in the Jimbaran *mapajar*, and in those of most other village *barongs*, involves Rangda asking her daughter, Rarung, to go to the cemetery to get the body of a dead baby. Rangda is going to pray and she needs an offering, *pabersihan*, which includes a baby's body. In the performance, Rarung goes to the cemetery and finds a baby (the red cloth that she cradles in her arms) and plays around with it, as one would with a live baby. While she is doing this Barong is hiding behind a tree watching her. Barong confronts Rarung and demands the baby. They fight, and Barong gets the baby. Rarung cries all the way back to her mother, who is furious — Rangda tells Rarung that she had been told to get a baby, but instead she has brought back an enemy. Rangda orders Rarung to go home and pray — in every shrine — that she, Rangda, will be the winner in the fight against Barong. Rangda then talks loudly to herself, summoning up her powers for the fight. Barong hears her voice and tells his followers to kill Rangda. But Rangda advances with her two *lelonteks* and her magic cloth, and she conquers the followers of Barong — but not, however, Barong itself.

Rangda is clearly the winner over Barong's followers, but not over Barong. The outcome is inconclusive. This is really all there is to the story, except it is said that after the confrontation, Barong and Rangda overcame their differences and made up once again. Please note that, after the confrontation between Barong and Rangda, nobody is *dead* — this is not a tragedy play. The performance is an enactment of the Hindu-Balinese notion of good-evil balance. There is no "winner" in the sense of a victor in the struggle for "good," and evil is not "vanquished." What makes Barong the source of such fascination is that it is a deity, with great religious and magical power, in a tangible, physical form. Rangda is equally powerful, and equally fascinating. Her power is perhaps of a darker kind, but this does not make her "evil" in our sense. In the performance, Rangda and Rarung speak in the ancient language of Kawi, unintelligible to most of the audience. The men who take the parts of Rarung and Rangda are not highly educated scholars. They say they know a little Kawi, but when they put on the masks and assume the personalities of those whom they portray, the words just come out, as if divinely inspired.

THE SANDAR-OMANG STORY is much more complex, at least as far as its history is concerned. I have unearthed at least a dozen completely different accounts, each purporting to explain the story and the symbolism. The religious leader of Jimbaran said he hadn't the faintest notion of where the story comes from. Nor, to my great surprise, did Sopir, the *pemangku* of the Dewa Ayu Barong. Nor did anyone else in Jimbaran. It was just a performance that was required as a prelude to the Rangda-Barong encounter.

Beryl de Zoete and Walter Spies' 1958 *Dance and Drama in Bali* has an account, with pictures, of Sandars used in connection with the *barong* performance at Tegeh Kuri, not far from Denpasar. But in Tegeh Kuri the Sandar-Omang part of the performance was stopped in the 1960s, and, in fact, the *barong* performance is now only an abbreviation of what de Zoete and Spies recorded 30 years ago. The masks are still there, but unused.

I Gusti Agung Gde Putra, who at the time I interviewed him was the director of the government's Department of Religion, Kanwil Departemen Agama Propinsi Bali, offered a theological explanation for the Sandar-Omang prelude. His story describes the purification of the world after its creation by Siwa and Uma.

After creation, the earth could not yet produce anything. Dewi Uma created the matter or material of all living things. And Siwa gave them all life or spirit. But Siwa and Uma became extremely attached, too attached (*terikat*) to their creations. This attachment was not good and built up too much energy in Siwa and Uma and they changed into strange and frightening forms. Uma changed herself into Durga in the shape of Rangda; Siwa changed into the form of Rudra, the symbol of human greed. Durga-Rangda and Rudra produced disease from the rays of their eyes. Whatever they looked at turned sick. Eventually the demons, *bhutas* and kalas, sprang from Durga, and she was surrounded by evil spirits.

In heaven, the gods smelled something bad going on. They called upon Begawan Wrespati, the priest of the gods, to help. He found in a *lontar* that only Sanghyang Tri Murthi — the Hindu triad of Brahma, Wisnu, and Iswara — could return the bad things on earth to normal. Sanghyang Tri Murthi met Durga and Rangda at the main crossroads. He hesitated to criticize them because Siwa, disguised as Rudra, was his teacher. It would not be polite for him to tell Siwa what to do. So to avoid the embarrassment, Sanghyang Tri Murthi performed a *wayang kulit*, a shadow puppet play, in order to show the two their mistakes. Brahma became the puppet master's lantern. Wisnu became the *gender wayang* player, and Iswara became the puppet master (*dalang*) and offered a parable about the creation of the earth.

The story did not tell Durga and Rangda to do anything specific, but was suggestive, indicating why a person should not become too attached to that which he has made. As they watched the performance Rudra and Durga became conscious of what they had done. Rudra recovered and again assumed the appearance of Siwa and went back to heaven. There he told his son, Ganapati, to go to earth and bring back his mother, giving him a special mantra and a *lontar* of predictions to help. When Ganapati met his mother she was furious because he was not respectful of her. He was not respectful, he said, because she had assumed the shape of Durga. He said he would be respectful when she changed back to her proper form. Durga got so angry that fire sprang from her body and burned half of Ganapati's *lontar*. He quickly recited a mantra from the *lontar,* and the fire went out. (But, it is said, the part of the *lontar* that predicted the future was burned, which is why we now cannot predict the future successfully.) Durga, seeing the power of the *lontar* and mantra, changed back to Uma

RANGDA CONJURING UP DEMONS

and returned to heaven.

But her followers, the *bhutas* and *kalas,* were still there, as was Sanghyang Tri Murthi. The demons spread out to all house compounds, causing myriad problems. To restore balance, Sanghyang Tri Murthi changed himself as follows: Iswara changed into a Telek (another name for a Sandar); Wisnu changed into a *barong;* and Brahma changed into a *tapel bang. Tapel* is Balinese for "mask" and *bang* is the high Balinese word for "red." When *tapel bang* is mentioned, it may refer specifically to a red mask that is rough and uncouth looking (*kasar* or *keras*), or it may refer to any of the group of Omang-type, rough characters that are associated with and companions of the *tapel bang.* Red is the color associated with Brahma. The Tri Murthi then went from gate to gate, purifying each house compound. When the *bhutas* and *kalas* saw them they left quickly.

Pak Putra is here talking about two kinds of *barong* performances. His story most closely describes the performance as it is given in the village of Jumpai, near Gelgel. The Jimbaran *barong* does not *ngelawang* — go from gate (*lawang*) to gate — as do many *barongs* in central Bali. Traditionally, *ngelawang* occurs during a 42-day period following Galungan — in another story, Durga was purified by sacrifices in this period. He mentions the Kajeng Keliwon performances celebrating the day of creation and refers to Tapel Bang. Although one of the Jimbaran masks is a *tapel bang*, the reference is more generally to what we in Jimbaran would call Omang. And what he calls Telek, we would refer to as Sandar.

The central idea, to one not used to fathoming such a variety of nomenclature and interpretation, is that the performance of the Barong, Rangda, Sandars, and Omangs is a reenactment of the task that Brahma, Wisnu, and Iswara performed when they drove the *bhutas* and *kalas* from the house compounds after their leader, Rangda, deserted them. In some villages it is done around Galungan, and for a period of 42 days thereafter. In some villages, like Jimbaran, it is done every 15 days, on Kajeng Keliwon.

Pak Putra's is one interpretation. There are many others. I interviewed four *pedandas* on the question of the Sandar-Omang aspect of the Barong, and put the same questions to the Dalem Pemayun of Puri Gede, Klungkung, a renowned religious scholar. The results were quite uneven. One *pedanda* talked at some length on how the Balinese love to make up stories, and how, especially if they are popular, other groups will copy them freely, until it becomes virtually impossible to find out where the story originated and what it represents. He said the Sandar-Omang story is a good example. In effect, the answer is that there is no answer — no story, no theme. Several of the *pedandas* stated outright that they just did not know. But Dalem Pemayun offered a story.

Siwa had a wife, Giri Putri, and he wanted to test her love. He pretended he was sick and told her only the butter of a bull(!) could cure him. He sent Giri Putri to earth to get the butter. She did, and looked everywhere, but could not find any. Then Siwa came to earth and changed himself into a *rareangon*, a cattle herder, and announced that he had a bull that could produce milk. Giri Putri asked for the milk, but the cattle herder, Siwa in disguise, said that the only way he would give her the milk would be if she had sex with him. Giri Putri didn't know what to do, being torn between loyalty to her husband and the need to cure his illness. So she moved her vagina to her heel, and told the cowherd that he could have sex there. He refused. Then she moved it to her knee. Still no. Finally she submitted, got the milk, and returned to heaven where Siwa, having already returned, was waiting for her.

Siwa and Giri Putri had two children, and he ordered the older one, Bhatara Gana, to find out how his mother got the milk. Gana did so through meditation and consulting a sacred *lontar*, and told his father. Giri Putri was embarrassed and angry, burned the *lontar*, and, in her anger, changed to Durga and went to earth, leaving her youngest baby behind. But Siwa wanted her to come back so that the baby could be given milk, and he sent Brahma, Iswara, and Wisnu to earth to find Giri Putri and bring her home. Iswara changed into the five directions — so that he could see everywhere and look for Durga. The five creatures that he turned himself into were Teleks or Sandars, and they were white because the color of Iswara is white. But they could not find Durga. Then Brahma came and turned himself into three red Jauks, Jauk Bang, since Brahma's color is red. Brahma couldn't find Durga either. Then Wisnu came to earth and turned into Banaspati Raja, Barong, but was no more successful than the others.

But one day Banaspati Raja came across Kalika, another name for Rarung, who was looking for a baby's corpse for Durga. Barong called to Rarung, but she didn't answer because she was using her magic powers to crack open the ground to find a baby. Barong interpreted the lack of an answer as rudeness, and the two had a fight, which Rarung lost. She ran home to tell her mother. Durga got very angry and fought Barong, defeating him. After the fight, all living things expressed their love for Wisnu/Banaspati Raja/Barong. They chased Durga, but they could not find her, and so they stabbed themselves in frustration.

Yet another interpretation offered for the Sandar-Omang story is that it is simply a symbolic reenactment of the battle between the gods and the demons at the time of the churning of the Sea of Milk, from the "Pamuteran Mandara Giri" story. The Sandars are the *dewas,* and the Omangs are the demons. Barong represents Naga Basuki, the snake whose body was used to spin Mount Mandara. This story is the official one used by the group that presents the *barong* ceremony at Desa Pemogan. Their *barong ket* is quite unusual, its coat made entirely of peacock feathers.

These tales are only the beginning. I have recorded at least again as many stories of the Omang-Sandar performance. Several were presented here just to demonstrate how difficult tracing these origins can be.

ULTIMATELY THE QUESTION OF THE ORIGIN of the *barong* story is quite irrelevant to the Balinese. Nor is it important that the "good guys" win, in the sense of a Western drama. The Barong-Rangda and Sandar-Omang stories are really the same, each symbolizing the struggle to maintain balance, to maintain an equilibrium of opposing powers. The Hindu-Balinese world view is complex, and interlocking, and the origins offered by various *barong* groups for their performances, though seemingly almost contradictory, do not differ in any essential way.

CHAPTER 28

Wayang Kulit

THE POPULAR BALINESE SHADOW PLAY

By Margaret Eiseman

A LARGE WHITE CLOTH is stretched in front of a low platform, illuminated by a flickering coconut oil lamp. A crowd of several dozen men sit patiently on the ground, little boys in the front row. Delicate, tinkling music drifts from behind the screen. It is late evening, and the show is about to begin. Shadowy figures appear on the screen, going in and out of focus. Their voices, all the product of the *dalang* puppet master's highly-trained vocal chords, range from groans to sweet tremolos and coarse barks. The audience titters, then roars at a choice remark. The little boys fall asleep, but are quickly awakened by the battle scenes and a final shout of approval when the villains fall and the heroes triumph.

Almost any traveler to Bali falls at once in love with the daily extravagant celebrations of faith for which the Hindu inhabitants of this tiny Indonesian island are justly famous. Likely to go unnoticed, however, mainly because it doesn't begin until long after dark, is an extremely important, popular, and common form of entertainment — the *wayang kulit* shadow play. Any visitor to Bali with more than a casual interest in the area should try to witness one of these performances because it represents, all at the same time, an entertainment, a morality play, and a form of religious experience.

Kulit in Indonesian means "skin" or "covering," and *wayang* refers generally to a puppet. The puppets are cut out of cow hide, filigreed into the equivalent of leather lace, painted, and braced with sticks. They have articulated arms and legs, sometimes even jaws, and these are supported by sticks that the *dalang* can manipulate. These puppets are, as representations of sacred figures, sacred themselves — they are always kept in elevated positions, and are given special offerings. The *wayang kulit* performance is a story told by a *dalang* through voice, shadows on a screen, and music. The *dalang* takes all of the parts, and the success or failure of the show depends entirely upon his skill and knowledge — he must impersonate a dozen or more characters, and have a complete knowledge of the stories that he tells.

The *dalang* sits cross-legged on a mat with his lamp just in front of his face. His box of puppets is at his left. He clutches a wooden hammer in the toes of his right foot with which he periodically strikes the puppet box — in single strokes or long rolls — either to emphasize points of the story or to signal the musicians. One assistant sits on each side, handing the required puppets to him and accepting those that have gone off stage. The oil of the lamp is constantly renewed. Behind the *dalang* sit four musicians playing the *gender wayang,* four xylophone-like instruments that are struck by small, round, wooden mallets, one in each hand. Unlike the usual *gong,* or percussion orchestra, where the tones of the bronze keys are damped with the left hand, *gender wayang* keys are damped with the knuckles of both hands almost at the same time the hammers are struck.

A group of men and boys will usually crowd the back of the screen as well as the front, for there is a fascination in the behind-the-scenes operations of the *dalang's* performance. But the space there is always very limited, and people have to crowd in uncomfortably. The sound of the *dalang's* voice, with its nearly unintelligible twisting and elongating of the vowel sounds, his foot clapper, and the background music of the four *gender* are integral parts of the experience. The musicians must play music befitting the scene, such as traveling music, love music, or battle music. They must work closely with the *dalang,* sensitive to every nuance, so that music and drama mesh perfectly. The *dalang* uses his clapper to cue the players.

A TALENTED *DALANG* MUST HAVE MANY SKILLS. He must know more than 100 stories and be willing to learn more. He must possess enormous stamina to sit and declaim for three to six hours without a break, and usually without any sort of electrical amplification. In addition to having a thorough knowledge of the ancient Javanese Kawi — the language in which the plays and all other important Hindu-Balinese texts are written — the *dalang* must also be fluent and literate in high, middle, and low Balinese. He will use them all in a performance: high Balinese for the gods, middle Balinese to address royalty, and low Balinese for the common characters. These are four distinct languages, the levels of Balinese being not dialects, but separate tongues. As an indication of just how demanding a linguistic task the *wayang kulit* presents, the *dalang* — like an English professor in the West — is considered the exemplar of correct pronunciation and proper language use.

The puppet master must narrate and speak the dialogue of the story figures with the peculiar declamation so unique to his art. Kawi is not really
spoken, but rather chanted and sung, and the *dalang* has to have a vocal
range from low and coarse to high and delicate. Each character must possess a convincingly unique voice and manner, and the *dalang* must maintain this uniqueness so that the listener can tell who is talking without even
watching. He must be able to evoke all moods, human and supernatural,
and to create all dramatic effects. He must be able to select an appropriate
story for the occasion. Most important of all, he must be able to improvise
with comedy and timely commentary, because it is principally this that the
audience comes to hear.

The *dalang* is actually a kind of priest. He is familiar with, and in contact
with, the religious stories and sacred traditions. The puppets must be
brought to "life" with special rituals and prayers. The *dalang* can make
holy water — this is done following a special daytime performance called a
wayang lemah (daytime) — which accords him a status much like that of a
pemangku, or lay priest. He is also a craftsman, a puppet maker, for the
dalang must be able to design, carve, and paint a complete set of puppets,
which can run to well over a hundred. And he must be a musician, able to
play the *gender* himself and skillfully cue the players during the performance. Last, but perhaps most important, the *dalang* must have the
instincts and charisma of a showman. He must love his work and he must
be able to project this love to his audience.

MAN'S FASCINATION WITH MOVING SHADOWS on a screen precedes by
many centuries the current worldwide craze for cinema and television.
Scholars do not agree on the historical origin of the shadow play, though
many think it had its beginnings in India. It has been known throughout
Asia from China to as far west as Turkey. Today, only vestiges of the tradition can be seen here and there — China, Thailand, Malaysia, the
Philippines, and occasionally in India. But its popularity has never flagged
in Java and Bali. The purpose and function of the shadow play has always
been to educate; to portray both good and evil human traits, with good
always triumphing over evil. Evil is never destroyed however, because
Hinduism does not suggest the existence of pure good. Good and evil
coexist, and Hinduism seeks to make it a peaceful partnership. The shadow
play is an important part of this religious tradition.

A great deal of modern Balinese culture, the shadow play included, has
come from Java. Driven from their homeland in the 14th century by the
pressure of advancing Islam, Javanese Hindus escaped across the narrow
strait to safety in Bali, taking with them their sacred palm leaf books, the
lontars, upon which the ancient stories were inscribed. Nothing escapes

change in Bali, however. Today the Balinese version of *wayang kulit* is quite
different from its Javanese precursor. The *lontars* also contain rules that
prescribe just how the shadow play must be presented, but interpretation of
these rules varies from village to village. The *lontars* are very sacred books,
passed on from father to son and studied with reverence. The shadow play
is loaded with symbolic meaning, with enough mystical overtones and eso-
terica to intrigue the most advanced scholars, ancient and modern.

The shadow play is performed primarily at religious functions. These
might include the important 42-day, 105-day, and 210-day ceremonies for
a newborn, a tooth filing ceremony, a wedding, a cremation, or a temple
odalan. An individual might commission a shadow play to fulfill a vow
made to a god, for example, in exchange for healing a sick child. It has
been performed in schools as an educational tool. And it has even been
used for political purposes. A *dalang* may be hired by someone just because

STAGING A WAYANG KULIT

he is fond of shadow plays. But the fan will have to be well-heeled. A good
dalang can command U.S. $75, as much as three weeks' pay on the island.
This is not to say that *dalangs* are rich, because the fee must be split with
the musicians and assistants, and must subsidize the transportation of the
performers and the equipment. The choice of a *dalang* is often regional.
Different puppet masters are favored in different parts of Bali, and the
Balinese have very strong and definite opinions about whom they prefer.
There are perhaps two hundred to three hundred *dalangs* in Bali's population of about 2.5 million, but of these only 20 or 30 are actually regularly
working *dalangs*.

ALTHOUGH THERE ARE HUNDREDS of stories regularly performed in the
wayang kulit, practically all of them are derived from the two Hindu epic
poems — the Ramayana and the Mahabharata. More often the Mahabharata, because the stories from the Ramayana require a more elaborate
instrumental ensemble. Originally written in Sanskrit, these poems were
later translated into Kawi. Since the main line of the story is always narrated
in Kawi, virtually none in the audience can understand it. The members of
the audience know the stories by heart, and they know what is going on,
but they cannot understand what the principal characters are saying. Thus
every Balinese shadow play includes four clownish *panasars,* playful and
bumbling characters who both entertain and translate. They indulge in
endless horseplay, make rude and often lewd jokes, and provide not only
the meaning of the story, but also the comic relief that every serious tale
requires. These four "translators," favorites with the Balinese, do not
appear in the original versions of the Hindu epics.

Panasar comes from the Balinese word for "servant," particularly the
servant of a king. The *panasar* is the principal secondary character of a
drama who supports the hero. Two of these characters support the side of
the hero. They are Twalen, and his son Wredah, sometimes called Merdah.
Twalen is the most important of all four. He is the symbol of knowledge,
openheartedness, and wisdom. Merdah is sly. On the side of the villains are
the principal, Delem, sometimes called Melem, boastful, impolite, and a
great coward, and his companion, Sangut, the epitome of the opportunist.
In fact, a Balinese will often speak critically of a person whom he doesn't
especially like by saying that he is, for example, "like Sangut," and the listener will know exactly what sort of character he means.

Each *wayang kulit* story is different, so it is impossible to give the first-
timer specific details — a libretto, so to speak. The stories share many common characteristics, however, and an understanding of their general nature
will illuminate any specific performance. I asked a friend of mine, the well-
known *dalang* I Wayan Wija of Sukawati, to pick a typical story from his

large repertoire that would illustrate the types of episodes that might be considered quintessential to the *wayang kulit*. Wija was a good choice. He has won many awards, including first place in the 1981 Ramayana Festival competition in Denpasar. He is a scion of a large family of *dalangs,* and is an especially creative and imaginative individual. He is a fine musician, an indefatigable maker of puppets, and a skilled artist. He has created a whole set of puppets to illustrate the Tantri stories, the Balinese equivalent of Aesop's Fables, and has generally been an innovator.

Wija selected the story "Bima Suci," literally "Bima Is Purified," or "Bima Becomes Holy." It is a tiny episode from the Mahabharata, a story about the conflict between two families, the Pandawas, and the Korawas, over the control of their kingdom. Bima is one of the five Pandawa broth-ers, perhaps the most popular of them all. He is the man of action who wades fearlessly into battle, is sent on impossible missions and returns suc-cessful, and is, generally, a crowd-pleaser. His puppet is large, painted black (although, of course, one can't see this from the shadow), and wears a headdress. Bima wears a snake around his neck like a necklace. The Balinese already know "Bima Suci" and most of the other shadow play puppet sto-ries very well, so the *dalang* need not dwell upon its details in the perfor-mance. But some general background is necessary for our purposes. This is the way the Balinese learned the story.

Long ago, in the kingdom of Astina in India, there lived a man named Pandu who headed the powerful Pandawa family. He had two beautiful wives, Kunti and Madri. While hunting one day, he found a pair of deer having sex and shot the buck. The deer then changed to the human forms of a priest and his wife. The dying priest put a curse on Pandu that he must never make love to his wives again or he would die.

Now, Pandu's wife Kunti had a special charm that made it possible for her to call any god to her bedroom. This charm could be used just five times. She had used the charm once before she was married to Pandu and bore a child, Karna, from the sun god. This child, left by a river, was found and reared by a chariot driver and later became an enemy of the Pandawa family. Pandu's curse gave Kunti a reason to try the gift again. In this way, three sons were born to her: the first, Yudistira, was born of the god Dharma; the second son, Bima, was sired by the god of the wind, Bayu; the third, Arjuna, was fathered by Indra, the king of the gods. When Pandu's other wife, Madri, saw this she begged Kunti to give her the fifth use of the charm. As a result of her calling upon twin gods, Madri gave birth to two sons, Nakula and Sahadewa.

Madri's beauty overcame Pandu one day and he made love to her, dying as a result of the curse. Madri felt responsible and killed herself to join Pandu in death. This was how the five Pandawa brothers, Arjuna, Bima,

BIMA

Nakula, Sahadena, and Yudistira came into being. Their fine, princely attributes made them very popular in the court, and they were the envy of their hundred cousins, the jealous and evil Korawa brothers. This was part of the cause of the great battles between the two families. There are endless deviations from the main story line of the Mahabharata, and "Bima Suci" is one. What follows is a description of some of what you would see in its performance by a *dalang*.

FIRST THE LAMP IS LIGHTED, and while the shimmering overture music of the four *gender* musicians fills the air, the *dalang* proceeds with his special rituals and prayers as he awakens the puppets and brings them to the screen. He waves a special puppet in the shape of a tree, the *kayon*, to signal the ritual start of the story. Later, the *kayon* will function as an indicator of scene changes, or it may represent some of the scenery itself, such as the sea or a house, or a forest. Then the opening chant begins:

> Thereupon day breaks
>> Drums, cymbals, and conches sound with a roar.
>> The shouting troops assemble
>> And set forth in procession.
>> The royal brothers have put on splendid garments
>> And travel in gleaming chariots;
>> King Yudistira is at the head,
>> Preceded by Bimasena,
>> Nakula, and Arjuna.

Now the *dalang* recites a few lines explaining the origin of the story, the eighteen books of the Mahabharata. Next he recites the background to the episode that will follow. After this, the *kayon* is removed from the screen and the story begins.

The Balinese audience needs no introduction to the characters, each of whom they recognize on sight from his characteristic shape, appearance, and headdress. The *dalang* picks out the dozen or so puppets from his collection that will appear in the story, puts the rest back in the box, and sticks the principals in the banana log at the base of the screen. The appearance of the chosen puppets tells the audience instantly just what episode is about to unfold. The good characters have refined, almost effeminate features. The bad ones have bulging eyes and fangs. Each has a distinctive headdress. Bima always has his snake necklace. The *dalang* places the evil characters to his left, and the noble ones to his right. The cast of Wija's story:

BIMA: a Pandawa, son of Kunti and Dewa Bayu, god of the wind, and breath of life.
DURYODANA: eldest of the 100 Korawa brothers, cousin of Bima.
DRONA: teacher from the court of Astina who teaches both the Pandawa and Korawa brothers.
TWALEN and his son, MERDAH: faithful attendants to the Pandawas.

They speak in Balinese to explain the story, often adding witty or bawdy commentaries; clowns.

DELEM and SANGUT: attendants of the Korawas, who represent the evil side; also clowns speaking in Balinese, they often point out the good of the other side.

DEWA INDRA: king of heaven.

DEWA BAYU: god of the wind; father of Bima.

DEWA RUCI: the all-pervasive god who loves mankind. This puppet must be handled with extreme care.

DEWA SIWA: God as the dissolver of life.

DEWA ASMARA: god of love.

DEWA WISNU: God as water, and God as preserver of life.

DEWA NAWA SANGA: the gods of the nine directions, being the cardinal points, the four intermediate points, and center.

In the Prologue the *dalang* tells that Duryodana has conspired with Drona to cause the death of Bima because they are jealous of the growing popularity of the Pandawas. Now the *kayon* is removed from the screen, and the action begins.

SCENE I: Bima is called to the court by his teacher, Drona, and ordered to go into a forest to find the holy water known as *tirtha kamandalu*. Delem attends Drona, and Twalen attends Bima. Drona thinks that, surely, Bima will be killed by fierce demons in the forest. Bima and Twalen travel to the forest, chatting about their forthcoming adventure, sometimes joking, sometimes fearful.

SCENE II: In the forest, Bima is accosted by two demons. A battle ensues in which Bima is victorious. The vanquished demons change into two deities, Dewa Indra and Dewa Bayu. These two had been under a curse by the Siwa as a punishment for an earlier provocation. Being vanquished by Bima has freed them of their curse.

SCENE III: Dewa Indra and Dewa Bayu tell Bima that there is no holy water in the forest, and that he should return to his own country. These two then give Bima a gift of strength.

SCENE IV: Back at the court, Bima and his attendant, Twalen, report to Drona and Duryodana that they found nothing in the forest. Undaunted, Drona says that they made a mistake. What Bima is seeking is really in the ocean. Bima is then ordered to go to the sea and departs with his two attendants. Upon entering the sea, he is engulfed and drowned by huge waves. (The *kayon* now represents the waves of the sea.) Twalen and Merdah are very sad and weep for their dead master.

SCENE V: Dewa Ruci appears, takes Bima from the waves of the sea and brings him back to life. Twalen looks on, rejoicing.

SCENE VI: Dewa Ruci has taken Bima and his servants to his abode. While there, Bima enters Dewa Ruci's body through his ear, and, in this manner, receives revelations of spiritual knowledge and wisdom. He is told of the foul trickery of his teacher and that he should return home at once. Bima is very brave and begs to continue his search for the holy water. He is told that it is in heaven, so he goes there under the protection of Dewa Ruci to meet with the god of love, Asmara. Asmara tells him that the holy water is guarded by nine gods and many dragons.

SCENE VII: In heaven, brave Bima encounters two of the nine gods who are known as Dewa Nawa Sanga, the gods of the nine directions. These two are Dewa Wisnu and Dewa Indra. Eventually a battle with all nine gods ensues. Bima is finally killed by Dewa Bayu, who is one of the nine gods. Bima doesn't know that Dewa Bayu is his father.

SCENE VIII: Dewa Ruci again appears and brings Bima back to life. But Bima and Dewa Bayu fight once more. This time Dewa Siwa intervenes and orders them to stop fighting.

SCENE IX: Bima explains his mission to get the holy water, *tirtha kamandalu,* to Dewa Siwa, who grants his wish and gives it to him. Suddenly the characters vanish, and the *kayon* appears, planted stage center. The story is ended! The audience leaves just as suddenly. There is no need to tell them the moral, because they already know it. What happens next will be continued in another story, another time. The puppets are put back to sleep in their chest.

THE ABOVE IS THE BAREST BONES OF THE STORY. The audience already knows it anyway, probably as well as the *dalang*. The story itself could be told in 15 minutes. The really popular parts of the performance occur when the four translators, or two or three of them, get together. Their conversations often have absolutely nothing whatever to do with the "Bima Suci" story. There is much slapstick comedy, people backing into each other, straight out of vaudeville, but never failing to get a laugh. There are references to topical subjects that only make sense to those who live in the immediate area. There are just plain dirty jokes. There even may be political references.

The sky is the limit as far as these scenes are concerned, and herein lies the test of a good *dalang* and the source of his reputation, because almost all of the dialogue is improvised on the spot. Each *dalang* has some favorite routines, but he is careful not to use the same material too often in one locality. I have seen audiences literally rolling on the ground with laughter, tears running down their cheeks. The whole atmosphere reminds one of an old-time comedy hour on the radio, except the laughter is genuine. The little boys like the battle scenes best. A good *dalang* is also known for his spears and arrows and anguished cries of the wounded. The assistants work lighting fast, handing more arrows and spears to the *dalang,* as he whips them across the screen in veritable barrages.

This can be only a short introduction to the flavor of a *wayang kulit* performance. You have to see many of them, study the sources from which the stories come, and even learn some Balinese in order to appreciate *wayang kulit* fully. But perhaps this will enable you at least to develop a taste for this very popular and entertaining art form.

CHAPTER 29

Gamelan Gong

TRADITIONAL BALINESE ORCHESTRA

By Margaret Eiseman

VISITORS TO BALI almost always come away with the sounds of the unique and flamboyant *gamelan* ringing in their ears. Something perhaps in the elaborate instruments — cast in bronze using centuries-old techniques and hand-fitted into elaborate wood and bamboo frames — gives the impression of antiquity, as if the visitor were seeing a bas relief from some ancient stone wall come to life. Well, the tradition of the *gamelan* is certainly an old one. But nothing in Bali survives unchanged for long. Even the stone wall that looks so old is probably younger than the person looking at it.

The *gamelan* has undergone some dramatic changes in recent times, probably the most important of which is the *kebyar* style of fast and syncopated playing which, first created in North Bali in the early part of this century, is now by far the most common style. The older styles of playing, more sedate, have begun to be forgotten. Entire *gamelans* — the *kebyar* style has its own instruments — have fallen into disrepair, literally rotting away. And to some critics, the Indonesian government's creation of special music schools, where the *gamelan* is studied and innovations in its performance are introduced, seems to have brought about a stifling uniformity of style on the island.

But some of these worries seem to mirror the paranoia that swept the United States in the late '50s concerning the destructive effects of rock and roll on music traditions. The form itself is, if anything, more popular than ever. One can buy *gamelan* music on cassette tapes now, and hear it on the radio. There are even efforts, as will be seen below, to restore old *gamelans* and in at least one important instance, the dance styles that went along with their unique instruments.

THE WORD *GAMELAN* IS SIMPLY the Balinese word for "orchestra," and there are many types of orchestras in Bali, just as there are everywhere else. *Gamelan* is a generic term, and there are a dozen or more completely different kinds of ensembles. That most commonly seen by visitors is called a *gamelan gong* and consists of from 25 to 50 men, most of them seated on the floor or on low stools, who play a group of xylophone-like instruments, assorted sizes of tuned gongs hanging in frames, some smaller single percussion instruments resembling inverted pots or cymbals, and two cylindrical, double-ended drums.

The xylophone-like instruments are called *gangsas*, and consist of a carved, and often gilded, frame containing bamboo resonators over which a series of bronze keys are suspended by hide lacing. It looks, for all the world, like the great-great-grandfather of the vibraphone. The *gangsas* have varying numbers of keys, from 4 to as many as 14, which are grouped in matching pairs according to size and number. A single, large *gangsa* is usually stationed in the center of the *gamelan*. This instrument is played by the orchestra's leader. His wooden hammer signals the start of the composition. He may raise it like a baton and bring the full orchestra to a start with a resounding sforzando, or he may improvise a delicate cadenza, during which, at some magic moment, the rest of the players burst into their parts. The precision is phenomenal, as the matching instruments seem to play as one, often with lightning speed.

The musician holds his mallet in the right hand, striking the keys of the *gangsa* and then immediately damping the note with the thumb and forefinger of his left. Imagine the dexterity required to do this at those lightning speeds, and the practice it takes to achieve this skill! From the time a little boy can hold a mallet in his hand he loves to sit in his father's lap while he is playing or rehearsing. And when fathers leave for a short break, the little boys flock in and create a very passable *gamelan* group. Most musicians get a very early start, and one is sometimes a bit shocked to see playing at a village ceremony a full-fledged *gamelan* in which half the musicians are mere children.

The *gangsas* always play unison melodies in a structured way, according to the size of the matching pairs of instruments. The lower sounding ones with large keys carry the main melody, while the smaller-keyed instruments, still playing in unison, play complicated little patterns or variations based upon the notes of the melody, often at a frantic pace. The net result is a big, full sound. Scattered through the orchestra are men playing singly, perhaps tapping a stick on an inverted bronze pot or clashing together some small cymbals. But the richest sound comes from the magnificent bronze gongs. A gong player often appears to be taking a nap until, at a mysterious moment, he suddenly reaches up and taps a deep, mellow tone with his cloth-covered mallet. The gongs punctuate the melodies and divisions of the composition. This is far from simple music. Foreigners often spend years in Bali learning to follow it, much less play.

The most whimsical instrument in the gamelan has the onomatopoeic name *ceng ceng*. It is a small wooden stand with several small bronze cymbals fastened to its top. The seated player holds a similarly sized cymbal in each hand and clashes them against the mounted cymbals in syncopated rhythms. The *ceng ceng* creates quite a chattering sound. Woodcarvers decorate the *ceng ceng* stands with the classic Balinese legends. Most often one sees the *ceng ceng* as the mythical turtle that is said to serve as the foundation of the world.

The instruments mentioned so far either play melodies in unison or strike simple, single notes. Only one instrument in the *gamelan* can be

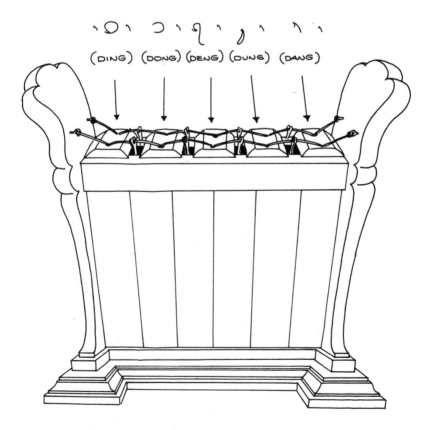

(DING) (DONG) (DENG) (DUNG) (DANG)

A JUBLAG, WITH THE PENTATONIC SCALE

described as playing harmony. It consists of a long frame holding a graduated series of a dozen or so inverted bronze pots, from each of which a small
knob protrudes. Four players sit in a row behind this *riyong*, or *riong*, and
each plays his segment of pots by striking two knobs simultaneously, the
adjacent pots tuned to complement each other. There are no instruments
like this one in the West. Often a second such instrument will be placed
center stage in front of the orchestra, with pots and a frame that are a bit
larger than those of the *riong*. This instrument, the *trompong*, is played by a
single musician with two long wooden sticks, their ends wrapped in string.
This player is the only true soloist in the *gamelan*. He improvises or para-
phrases the melodies. In spite of the rich sound of the full orchestra, the
trompong melodies stand out, producing a sort of doleful sound. The player
is an honored musician, second only to the drummers in skill and training.
Long arms and dexterity are required of this man as he must strike intricate
melodies while reaching across a span of more than two meters.

Two other kinds of instruments may be seen in the *gamelan gong*. There
may be some flutes, *suling*, playing high-pitched versions of the melody,
singing out above the orchestra. And occasionally one may see a strange little two-stringed instrument, its player bowing it something like a cello.
One strains one's ears to hear it above the rest, but usually the sound is too
soft to be heard distinctly. This is the *rebab*, an ancient instrument that is
believed to be the ancestor of our modern violin. The *rebab* can produce
quite a lovely viola-like sound if you can hear an expert play it by itself.

The real heart of the *gamelan gong* is the pair of drums, called *kendang*.
One drummer is the principal player. With flourishes of his hands and head,
he communicates with musicians and dancers as he taps out intricate
rhythms. Sometimes he uses just his hands, sometimes a stick. In fact, the
rest of the orchestra could just as well pack up and go home, leaving just
the drummers to accompany the dancers. The dance performance would be
just as complete. Dancers or other performers often rehearse only with the
drums — generally only a single drum. The principal drummer is the most
important and most advanced player in the *gamelan*, and he must master
all the other instruments before he is allowed to take over the drum.

In addition to the character of the instruments, the distinctive sound of
the *gamelan* is also a product of the choice of tones used in the musical
scales. Any of us who had to practice our eight-note scales in early music
lessons learned to start on each one of the twelve notes in the octave. In
fact, much of the richness of Western music results from the ability of
almost all of the instruments of the orchestra to do this. Western compositions derive much of their variety and color by being able to roam through
these different "keys." But this is not the case with the *gamelan*. Music
teachers here will say there are a total of seven tones available to Balinese

music, but only five of the tones are frequently used — a pentatonic scale. All that music comes from only five tones arranged from low to high pitches throughout the group of instruments. Actually, the Western ear will probably recognize two distinct five-tone scales, but a Balinese musician will tell you that there are many more than that. It requires some ear training and study for a foreigner to recognize these nuances. And sometimes it is a bit difficult to communicate with Balinese musicians who have not had Western training, because their entire concept of the idea of scales and keys, and the terminology used is so different than that understood in the West.

Most of us have heard the concertmaster of a symphony orchestra sound the standard, 440-hertz pitch of the note A to tune up before the conductor strides onto the stage. Violinists adjust strings, trumpet players adjust their mouthpieces, flutists stretch or shorten their instruments to conform. This does not take place in the *gamelan*. Except for the lonely *rebab*, all the instruments have fixed pitches, tuned once and for all when the instrument was made. The choice of the five or seven tones is made when the group of instruments is constructed, and every *gamelan* is different. Standardization is heard of, but according to some musicians is undesirable. Lack of a standard concert pitch, they say, permits a variety of sound and color, even within the same types of *gamelans*.

Although the instruments in a symphony are all tuned to the same note, the tonal characteristics of each combine to produce the lush sound Westerners love to hear — although both may be playing middle C, a cello is warmer than, say, a clarinet. In a *gamelan*, each of the paired instruments, such as the *gangsas*, is tuned differently from its partner. Even in single instruments with more than one octave range, the octave notes may be deliberately tuned slightly higher than the matching lower tone. All Balinese will tell you that when the pairs of instruments so tuned are played in unison the sound produced will be rich and appealing. This is caused by the fact that when two notes are struck that differ very slightly from each other in pitch, a third note, called the beat note, is produced that has a frequency that is the difference between the two notes sounded. The beat note adds a kind of throbbing sound to the other two notes, not unlike the vibrato a trained singer uses, or that produced by the player of a stringed instrument when he wiggles his left hand over the stops of the strings.

ENTERTAINING BALI'S VISITORS is only a secondary function of any *gamelan*. The group's primary function is to assist in the myriad of ceremonies required during each 210-day cycle of the Balinese Pawukon cycle, as well as those involved with the lunar calendar. These activities range from massive, villagewide temple ceremonies to private family observances such as weddings or the dedication of new buildings. The musicians must be able to play at any hour of the day or night or both, as demanded by the ceremony in progress. They may accompany a priest in his devotions, or they may accompany entertainments, such as temple dances. There is no such thing as a professional musician in Bali. The *gamelan* players are rice farmers or village artisans or work at some sort of job — they are musicians during their time off.

A small group within the main *gamelan,* consisting of the percussion and gong players, forms a marching band that must accompany any religious procession. Nearly every ceremony calls for a procession somewhere, often more than one. The cremation procession, one most often seen by the visitor to Bali, is accompanied by the cacophonous, jazzy sounds of the marching band as it follows the bearers of the ashes of the deceased to the sea, to be thrown therein so that the soul can be released. The music is nothing like a dirge.

The *gamelan* is generally owned by a village neighborhood organization called a *banjar.* A club that desires to play forms within a *banjar,* a group of instruments is obtained, if there is none, and a teacher or a good leader is chosen to see that all the required music is perfected and memorized. This is accomplished through endless rehearsal, often several times a week. Music is not written down in Bali. And remember, except for perhaps some of the *trompong* player's riffs, nothing you hear a *gamelan* play is spontaneous or improvised. Everything is always performed the same way once a piece is committed to memory. There is no variation. New pieces, yes — many. But once a new piece is learned, it is always played the same way.

A *gamelan* may have a talented member who can compose new music. A few composers become famous, and their compositions are eagerly sought by other clubs. Talented young players will often be sent to one of the two well-known conservatories in Denpasar for training. The two conservatories are generally known by their acronyms: KOKAR for high school–level students, STSI for university-level students. While attending these schools students must learn all the related forms of music, dance, drama, and art. Most of them return to their village *gamelans* to perform and teach. But some especially talented people stay on to become teachers at the conservatories. A few of the latter go off to teach about Balinese music and learn about Western music in foreign universities, always returning to their villages with fresh ideas to participate when they can. STSI and KOKAR have been the leading forces of innovation in Balinese music and dance in recent years, and their influence is felt all over the island.

Before the Dutch and independence, the Balinese rajas maintained the great *gamelans* and the traditions of dance and drama. As these kingdoms gradually ceased to exist, there were few individuals who could afford to maintain these activities. It then fell to the *banjars* to shoulder the responsibility. A *banjar* club may break up, however, leaving a *gamelan,* unused, to fall into terrible disrepair. The trend, one might imagine, would be for the form to disappear. But *gamelans* are extremely competitive, and most groups actively seek to improve their skills and maintain their equipment. This competitiveness is actively fostered by the Indonesian government, which sponsors yearly festivals or competitions in which groups or individuals compete to be best or among the top three winners. Nearly any activity is an excuse for a competition. Local winners are often invited to Jakarta, to compete nationally. A Balinese musician loves to tell you about the year he won first prize; a *gamelan* group might tell you that they are striving to be in first place next year.

NOT FAR FROM DENPASAR is the small village of Ubung where a *banjar* owned a decrepit, old-style *gamelan.* The club was bored with it, though it continued to serve at all the ceremonies. The club wanted to have it melted down and made over into a more contemporary type of *gamelan gong.* A member of the club recognized, however, that this *gamelan* represented an extremely rare classical type known as *semar pegulingan.* This produces sounds that are more delicate, sweeter than those of a *gamelan gong.* Based on seven tones, the *semar pegulingan's* principal difference from the usual *gamelan gong* is in the type of metallophone used. Replacing the *gangsas* described earlier are xylophone-like instruments called *gender* (unlike our "gender" it has a hard *g* and the accent is on the last syllable). The musician, seated on the floor, strikes the bronze keys with a mallet in each hand — each mallet having a disc-shaped head. In order to stop the sounds of the notes so that they won't run together, the player must lower his knuckles to touch the key after each note is played. Again, amazing skill is required. Other than musical style and the use of the *gender,* the rest of the instruments are the same as the *gamelan gong.* But this old-type gamelan and its repertoire can hardly be found any more in the wake of the more popular, fast-paced *gong kebyar* style.

The man who was so concerned about the Ubung *gamelan* was I Wayan Sinti, M.A., now a master teacher at KOKAR conservatory. Affectionately known as "Pak Sinti" (Pak is a term of respect for an elder or a master), Sinti was born in the 40s in the village of Ubung, and was sent to KOKAR as a child, when his musical talent was noticed. He became a famous *trompong* player and top-notch drummer. He later joined the faculty at KOKAR, and was finally chosen to attend music school in the United States, where he both taught and earned a graduate degree. He returned to KOKAR to be a master teacher, always journeying to his village when it was time for important ceremonies. Now he appreciated more than ever the need to save the old *gamelan.*

Pak Sinti had to convince his club and his *banjar* first. The cost of restoration and replacement would be the worst problem. He decided to produce a performance of the nearly forgotten *legong keraton* palace dance for foreign tourists, which would — at the same time — raise money, revive a disappearing music and dance form, and create an interesting activity for the *banjar*. Sinti knew the *banjar* would have to hire a teacher to train the musicians. Another teacher would be needed to train the dancers, and the costuming would have to be commissioned. Pak Sinti himself would be one teacher, and he knew of some famous old compositions. When he was able to interest the Ford Foundation in giving a grant for the project, his idea began to be accepted. With a lot of work and help from the *banjar*, the project was launched and became a reality.

I Made Gabeleran, of Blahbatuh Village, Gianyar, is Bali's most celebrated instrument maker. He learned his craft from his father, who learned it from his father, and so on further back than anyone can remember. He studied with other experts in Java. Not only is his knowledge of bronze smithing considered to be superb, but he is admired as a walking encyclopedia of Balinese music.

Pak Gabeleran's instrument factory resembles Santa's workshop more than anything else I can think of. On a lucky day, a visitor might see copper and tin, carefully proportioned, melted into bronze. Or he might see a heat-reddened bronze disc being forged into the shape of a *trompong* pot, as a man takes it carefully from the hot coconut charcoal fire with tongs to be hammered again and again by two or three strong men pounding in rhythm. An old man patiently pumps air into the fire by pushing feathered plungers up and down in large bamboo tubes. Or one might see workers casting the bronze keys in molds lubricated with coconut oil and covered with peels of banana tree stem. Someone else might be scraping newly cast keys with a file, bringing them to a golden sheen, every now and them tapping them with a stick and bringing them to his ear, to see if the desired pitch has yet been achieved.

Gabeleran, somewhere in his 60s, is the antithesis of Santa in appearance. He is the final judge of the tuning. He and the future owners of the *gamelan* consult on the exact tuning desired. Since there is no standard concert pitch, and since the *gamelan* that is to be made will not (and indeed, *cannot*) be played with any other *gamelan*, the tuning need only be consistent within the orchestra. But the type of scale has to be determined, and Gabeleran will make suggestions, based upon how the *gamelan* is to be used. He fashions a set of bamboo sticks to serve as tuning forks. The workers match the tones of their bronze keys or pots with the barely audible tones of the sticks by striking the stick and the bronze together, listening and then filing some more. To raise the pitch of a key, they file a bit off each end. To lower the pitch, they remove material from the back. Keys for the matched pairs of *gangsas* or *genders* must be deliberately mistuned a tiny bit in order to produce the desired beat note vibrato.

The woodworking shop is in a separate courtyard, and there carvers chip, chisel, and saw the ornate stands and frames for the instruments. The yellowish wood from the jackfruit tree, called *ketewel,* is the favorite material. It is strong, easy to carve, and turns a lovely brownish-tan color when stained with varnish. Clubs with limited resources, however, must choose very plain frames. The really fancy ones have scenes from the Hindu epics carved in panels on their sides to cover up the bamboo resonators, and some are elaborately gilded. In the display room, one might see a nearly completed set of instruments waiting for its owners to pick it up. It will be one of five or six sets that Pak Gabeleran makes in a year. One set was recently shipped to a large university in the United States. Another went to Japan. Occasionally a foreign student will scrape up enough money to bring a set back home. The 1985 price for a fine, complete *gamelan* was about U.S. $5,000, not including shipping. It could be more if an extra fancy finish is required on the frames.

Pak Sinti's club sought out Pak Gabeleran, agreed upon the kinds of instruments needed and the tuning, and waited patiently for many weeks until the project was finished. Then the musicians came to Blahbatuh, loaded their new instruments into a large truck, and hauled them across the island to Ubung village. The very first thing they had to do after bringing the instruments home was to hold an elaborate religious ceremony to inaugurate the *gamelan* before it could be played.

After many lessons and much practice, the first performance was held for a delighted audience. Now an interested visitor or group of them can contact Pak Sinti at KOKAR and arrange for a private performance of this outstanding *legong keraton.* It is not usually performed on a regular schedule, but rather, held for groups when they so desire. However, anyone is welcome to attend the regular weekly rehearsals, and one should contact Pak Sinti to determine time and place.

SOME PEOPLE ARE CONCERNED that there will be too much innovation in Balinese music in the next few years, as more and more teachers go to foreign universities for their training and master's degrees, as more and more rock-and-roll cassettes are imported and played, as more and more Balinese work in the tourist industry and come into contact with new and strange ideas. Some people feel that KOKAR and STSI are having undue influence upon the development of music and dance in Bali, since, as their students spread over the island, they take with them the things that they learned from their innovative and creative teachers. One has but to look, they say, at the impending disappearance of musical and dance traditions of other cultures of the world, where outside influence has crept in and gradually replaced native dance and music.

But I think that there is great hope for Bali. Music and dance were never more popular than now. I don't mean in tourist shows, I mean in the villages themselves. Traditional music — whatever "traditional" means — played by the Balinese for the Balinese. Balinese culture has never been static. It is one of the most dynamic cultures on earth, trying everything new it can get its hands on and adopting as its own that which it feels is valid and interesting. Music is no exception. With many foreign students devoted to learning the music of Bali, the *gamelan* inevitably enters into the musical thought of player and composer and becomes part of the mainstream of world music. Influence can work both ways, into Bali and out — imports and exports. Pak Sinti and Pak Gabeleran are missionaries too.

CHAPTER 30

Byar!

THE ENERGETIC MODERN MUSICAL STYLE

THE AUDIENCE LEANS FORWARD EXPECTANTLY. The lead player flourishes his wooden mallet over his head, *BYAR!* — 25 hammers descend as one on the bronze keys, the great gong booms out, and a shimmering cadence begins that sends chills running up your spine. This is by far the most popular music in Bali, played by the *gamelan gong kebyar* and heard at dances, temple ceremonies, luxury hotels, and on the radio. It might seem, to Western ears, somehow "traditional." But this is modern music, with its beginnings in the 20th century. The Balinese call this musical style *kebyar*, an onomatopoeic word derived from *byar*, or *biyar*, meaning, variously, a sudden intense sound, a sudden bursting open of a flower bud into bloom, the flaring up of a fire, a sudden flash of light. Any of these is an apt simile for the way most *kebyar* music begins. It is flashy, highly embellished, and complex music, full of sudden stops and starts, lightninglike. One author calls it "almost supercharged."

Kebyar is certainly not the sort of music that travelers heard in Bali before World War I. Nor is it the kind of traditional music heard today in Central Java, where Balinese musical traditions got their start some 500 years ago. The style was created by independent musicians near Singaraja in the early part of the century and within 80 years has become by far the most popular style on the island.

Well into this century the Balinese musical scene was dominated by the grand old *gong gede* orchestras of the rajas and the large temples, and the smaller versions of them, called *gamelan gong*, found in the villages. The word *gamelan* simply refers to orchestra; *gede* means "big." The melodic instruments of the *gong gede* are like xylophones, each having five large, platelike bronze keys that are struck with a large wooden hammer. The keys of the lower-pitched instruments are suspended above hollow bamboo resonators. But the keys of the small, melody-playing *saron,* which are in the majority, are suspended, with no resonators. The tone of the *saron* is brassy and harsh, full of harmonics. Its sound does not resonate or "sing."

The music of the *gong gede* is stately, majestic, and reserved, sort of "Pomp and Circumstance" music. The melody is usually introduced by a man playing one of the two *trompongs,* instruments consisting of inverted bronze pots that are struck by large sticks, the ends wrapped in string. After the slow solo introduction the huge gong booms out, the drums signal the start, and the smaller instruments slowly pound out their stately compositions. It is quite a contrast to the flamboyant *kebyar* style.

THE FIRST PERFORMANCE OF *KEBYAR* music took place around 1915 in North Bali. The place and time are not insignificant. Bali's northern port, Singaraja, served as the Dutch headquarters after 1914 when the European state had succeeded in conquering or forcing the cooperation of the last of the Balinese rajas. Thus Singaraja was the first point of contact with the West. Imagine the shock the North Balinese felt when the Dutch required a high caste boy to sit next to a low caste girl in school. And this is just one example. The cultural shakeup was tremendous. Even before the Dutch, North Bali was a bit of a maverick region — artistically, culturally, and religiously. In the rain shadow of the great east-west mountain ridge and a difficult journey from the fertile and populous South, North Bali was always relatively apart from the bitter and bloody political and economic competitions afflicting the rajadoms of the South.

Before the innovation of *kebyar,* not all *gong gede* music was steady and stately. Sometimes this orchestra was (and is) used to accompany ceremonial dances in the temples. And when accompanying a dance, the *gong* must play complex syncopated accents called *angsels.* These rhythms are executed simultaneously by dancer and *gong,* and each pattern ends in a sudden pause — both musicians and dancers stop for an instant. These *angsels* provide one of the probable roots of *kebyar.* And at the time the new style was created, there was intense musical competition between two neighboring villages in the Singaraja area: Jagaraga and Bungkulan. Both villages are known to have had talented and imaginative musicians, and historians of music credit the efforts of these musicians to distinguish themselves with the development of the new style.

Kebyar cannot be played on a *gong gede.* In general, the instruments are too large and the mallets too heavy to encourage fast playing. And the *saron,* without resonators, does not allow the "singing" quality of *kebyar* to be produced. But perhaps most important, the five keys of the *gong gede* instruments do not allow for quick movements up and down the scales. The musicians of North Bali found the raw materials for their new sound in ancient instruments that, although rarely used in those days, had more than five keys. In order to pack a large number of keys into one frame, these instruments had keys that were cast in thick ingots, trapezoidal in cross section — this retained enough mass to produce a low pitch, while also saving space. Gradually, a whole new series of instruments came into being — instruments that were played with light, easily movable hammers on closely spaced keys. And the number of keys on the melodic instruments was increased from five to ten by adding a second octave, allowing much greater freedom of expression and rapid movement. These changes were evolutionary, and some of the *gong gede* instruments were retained, particularly the lower-pitched ones and the drums.

THE COLLECTION OF INSTRUMENTS that you are most likely to see and hear today is the *gong kebyar,* the result of decades of experimentation and evolution. Most of the *gong gedes* have been melted down and recast into this modern ensemble. In fact, the popularity of the *kebyar* style threatens the very existence of the more traditional *gamelan* groups. There are only three or four *gong gede* groups left in all of Bali. A recent search of the cassette shops in Denpasar revealed not a single *gong gede* tape amid shelves full of *kebyar* cassettes. This situation, however, seems about to change, as a group of Balinese scholars, shocked at the disappearance of a fine, old tradition, are trying to revive interest in the *gong gede.* They are planning to sponsor concerts and competitions, and to see that tapes are made commercially available. (See CHAPTER 29.)

Gong kebyar music is pentatonic. As has been mentioned, some instruments have ten keys, but these just cover two five-note octaves. The scale is tuned several ways, but the internals of the most common would be something like: E, F, G, B, and C. This narrow range of notes produces the relative monotony of the *gong gede.* The *gong kebyar* escapes this, using the same scale, by rapid changes in tempo, rhythm, and dynamics, by frequent *angsels,* and by allowing instruments to take turns at solos, almost like a Western concerto grosso. None of the music is spontaneous, or improvised. The compositions are practiced over and over again until, as the Balinese say, "they are part of the body." Once a piece has been learned it is invariably played the same way. It may look spontaneous, but it most certainly is not. The musicians are not full-time professionals. They are farmers, taxi drivers, and shopkeepers, just like everyone else.

The *gong kebyar* consists of four main instrumental groups. One plays the melody; another ornaments the melody; a third punctuates the composition; and the fourth, the two drummers, leads the orchestra and controls

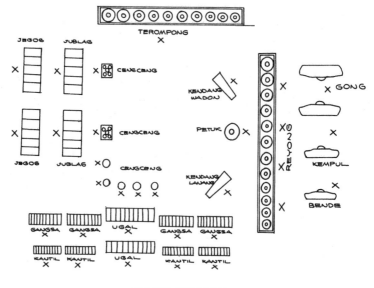

GONG KEBYAR

its tempo and dynamics. The drummers are the leaders (and often the teachers) and the best musicians of the group. They know how to play every instrument in the *gong* — well. They hold double-ended, more or less cylindrical drums in their laps as they sit cross-legged on the ground and produce an enormous variety of sounds by slapping and pounding various parts of the drum heads with palms, fingers, and sticks. Their rhythms are exceedingly complicated. They use head movements and body language to supplement the signals sent by their drum beats. If the *gong* is accompanying a dance, the lead drummer watches the performer with intense attention, responding to the dancer's cues by sending audible signals to the rest of the musicians — change tempo, rhythm, or perform an *angsel.* In some dances the signals run the other way, and the *gong* controls the dancer. This is especially true when the dancers are performing a less-exacting, well-known dance at some distance from the *gong.* Some *gongs* employ only a single drummer, using a stick instead of his hand. This is required for certain types of music and creates excitement.

There are two groups of xylophone-like instruments. All have bronze keys suspended over bamboo resonators. The resonators are often not visible, being concealed by elaborately carved and painted panels. The two larger ones have only five keys each and are the same instruments used in the *gong gede.* The larger of these is the *jegog,* and the smaller is the *calung* or *jublag.* They are played rather slowly, supporting the basic skeleton of the melody and occasionally playing the melody itself. The smaller xylophones are called *gangsas*. All have ten keys, two octaves of five notes each. Some musicians insist that the word *gangsa* be used only for these ten-note xylophones, while others include the *jegog* and *jublag* as *gangsas*. Each of the ten-note *gangsas* is stuck by a single musician using a small wooden hammer held in his right hand. He strikes the keys and immediately damps them with the thumb and forefinger of his left hand. The smaller the *gangsa*, the faster it is played, ornamenting the basic melody. The lightning speed with which the smallest *gangsas* are hit and damped requires enormous dexterity, often acquired at a surprisingly early age. The three sizes of *gangsas*, from largest to smallest, are the *pengugal* (also *giying*, or *penyerog*, or *pengenter*), the *pumade*, and the *kantilan*. There are often two pairs of the tinkly *kantilan*.

All of the *jegog* and *jublag*, and all the *gangsas*, come in pairs. Both are played in unison, but the keys of each of the instruments in the pair are tuned to slightly different pitches, producing a shimmering, vibrato sound, like a violinist waggling his left hand on the strings. There may be only one *pengugal*. This instrument is placed prominently in the front row and the man who plays it gives the signal to start the composition and periodically gives directions to the other players with flourishes of his hammer. The drummers are the real leaders, but often the *gangsa* players can't see them. The lead *pengugal* player thus acts as a kind of conductor, but he, in turn, takes signals from the drummers.

Most *gong kebyars* have one *trompong* — this is like that described previously for the *gong gede* except it has 10 notes. The *gong kebyar* rarely uses this *trompong* in the purely musical sections of the performance. It may sit, unused, stage center up front, or it may be hauled in from the wings when needed as the show piece for the *trompong duduk* — a special dance/*trompong* performance by a solo artist. This is a standard part of every tourist show, but it is never given in the villages. For tourist shows the *trompong* is sometimes placed in a prominent position, and the *gong* plays overture music, similar in structure to *gong gede* music, though completely different in style. The *trompong* player, always a very gifted musician, opens the composition with a short solo, just as in *gong gede* compositions, and is then joined by the rest of the *gong*. Even villages that own *gong kebyars* sometimes use the *trompong* in this way, simulating the *gamelan gongs* of old, because the musicians feel that this traditional introduction is more appropriate for accompanying religious ceremonies.

Another holdover from the *gong gede* is the *riyong*, which looks like a small version of the *trompong*, with 12 inverted pots (the traditional *gong gede riyong* has only four). The *riyong*, unlike the *trompong*, is played by four men who beat the knobs of the pots in front of them, each man using two sticks. The result is the only instrument in the *gamelan* that can actually play chords. Different effects are produced by hitting the pots on the knob or on the edge. Also holdovers from the *gong gede* are the *kempli*, a single pot struck with a stick, and the chattering little *ceng ceng* cymbals. And of course, every *gong kebyar* must have a gong, and most have two — the larger often 75 centimeters or more in diameter. The rich, vibrant tones punctuate each phrase or section of the music. The largest gong is always sounded at the beginning and end of each piece. Some *gong kebyars* include an intermediate-sized gong, and some have only one. Gongs are always struck rather gently upon the knob with a cushioned mallet. The usual two gongs are hung vertically from wooden frames, facing each other, and one man plays them both. The larger of the pair is called gong *wadon*, and is considered female; the smaller, gong *lanang*, is considered male.

Occasionally the gong will include nonpercussion instruments. The shrill sounds of the *suling*, a flute, may be difficult to hear above the clanging of the *gangsas*. The flutes are more like what a Westerner would call a recorder, held parallel to the body rather than transversely. The *rebab* is the only instrument in the ensemble that can be tuned. It is a two-stringed ancestor of the violin, held in an upright position like a cello and played with a very loosely strung bow. It has a lovely, plaintive sound when heard as a solo instrument, but it is likely to get lost in the din of the loud *gangsas* that dominate the *gong*.

GONG KEBYAR MUSIC IS NOT SIMPLE. What it lacks in polyphony and varied harmonies it makes up for in complex rhythmic patterns, sudden *angsels*, and great dynamic range. When you hear it, try to pick out the opening part of the piece, the body, and, as the Balinese call it, the "tail." See if you can catch the number of beats per measure. It is always even — listen for the gong. Pick out the real melody, which is often surprisingly slow. See if you can anticipate the *angsels*. Notice how the drummers exchange signals with dancers and musicians, and try to follow their complex polyrhythms. Look for the flourishes of the lead *gangsa* player's hammer as he signals his fellow musicians. All this — with five notes and percussion instruments! Note that the *gangsa* players, their hands flying on the keys, affect a bored look, and stare off into space. See if you can anticipate when the big gong will sound to end the piece — it is seldom the "home base" note of Western compositions. There is no build-up, no drum roll and cymbal crash. Just a gong beat, fading slowly into silence.

Glossary

ADAT. Customary, according to traditional cultural values as opposed to following civil law. *Chapter 7.*

ALUS. Refined; opposite of *kasar* — ill-mannered, coarse. *Chapters 11, 23, 26, 27.*

ANAK AGUNG, COKORDA. Titles of men of the Ksatriya caste. *Chapter 3.*

ANGGAR(A) KASIH. Day when Anggara (Tuesday) of the Saptawara (7-day week) coincides with Keliwon, the 5th day of the Pancawara (5-day week) *Chapter 17.*

ANGKER. Terrifying, fearsome because of magical power. *Chapters 13, 26.*

ARAK . A clear, colorless brandy; distilled from *tuak,* the fermented juice of the coconut or *lontar* palm flower. *Chapters 16, 19, 26.*

ARECA. A kind of tall, thin palm tree that produces nuts, commonly called betel nuts, that are used symbolically in offerings and are the principal ingredient in a masticatory. *Chapters 11, 19.*

ARI-ARI. The placenta; treated with great respect because it is symbolic of one of the *kanda empat,* the four brothers or sisters of the newborn child. *Chapters 9, 10.*

ARJA. A common traditional form of entertainment at religious festivals in which girls, dressed as men, sing and dance simultaneously. *Chapter 25.*

ARJUNA. One of the five Pandawa brothers (the others are Yudistira, Bima, Nakula, and Sahadewa) who are the heroes of the Hindu epic, the Mahabharata. *Chapters 2, 28.*

ASTA KOSALA KOSALI. Principles of Balinese architecture which seek to harmonize a building's measurements with the body measurements of the owner. *Chapter 1.*

ASTI. Acronym for Akademi Seni Tari Indonesia, the university-level conservatory in Bali. Recently renamed: Sekolah Tinggi Seni Indonesia (STSI). *Chapters 25, 29.*

BABUTEN. One who habitually goes into trance because of the influence of *bhutas* and *kalas*. *Chapters 15, 26.*

BALE. House, pavilion — usually refers to an open structure within the house compound. *Chapters 1, 12, 23.*

BALIAN. Shaman, medicine man, healer; often has a knowlege of occult practices. In Indonesian, *dukun*. *Chapters 3, 14, 15.*

BANJAR. Neighborhood association. *Chapters 1, 3, 22.*

BANTEN. General term for offering. *Chapters 19, 24.*

BARIS. Any of the many types of male dances that are based upon the mimicry of the movements of a soldier; usually a characteristic pointed helmet is used. *Chapters 12, 21, 25.*

BARONG. A mask and costume representing a mythical, supernatural creature; the most common *barong* has a costume that looks like a Chinese lion (*barong ket*) and is animated by two men, one manipulating the mask, the other the hind end. *Chapters 1, 15, 19, 22, 25, 26.*

BEDAWANG, BEDAWANG NALA. The world-turtle that supports the earth on its back. *Chapter 1.*

BEDUGUL. Shrine that is usually found in rice fields. *Chapter 24.*

BETARA-BETARI. A general term for gods, respectively, male and female. *Chapter 19.*

BHAGAVAD-GITA. Part of Book VI of the Mahabharata in which Arjuna, leader of the Pandawas, converses with his charioteer, Krishna, who is transfigured and lectures to Arjuna about the role of the duty of a warrior. *Chapters 3, 19.*

BHAKTI, BAKTI. Worship. *Chapter 2.*

BHATARA YANG, also NENEK MOYONG, DEWA HYANG, PITARA HYANG. Various equivalent names for the deified ancestors of a family group. *Chapter 24.*

BHOMA, BOMA. Son of the forest, the fanged face of whom appears above many gate-entrances to the inner courtyards of temples, its function being to prevent evil spirits from entering. *Chapters 1, 12.*

BHUANA AGUNG/ALIT. The macrocosm/microcosm; the universe as a whole and man as he is related to that universe. *Chapter 1.*

BHUR, BUWAH, SWAH (LOKA). The cosmos — respectively, the underworld; the world of man; the world of the gods. *Chapter 1, 12.*

BHUTA KALA, BHUTAS and KALAS. General terms for the disruptive, negative forces of the earth; demons who torment man; evil spirits. *Chapters 1, 9, 15, 20.*

BIMA. One of the Pandawa brothers who figures prominently in many *wayang kulit* stories. *Chapters 2, 28.*

BINTANG. Star; refers figuratively to one of the 35 days of the Balinese astrological chart and the characteristics of one born on that day. *Chapter 18.*

BRAHMA, WISNU, SIWA. The Hindu triad, or *trimurthi*; God as creator, preserver, and dissolver/recycler of life; temples dedicated to them are the Pura Desa, the Pura Puseh, and the Pura Dalem; their directions are south, north, and center; *Chapter 2.*

BRAHMAN. Early Hindu concept of a single all-pervading, unknown, and unknowable life force in the universe. *Chapter 2, 23.*

BRAHMANA. A member of the highest, priestly, caste. *Chapter 3.*

BREM. Rice wine made by fermenting sticky white and black rice, *ketan* and *injin*.

BUDA CEMENG. The day upon which Buda (Wednesday) of the Saptawara (7-day week) coincides with Wage, the fourth day of the Pancawara (5-day week). *Chapter 17.*

BUJANGGA WESNAWE. Member of a group that holds itself free from caste and that simplifies the complex rituals of more traditional Balinese Hindus; Wisnu is the principal focus of this group's religious attention. *Chapter 7.*

BUNGBUNG. A length of bamboo from just below one node to just below the next adjacent node; a container, often used for holy water, made from a *bungbung;* a musical instrument, the keys of which are made from *bungbungs*. *Chapters 5, 25.*

BUSUNG and SELEPAN. Coconut leaves; *busung* are the yellowish-white immature leaves widely used to make offerings; *selepan* are mature green coconut leaves used for a variety of purposes, such as making mats. *Chapters 5, 16, 19.*

CAKRA. The discus-like weapon of Wisnu. *Chapter 6.*

CALONARANG. A drama depicting the story of Mahendradatta, a.k.a. the Widow of Girah, who became the witch Rangda and tried to destroy the kingdom of Erlangga, only to be defeated by Empu Pradah. *Chapters 25, 26, 27.*

CANANG. A common, small, everyday offering in the shape of a shallow square tray containing a *porosan*, fruit, flowers, and a *sampian*. *Chapters 5, 11, 19, 20, 22.*

CANDI BENTAR. Split gate without a top, often at the entrance to the outer courtyard of a temple. *Chapters 1, 23.*

CARU. A blood sacrifice with the purpose of purification by attracting *bhutas* and *kalas* and satisfying their hunger so that they will not adversely affect the affairs of man. *Chapters 7, 13, 19, 20, 24.*

CASTE. Various meanings, the most usual of which refers to birth-dictated station; the castes in Bali are, in order of greatest to least privilege, Brahmana, Ksatriya, Wesya, and Sudra. *Chapters 2, 3.*

CATUR WANGSA. The four castes: Brahmana, Ksatriya, Wesya, and Sudra. *Chapter 2.*

CENG CENG. A musical instrument consisting of a set of small cymbals attached to a base. *Chapter 29.*

DAKSINA. An important type of offering that consists of a more or less cylindrical basket made of coconut leaves containing a shaved coconut, a *porosan*, and various leaves, fruits, and rice. *Chapter 19.*

DALANG. The puppeteer of the *wayang kulit* shadow play. *Chapters 2, 17, 28.*

DANGHYANG NIRARTHA, also PEDANDA WAWU RAUH or DWIJENDRA. An influential Siwaist priest who came to Bali at the time of Watu Renggong (1550–1570) and who built many temples and shrines. *Chapters 4, 23.*

DAPDAP. A common tree that grows very rapidly and is used as a symbol of ever-lasting life and strength. *Chapter 9.*

DESA. Village. *Chapter 8.*

DEWA. General word for a god. *Chapters 2, 20, 26, 28.*

DEWA SINTIA (CINTYA, ASINTYA), DEWA RUCI. Representation of the unknown, unknowable, and un-representable supreme god, Sanghyang Widi; a single puppet in the *wayang kulit* shadow play can represent either of these, or other manifestations of the same idea. *Chapter 28.*

DEWASA. Auspicious or inauspicious days for various activities. *Chapters 17, 18.*

DHARMA. Religious duty, according to one's caste. Adharma is the lack of observation of this duty. *Chapters 2, 3.*

DUK. The black fiber from the sugar palm, *punyan jaka;* used for twine and the preferred roofing material for shrines. *Chapters 23, 24.*

DULANG. A container used to carry offerings; usually of clay, with a flared top and bottom. *Chapters 5, 19.*

DUPA. Incense. *Chapter 19.*

DURGA. The evil counterpart to Siwa, usually represented as his wife. *Chapter 13.*

EKA DASA RUDRA. A large series of ceremonies, the purpose of which is to purify the universe; held once every 100 years, the climax takes place on the last day of a year that ends in two zeros in the Saka calendar; last held in 1979, with its climactic day on March 28. *Chapters 5, 17, 20, 21.*

GALUNGAN. Buda (Wednesday) of the week Dunggulan; a religious festival that takes place around this day and which celebrates the victory of dharma over adharma; the most important festival of the Balinese Hindu cycle. *Chapter 17.*

GAMBUH. A dance given in the inner temple; considered to be ancestral to all other Balinese dances; the *gamelan* used features very long flutes. *Chapter 21, 25.*

GAMELAN. A general word for any of the many types of Balinese orchestral groups. *Chapters 22, 25, 29, 30.*

GAMELAN GONG KEBYAR. A large group of instruments that plays highly ornamented music with complex rhythmic patterns; the style was created in the early part of this century. *Chapters 29, 30.*

GANGSA. Any of the various Balinese musical instruments with bronze keys that are struck with a hammer or mallet. *Chapters 29, 30.*

GARUDA. The eagle-like vehicle of Batara Wisnu, frequently the subject of intricate and colorful wood carvings. *Chapters 4, 21.*

GEDEBONG. The stem of a banana plant. *Chapter 19.*

GENDER. A type of *gangsa* tuned to the *slendro* scale and played with two round mallets, the keys being damped with the knuckles of the hand that holds the mallet; four of these are used to accompany *wayang kulit* performances, the group being called *gender wayang. Chapters 11, 28, 29.*

GONG. A circular percussion instrument, usually made of bronze, with a knob that is hit with a mallet; any musical group or orchestra in Bali. *Chapter 5, 22, 29, 30.*

GUNA. Talent or aptitude; use. *Chapters 3, 24.*

GUNUNG AGUNG. The highest mountain in Bali, located in the east central part of the island; elevation 3,142 meters (10,308 feet). *Chapter 1.*

GUSTI. Title often, though not necessarily, used by a member of the Wesya caste. *Chapter 3.*

HANUMAN. General of the monkey armies in the Ramayana and ally of Rama in the battles to recapture Sita, Rama's wife, from the evil Rawana; a very popular hero with the Balinese, especially children. In Balinese, Anoman. *Chapter 2.*

IDER-IDER. Strips of cloth attached to the eaves of a *bale* for decoration during a festival; usually made of *prada*, a colored cloth decorated with gold paint or gold leaf. *Chapters 1, 9.*

JABA, JABA TENGAH, and JEROAN. The three courtyards into which many, but not all, temples are divided — the *jaba* is the outermost, secular area, the *jaba tengah* is the middle courtyard, and the *jeroan* is the inner and most sacred courtyard. *Chapters 1, 8, 23, 25.*

JAJA. Cake, usually of rice dough; those used in offerings are usually highly colored, crisp, dry, and relatively tasteless; those made for daily consumption are less colorful, but more tasty; there are dozens of varieties. *Chapters 17, 19, 21.*

JANGER. A modern type of dance involving a dozen or so young men and women who sing sometimes as a single chorus, sometimes as two separate choruses, accompanied by a *gong batel* of rhythm instruments; purely a social dance with many variations. *Chapter 25.*

JAUK. A dance featuring a *kasar* mask with a tall, pagoda-like helmet; the male dancer's movements are sudden and demonic. *Chapter 26.*

JOGED BUNGBUNG. A social dance in which a solo female dancer, accompanied by a *bungbung* orchestra, selects men from the crowd of onlookers and dances with them in a provocative way. *Chapter 25.*

KAJA and KELOD, KANGIN and KAUH. The cardinal directions on Bali: mountainward and seaward, east and west; since Bali's mountains are approximately in the island's center, *kaja* and *kelod* vary according to where in Bali one is; *kangin* and *kauh* are always east and west. *Chapters 1, 20, 24*

KAJENG KELIWON. A coincidence day between Kajeng, the third day of the

Triwara (3-day week), and Keliwon, the fifth day of the Pancawara (5-day week); occurs every 15 days and is especially important for making offerings to *bhutas* and *kalas. Chapter 17.*

KAKAWIN. A staged reading from sacred *lontars* that is a common adjunct to many ceremonies; one man reads the *lontars* in the original Kawi with a singsong voice and another translates into the vernacular. *Chapter 22.*

KALA RAUH (RAU). The eclipse demon from the Pamuteran Mandara Giri story; the demon stole the holy water of immortality and succeeded in swallowing a little before Wisnu, informed of the theft by the sun and moon, beheaded him with his magic *cakra*; the demon's head was already immortal, however, and it chases after those who informed on it, periodically swallowing them in an eclipse. *Chapter 6.*

KAMBEN. The standard waistcloth used by both men and women; the cloth is usually 2.5 meters long and 100 to 110 centimeters wide, made of *endek* (string tie-dyed cloth) or batik; it is wrapped around the waist counterclockwise for men, clockwise for women. *Chapters 11, 23, 26.*

KANDA EMPAT. The four brothers or sisters who are born with a baby and accompany him throughout life and the hereafter, guarding and helping him if treated properly, causing problems if not; they change names and duties early in the child's life; they can be used for either noble or evil ends, depending upon the individual. *Chapters 9, 10, 24.*

KARMA-PALA (or PHALA). The doctrine that one's deeds during life, karma, produce results, *pala* (literally 'fruit') that are rewarded or punished according to how closely these deeds followed the dharma of the individual. *Chapters 1, 2, 3.*

KASAKTIAN. The magical forces or powers that pervade the universe. *Chapter 13.*

KAWI. A literary language, based upon Sanskrit, that evolved in South India and was transmitted to Java; many sacred Balinese *lontars* are written in Kawi, which is unintelligible to the average person and must be interpreted; the heroes and heroines of the epic poems speak in Kawi. In the lower case, *kawi* means "creative force," "to write or compose prose or poetry." *Chapters 15, 26, 27.*

KAWITAN. Origin, root, ancestral connection; often used to refer to the temple of origin of a family or clan. *Chapter 15.*

KEBO. Water buffalo. *Chapter 20.*

KEBYAR. A style of modern Balinese music that features sudden changes in rhythm, embellishments and ornamentations, and varied instrumental performances. *Chapters 29, 30.*

KECAK. A chorus of men who utter the syllable "c(h)ak" with many variations and without instrumental accompaniment; originally accompanied *sanghyang* dances in the villages, but was adapted by Europeans to a new form called, popularly, "Monkey Dance" that is performed for tourists. *Chapter 25.*

KEKIDUNG. A slow, sacred chant performed by a chorus of men at many ceremonies; words are in Kawi. *Chapter 22.*

KEMULAN, KEMULAN TAKSU. An important roofed shrine, usually on the *kangin* side in the family temple; it has three horizontal compartments for which various explanations are offered: Brahma, Wisnu, and Siwa; Brahma, Wisnu, and Iswara; Brahma, Betara Guru, and Wisnu. *Chapter 24.*

KEPUH. A very large tree, *Bombax malabaricum*, related to the *kapok* tree; found very often in cemeteries, magical power is ascribed to it and its wood; the tree produces large, bright red flowers and many seeds covered with white, cottony filaments that aid in their dispersal. *Chapter 24.*

KRIS. A short sword that possess considerable magical power and must be treated with great respect; some have wavy and/or Damascus steel blades; worn by male dancers slung across the back, handle to the right; an important part of traditional formal Balinese male dress. *Chapters 8, 16.*

KETIPAT BANTAL. A ceremony performed after a wedding in which the family of the man visits the family of the woman; *bantal* is the name of an elongated cake, wrapped in *busung*; *ketipat* is the name of a large variety of sizes and shapes of loosely woven busung containers which are filled with rice and cooked; in the *ketipat bantal* ceremony, a single *bantal* is tied to two small *ketipats*, with obvious reference to the male genitalia. *Chapter 9.*

KOKAR, SMKI. Acronym for the Sekolah Menengah Karawitan Indonesia, the high school–level musical conservatory, located in Batubulan. *Chapters 25, 29.*

KORAWAS, KAURAWAS, KURUS. Cousins of the Pandawas, their war with whom is the central theme of the Hindu epic, Mahabharata. *Chapter 2.*

KORI AGUNG. The large gate that leads from the middle courtyard (*jaba tengah*) to the inner courtyard (*jeroan*) of a temple; often very elaborately carved, especially in North Bali; often decorated with the head of Bhoma above the entrance. *Chapters 1, 23.*

KRISHNA. A complex and many-faceted hero of the Mahabharata, the Puranas, and many other Hindu tales; one of the most popular of the Hindu folk hero–gods; his most noteworthy appearance is as Arjuna's charioteer who, just before the battle between the Pandawas and Korawas, reveals himself as Wisnu and lectures to Arjuna about the role of duty in a military leader — this section of the Mahabharata being known as the Bhagavad-Gita. *Chapter 2.*

KSATRIYA. The second caste, consisting, originally, of soldiers and rulers. *Chapters 2, 3.*

KULKUL. A signal drum or bell that is made from a hollow log with a slit down one side and is used as a summons to temple or *banjar* events. *Chapter 22.*

KUNINGAN. An important religious day, Saniscara (Saturday) of Week 12; it marks the end of the 10-day Galungan period; the word is related to *kuning*, which means yellow, and is derived from the fact that rice used in offerings on this day is dyed yellow with *kunyit*, turmeric. *Chapter 17.*

LAMAK. Woven coconut leaf mat, usually in the form of a long strip that may be up to several meters in length, decorated with colored cut-outs, and used to decorate many kinds of shrines — even automobile grilles when the cars are blessed. *Chapters 17, 19.*

LEGONG. A traditional classical dance, usually, but not always, performed by three girls; there are many modern variations of *legong*, several consisting of shortened versions created especially for tourists. *Chapters 4, 25, 29.*

LELONTEK. Very long, thin, triangular flags that taper to a point on top, attached to long bamboo poles; used, for example, by Rangda in the Barong performance. *Chapters 15, 26.*

LEMBU. The bull that is used as a sarcophagus at cremations; technically allowed only to upper caste families, but this rule is not often observed. *Chapter 12.*

LEYAK. One who practices "black magic"; a spook or witch; the "black magic" itself. *Chapters 13, 14.*

LINGGAM, also LINGGA, LINGA. The symbol of Siwa as recycler of life; it is phallic in shape. *Chapter 2.*

LIS. A wand used to sprinkle holy water; made of young coconut leaves cut into decorative patterns. *Chapter 5.*

LONTAR. A book of inscriptions, often written in Kawi or old Javanese; the text is scratched upon the leaves of the *lontar* palm and the book is bound with boards on either side by strings that pass through holes in the leaves; the books and their contents are considered sacred. *Chapter 19, 28.*

LUAN and TEBEN. Paired directions: *luan* is the intercardinal point between *kaja* and *kangin* and is sacred; *teben* is *kelod–kauh* and is less sacred, even profane. *Chapter 1.*

MAHABHARATA. A very long, rambling Hindu epic, the central theme of which is the war between the Pandawa brothers and their cousins the Korawa brothers. *Chapter 2, 19.*

MAHAMERU. A fabled mountain located in the center of the earth, at the top of which is *suarga*, heaven; identified rather vaguely with the Himalayas; also identified with Mount Semeru in East Java. *Chapter 1.*

MAJAPAHIT. A Siwaist-Hindu-Buddhist Kingdom of East Java (1294-1520) that was eventually defeated by Islamic armies and forced to flee; Bali derives a good deal of its culture from the remnants of this kingdom. *Chapters 2, 3.*

MANUSA YADNYA. Religious ceremonies carried out for human beings, rites of passage; the other *yadnyas: bhuta yadnya*, ceremonies to propitiate evil spirits; *dewa yadnya*, ceremonies for the gods; *rsi yadnya*, ceremonies for holy Hindu prophets; and *pitra yadnya*, ceremonies for the spirits of ancestors. *Chapters 5, 9.*

MAPAJAR. Literally "speak" or "talk," but used to mean a performance of a ceremony in which there will be some sort of dance; the usual word used in Jimbaran to refer to the performance of our *barong*; the correct use of the word is "Dewa Ayu mapajar" — Dewa Ayu (the name of our *barong*) is performing. *Chapters 15, 26.*

MARERAUHAN(G). A ceremony in which one or more people who are susceptible to going into trance (*sadegs*) do so in order to communicate with a god to determined if the god is pleased with earthly arrangements. *Chapters 15, 26.*

MASAUDAN, MASASAUDAN. To promise a god that some sort of offering will be made or some sort of action taken, often requiring considerable trouble and expense, if the god will grant a wish from the supplicant. *Chapter 14.*

MASIMPEN. Literally "stored"; used in Jimbaran to refer to a period of time during which our *barong* has been taken apart and is not performing. *Chapter 26.*

MATABUH. Pouring *brem* and/or *arak* on the ground as an offering to *bhutas* and *kalas;* the liquid itself is called *tabuh. Chapters 19, 20.*

MATANGI. Literally "awake"; used in Jimbaran to refer to the period during which our *barong* has been assembled and performs regularly. *Chapter 26.*

MAYADENAWA. An evil king, son of Sri Jaya Kesunu, who is said to have ruled over Bali in the 6th century A.D.; he prohibited the worship of the gods, destroyed shrines, and tried to wipe out all religion and as a result Bali fell upon evil days;

Mayadenawa was eventually killed after a series of fierce battles by Indra; it is often said that the victory over Mayadenawa is the source of the important Galungan celebration, although many other explanations exist. *Chapter 4, 7.*

MELASPAS. A dedication ceremony in which a house or other building is "brought to life" with offerings and mantras so that it can be lived in and used. *Chapter 20, 24.*

MELASTI, also MELIS. A procession to the sea or to a holy spring in which the village gods in their *pratimas* are carried to the source of water and ceremonially sprinkled with holy water; the ceremony is a general purification of the village and its deities; *melasti* always occurs just before Nyepi (New Year's Day), but it can be held at other times for unrelated ceremonies. *Chapter 5.*

MERAJAN, PEMERAJAN. Family temple of an upper caste family. *Chapter 24.*

MERU. A tall, pagoda-like shrine with an odd number of roofs that diminish in size toward the top. *Chapters 12, 21, 23, 24.*

MOKSA. Union of the atman with God after death and freedom from the cycle of reincarnations. *Chapters 2, 12, 23.*

NAGA. Snake or dragon-snake; Naga Basuki and Naga Anantaboga are the two dragon-snakes that attend the world-turtle Badawang; they symbolize man's earthly needs; they are often depicted on *padmasana* shrines. *Chapters 1, 6, 12.*

NANGKA and KETEWEL. *Punyan nangka* is the jackfruit tree; *ketewel* is the wood of this tree, often used in musical instruments and fine woodcarvings. *Chapter 29.*

NATAB and NGAYAB. *Natab* means to waft the *sari* ("essense") of and offering toward oneself or toward another person, such as a baby, as in a *manusa yadnya* ceremony; *ngayab* means to waft this essence toward the gods, normally away from oneself. *Chapters 9, 19, 20.*

NAWA SENJATA. The nine weapons of the nine gods of the nine directions; often depicted as a sort of compass. *Chapter 7.*

NGABEN. To cremate a body, low Balinese; the noun is properly *pengabenan*, but the transitive verb is commonly used to mean "cremation"; *palebonan* is the equivalent in high Balinese. *Chapter 12.*

NGEROROD, also MALAIB. Marriage by elopement; it is much more common than *mamadik*, a traditional arranged marriage. *Chapter 9.*

NGUNALATRI. A single calendar day that contains two lunar days; this correction, which comes every 63 days in the Saka calendar (currently always Wednesday) is necessary to preserve the rule that there be 30 lunar days between two successive moon phases, whereas there are actually about 29 1/2. *Chapter 17.*

NGURAH. A common title for members of the Wesya caste, although sometimes used by others. *Chapter 3.*

NISKALA. "Intangible," "occult"; opposed to *sekala* — "tangible," "visible." *Chapters 5, 13.*

NUNAS. Literally "beg"; a very common verb used by an inferior when speaking to a superior or when talking about religious matters; *nunas tirtha* means to beg or obtain holy water. *Chapter 5.*

NYEKAH. A ceremony, sometimes called a "second cremation" although it is not, held after the regular cremation; its purpose is to consign the spirit of the deceased to heaven for reward and punishment so that it may ultimately be reborn upon earth. *Chapter 12.*

NYEPI. The first day of the 10th month, Kedasa, generally in March; a day of meditation when one is not supposed to be outside of the home; it is the first day of the Balinese Saka year, following ceremonies the preceding day that were designed to appease the evil spirits and restore the balance of good and evil. *Chapters 17, 20, 21.*

ODALAN. The annniversary festival of a temple; it may fall once every 210 days if set by the Pawukon calendar, or it may occur once every lunar year, if it is set by the Saka calendar. *Chapters 5, 19, 22.*

ONGKARA. A written symbol that combines the symbol called *ulu candra*, pronounced "M," with the long vowel, *au*, producing the combination *aum*, usually pronounced "OM." This is a very sacred sound and syllable that occurs in all mantras since it signifies the unknown and unknowable god. *Chapters 9, 10.*

OTON. The ceremony held 210 days, one Pawukon cycle, after the birth of a baby; some families hold similar ceremonies for the first three *otons* at 210 day intervals, and some celebrate every *oton* throughout life with offerings that differ in size and elaborateness. *Chapter 9.*

PADMASANA. An important shrine that is found in many temples; it has an empty chair for Sanghyang Widhi (some say for Batara Surya) on top; the shrine should have an eight-leafed lotus, one leaf for each of the gods of the eight directions; often the world-turtle is depicted at the bottom, with the two attendant *nagas*. *Chapters 19, 23, 24.*

PAGERWESI. An important religious holiday, especially in North Bali; occurs on Buda (Wednesday) of Sinta (Week 1) of the Pawukon cycle; second only to the Galungan-Kuningan festival in importance; like Galungan, it celebrates the victory of dharma over adharma. *Chapter 17.*

PALINGGIH. Shrine, holy place; literally "seat" (for a god). *Chapter 24.*

PAMUTERAN MANDARA GIRI. "Spinning Mount Mandara"; The story of how the gods and evil spirits used Mount Mandara Giri to churn the Sea of Milk in order to obtain the holy water of immortality. *Chapter 6.*

PANASAR. "Servant"; Twalen, Merdah (Mredah), Delem, and Sangut are the *penasars* in the *wayang kulit* shadow puppet plays. *Chapter 28.*

PANCA MAHA BUTHA. The five elements of the macrocosm that have been temporarily formed into the microcosm of man: fire, earth, air, water, and space; these are returned to the macrocosm upon cremation. *Chapter 12.*

PANDAWAS. The heroes of the Mahabharata, sons of Pandu: Yudisthira, Arjuna, Bima, Nakula, and Sahadewa; their battles with their cousins, the Korawas, are the central theme of the Mahabharata. *Chapter 2.*

PANDE. The clan of smiths. *Chapters 3, 8.*

PARAS. A soft, gray stone from which Balinese stone carvings are cut; technically it is tuff, a volcanic ash sandstone. *Chapter 4.*

PASEK. An important clan to which over 60 percent of Balinese Sudras belong; the clan traces its origin back to the Brahmana caste in Java. *Chapter 3.*

PAWINTENAN. *Manusa yadnya* ceremony of purification so that one will be protected in the study of potentially dangerous matters. *Chapter 9.*

PAWUKON. The Balinese 210-day calendar that governs most, but not all, anniversaries, auspicious days, and religious events; successive Pawukon cycles are not named, numbered, or otherwise kept track of. *Chapter 17, 18.*

PECATU. A village on the Bukit between Jimbaran and Pura Uluwatu; Pecatu is a *desa*, administrated by a *kepala desa*. *Chapter 26.*

PEDANDA. A high priest of the Brahmana caste; may be male or female. *Chapters 2, 3, 22.*

PELELINTANGAN. The Balinese astrological calendar; a chart of the 35 days that are combinations of the 5- and 7-day weeks; a person born on any one of these days acquires certain characteristics from his birth day, and these are symbolized and indicated on the *pelelintangan. Chapter 18.*

PEMANGKU. Lay priest and custodian of a temple; usually of the Sudra caste. *Chapters 5, 9, 15, 19, 20, 21, 22, 23, 26.*

PENAMPAHAN. The day before Galungan, Tuesday, of the 11th week, Dunggulan, when it is traditional to prepare a feast of *ebat* (a kind of hash made of turtle meat) for the upcoming Galungan celebration. *Chapter 17.*

PENDET. A common, traditional welcoming dance that is presented in the *jeroan* of a temple at the time the temple gods are invited to descend; the dance is for the entertainment of the gods; it may consist of any of a variety of different dances, all of which, however, have a common general style. *Chapters 21, 25.*

PENJOR. An offering consisting of a bamboo pole with decorations; the arched top represents Gunung Agung, the body is a river that flows from the mountains to the sea, and along its route are the products of the harvest, tied to the pole; at the foot of the pole is a temporary shrine; *penjors* are found everywhere at Galungan time, but are also commonly erected for many other important religious festivals. *Chapters 17, 21.*

PERAKSOK. A fiber made from the long, thin leaves of a plant that resembles agave or *pandanus;* the leaves are soaked in mud or water for an extended period, then combed out into fibers that are commonly used for the "fur" of a *barong. Chapter 26.*

POROSAN. A small container in which are placed small amounts of *areca* nut, lime, and *base* (the leaf of a species of pepper) — the ingredients of the betel chew; these substances serve as temporary places of residence of the Trimurthi: Brahma, Wisnu, and Siwa, within the offering, because each is attracted toward its preferred color and direction. *Chapter 19.*

PRAMADA. Insubordination; the widespread feeling that one must not engage in certain activities, lest it be interpreted by the gods as rude behavior and the individual punished accordingly; the most important of these prohibitions are again asking questions about or discussing religious matters, using the name of a superior, adult, or god and acting or talking in a pretentious way beyond one's dharma and social status. *Chapters 14, 16.*

PRATIMA. A small statue, usually in the shape of a human figure, in which the spirit of a god is invited to reside for the duration of a ceremony; each of the *pratimas* itself has a larger, more ornate carving associated with it which serves as the god's vehicle. *Chapters 3, 5, 21, 22.*

PUPUTAN BADUNG. Mass ritual suicide of the court of the raja of Badung that took place on September 20, 1906 when a Dutch army advanced upon Denpasar from Sanur. *Chapter 17.*

PURI. The home of the raja and his court; sometimes used to mean the home of any member of the upper castes. *Chapter 3.*

RAKSASA. General name for a large and varied class of demons. *Chapter 10.*

RAMA and RAMAYANA. Rama is the name of the hero of an extremely popular Hindu epic poem, the Ramayana, which chronicles his efforts to recapture his wife Sita who was stolen by the evil Raksasa Rawana, king of (Sri) Langka; Rama represents ideal man — loyal, brave, and heroic; he is considered one of the several incarnations of Wisnu. *Chapter 2.*

RANGDA. Literally "widow"; Rangda is one of the two central figures in the *barong* play, representing the negative side of man; Rangda is also related to Durga, wife of Siwa, who represents his destructive side. *Chapters 26, 27.*

RARAHINAN, RAHINAN. Festival day, important religious day. *Chapter 24.*

RAWANA. The evil ruler of (Sri) Langka who in the Ramayana arranges for the capture of Rama's wife Sita; he is defeated and killed by the combined armies of Rama and the monkey king, Sugriva. *Chapter 2.*

RUDRA. The destructive aspect of Siwa; his home is in the southwest and his color is orange; Pura Uluwatu is dedicated to Rudra. *Chapters 21, 23.*

RWA BHINEDA. The Hindu principle of opposing positive and negative forces which must exist in harmony and equilibrium. *Chapters 1, 20.*

SAD KAHYANGAN. The six most important temples in all of Bali; lists vary, but the Department of Religion recognizes these: Pura Lempuyang, Pura Batukaru, Pura Penataran Agung at Besakih, Pura Gua Lawah, Pura Luhur Uluwatu, Pura Pusering Jagat. *Chapters 3, 8.*

SAD RIPU. The six "enemies" of mankind that are symbolically removed when one has his teeth filed: *kama*, "lust"; *lobha*, "greed"; *krodha*, "anger"; *mada*, "drunkenness"; *moha*, "confusion"; *matsarya*, "jealousy." *Chapter 11.*

SADEG. A person, usually a man and usually a *pemangku*, who goes into trance easily and who is invited to do this in order to communicate with a particular god to ascertain its wishes. *Chapter 26.*

SAKA CALENDAR. The Hindu-Balinese lunar calendar; the Saka normally has 12 months, each of which ends on new moon, Tilem; a 13th intercalary month is added every 3 or 4 years; calendar numbering is 78 or 79 years behind Gregorian year numbering. *Chapters 17, 21.*

SAMPIAN. A decorative part of some offerings consisting of intricately cut young coconut leaves "sewed" together with bamboo skewers; size and degree of elaboration varies greatly. *Chapter 19.*

SAMSARA. Reincarnation; doctrine that after death, a person's spirit is rewarded or punished according to the doctrine of karma-*pala* and then reborn into a new status befitting the degree to which karma achieved dharma in previous incarnations. *Chapter 2.*

SANDAR and TELEK. A refined, *alus,* female character with a white mask and a tall Jauk-like headress that performs before the *barong mapajar* in some villages; part may be taken by males or females, but the gestures and character are female. *Chapters 26, 27.*

SANGGAH. Any sort of shrine, but the word is usually used to refer to the set of shrines in the family temple, hence the family temple itself in a low caste home; the family temple of a high caste home is usually referred to as a *merajan* or *pemerajan.* *Chapters 5, 20, 24.*

SANGGING. A tooth filer; artist who uses a chisel, e.g., a sculptor. *Chapter 11.*

SANGHYANG. An honorific term for a god, such as Sanghyang Widhi; any of several types of dances that are directed toward purification from evil spirits and that involve trance. *Chapters 4, 9, 25.*

SANGHYANG WIDI (WIDHI) WASA. The unification of all manifestations of God into one single, all-powerful God, more or less equivalent to the Christian God and the Islamic Allah. *Chapter 4.*

SAPUT. A wide piece of cloth of almost any type that men wear wrapped around their hips and upper legs; it is worn over the *kamben,* usually only when participating in a temple ceremony; also means "blanket." *Chapter 1.*

SARASWATI. Wife of Brahma and the deity of books, knowledge, and learning; the last day of the Pawukon cycle, Saniscara Watugunung, is devoted to her worship; often depicted playing a musical instrument and astride a swan. *Chapter 17.*

SARI. The essence of an offering; that part of an offering that the gods consume, leaving the material offering for people to eat; also, generally, "essense," "gist." *Chapters 19, 22.*

SATÉ. A dish that consists of pieces of meat or fat skewered onto a short length of bamboo or a paste of meat or fish molded and wrapped around such a stick; molded or wrapped *saté* is called *saté lembat;* skewered *saté* for ordinary food is called *sate serapah;* skewered fat and omentum that is used to make offerings is called *saté renteng. Chapters 9, 19, 21.*

SEGEHAN and BELABARAN. Offerings of rice and relishes put down at the entrance of a house compound and other places for *bhutas* and *kalas; segehan* is the low Balinese word, *belabaran* is medium Balinese; the offering is usually in the form of a small triangular container made of *selepan* in which are placed, among other things, onion, ginger, and salt. *Chapters 13, 19, 20.*

SEKA, SEKEHE. Club, society, or group; when used as an adjective the letter N is added at the end of the word — for example *sekan barong, sekehan barong. Chapters 15, 26, 27.*

SEKALA. Tangible, able to be perceived by the senses; contrast with *niskala. Chapter 5, 13, 26.*

SENGGUHU. Low-caste priests who specialize in *caru* offerings, but who are not bona fide Ida Bujangga Rsi, (Bujangga Wesnawe priests); often called Jero Gede. *Chapter 7.*

SIDA KARYA. The most important mask used by a *topeng pajegan* performer; it is danced last in the *jeroan,* often at the same time the climax of the temple ceremony occurs; the term means "the work can be accomplished" and indicates that this sacred mask can insure the efficacy of the ceremony; also the name of an important temple in Sesetan in the south part of Denpasar; also a *desa adat* in South Denpasar. *Chapter 26.*

SITA. Wife of Rama, the heroine of the Ramayana epic who was captured by an agent of the demon Rawana and forced to live in (Sri) Langka; rescued by Rama and Hanuman, but under suspicion of infidelity and so returned to her mother furrow in the earth. "Sita" comes from "furrow." *Chapter 2.*

SONGKET. A type of brocade in which silver or gold threads are woven into a cotton fabric used for traditional dress; widely faked nowadays with a cheap, machine-made cloth. *Chapter 11.*

SUARGA and NERAKA. Heaven and hell, respectively; places of reward or punishment for a spirit, according to karma. *Chapter 1, 12.*

SUDRA, JABA. The lowest of the four castes, originally designated as assistants to the other three; over 90 percent of the Balinese are Sudras. *Chapters 2, 3.*

SUGIAN. The three days Rebo through Sukra, (Wednesday through Friday) of the 10th Pawukon week, Sungsang, are called Sugian (or Sugi) Tenten, Sugian Jawa, and Sugian Bali; Sugian Tenten is the day for awakening oneself to the approaching festival of Galungan; Sugian Jawa is for meditation and thanks for those Javanese who helped in the overthrow of Mayadenawa and the restoration of harmony; Sugian Bali is similar, except it is for the Balinese who overcame adharma; the goal of all three days is purification. *Chapter 17.*

SURYA. The sun; Betara Surya is god manifested in the sun; *surya* is also used to mean the high caste patrons of a low caste family, the family being the *sisya* of the high-caste *surya*. *Chapters 1, 3, 24.*

TAJEN. Cockfight. *Chapter 20.*

TAKSU. A shrine in the family temple dedicated to the spirit that gives one the power to perform certain acts; it can be taken as the spirit of one's profession or talent; or it can be taken to mean the spirit that allows one, for example, to communicate with supernatural forces; the shrine is properly called the *palinggih taksu.* *Chapters 14, 15.*

TAPEL. Mask. *Chapter 27.*

TAUR. The word means, literally, "to pay," but is generally used to refer to a variety of *bhuta yadnya* ceremonies which feature a large *caru* or sacrifice for purification from the influences of evil spirits. *Chapters 7, 20, 21.*

TENGET. Mysterious, charged with supernatural power. *Chapters 13, 26.*

TIKA. A calendar for keeping track of the 210 days of the Pawukon cycle; consists of 7 horizontal rows, one for each day of the Saptawara (plus a heading and a footing row) and 30 vertical columns, one for each of the 30 weeks of the Pawukon. *Chapter 17.*

TILEM and PURNAMA. Tilem is new moon, Purnama is full moon, as shown on the Saka calendar; these may differ from the actual astronomical new or full phase by one day. *Chapters 17, 21.*

TIRTHA, TOYA, YEH. Three words for "water" in high, medium, and low Balinese; *tirtha* and *toya* are sometimes used as being synonymous with holy water; *tirtha kamandalu* is the holy water obtained by the gods and demons when the Sea of Milk was churned with Mount Giri. *Chapters 1, 5, 6, 20, 28.*

TOPENG. Mask; masked dance performed either by one actor, *topeng pajegan,* or by a troupe of performers, *topeng panca. Chapters 21, 25.*

TOYA PENGALUKATAN. An important type of holy water prepared by a *pedanda* for purification. *Chapter 5.*

TRIMURTHI, TRIMURTI. The Hindu triad, Brahma, Wisnu, and Siwa; sometimes Hindu legends collectively referred to them as Sanghyang Trimurthi. *Chapter 2.*

TRISANDHYA. One of the most common Hindu mantras, having its origin in ancient Aryan times in India; a Hindu is supposed to recite it three times a day. *Chapter 2.*

TRIWARA, PANCAWARA, SAPTAWARA. The three most important weeks of the Pawukon cycle, containing, respectively, three, five, and seven days each; these three weeks, and seven others ranging in length from one to ten days, all run concurrently. *Chapter 17.*

TROMPONG. A musical instrument that consists of a row of 10 bronze "pots" that have protruding knobs, suspended from a long wooden frame; the performer strikes the pots with two long sticks, one held in each hand; generally considered an old-fashioned instrument and not commonly used in *gong kebyar* style performances. *Chapters 29, 30.*

TUAK. Palm beer or toddy produced by fermenting the sap of the young flower stalk of a coconut or *lontar* palm; the sweet, mildly alcoholic drink is bubbly, and white to pale pink in color. *Chapter 20.*

TUGU, PENUNGGUN KARANG. A shrine, usually roofless and open and made of stone or brick, that is found in the *kaja-kauh* corner of the house compound; offerings are made in it to Betara Kala (Kala Raksa) as guardian of the house and property, the watcher of the dwelling complex; *tugu* are also erected near especially *tenget* places outside of the house compound, to serve as dwelling places for the spirits of those places. *Chapter 24.*

TUKANG. Craftsman, expert, practitioner; a *tukang uut* is a traditional massage expert, a *tukang ukir* is a carver. *Chapter 14.*

TULISAN BALI. A form of traditional writing based on the old Javanese alphabet; it is usually used only for sacred manuscripts, almost never in everyday life; the contents of *lontars* are usually written in Tulisan Bali. *Chapter 14.*

TUMPEK. Any of six coincidence days when Keliwon, the fifth day of the five-day week, falls upon Saniscara (Saturday); Tumpeks occur every 35 days and are, in order: Landep, Uduh, Kuningan, Krulut, Kandang, and Wayang; some go by other names. *Chapters 16, 17.*

TWALEN, MERDAH (MREDAH), DELEM, and SANGUT. *Panasars,* servants of the principal characters in many Balinese epic tales who translate the unintelligible Kawi spoken by these heroes and heroines into understandable colloquial Balinese, adding their own comic interludes in episodes that have nothing to do with the main story; the first two are on the side of the good guys; the last two are on the side of the bad guys. *Chapter 28.*

UDENG. Traditional headcloth worn by men; called *dastar* in high Balinese. *Chapters 1, 17, 26.*

URIP. Ritual number assigned to various objects such as days of weeks; literally "living." *Chapter 17.*

VEDAS. Four holy books of the Aryans, dating from about 1,000 B.C.; the Aryans were not Hindu, but they laid some of the most important foundations of Hinduism; the Vedas are considered sacred by Balinese Hindus; the Rig Veda is the best known of the four and is probably the oldest religious text in the world. *Chapter 2.*

WADAH. The word means "container," but is usually used to refer to a cremation tower, in which the effigy or body of a dead person is carried to the cemetery; the tower is also called a *bade. Chapter 1, 12.*

WANGSA. Genealogical descent, lineage. *Chapter 3.*

WAYANG KULIT. Shadow puppets. *Chapters 2, 22, 25, 28.*

WESYA. The third and lowest of the upper three castes, originally assigned to merchants and traders. *Chapter 3, 22.*

Index